Population Statistics

Population Statistics

Nitin Johari

RANDOM PUBLICATIONS
NEW DELHI (INDIA)

Population Statistics

ISBN 978-93-5111-392-8

Published in 2014 in India by

RANDOM PUBLICATIONS

4376-A/4B, Gali Murari Lal, Ansari Road
New Delhi-110 002
Phone : +91-11-43580356, +91-11-23289044
e-mail: randomexports@gmail.com, sales@randompublications.com, info@randompublications.com

Reprinted 2022

Type Setting by : Keystoneprintads, Delhi-110051
Digitally Printed at : Replika Press Pvt. Ltd.

Preface

Population statistics is the use of statistics to analyze characteristics or changes to a population. It is related to social demography and demography. Population statistics can analyze anything from global demographic changes to local small scale changes. For example, an analysis of global change shows that population growth has slowed, infant mortality rates have declined, and there have been small increases in the aged.

National population statistics are usually collected by conducting a census. However, because these are usually huge logistical exercises, countries normally conduct censuses only once every five to 10 years. Even when a census is conducted it may miss counting everyone. Also, some people counted in the census may be recorded in a different place than where they usually live, because they are traveling, for example. Consequently, raw census numbers are often adjusted to produce census estimates that identify such statistics as resident population, residents, tourists and other visitors, nationals and aliens. For privacy reasons, particularly when there are small counts, some census results may be rounded, often to the nearest ten, hundred, thousand and sometimes randomly up, down or to another small number such as within 3 of the actual count. Between censuses, administrative data collected by various agencies about population events such as births, deaths, and cross-border migration may be used to produce intercensal estimates.

Population estimates are usually derived from census and other administrative data. Population estimates are normally produced after the date the estimate is for. Some estimates, such as the usually resident population estimate who usually lives in a locality as at the census date, even though the census did not count them within that locality. Census questions usually include a questions about where a person usually lives, whether they are a resident or visitor, or also live somewhere else, to allow these estimates to be made. Other estimates are concerned with estimating population on a particular date that is different to the census date, for example the middle or end of a calendar or financial year. These estimates often use birth and death records and migration data to adjust census counts for the changes that have happened since the census. Population projections are produced in advance of the date they are for. They use time series analysis of existing census data and other sources of population information to forecast the size of future populations. Because there are unknown factors that may affect future population changes, population projections often incorporate high and low as well as expected values for future populations. Population projections are often recomputed after a census has been conducted. It depends on how conjusted the area is in the particular demarcation.

I thank all members of my team who have helped in the preparation of the book. My special thanks go to "Random Publications" who have published the book.

– Nitin Johari

Contents

1

Introduction

THE CHALLENGE OF DEMOGRAPHY

Demography, the study of the size, structure and development of human populations, is finally beginning to receive more attention among ancient historians. Yet we still have a long way to go, not only in establishing even the most basic features of ancient populations but even more so in applying this information to our interpretations of all aspects of the Greco-Roman world. Concerned with birth, death and migration and desperate to measure, model and quantify, populations studies may seem both forbiddingly technical and safely remote from the humanistic interests and skills of most students of antiquity.

Moreover, usable evidence is scarce, and generally requires comparative and interdisciplinary approaches to make any sense at all. At the same time, however, we must bear in mind that demography is much more than just numbers, and relevant to much of what we seek to know and understand about the distant past. In pre-modern societies, population size was the best indicator of economic performance; the distribution of people between town and country was instrumental in the creation of collective identity and may reflect the scale of division of labour and commerce; human mobility mediated information flows and culture change; mortality and morbidity were principal determinants of well-being and determined fertility, investment in human capital, and economic productivity, and more generally shaped people's hopes and fears.

The same is true of marriage customs and household structure. Classical civilization was the product of a thoroughly alien environment of frequent pregnancy and sudden death. Along with technological progress and scientific discovery, it was demographic change that separated the modern world from the more distant past. Archaic patterns of marriage, reproduction and death seemed as natural and immutable then as they are exotic to us, and we cannot hope to approach ancient history without a solid understanding of what these conditions were and how they permeated life.

This is the true challenge of demography. All I can do here is provide a short road map of recent progress, abiding problems, the principal areas of controversy, and the broader historical implications of ancient population studies.

DEATH AND DISEASE

Thanks to modern advances in public health, medicine and nutrition, mean life expectancy at birth today exceeds 80 years in Japan and reaches the high 60s for the world as a whole. These conditions represent a dramatic break even from the fairly recent past: averages of less than 30 years still prevailed in parts of eighteenth-century France, nineteenth-century Spain and Russia, and early twentieth-century India and China. This leaves no doubt that ancient societies must have experienced similarly low levels of life expectancy. Precision is beyond our reach: modern estimates are guided by the fact that at levels below 20 years, even very fertile populations would have found it difficult to survive, and that comparative evidence rules out levels of well above 30 years for the ancient world overall. Considerable variation may have occurred within this range, from particularly high mortality in large unhealthy cities and malarious lowlands to significantly better odds of survival in sparsely settled and salubrious areas, especially at higher altitudes.

Empirical data are rare and of uneven quality. Several hundred census returns from Roman Egypt from the first three centuries AD that have survived on papyrus and list the members of individual households with their ages and family ties provide the best demographic evidence for classical antiquity. The aggregate age distribution of the recorded population is consistent with a mean life expectancy at birth of between 20 and 30 years. Human skeletal remains have been unearthed in large numbers but are of limited value for demographic analysis: despite ongoing progress, it remains difficult to determine the precise age of adult bones, and, more seriously, we cannot tell whether the age structure of cemetery populations matched that of actual living groups or was distorted by burial customs or migration.

Owing to selective funerary commemoration governed by age and gender, the tens of thousands of ages at death recorded on Roman tombstones do not permit us to infer levels of life expectancy. Differential mortality is almost impossible to trace: all we know is that Roman emperors who died of natural causes and other elite groups seem to have experienced a mean life expectancy at birth in the high 20s, which suggests that the rich and powerful could not expect to live signicantly–if at all–longer than the general population. The health hazards of urban residence may have been to blame.

Faced with such inadequate sources, ancient historians have increasingly embraced model life tables to arrive at a better idea of the probable age structure of ancient populations. Models for high-mortality environments are derived through algorithmic extrapolation from known historical population structures. Unfortunately, this method requires reliable base data that are only available for relatively recent populations that had already overcome pernicious diseases such as endemic smallpox or plague, malaria and tuberculosis that used to wreak havoc in earlier periods of history and distorted age structures in unpredictable ways.

Growing awareness of this problem has encouraged attempts to create high-mortality models that accommodate such factors and might offer a more realistic approximation of ancient conditions. Even so, as suggested, always have to allow for wide margins of uncertainty. For all these reasons, it seems unlikely that our knowledge of ancient mortality will ever progress much beyond the most basic features: that infant mortality was very high, perhaps around 30 per cent; that maybe half of all people died before they were old enough to bear or father children; that death was as much a phenomenon of childhood as of old age; and that ancient populations were therefore necessarily very young, similar to those of developing countries today.

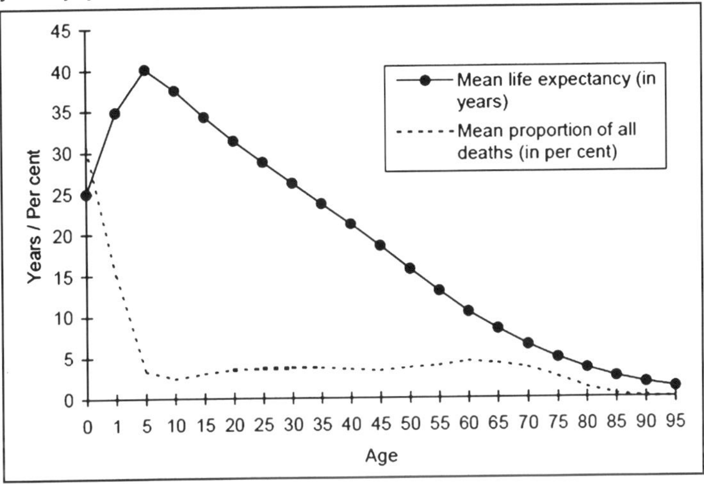

Fig. Mean Life Expectancy at Age *x* (0, 1, 5, etc) and Mean Proportion of all Deaths Occurring between Ages *x* and *x+n* (0-1, 1-5, 5-10, etc) in a Model Population with a Mean Life Expectancy at Birth of 25 years

At the same time, two areas in particular hold considerable promise: the study of the causes of mortality, and our understanding of its broader historical implications. Ancient demography and medical history, usually two separate fields, have finally begun to merge. Dates of death recorded in epitaphs allow us to reconstruct the seasonal distribution of mortality which is indicative of the underlying causes of death, especially infectious diseases which tend to be seasonal in character: this approach has produced new insights into the disease environments of ancient Rome, Italy, North Africa and Egypt. Moreover, rich literary evidence for the prevalence of malaria and its effects in Italy from antiquity to the recent past has made it possible to account for demographic variation in the peninsula. DNA recovered from ancient skeletons increasingly provides direct evidence of ancient pathogens: recent findings include the discovery of malignant tertian malaria in a late Roman child cemetery in Italy and the identification of typhoid fever in an Athenian mass grave that has been linked to the plague of 430 BC famously described by Thucydides. Epidemiological computer simulations have been marshalled to model the likely demographic impact of the so-called 'Antonine Plague' that spread through the Roman world in the late second century AD and scientific knowledge can also be brought to bear on the plague pandemic of the sixth century AD or the gradual dissemination of leprosy. Further progress will depend on the extent of transdisciplinary collaboration between ancient historians and scientists.

More traditionally-minded historians will want to focus on the manifold consequences of high and unpredictable mortality: the destabilization of families, the ubiquity of widows and orphans, disincentives to investment in education, the disruption of trust networks that sustain commerce, and more generally the social and cultural responses to pervasive risk and frequent loss, including religious beliefs. For these purposes, even rough models of ancient mortality proffer a useful approximation of demographic conditions, and comparative source material from the more recent past–shaped by similar experiences–is abundant yet still largely neglected by students of antiquity. Ancient social, economic and cultural history can only gain from an enhanced appreciation of how pervasively mortality regimes shaped all aspects of people's lives.

REPRODUCTION AND FERTILITY CONTROL

High mortality logically implies high fertility. For instance, a mean life expectancy at birth of 25 years compels–on average–every woman surviving to menopause to give birth to approximately five children to maintain existing population size. The corresponding rate was higher still for married women: one reconstruction posits a lifetime mean of 8.4 births for continuously married women in Roman Egypt. Whilst allowing for short-term variation, the balance of births and deaths must have been fairly stable in the long run: even a seemingly moderate net shortfall of 1 birth per woman would have halved a given population within three generations whereas a net surplus of 1 birth per woman would have doubled it, neither of which was at all likely to happen.

At the same time, even high fertility was mediated by an array of reproductive strategies. While the modern concept of family planning cannot be transposed to early societies, various mechanisms of fertility control were available and employed to varying degrees. Historically, female age at first marriage and the overall incidence of female marriage as well as remarriage used to be crucial determinants of fertility levels. Means of control within marriage include birth-spacing through lactational amenorrhea or abstinence, chemical contraception, and more invasive forms of intervention such as abortion, exposure, 'benign neglect', and outright infanticide.

While changes in marriage age or frequency may well have been important, we are unable to observe them in the record. By contrast, fertility control within marriage is at least dimly perceptible: the Egyptian census returns show multi-year intervals between births that must have been determined by cultural practices. Some of the contraceptives and abortifacients discussed in ancient literature may indeed have been effective, yet we cannot tell whether married couples would have resorted to such hazardous means or would even have wished to have fewer children in the first place. For the most part, ancient concerns about deliberately low fertility are best understood as moralizing rhetoric: there is no sign that ancient populations shrank out of sync with available resources.

Comparative evidence suggests that elites may have been most likely to curtail family size in order to preserve their estates and attendant status. Roman emperors can be shown to have reproduced at replacement level but the representative value of this sample remains unclear. At the other end of the social spectrum, the reproductive performance of slaves is largely unknown. Exposure, whilst reducing family size, did not always depress overall reproductivity since some babies were picked up and raised as slaves: the scale of this practice is obscure but may have been considerable. Overall, the potential of postnatal intervention to ease population pressure is a big unknown for ancient historians.

Sex selection is a related problem. Even today, femicidal practices are known to create imbalanced sex ratios and anthropological evidence for this custom is not uncommon: some scholars have used records of male-biased sex ratios to argue that something similar may have happened in the ancient world, especially among the Greeks. However, we cannot normally tell if such imbalances reflect actual femicide or merely discriminatory underreporting. Moreover, if femicide did indeed occur, it may have aimed to offset male excess mortality in violent conflict, analogous to strategies observed in some tribal cultures.

In the end, postnatal intervention for the purposes of fertility control or sex selection *may* conceivably have been an important determinant of social relations and even economic development but is almost impossible to investigate. This serves as a powerful reminder that demography mattered even when we cannot hope to find out how.

MARRIAGE, FAMILIES AND HOUSEHOLDS

Moving beyond impressionist accounts derived from literary sources, demographic study of the ancient family now focuses on quantifiable features such as marriage age and household structure. In general, and in keeping with later Mediterranean practice, early marriage for women and late marriage for men appears to have been common among Greeks and Romans. Like other elites in history, Roman aristocrats entered unions at unusually young ages, in the early to mid-teens for women and the late teens for men. Non-elite customs can only be assessed indirectly, by measuring shifts in commemorative patterns in epitaphs: thus, the age at which spouses replaced parents as commemorators for young adults is taken to reflect the age of first marriage. This method implies a substantial gap between a mean female marriage age of around age 20 and male marriage around age 30 in the western half of the empire.

However, as the available evidence is largely limited to urban environments and the first few centuries AD, we are left wondering about marriage practice in the countryside–where men may have married earlier–and about conditions in Republican Italy. The latter is particularly vexing because our understanding of the social impact of Roman mass conscription of young men critically depends on the average age of first marriage: if recruits had already acquired spouses and children, their absence might have been more disruptive than in the event of delayed marriage. As it is, the current model of late male marriage papers over big gaps in our knowledge but is simply the best we have got. By comparison, the Roman Egyptian census returns indicate slightly less delay, with first marriage in the late teens for women and from the early twenties onward for men.

The same census documents allow us to determine the mix of nuclear and complex households in that province: well over half of all recorded individuals belonged to extended-family or multi-couple households. While the Greek evidence is meager, Roman conditions are once again inferred from funerary epigraphy: since most deceased free civilians were commemorated by members of the nuclear family, single-couple households are thought to have been common. Urban bias, however, raises the possibility that rural households may have been more complex, as they were in Roman Egypt. Complex households are likewise known from other eastern provinces of the Roman empire.

Household composition matters because it is associated with the degree of autonomy of married couples–who may strike out on their own or remain embedded in extended families–as well as economic performance. Extended families provide better safeguards against risk but also are also conducive to higher fertility that may lower living standards, whereas neolocality would make it harder for widows and orphans to cope. These broader consequences of ancient marriage and household patterns have gradually begun to atract attention among historians. The later men married, the more likely their wives were to be widowed and their children to grow up fatherless. In Roman society, paternal mortality severely constricted the actual scope of *patria potestas*, a father's absolute authority over his household. Divorce, generally easier to come by than in the recent past, would have added further to the instability of families.

All in all, we end up with a picture that has much in common with modern conditions of fluidity and hybrid reconfiguration: step-parenting and adoption of relatives was common, creating complex arrangements that can only be documented for elite circles but would likely have occurred across all classes. Stereotypical ideologies of patriarchy were hard to reconcile with demographic realities.

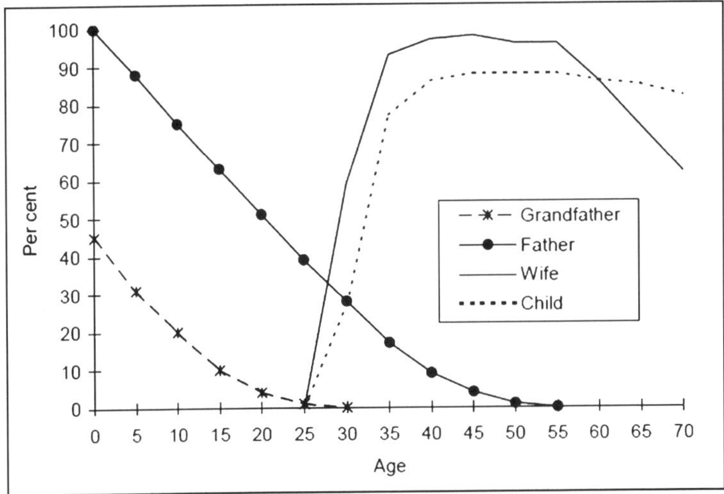

Fig. Approximate Proportion of Roman Men at Age x with at Least one Living Relative in a given Category

Meanwhile, what is arguably the single most striking feature of Greco-Roman marriage has failed to raise any curiosity at all–the fact that Greeks and Romans were strictly monogamous regardless of their socio-economic status, just like modern westerners but unlike most other early civilizations.

While our own experience might tempt us to take this for granted, we must ask how this principle came to be so firmly established even among elites–the egalitarian ethos of the city-state is a plausible candidate–, how it co-existed with de facto polygyny facilitated by sexual congress with chattel slaves, and how it became entrenched in Christian doctrine that survived the fall of the Roman state and ensured its survival and spread in later European history. In this strangely neglected area, ancient history has a vital contribution to make to our understanding of the global evolution of marriage.

POPULATION NUMBER

Questions of size have long occupied center stage in the study of ancient population reaching back at least as far as David Hume in the eighteenth century. Following a shift in focus from size to structure in the 1980s and 1990s, controversies over population number are now experiencing a comeback and force us to reconsider our most fundamental assumptions about the character of ancient societies. Studies of particular locales or groups can take us only so far, increasingly for want of anything new to say: this is certainly true of the perennial favourites, the debates about the size of the number of residents of classical Attica and the imperial metropolis of Rome.

The key question for Athens is whether, when and to what extent its population outstripped local food production and relied on maritime grain imports, an issue that is of more than antiquarian interest since it shapes our understanding of the driving forces behind political and military developments. By contrast, Rome's utter dependence on imported food has never been in doubt: here, the main problem is how to reconcile the huge population size implied by the recorded number of recipients of the grain dole with the limited extent of residential areas within the city boundaries: a grand total of up to 1 million would imply extremely high–though perhaps not impossible–settlement density. Much depends on the question of whether the *suburbium* was demographically integrated into the urban core.

Attempts to gauge the numerical size of social groups face even more formidable obstacles: thus, questions about the number of slaves in Attica or in Roman Italy, to name just two of the most prominent examples, are ultimately unanswerable, and can only be addressed on the basis of probabilistic modeling of demand for labour that puts some constraints on otherwise completely free-floating guesses. Similar problems bedevil the demographic study of religious groups such as Jews or early Christians in the Roman empire.

In any case, all these debates are dwarfed in importance by more general questions about the gross population of the core regions of the ancient Mediterranean world. A new comprehensive survey of all the evidence for the size of Greek poleis has prompted a higher estimate of the total number of all Greeks: we may now have to reckon with some 7 to 9 million people, albeit including assimilated indigenes, resident aliens, and slaves. Indeed, on some readings, parts of classical Greece such as Boeotia or Aegina were more densely settled than in any subsequent period prior to the twentieth century. These observations raise profound questions about the scale of Greek population growth between the nadir of the Early Iron Age around 1000 BC and the classical period 500 years later about the relative demographic strength of the Greeks and their competitors and most importantly about economic performance.

If the Greeks of the archaic and classical periods grew to be very numerous and even added to natural growth by importing lots of slaves but nevertheless experienced substantial improvements in living standards, their economies must have been unusually strong by pre-modern standards, which makes it necessary to revisit long-standing debates about the nature of 'the ancient economy'.

Roman population size is an even greater conundrum. While the number of Roman citizen—and hence the population of Italy as a whole–may seem unusually well documented thanks to a series of surviving census tallies stretching from the early Republic into the first century AD, on closer inspection these records create more problems than they solve. These counts, traditionally confined to adult men, rise gently in the second century BC but jump tenfold between 114 and 28 BC before returning to much slower growth to 5 million in AD 14 and 6 million in AD 47.

As this cannot possibly be read as a straightforward demographic progression, we have to choose between two ways of making sense of these figures. What we might call the 'low count' assumes that the Republican figures are broadly correct and the later ones are so much higher because of an undocumented switch to the registration of all men, women and children of citizen status, and allows us to read the apparent tenfold increase as a tripling or at best quadrupling of the citizenry caused by the enfranchisement of the Italian allies and residents of northern Italy and the beginning spread of citizenship to the provinces.

Conversely, the 'high count' is based on the belief that coverage remained unchanged but holds that Republican counts were increasingly defective and thus exaggerated the apparent scale of the first-century BC increase. In this scenario, 4 to 6 million adult male citizens most of them located in Italy proper, translate to a final Italian population of anywhere from 15 to 20 million including women, children, aliens and slaves and, therefore, a regional population density not encountered again until the nineteenth century.

Unfortunately, both interpretations raise logical problems. Hence, the 'low count' requires very high levels of popular military mobilization in the Republican period, very high levels of urbanization and metropolitan primacy, and high levels of mobility and suggests that Roman population numbers fell short of those of the High Middle Ages. The 'high count', on the other hand, renders Roman Italy exceptionally densely populated by pre-modern standards, calls for a massive demographic collapse at the end of this period, and leaves us wondering why Romans imported millions of slaves at a time of rapid indigenous population growth when they already faced conflict over access to land and underemployment–and why these conflicts ceased in the Principate even as population would at least initially have continued to grow.

Perhaps most crucially, it likewise raises questions about the size of the empire's population as a whole: while the 'low count' envisions some 60 to 70 million imperial subjects with one-tenth of them located in Italy itself, the 'high count' must assume either that the imperial heartland was massively overpopulated relative to its provinces or that the entire empire was much more populous than commonly assumed, presumably in excess of 100 million.

It does not help that independent consideration of provincial population size is largely unfeasible outside Egypt, and fails to yield unequivocal results even for that province. If the ancient Greek experience is anything to go by, a 'super-sized' empire is by no means impossible: in fact, it is widely accepted that the Asian and African parts of the empire did not re-attain Roman population densities until the nineteenth century. The key question is whether the same was true of Italy as well, and how other parts of the Mediterranean measured up.

In the end, just as for the Greek poleis, if we could be certain about population size, we would be e better able to compare economic performance in antiquity to conditions in the medieval and early modern periods. Archaeological data may hold the key to this issue: while field surveys can cast some light on patterns of land use in different periods, physical indices of well-being such as body height and dietary regimes may reflect the extent of population pressure. In this sphere, despite an abundance of published local field work, major synthetic analyses are only beginning to appear. These questions will continue to occupy ancient historians for some time to come, all the more so as they are of fundamental importance for our understanding of classical civilization: how good were very different kinds of ancient states–Greek city-states on the one hand, the Roman mega-empire on the other—at fostering economic development, how many people could these economies support, and in what style?

DISTRIBUTION AND MOBILITY

The urban-rural split of ancient populations is a closely related issue. More than most pre-modern societies, the Greco-Roman world was dominated by cities. Moving away from old debates about the economic character of ancient cities demographic research needs to concentrate on the degree of urbanization and its social and political consequences. While urbanization is usually regarded as an indicator of economic development, we often cannot tell whether urban residence was linked to non-agrarian occupations: if many farmers lived in urban settlements, a high level of urbanization might create a misleading impression of economic progress. Thus, if it is true that perhaps half of all Greeks in the classical period lived in towns, this would tell us a lot about the foundations of civic identity but little about division of labour or agricultural productivity.

The contrast between Greece and Roman Italy on the one hand and Roman Egypt on the other is particularly telling: most of the 1,000-odd poleis of the classical Greek world or the over 400 towns of Roman Italy must necessarily have been small and somewhat agrarian in character, whereas the 50 or so cities of Roman Egypt co-existed with numerous and sometimes massive villages that in Greece or Italy might well have been classified as urban communities. Ancient urbanization defies straightforward categorization and hinders cross-regional comparisons even within the same timeframe, let alone with later periods. Greco-Roman urbanism often needs to be studied on its own terms.

Even more than other branches of ancient demography, the study of population movements suffers greatly from the paucity of quantifiable evidence. Qualitative impressions simply will not do, and parametric models of putatively plausible flow volumes push us onto thin ice: my attempts to quantify Greek colonization, migration from and within Roman Italy, and the Roman slave trade give an idea of what can and cannot be expected from this conjectural approach. Luckily, an entirely new source of information has been opened up by the study of the genetic properties of current populations that allow us to infer earlier migration patterns. Earlier studies of blood group gene frequencies already produced tantalizing results, for instance regarding the extent to which ancient Greek immigrants came to demographically dominate Sicily and southern Italy. Research on mitochondrial DNA and the Y-chromosome are now the principal means of mapping migratory trajectories, although the ancient Mediterranean has only begun to be covered by this kind of work.

Other methods add to the scientific armory, such as stable isotope analysis that helps establish where interred individuals had been raised–and thus indicates migration when the isotope signatures associated with their place of origin differ significantly from those of their place of burial: for example, it has been shown that many individuals buried in the Isola Sacra necropolis near the ports of imperial Rome had moved there from other regions. Science stands to make a major contribution to our understanding of ancient population movements.

OUTLOOK

Beginning in the 1960s but primarily since the 1980s, ancient population history has been revolutionised by the adoption of the concepts, methods and questions of the historical demography of the more recent past. This has helped us integrate ancient demography into the wider field of population studies and draw on demographic insights to re-shape our vision of the ancient world. Further progress will result from more synthetic studies of archaeological remains and the application of scientific techniques from anthropometry to genetics.

Our ultimate goal is a better appreciation of the 'demographic regimes' of the ancient past, that is the culturally and ecologically specific configuration of demographic factors that governed people's lives, and of how they changed over time. This would make it easier to merge demography with social, economic, cultural and environmental history, and bring us a step closer to a truly integrative 'total history' of the ancient world. Unfortunately, this goal may never be achieved: much of what we would need to know about ancient demography will forever remain out of reach, even as comparative history teaches us how much it would matter in principle. This may seem frustrating, but it also means that demography will keep ancient historians on their toes–and that is a good thing.

2

Social Contract and Demography

INTRODUCTION

Since the founding of the United States as a sovereign nation, population diversity has challenged the values of inclusiveness and equality. Historically, these tensions manifested themselves in debates over taxation and representation; apportionment; and suffrage.

In modern times these values are disputed in controversies about the differential undercount and census adjustment; immigrants' rights to representation; access to higher education; and the entitlements of citizenship, among many other social issues. Essentially the question is about the rights of membership in a liberal democracy and whether citizenship is a special membership status.

The antecedents of the debate over membership date back to classical political theorists, particularly Thomas Hobbes, John Locke, and Jean-Jacque Rousseau. Their notion of membership derives from consent to be governed: individuals willingly concede some of their personal freedoms in exchange for security and other social benefits. Members maintain autonomy and avoid being subjected to the will of others by obeying laws they give themselves.

Ideally, the "general will" creates unity by subordinating individualism in the interest of the collective well-being. However, recognizing the challenge of forging unity from diversity, Rousseau warned of special interests—"partial societies"—within the state, which could undermine the ability of the general will to serve the common good. To prevent the emergence of social cleavages, Rousseau argued for democratic equality. Should factions arise, maintaining equality among them was essential to prevent the general will from dissolving into particular interests and undermining shared interests.

Of course, the real world is far more complicated than 18 century political theorists envisioned, yet these simple premises bear profound sessions for understanding the civic implications of recent demographic trends. The ideals of American democracy, which have influenced liberal democracies around the world, rely crucially on the notion of consent as the basis of citizenship even though few have specified what precisely constitutes consent.

Modern political theorists and legal scholars have elaborated the primitive Rousseauean vision of social contract theory, making distinctions between nominal citizenship, which is based on participation in social life, to formal citizenship, which guarantees the right to vote and to exercise political power.

And while the U.S. political system has been heralded as the gold standard of liberal democracy, according to Rogers M. Smith, "…for over 80 per cent of U.S. history, American laws declared most people in the world legally ineligible to become full U.S. citizens solely because of their race,…nationality or gender." In short, American democracy has violated the sacred values of inclusiveness and equity.

Against a backdrop of rising income inequality since 1973, the historically unparalleled diversification of the U.S. population compels a reexamination of the social contract to ask whether the terms of membership are qualified as heterogeneity increases, and if so, for whom and why. I argue that, as the principle motor of contemporary and past population diversity, immigration strains commitment to the democratic principles of inclusion and equity by redrawing the boundaries of membership based on ascription and an ever more narrow definition of citizenship. As long as membership confers different rights to different groups, future progress towards reducing social and economic inequality will be stymied. I conclude that population diversification warrants a realignment of democratic ideals with demographic realities.

In order to illustrate the powerful role of demography for understanding the evolution of social justice in the United States, I first sketch 20 century immigration trends and highlight nativity differentials in poverty and educational inequality. Historical debates about membership, as played out in controversies about representation and immigrant suffrage, illustrate some potentially deleterious civic consequences of recent demographic trends.

I also identify several contemporary issues that show how immigration has sharpened group boundaries and strengthened civic hierarchies. This need not be so if the rules of membership are made more inclusive and the commitment to equity renewed.

My conception of citizenship as a social contract conceding the right to be governed in exchange for privileges, rights and social obligations emphasizes the liberal ideas of T.H. Marshall, who considers equity and social welfare as core features of mature citizenship; Jamin Raskin, who differentiates among citizenship as presence, as integration, and as standing; and Rogers Smith, who views citizenship as an institution for distributing life opportunities. In what follows I argue that the relative openness of U.S. borders makes immigration central to the project of democracy for the 21 Century.

DEMOGRAPHY OF DIVERSIFICATION

The ebb and flow of immigration during the 20 century is evident in the changing race, ethnic, and nativity composition of the U.S. population.

In 2001, over 10 per cent of U.S. residents were foreign born; this share has more than doubled since 1970. The absolute number of immigrants is much larger now than at the turn of the century because the population base was much smaller. Both at the turn of the 20 and 21 centuries, immigration was and is a highly politicized social issue.

Four decades of high-volume immigration from virtually every country, rising intermarriage, and persisting fertility differentials have transformed the United States into the most demographically complex country in the world. Since in 1960, the changed source countries of immigrants have visibly altered the U.S. ethno-racial landscape, just as the shift in source countries from Western to Eastern European countries did during the latter half of the 19 and early 20 century.

At the turn of the 19 century, 12 per cent of the U.S. population was black and an additional 1 per cent combined either Hispanic, Asian, or American Indian. Half a century later, these same groups combined accounted for 13 per cent of the U.S. population, except that the black share had fallen from 12 per cent to 10 per cent. Yet, over the next 50 years the combined share of blacks, Hispanics, Asians, and Native Americans swelled to just under 30 per cent of the total population.

Table. Changing Population Composition, 1900-2000

	Race and Hispanic Origin					
Year	**Whites**	**Blacks**	**Hispanics**	**Asians**	**AIND**	**Total FB %**
1900	87.9	11.6	–0.2	0.3	13.6	
1950	89.5	10.0	–0.2	0.2	6.9	
1960	88.6	10.5	–0.5	0.3	5.4	
(%FB)	5.9	0.7	–31.9	0.0		
1970	83.5	11.1	4.5	0.8	0.4	4.7
(%FB)	4.2	1.1	19.9	35.7	1.9	
1980	79.7	11.7	6.4	1.6	0.7	6.2
(%FB)	3.9	3.1	28.6	58.6	2.5	
1990	75.6	12.0	8.8	2.9	0.8	7.9
(%FB)	5.0	4.9	35.8	63.1	2.3	
2000	70.6	12.3	12.5	4.0	0.7	10.4
(%FB)	3.6	6.2	39.0	61.4	-	

Note: (per centFB) = Per cent Foreign-Born. all percentages may not Sum to 100 Due to Rounding and Estimation.

The force of immigration is evident in the changing nativity composition of these pan-ethnic groups. Whereas only one-third of Asians were foreign born in 1960, this share rose to 63 per cent during the 1990s. In like fashion, the foreign-born share of the Hispanic population nearly doubled from 1970 to 2000. By contrast, the foreign-born share of the non-Hispanic white population has declined slightly, from six to three percentage points, while the black share has risen from 1 per cent-6 per cent. Although differential fertility also has altered the ethno-racial composition of the U.S. population, I focus on immigration because it is the single most powerful force driving the demography of diversification, and because nativity differentials at best maintain or at worst increase aggregate socioeconomic inequality.

A brief overview of poverty and educational differentials suffices to make this point. The decline in poverty, from 22 per cent to 17 per cent between 1960 and 1965, and to 12.3 per cent a decade later, is one of the stellar achievements of the War on Poverty. However, sizeable nativity differentials persist.

In 1999, when 11.8 per cent of the U.S. population was poor, immigrant poverty exceeded that of natives by 5.6 percentage points—16.8 per cent versus 11.2 per cent, respectively. Moreover, recent immigrants are more likely to be poor than earlier arrivals, and noncitizen poverty is over twice that of naturalized citizens. Specifically, just over one in five noncitizens were poor in 1999 compared to less than one in ten naturalized citizens.

Immigrants from Latin America are much more likely to be poor than those hailing from Europe, Asia, or Africa. In 1999, less than 10 per cent of European immigrants lived in poverty compared to 13 per cent of those from Asia and Africa, and over one-in-five immigrants from Latin America. Mexicans and Central Americans are the poorest among the foreign born, with one in four below the poverty threshold in 1999. Because Mexicans now account for over one-quarter of the foreign-born population, up from 8.2 per cent in 1970, their high poverty rate weighs heavily on the aggregate immigrant poverty rate and especially the poverty rate for Latin Americans.

To a considerable extent, differentials in economic well-being are rooted in large and persisting educational disparities among demographic groups, which are exacerbated by the influx of immigrants with very low and very high educational levels. Among college graduates, there are small differences between native and foreign-born adults because the majority of immigrants who gain admission under the occupational preferences are highly selected towards advanced degrees. However, the nativity differential in high school graduation is appreciable: 87 per cent of native born persons ages 25 and over are high school graduates, compared to 67 per cent of the foreign-born. Aggregate differentials in high school completion reflect the comparatively low educational levels of recent immigrants from Central and South America, but especially Mexico.

The diversification narrative would be of little socioeconomic or civic consequence if the promises of the Great Society had been delivered. Some were; others were rescinded; and still others have been threatened by restrictive legislation that deprives immigrants of their full rights of civic membership. By comparison with studies of socioeconomic inequality, demographers have paid considerably less attention to what Milton Gordon characterized as civic assimilation—that is, membership, statutory citizenship, and political participation. These primary rights are pillars of a liberal democracy committed to the values of inclusion and equality, and essential for preventing the re-emergence of what Rogers M. Smith dubbed "ascriptive democracy"—that is civic hierarchies defined by race, birthplace, sex, and age, with their attendant social and economic consequences.

U.S. immigration history dramatically illustrates ascriptive democracy in play. This story has been thoroughly scripted and warrants no elaboration except to underscore three points. First, the 1924 Immigration Act, frequently called the National Origins Act, set the first numerical limits on immigration, set country quotas based on 2 per cent of resident nationalities according to the 1890 census, and established a commission to determine the country quotas. However, heated debate ensued about whether to apportion the quotas using the 1890 census as the law stipulated, or the 1920 census. This controversy centered fundamentally on protecting a Tocquevillian image of American national identity as white and Anglo Saxon.

The 1890 census did this, but the 1920 census did not because almost 90 per cent of all immigrants enumerated in 1890 were from Northern and Western Europe or Canada, but by 1920 only 45 per cent were. Originally scheduled to go into effect in 1927, the political struggle over the apportionment of quotas delayed implementation of the 1924 Immigration Act until 1929. In the end, quotas were based on the 1920 census. Second, the 1952 Immigration Act, which was passed over President Truman's veto, repealed the Asiatic exclusion clause that had damaged American prestige overseas, but retained the 1920 census as the basis for apportioning quotas.

This legislation reinforced the pro-European bias of U.S. visas by explicitly restricting Eastern European immigration through numerical ceilings. As a concession to the social value of inclusiveness, this legislation ended the ban of nonwhite immigration imposed in 1790.

If the architects of the 1924 Immigration Act were in denial about demography in America, they were even more naïve about how the politics of exclusion extol their price as unintended consequences. References to the restrictions imposed by the 1924 legislation emphasize the quotas imposed to exclude groups by limiting new admissions to tiny shares of the resident national origins, yet its long term impact derives more from the groups exempt from the quotas.

Explicitly excluded from the numerical quotas were immigrants from: Canada, Newfoundland, Mexico, Cuba, Haiti, the Dominican Republic, the Canal Zone, and the independent countries of Central and South America, along with their immediate dependent family members. Since 1980, Mexico has been the leading source country of U.S. immigrants, and along with Haiti and the Dominican Republic, is a major contemporary source of undocumented immigration. Third, the heightened volume and changed composition of U.S.-bound migration since 1970 was seeded in the 1924 Act, and bolstered by the 1965 Amendments to the 1952 Immigration Act. Designed to atone for the discriminatory foundations of the 1924 national origins quota system, the 1965 Amendments accomplished several things. One, by abolishing the quota system, the Amendments opened doors to immigration from countries previously excluded, notably Asian and African nations, albeit with strict country limits.

Two, an annual ceiling of 120,000 was extended to Western Hemisphere immigrants and individual countries were subjected to the 20,000 annual country maximum to which Eastern hemisphere countries had been subjected. Finally, the 1965 Amendments shifted the emphasis of the visa allocation preference system from labour market priorities to family reunification. Initially, 74 per cent of total visas available each year were reserved for relatives of U.S. citizens and permanent resident aliens, but this share of the numerically regulated visas was raised to 80 per cent in 1980.

Co-sponsor of the 1965 immigration legislation, Emanual Celler argued during the floor debate that few Asians or Africans would enter the country because they had no family ties to the United States. In signing the bill into law, President Lyndon Johnson reassured his critics of benign consequences: "This bill that as suggested, sign today is not a revolutionary bill. It does not affect the lives of millions.

It will not reshape the structure of our daily lives". Then Attorney General Robert Kennedy predicted approximately 5,000 immigrants from the Asia-Pacific triangle and very few thereafter; Secretary of State Dean Rusk anticipated 8,000 immigrants from India over 5 years; Senator Edward Kennedy argued that the ethnic mix of the country would not be upset. History scripted otherwise, as European immigration plummeted following post World War II reconstruction, while rising inequality and political strife in Latin America and Asia swelled the ranks of workers aspiring better opportunities for earning a living.

Not only did the 1965 Amendments usher in a new period of mass migration, but the law did affect the lives of millions of residents already here and those yet to come. Immigrants from the Americas comprised about one-third of those admitted during the 1930s and 1940s and nearly 40 per cent of new arrivals during the 1950s. Since 1960, roughly half of all immigrants admitted hail from the Americas, and about one-third from Asia.

Owing to the legalization programme authorized by the 1986 Immigration Reform and Control Act, during the 1990s, the number of legal immigrants exceeded nine million, of which 42 per cent originated in Latin America. If the diversification narrative broadened the cultural space to forge a core American identity from many race and ethnic strands, participation in the reformulated "WE" required rewriting the social contract to realign democracy with demography. This is the project of U.S. democracy for the 21 century—forging and governing a "world nation" within a framework of social justice.

As such, historical and contemporary debates over apportionment and suffrage provide key sessions about how changing population composition evolved into civic hierarchies that undermine the commitment to values of inclusiveness and egalitarianism, and they highlight future challenges to civic integration of the foreign-born. I discuss each in turn.

APPORTIONMENT, SUFFRAGE, AND THE POLITICS OF EXCLUSION

Constitutional guarantees of representation and suffrage were integral to forging the social contract, yet both rights have been contested terrain since the nation's founding. The 14 Amendment of the U.S. Constitution clearly states that, "Representatives shall be apportioned among the several states according to their respective numbers, counting the whole number of persons in each state, excluding Indians not taxed."

That all persons residing in the United States are counted for the purposes of apportionment, but only citizens are permitted to vote in national elections, presumes that the right to representation is more fundamental than the right to exercise the franchise.

However, the value of representation is eroded to the extent that growing numbers of "new Americans" have no voice in selecting who represents them. This need not be so, and for a large part of our history, including most of the last period of mass migration, non-citizens were allowed to vote. Although the landmark "one-person, one-vote" decision responded directly to inequities in representation and exercise of the franchise, the presence of immigrants continues to defy the value of inclusiveness.

APPORTIONMENT

The method used to apportion the seats in the U.S. House of Representatives conveys commitment to equality as a social value; the question of who should be included in the apportionment population conveys the value of inclusiveness. Since 1790, five different methods have been used to allocate the seats among states.

All methods emphasize equity relative to population size; the current method of equal proportions in use since 1940 has the advantage of minimizing the proportional difference in the average district size between two states, with a bias favouring small states. Because the Constitution neither requires apportionment after every census nor specifies how to apportion, these decisions are entirely within the purview of Congress.

The matter of who should be included in the apportionment base has been controversial since the Constitution was ratified, so it is remarkable that its provisions for representation have withstood the test of time and numerous legal challenges. The Civil War raised the value of slaves from 3/5 to full persons for purposes of representation; the 14 Amendment defined statutory citizenship, provided equal protection for all persons, and reaffirmed the principles of representation on the basis of persons, including non-citizens.

Since that time, the collision of political interests with the moral principles of justice and fairness has precipitated several legal challenges to the practice of including immigrants—both legal and undocumented—in the apportionment base. For example, to support claims that the framers of the Constitution were unable to envision the emergence of undocumented immigration, advocates of a citizen-only apportionment base argue that the absence of immigration policy prior to 1875 made this category inconceivable in 1787, and that the words inhabitants, persons, and citizens are deliberately used interchangeably in the Constitution.

However, Gerald Neuman dismisses these claims because prior to 1875, legislation regulating foreign admissions was largely a state concern, and once slavery ceased to be a divisive issue, systematic federal regulation was possible.

The first major 20 century apportionment controversy involved the 1920 census, which singled out immigrants as a source of "distortion" in the rural-urban population distribution. Representatives from rural states slated to lose Congressional seats to urbanized states with large immigrant populations proposed a panoply of reapportionment bills designed to correct the alleged immigration distortion. Even though they paid taxes and had been legally admitted to the United States, the anti-immigrant Representatives considered immigrants unworthy of representation in Congress.

The ensuing vitriol found ample pseudo-scientific support in the 42-volume Dillingham Commission Report, which claimed that immigrants from eastern and southern Europe were intellectually inferior and unworthy of naturalization. Kansas Representative Homer Hoch argued that exclusion of non-citizens from apportionment not only would alter the allocation of seats in 16 states, but would allow farming states to retain their seats.

The bitter and protracted political struggle culminated in several unsuccessful Constitutional Amendments to exclude all aliens for purposes of apportionment. In the end, the rural states won the debate because there was no reapportionment based on the 1920 census. Although, the balance of power was preserved, the passage of restrictive immigration legislation in 1924 testified that the admission of foreigners had assumed center stage in Congress.

In anticipation of the 1930 census and to avoid a similar spectacle, in 1929 Congress passed legislation requiring reapportionment after each census. Apparently the sessions from the 1920 apportionment dispute faded quickly because the 76 Congress again debated the immigration-apportionment question.

New York Representative Hamilton Fish, conceded that "it is one of the most difficult problems for the House to solve on a fair and nonpartisan basis". Not surprisingly, Representatives from New York and Illinois, two states where immigration had figured prominently in population growth, strongly supported including aliens in the apportionment base. By contrast, Representative John Elliot Rankin, a Mississippi Democrat, claimed that "... the reapportionment must be based upon persons, and that means American persons; it does not mean alien persons who owe no allegiance to the United States"

On matters of immigration, political interests did not follow partisan lines. The fight was not about the disappearance of a Jeffersonian agrarian society; at stake was the balance of power between those states growing rapidly through immigration, and the sparsely populated rural states. Combined, the six immigrant-receiving states gained 16 seats in the House between 1900 and 1910, signaling a shift in political power that threatened the interests of rural states should immigration continue. And continue it did, until Congress passed legislation to restrict who and how many were admitted. Between 1960 and 2000, these same six states, which currently house 75 per cent of the foreign-born population, increased their share of House seats from 153 to 171, so that currently they hold nearly two of every five seats. There are 435 seats in the House of Representatives—a number that has been fixed since 1911, but variable before that time.

Given how much ink and energy have been expended on the politics of immigrant exclusion in matters of representation, and in light of the growing political dominance in the U.S. House of Representatives of the six immigrant receiving states, it is instructive to imagine how representation and apportionment would have changed if a Constitutional Amendment to exclude all immigrants from apportionment had succeeded; if the restrictionists in Congress had succeeded in averting the two great waves of 20 century immigration; or if rural states had succeeded in eliminating non-citizens from apportionment.

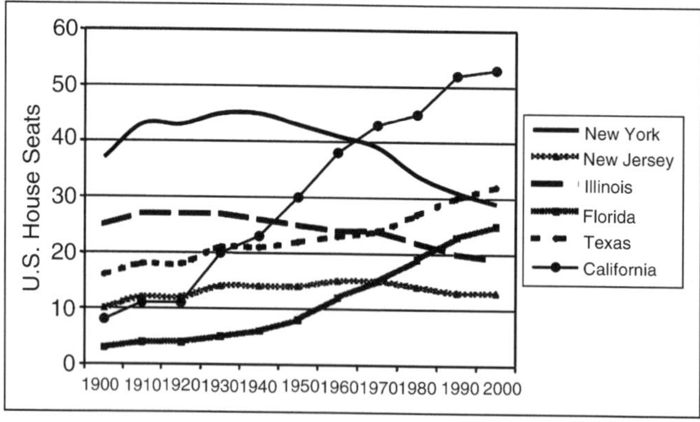

Fig. Seats in u.s. House of Representatives Held by Six Leading Immigrant Receiving States, 1900-2000

To develop these counterfactuals, I simulated three scenarios each for the period 1900 through 1930, which covered the first wave of 20 century mass migration, and from 1960 to the present, which represents the second wave of 20 century mass migration. These three scenarios simulate the world that the politics of exclusion sought to create under the banner of ascriptive democracy, namely: apportionment restricted to the native-born designated "natives only;" apportionment assuming no immigration between 1900 and 1930, and none again after 1960 denoted "halt immigration;" and apportionment that excludes non-citizens dubbed "citizens only." Stopping immigration in 1900 or 1960 is not only less stringent than excluding all of the foreign-born from apportionment, but also is more in keeping with liberal ideology to embrace those already here, while lifting the gangplank to future arrivals. "Citizens only" is the least restrictive of all, implicitly stipulating a "qualified membership" for those who do not pledge allegiance.

That the total number of reshuffled seats for a given scenario is usually less than the number of states affected reflects the high residential concentration of immigrants, the highly unequal populations of the 50 states, and the small state bias of the formula used to apportion seats in Congress. To simplify the exposition, I summarize the results for each period by counterfactual, beginning with the most restrictive scenario and concluding with the least restrictive. This strategy helps illustrate how layers of qualified membership undermines the spirit of equal representation.

FIRST PERIOD OF 20 CENTURY MASS MIGRATION

Had apportionment excluded all immigrants in 1910, when 15 per cent of the population was foreign born, 24 seats would have been reshuffled among 29 states, with 17 states gaining and 12 losing seats.

As the primary hub of European immigrants during the 19 century, New York would have sustained the greatest losses, with eight fewer seats than were actually assigned, and Mississippi would have claimed two of the reshuffled seats. For 1920, the "natives only" scenario would have reallocated 22 seats—two fewer than in 1910—among 28 states, with 15 gaining and 13 losing seats.

Following a decade of numerical restrictions on immigration, by 1930 only 15 seats would have been reshuffled among 20 states had apportionment been restricted to native born persons. Seat losses affected eight states, with New York sustaining over one-third of the losses, while 12 different states would have increased their congressional power.

A less stringent scenario, "halting immigration in 1900," excludes recent immigrants from the apportionment. Because two-thirds of the resident foreign born in 1910 arrived prior to 1900, stopping immigration in 1900 would have reshuffled only eight seats among 14 states in 1910, with eight gaining and six loosing seats in the U.S. House of Representatives.

Table. Reapportionment Summary for Three Scenarios about Representation of the Foreign-born

	Natives Only				Stop Immigration*			Citizens Only	
	Seats Reshuffled	States Affected		States Reshuffled	States Affected		States Reshuffled	States Affected	
		Gainers	Losers		Gainers	Losers		Gainers	Losers
Period 1									
1910	24	17	12	8	8	6	7	7	6
1910	24	17	12	8	8	6	7	7	6
1920	22	15	13	12	8	9	12	9	8
1930	15	12	8	12	12	8	7	7	5
Period 2									
1970	6	6	3	3	3	3	3	3	3
1980	8	8	3	6	6	3	6	6	3
1990	12	12	4	11	11	4	8	8	4
2000	16	16	5	14	14	5	9	9	4

* In Period 1, Recent Immigrants are defined by those who arrived after 1900, while in Period 2 Recent Immigrants refer to those who arrived after 1960.

Under this scenario, New York would have lost three instead of eight seats, and Mississippi would have reclaimed one seat. Had there been no immigration after 1900 and had Congress actually been reapportioned in 1920, 12 seats would have been reallocated among 17 states, with eight gaining and nine losing votes in congress.

Because immigration restrictions were actually implemented during the 1920s, a 1930 reapportionment that assumed no immigration after 1900 would have reshuffled the same number of seats as in 1920, except that 20 rather than 17 states would have been affected, with 12 gaining and eight losing seats. New York alone would have lost five seats if 2.3 million immigrants who arrived after 1900 had been excluded from the 1930 reapportionment, while California, Connecticut, Illinois, Massachusetts, Michigan, New Jersey, and Washington would have each lost one seat.

The third scenario, which responds to Representative Rankin's views about representation and citizenship, restricts the apportionment to "citizens only." This counterfactual produces the smallest effects on reapportionment because naturalization rates were relatively high at the beginning of the 20 century, particularly following the Americanization movement to naturalize the foreign born. Only seven seats would have been reshuffled in 1910 by restricting congressional apportionment to citizens, with seven states gaining and six losing seats. Under this scenario New York would have only lost two seats.

By 1920, however, the "citizens only" counterfactual would have reallocated 12 congressional seats among 17 states, with nine gaining and eight losing votes in Congress. Iowa, Maine, Missouri, Pennsylvania, Rhode Island, and Vermont would each have lost one seat, while Massachusetts and New York would have lost two and four seats, respectively, had congressional representation been restricted to statutory citizens. Because the Americanization movement to increase naturalization rates was relatively effective in reducing the number of resident aliens, excluding non-citizens from the 1930 reapportionment would have reshuffled only seven seats, costing New York three and assigning one of these to Mississippi.

SECOND PERIOD OF 20 CENTURY MASS MIGRATION

The hiatus in immigration following the Great Depression reduced the foreign-born share of the national population to around 5 per cent by 1960, where it stabilized until after 1970. Therefore, the reapportionment simulations are less dramatic—at least until the second wave of mass migration unfolded. Thus, rather than decrease over time, the impact of immigration on the distribution of congressional power rose during the second period of mass migration. A second difference between the first and second periods of 20 century mass migration is that the states gaining and losing political power due to immigration changed, signaling a shift in congressional influence from the East and Midwest to the South and West.

Using the most restrictive "natives only" scenario for assigning congressional seats in 1970 would have reshuffled six seats among nine states, with six gaining and three losing seats. New York alone would have shouldered half of the lost seats, with California and Florida rounding out the losses at two and one, respectively. Beneficiaries of a 1970 reapportionment that excluded immigrants include Alabama, Maryland, Oregon, Pennsylvania, Tennessee, and Wisconsin—each with one additional seat. However, the increased volume of immigration over the next decade had more sizeable consequences for the 1980 distribution of power in Congress, as eight seats would have been reshuffled if apportionment had been restricted to natives.

California, New York, and Florida would have lost four, three, and one seats, respectively. Of the eight states gaining seats under this scenario, five are in the South and three in the Midwest.

The rising momentum of immigration during the 1980s and 1990s, which included the legalization of 2.7 million undocumented immigrants, had a more sizeable impact on the distribution of congressional power compared to the prior two decades. In 1990, the "natives only" counterfactual implies a reshuffling of 12 seats, of which 11 were due to post-1960 immigrants. In the most recent apportionment, 16 congressional seats would have been reshuffled among 21 states if the apportionment were based on the "natives only" scenario. Five states would sustain seat losses while 16 states would gain one seat each.

Because the 1965 Amendments to the Immigration and Nationality Act did not go into effect until 1968, the volume of immigration during the decade was relatively low. Therefore, "halting immigration in 1960" would have had a very modest effect on the 1970 distribution of congressional power—

reshuffling only three seats among six states. Moreover, reapportionment based on "citizens only" would have identical effects because in 1970 nearly 66 per cent of foreign born residents were naturalized citizens. But as the volume of immigration increased, so too did its consequences for the distribution of congressional votes among states. Owing to low naturalization rates among recent immigrants, for 1980 both the "halt immigration" and the "citizens only" scenarios would have reshuffled six seats among nine states, with six gaining and three losing seats. Under both counterfactuals, California would have borne the lion's share of the losses by forfeiting three seats, and New York would have lost two seats and Florida one seat.

In the 1990 reapportionment, the "halt immigration" scenario would have reshuffled 11 seats among 15 states, with California losing seven seats, New York two seats, and Texas and Florida one a piece. By 2000, the impact of recent immigration on the distribution of congressional power approached the magnitude witnessed in 1930. Apportioning seats assuming no immigration after 1960 would have reshuffled 14 congressional seats among 19 states in 2000, with California alone forfeiting eight seats, Florida and New York two each, and Texas and New Jersey one a piece. The 14 beneficiaries of the reshuffled seats, each receiving one additional vote in Congress, were dispersed throughout the country, and included Montana, Utah, and Oklahoma, among other states.

Because the naturalized share of the foreign-born population had fallen to 40 per cent by 1990, reapportioning using the "citizens only" scenario would have reshuffled eight seats among 12 states, with California alone forfeiting five, and Florida, New York and Texas each giving up one seat for the benefit of three southern states, along with four states in the north central region and Pennsylvania in the East. Confining the 2000 apportionment to birthright and naturalized citizens would have reshuffled one more seat than in 1990—with California forfeiting the additional seat. However, the profile of beneficiary states in each year differed. Owing to shifts in population distribution and the small state bias of the apportionment formula, Oklahoma, Indiana, Utah, Mississippi, and Wisconsin would have gained a seat in 2000 had apportionment been restricted to statutory citizens, but Georgia, Kansas, Louisiana, and Ohio would not.

Of course, these counterfactuals produce very conservative estimates of the impact of immigration on the distribution of Congressional power because they ignore the compounding demographic effects from immigrant fertility and internal migration in response to immigration. Moreover, because the Supreme Court unequivocally ruled that all persons are to be included in the population base for purposes of apportionment, these scenarios will not materialize. Nevertheless, they provide several important sessions. First, the effects of immigration on Congressional apportionment of immigration declined from 1900 to 1930 as political anxiety about the impact of the foreign born on representation rose, but the impact has risen appreciably since 1960 and particularly after 1980. This is also evident by comparing the difference between the "natives only" and "halt immigration" scenarios in Table. Furthermore, the states losing seats are more concentrated during the latter period, reflecting the higher concentration of immigrants in six states.

Second, based on the number of seats and states involved, the impact of immigration on the distribution of congressional power is most similar in 2000 and 1930 across all scenarios, except that there has been a shift in the balance of power among the six immigrant receiving states to California, Texas, and Florida from New York, New Jersey, and Illinois, at the expense of other states. In 1930, New York, New Jersey, and Illinois collectively held one in five House seats; currently, California, Texas, and Florida combined hold one in four House seats. These conditions are ripe for another round of restrictions on immigration to stem the flow, as well as new variants of ascriptive democracy.

Third, the consequences of the "citizens only" scenario rise before declining during the early period, but rise continually during the latter period. As Figure shows, this is because the proportion of naturalized immigrants was relatively high at the turn of the century, ranging from a low of 46 per cent to a high of 60 per cent during the first period of mass migration. Although the Americanization movement during this period was partly responsible for the high naturalization rates, naturalization rates declined during the most recent period, falling about 50 per cent from almost two out of every three immigrants in 1970 to just over one in three by 2000.

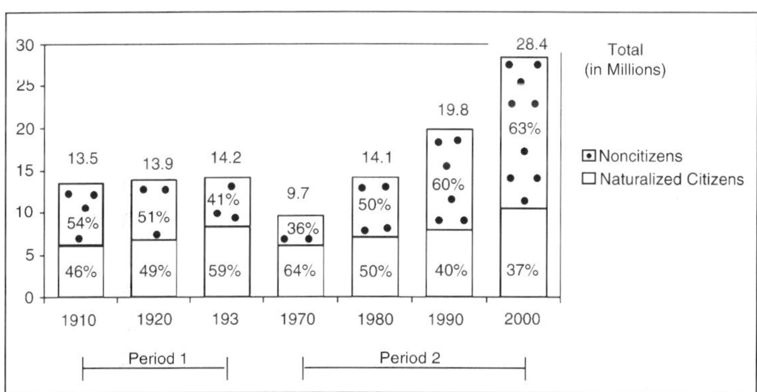

Fig. Citizenship Status of Foreign-Born Population for Two Periods Of Mass Migration

Fourth and more important, the "citizens only" scenario raises a real moral dilemma because non-citizens, who are a growing share of the immigrant population, do not have a voice in selecting their Representatives and because residential concentration of immigrants creates serious problems of malapportionment. For example, Illinois did not redraw congressional districts between 1900 and 1940, and although its number of Congressional seats held relatively stable, the disparity between the smallest and largest Illinois Congressional district rose from 105 thousand to 752 thousand persons. Nationally, the problem of malapportionment increased such that by 1960, the 20 most populous districts represented a combined population of 14 million compared to 4.6 million residents for the smallest 20 districts. Although disparities in the sizes of congressional or legislative districts size are not due entirely to immigration, problems of malapportionment are particularly harsh for districts containing large numbers of immigrants who can't vote because they are not citizens.

The problem of unequal voice has two solutions: one is to equalize the voting power across districts; the other solution is to strive for truly equal representation by allowing non-citizens to vote. However, both solutions are problematic from an operational or a legal standpoint. Equalizing voting power would appear to be straightforward, but immigration complicates the solution because the residential concentration of the foreign-born poses moral and practical dilemmas for achieving equal representation.

Essentially, the solution involves a choice between an exclusive apportionment that protects citizens' right to voting equality, and an inclusive apportionment that ensures equal representation for all persons, including non-citizens. The dilemma is moral because decisions about inclusion or exclusion of non-citizens from congressional and state legislative districts invoke issues of fairness, the spirit of equal representation, and the fundamental rights of membership implicit in the social contract; it is practical because population-based allocation of state and local monies could perpetuate inequities between the included and excluded residents, thereby effectively blocking the emergence of a Marshallian conception of social citizenship.

Figure for Los Angeles County illustrates the dilemma of balancing the democratic values of electoral equality and representational equity in districts with a high concentration of noncitizens. Electoral equality emphasizes proportionality of registered voters across districts, while equal representation dictates redistricting using population proportions as the base. Applying electoral equality on the basis of citizenship produced districts in

Los Angeles County with highly unequal populations: in 1971, district 4 had a population 70 per cent larger than district 9, despite similar proportions of registered voters. But an alternative plan proposed for 1990, which balances total residents without taking direct account of differences in citizenship, violates the spirit of "one-person, one-vote" by weighting more heavily the votes of citizens residing in districts with larger shares of unnaturalized immigrants compared to those with few immigrants. In effect, representational equality is traded for electoral inequality; that is, demographic equity implies unequal membership in a democratic society. An alternative solution to the problem of malapportionment in places with large immigrant populations is to equalize voting privileges.

The difficulty here is that the Constitution explicitly restricts voting in national elections to citizens, but not necessarily in state and local elections. Legislation passed in 1996 made alien voting in federal elections a felony, and voting in violation of any federal, state or local law grounds for removal. However, states retain great latitude in their local apportionment and voting criteria, provided that they do not engineer discriminatory impacts in violation of the Voting Rights Act.

Voting equality is possible at the state and local level if non-citizens are allowed to vote legally. This requires going beyond citizenship as presence, which recognizes that the resident foreign-born shape the lives of their communities and embracing Raskin's concept of citizenship as integration, which involves socializing newcomers in the activities that lead to formal citizenship, including participating in the governance of their communities. A review of alien suffrage makes this point more forcefully.

CITIZENSHIP AS PRESENCE AND STANDING

As a master status, citizenship defines membership, confers rights and privileges, and distributes life opportunities. The right to hold public office and the franchise are two of the most sacred privileges of citizenship, which distinguish this status from aliens, including those admitted as legal residents. The 14 Amendment, ratified in 1868, defines citizens as "All persons born or naturalized in the United States...," while the 15 Amendment guarantees all citizens the right to vote. Congress legislated itself power to enforce voting rights, but enforcement was irresponsibly lax until the Voting Rights Act of 1965 and its various reauthorizations put teeth into monitoring activities.

The stage of African American's quasi-citizenship has been well documented in legal and academic scholarship. Less well known is the story of immigrant suffrage and its role in nation-building, particularly how states used the state franchise instrumentally to increase population and gain seats in Congress. In fact, non-citizen voting was common through the early 20 century because federalism permits considerable discretion in civil matters, including specifying the privileges of state citizenship and deciding matters of legislative apportionment.

Although the federal Constitution restricts the national franchise to citizens, "categorical denial of noncitizens' voting is neither constitutionally required nor historically normal". But, the story of alien suffrage was neither linear nor smooth, involving periods of expansion and retrenchment along the way. During the Colonial Era, non-citizens not only voted, but also held public office. Neuman claims that the early instances of alien suffrage occurred because of the confused relationship between state and federal citizenship, which was only partly clarified by the Fourteenth Amendment. According to Rousseau, such ambiguity in the boundaries of political communities are natural to emerging states, whose values and principals are being forged in their social contract. Historically, access to the franchise not only excluded blacks, women, and the young but also selected non-Protestant groups. Rhode Island precluded Jews from voting until 1842; Catholics and Jews were denied the franchise in most colonies, while Quakers and Baptists could not vote in others. On the eve of the Civil War in 1860, aliens were allowed to vote in as many states as blacks—six. As barriers of property, race, sex, literacy, age, and other impediments to universal suffrage were eliminated through Constitutional Amendments and legislative acts, the suffrage rights of noncitizens were eroded and ultimately terminated, except for a few localities.

Secondary sources on the subject of alien suffrage disagree about how many, which, and when states allowed non-citizens to vote. A tally based on certain end-dates indicates that at least 22 states and territories allowed non-citizens to vote in the nineteenth century and that several permitted aliens to vote and hold public office during the early post-Colonial period. Thus, a count of all states recognized for ever permitting noncitizens to vote produces an upper limit of 35.

When the right to vote was linked mainly to property, age, sex, and race rather than to citizenship, and before the 14 Amendment was ratified, a legal interpretation of "inhabitants" easily included immigrants. As the United States consolidated its state and national identities during the late 18 and through most of the 19 centuries, state citizenship was a salient identity from which immigrants benefited and to which they contributed. The militant nationalism and xenophobia following the War of 1812 precipitated the first retrenchment of alien suffrage, largely involving the relatively well-populated eastern states, including New York, Vermont, Tennessee, Pennsylvania, and Massachusetts.

According to Porter, between 1820-1845 state suffrage debates lost sight of the foreigner, especially those occupied with the "free Negro" and reaming property tests. Even as the franchise was being rescinded in some states, other states capitalized on the paradigm of strong electoral federalism for instrumental purposes by declaring unnaturalized aliens as state citizens—assuming, of course, that they were white men 21 years and older. At that time, women and persons under 21 were ineligible to vote. Neither, of course, were slaves, and naturalization was closed to most Asian nationals until 1952. Despite the ratification of the 14 and 15 Amendments, in many southern states, African Americans were voiceless until the enactment and enforcement of the Voting Rights Act.

Even after the federal government's exclusive power to naturalize aliens was clarified, distinctions between state and national citizenship permitted states to grant aliens the franchise, by declaring them state citizens. Beginning with Wisconsin in 1848, states that allowed immigrants to vote required declarations of an intention to become U.S. citizens as a condition for voting, and several imposed a minimum residency requirement. Thus, at least during the mid to late 19 century, non-citizen voting was pre-citizen voting. Williams suggests that "naturalization was practically a state affair" until 1882 because of lax federal supervision over the records and procedures. Moreover, vigilance over the process by which first papers were filed was also weak to nonexistent. In Nebraska, or example, immigrants who took out their first papers for national citizenship were allowed to vote in national elections even before the 6-month waiting period.

The issue of non-citizen voting was embroiled in the national division over slavery: the North wanted to expand the privilege, while Southerners wanted to restrict suffrage to limit the political influence of the North. Alien suffrage actually expanded during the tense pre-war period, but during the Civil War alien suffrage carried an enormous price—namely, conscription, which was apportioned among states based on the apportionment population. Immigrants who attempted to rescind their declarations to become citizens in order to avoid conscription faced deportation.

After the Civil War 13 new states, including former Confederate states, adopted declarant alien suffrage as a way of repopulating their states, settling public debt, and regaining political power in Congress. The contraction of alien suffrage gained momentum in the wake of the 1890s recession, when several states repealed provisions that granted non-citizens voting rights, yet as late as 1900, 11 states still permitted noncitizen voting. The resurgence of nativism coupled with legal changes in voting rights of other citizen groups during and after World War I led to further contraction of alien suffrage, which terminated completely in the late 1920s. Thus, the suffrage stage of immigration history illustrates how the boundaries of membership were expanded and then contracted as matters of economic and political expediency within the guise of democratic values.

If in the past the instrumental goals of attracting immigrant settlers to populate newly admitted states and settle debt motivated political leaders to offer the franchise to non-citizens, democratic principle might compel a similar state and local policy in the 21 century. For blacks, the 13 and 14 Amendments formalized a social contract of rights and responsibilities by declaring them full-fledged citizens; the process of naturalization does the same for immigrants by formalizing their statutory status. For non-citizens, voluntary immigration provides more explicit consent to be governed than birthright citizenship.

Therefore, and in contrast to ancient democracies where the distinctions between citizens and foreigners were sharply defined and rigid, in a liberal democracy non-citizens should be virtually indistinguishable from citizens because legal admission ostensibly guarantees equal access to the privileges, rights, and civil guarantees accorded to citizens, save the franchise. However, in practice the citizen-alien distinction appears to be deepening. This need not be so. The citizen-alien distinction can be blurred because both are entitled to representation in Congress; because both are required to pay taxes; because both serve in the armed forces; and because both are bound by the same laws and obligations. Hence both are putatively eligible for the rights and privileges enjoyed by citizens through birthright or naturalization, except voting in federal elections, and where stipulated by law, also state elections. That states retain authority to grant non-citizen voting in state and local affairs is a socially meaningful way to fade the distinction between aliens and citizens. Some have argued that the citizen-alien distinction should be blurred because it is morally consistent with the values of equity and inclusiveness professed by a liberal democracy, and because political participation in local affairs ostensibly can prepare aliens for statutory U.S. citizenship. But as the history of black suffrage testifies, morality is never sufficient to compel compliance with the letter, let alone the spirit, of the law.

Not only are concerns about conflicts of allegiance less relevant in local compared to national politics, but the expansion of dual citizenship among immigrant sending countries renders moot the question of loyalty to either source or host country. More generally, as the era of mass migration unfolds throughout the world, the meaning of national citizenship comes into sharp relief and questions the relationship between rights and membership. According to Linda Bosniak, non-citizen residents as a social class render problematic "citizenship-as-rights" and "citizenship-as-status." Her perspective parallels Raskin's notion of citizenship as integration and as standing, which the 1992 Maastricht Treaty on the European Union brings into sharp relief.

As economic imperatives and adoption of a common currency compel making national boundaries porous in order to harness the benefits of scale in matters of trade and labour market specialization, questions of nationality and strict allegiance to a nation-state assume back stage, even in the face of persisting cultural and language diversity. The underplaying of national boundaries against the backdrop of pan-European citizenship is evident in the movement to increase the portability of political rights that EU citizens can use in any member country. The Maastricht Treaty commits member states to grant nationals of other member states the right to vote and run for office in municipal elections. Currently, 5.5 million EU citizens hold limited political rights throughout Europe, but the extension of suffrage and other privileges of citizenship do not extend to resident aliens and third-country nationals.

This unique social experiment, and its historical antecedents, bears important sessions for the political incorporation of U.S. immigrants. In the 1980s, Sweden seriously considered an initiative that would grant foreigners the right to vote, but these efforts were stymied by ardent nationalists. Eventually Sweden, along with Norway, Finland, Denmark, the Netherlands, and Ireland, granted active and passive local and regional voting rights to foreigners. In France and Germany the debate over extending the local franchise to noncitizens did not favour immigrants. Moreover, in the fall of 1990, Germany's Federal Constitutional Court reversed the statutes of two states that allowed resident aliens to vote in municipal matters, and reconfirmed the exclusivity of political voice for citizens only. Despite the efforts of the German government to revise its inefficient naturalization process, the privileged position of German ancestry immigrants remains in tact, reifying a membership hierarchy within the subset of foreigners.

The EU is not alone in limiting the national franchise to statutory citizens. A recent study by Blais and colleagues found that 76 per cent, or 48 of 63, of the democratic countries in their sample restricted the right to vote to citizens. Moreover, among the countries that did permit non-citizen voting, many imposed extended residency requirements. For example, while New Zealand grants permanent residents the franchise, in Uruguay non-citizens must reside in the country for 15 years before they can vote. At least 11 countries relax the citizenship requirement for suffrage for nationals from specific countries. This practice is particularly common among many former British colonies and Portugal. Notwithstanding its symbolic value of full membership, only when exercised is the franchise is socially and politically meaningful. When granted the right to vote, non-citizens are less likely than citizens to exercise the franchise and naturalized citizens are less likely to vote than native-born citizens.

In raising the issue of qualified membership, I am not advocating non-citizen voting. Rather, my purpose is to illustrate how, in the shadows of a history of ascriptive democracy, national but especially local interests are not well served by muffling the voices of a growing share of the U.S. population. "Because aliens are a significant part of many contemporary political communities, their presence inevitably shapes the nature and practice of citizenship within". Hence, if recent laws that explicitly prohibit immigrant voting disadvantage legal immigrants as a class, the political salience of citizenship through naturalization is bound to increase and it has. More significant, however, is that concerns about fairness in governance will become more discordant with the principles of equity and inclusion as long as entire communities remain voiceless in decisions that govern their life options and those of their children. But, for immigrant rights to become the civil rights of the 21 century, as Raskin claims, requires a realignment of democracy with demography.

ALIGNING DEMOCRACY WITH DEMOGRAPHY

Admittedly, the United States would be a very different country had immigration been stopped at the turn of the 20 century; or had the second era of mass migration not materialized after 1970. History scripted otherwise, and the future promises to do so even more. The U.S. Census Bureau predicts that 36 per cent of the U.S. population will consist of minority groups by 2020, and 47 per cent by mid-century. Immigration will play a major role in this future diversification. Even if immigration levels are cut, the offspring of immigrants will maintain the force of diversification for at least 30 to 40 years—the time required for significant changes in the childbearing behaviour of the foreign-born. Although the children of immigrants are citizens by birth, their place in the status hierarchy will be shaped by the reception and rights accorded their parents.

According to Linda Bosniak, "...the category of alienage poses a special challenge to the liberal vision of citizenship, because the concerns with status and rights which lie at the heart of this vision necessarily engage the questions of how far—and, especially, to whom—the liberal-democratic project of universality should be understood to extend." Fortunately, history provides sessions about how to prepare for that future within a framework of social justice. The main sessions are about how immigration challenges commitment to values of inclusion and equality given voice in the Declaration of Independence and the U.S. Constitution by requiring a broadened conception of membership that embraces both T.H. Marshall's notion of social citizenship and Raskin's notion of citizenship as integration. Maximal civic incorporation of immigrants is crucial for reinvigorating the shared commitment to values of liberty, democracy and equal opportunity. At a minimum, social justice dictates that non-citizens be treated as functional citizens.

However, several legislative measures targeting the foreign-born threaten the social contract and expose the vulnerability of immigrants' rights to political manipulation. For example, in 1980 the Supreme Court denied a lawsuit initiated by FAIR against the Commerce Department that aimed to exclude undocumented immigrants from the apportionment base. Former counsel to the Senate Judiciary Committee on immigration, Charles Wood, alleges that both the Constitutional provisions to include undocumented immigrants in the apportionment population and the provisions that grant birthright citizenship to children of undocumented immigrants are cracks in the social contract that will "undermine the civic foundation of national unity". He proposes to seal these cracks by excluding undocumented immigrants from the apportionment population and denying birthright citizenship to their offspring. Both objectives requires constitutional amendments, which to date have not succeeded. Once again, history teaches that inclusive approaches to sealing cracks in the contract are not only more enduring, but also consistent with the values of a liberal democracy.

Legislative measures targeting the foreign-born expose the vulnerability of immigrants' membership to political manipulation. Some have been revised or rescinded after public scrutiny and legal review, while others have been allowed to stand. If anti-immigrant initiatives in California, Florida, and Texas are the bellwether of the future, prospects for equality between natives and immigrants, and between citizens and non-citizens are worrisome. For example, passed in November 1994, by a 59 per cent majority of California voters, Proposition 187 targeted both legal and undocumented immigrants by advocating that children of non-U.S. citizens be denied access to public schools as well as health and social welfare benefits except in cases of emergency. That it was declared unconstitutional does not erase the strong symbolic message about membership and inclusion—rather, alienage and exclusion—and the strong popular support adds an aura of legitimacy to the intent.

Temptations to muffle immigrants' voice and limit social participation show no signs of abating. Even the extra protections afforded by statutory citizenship were threatened when INS interpreted a provision in the 1990 Immigration Act as granting the agency the ability to revoke citizenship as an administrative rather than a judicial matter. Although the practice of "administrative denaturalization" as proposed by the Attorney General's Office was declared unconstitutional, accusations of election fraud or partisan politics could lead to similar initiatives in a climate where nativism has re-sharpened boundaries between citizens and unnaturalized immigrants. According to Gopal, the current system of administrative denaturalization renders the revocation of citizenship easier than ever and with fewer safeguards for naturalized citizens.

In 1996 President Clinton signed the Personal Responsibility and Work Opportunity Reconciliation Act into law, which restricted the eligibility of some groups of legal immigrants from federal, state, and local benefits and services. This flagrant anti-immigrant legislation was further buttressed by the Illegal Immigration Reform and Immigrant Responsibility Act of 1996, which restricted access to social benefits for undocumented immigrants, including in-state tuition for postsecondary education. As Peter Schuck aptly notes, "Until the statutory changes adopted by Congress in 1996, the differences between the legal rights enjoyed by citizens and those enjoyed by LPRs were more political than legal or economic, and those differences had narrowed considerably over time." Both Acts deepen the divide between statutory and functional citizenship and underwrite inequality between immigrants and natives. In view of the volume of immigration in the recent past, sealing cracks in the social contract are essential to prevent the demography of difference and foreignness to shape the contours of inequality.

On a more positive note, there are several signs that democratic values are being realigned with the demographic realities of immigration. Local initiatives to promote inclusion by permitting noncitizens to vote in school board and municipal elections are an important stride towards building a sense of community by giving voice to immigrants and reducing the salience of foreignness. Several localities currently permit non-citizen voting. In Chicago and New York City, non-citizens have voted in school board elections for a long time. More recently Takoma Park, Maryland granted non-citizens, including undocumented immigrants, the right to vote in local elections. Yet these cases currently are the exception, not the norm. Similar initiatives have been proposed in several other localities with mixed success, and some opposition comes from members of the African American community, whose opportunities to gain seats on school boards and hold municipal office may be diminished if the local franchise is granted to Latino, Asia, and Arab parents. How diversity will play out in local politics will shape the contours of the national agenda about inclusion and equity.

Another powerful gesture towards the twin goals of equity and inclusiveness is recent legislation that grants in-state tuition privileges to undocumented immigrants who graduate from U.S. high schools. That Texas and California along with Utah have assumed leadership in authorizing this benefit is all the more impressive because these states contain over half of the undocumented population; because these states achieved notoriety during the mid-1990s for their anti-immigrant and anti-affirmative action legislation; and because their decisions defy the federal ban on in-state tuition benefits for undocumented aliens included in the 1996 Illegal Immigration Reform and Immigrant Responsibility Act. Other states have proposed similar initiatives, which have been defeated.

In a world where the value of college education signals large differences in lifetime earnings and general well-being, denying youth the opportunity to maximize their educational investment will surely compromise a future where immigrants' and their offspring will be major contributors to economic productivity.

Philosophically, denying children of undocumented immigrants equal access to public education not only falls short of a liberal conception of social citizenship that includes social welfare rights along with full civic membership, but by raising the threshold of the tolerable limits of inequality, also breaches the social contract.

3

Guidance for Population with Special Needs

INTRODUCTION

Children who have been determined to require special attention and specific necessities than other children. Special needs children face a lot of emotional, social and psychological problems due to their disability. A teacher can prove to be very helpful to students in providing personal and academic support. A little help and concern from a teacher can help them stabilize their emotional, social and psychological levels into a more balanced learner in the classroom. Under a teacher's guidance, students will feel secure and more engaged in the learning process. Teacher guidance can help students with special needs express their feelings and communicate their needs freely in the classroom which will create a more constructive student/teacher engagement and understanding. Therefore by providing guidance to students with Special needs, teachers can effectively help students towards a greater academic and social adjustment to their learning environment.

MENTALLY CHALLENGED LEARNERS SLOW LEARNERS: MEANING

Slow-learners are those who fail in school because of their low intellectual abilities. Their IQ ranges from 55 / 60 to 85 / 90. They have a wide range of abilities and a variety of characteristics depending on their background. The term Slow-learners is used to cover various group of students otherwise referred to Dull', Retarded' or Educationally Subnormal'. Now the term Slow-learners is used more widely to indicate the fairly large group of children whose learning is slowed down by one or more factors of which limited ability may be one even though their intellectual potential may be considerably higher. Definitions Knoff– Slow Learner is the one who learn or underachieve, in one or more academic areas, at a rate that is below average yet not at the level considered comparable to that of an educable mentally retarded student.

Types of SL:

- Very Backward – Due to retarded mental development accompanied by psycho-social deficiency.

- Ability not quite limited but having difficulty in learning than average children due to school, family or personal factors.
- They may derive benefits from special classes not limited in intelligence but have
- problems in reading and writing where as arithmetic and other subjects are high. Their causes may range from specific perpetual difficulties to emotional maladjustment. For them some kind of remedial teaching is required.
- In some schools there are many SL, for them sometimes special class is required. The children receive education in special school or class move to a regular school after the backwardness is removed.
- These children are hard to identify as they even manage in a less advanced society and do not drew attention easily as deaf, blind or physically handicapped do.
- The period at which their limitations arise are most obvious is that of school years.

SPECIAL PROBLEMS OF THE SLOW-LEARNERS

- Since in physical appearance they look like normal children, parents and teachers have the same expectations from them as from the latter.
- When they are not able to live up to these expectations, parents and teachers scold and punish them instead of trying to find out the reason behind their failure.
- Their classmates make fun of them.
- Consequently, they are bewildered and confused, wondering what wrong they have committed.
- Since their basic needs of being loved, accepted and recognised are not met, they develop emotional problems and behaviour difficulties.
- They generally have a low self-concept due to their limited experience of success and due to the low opinion expressed of them by parents, teachers and others around them.

CHARACTERISTICS

- In physical appearance they are no different from normal children and therefore likely to get admission into schools for normal children where the curriculum is drawn up to meet the needs of average children. So they find it extremely difficult to cope with the education imparted in these schools, unless special provision is made for them and the curriculum is oriented towards practical and real life activities.
- They are capable of being educated in ordinary schools and even achieving a moderate degree of success, if they are allowed to proceed at a slower pace and the syllabus is adapted to suit their abilities.

- But, they will not be able to keep pace with the average children and never be able to learn all the things we expect normal children to master by the time they leave school.
- They will not be able to go for higher studies despite all the guidance and educational facilities made available to them.
- They have poor memories. Their attention span is short and they cannot concentrate on one topic
- Weakness in thinking capacity, finding out relationships, similarity, familiarity, reasoning, object characteristic observing, poor language and number concept development.
- Poor verbal ability, Brief vocabulary.
- Difficulty in abstractions.
- Weakness in the memory.
- Constant Feeling of Insecurity.

Physical Characteristics

- Poor in dressing, using drawing & writing materials and tools.
- Need large practice in climbing, jumping, dancing, skipping, games etc.
- Sometimes SL have better physical development than mental development.
- Their capacity to learn is reduced because of sickness, minor ailments, malnutrition etc.
- Causes
- Poorer powers of retention.
- Weakness in Attention
- Physical or mental personal inadequacy.
- Having limited capacity for taking responsibility
- Unable to control feelings of aggression or outburst.
- Solation.

Showing the sign of slow learner doesn't mean that the child is slow learner, there are other factors that could cause the process of slow learning.

Emotional Growth

Children react to their environment in early stages and he learns from the environment in which they grow. Create a safe environment for them and reduce the stress on your child and remove the things which are physical threats to the children e.g.: abusive behaviour and unsafe toys etc With whom the child is spending his time, what is their intellectual level. And how they treat the child, when children have a secure environment, it flourishes their abilities in positive direction. Studies show those children who have better environment show better confidence in life and in education.

Growth and Opportunities of Learning

Opportunities of learning is very necessary for the development of children cognitive abilities, Parents should provide rich learning environment to their children and open new windows of learning opportunities for them. They need simple playable activities and games to develop their brains, Show them new things and arrange new activities for them to enhance their thinking skill.

Absenteeism

Absenteeism from the school is another factor which can affect the ability of learning of a child, when a child is often absent from the class, he could catch with other student in school, he need extra home work with the help of parents to cover his short coming other wise he lose his self confidence

EDUCATIONAL PROVISIONS

- Use of appropriate methods of learning
- Motivation
  - Learning Readiness
  - A practical approach
  - Concept formation
  - Grading of work
  - Assessment of progress
  - Consolidation
  - Active methods
- Individualization of treatment
- Cooperation between various professionals
- Parent Education and Guidance

There are several other strategies that are useful. Computers are great to use in the classroom. Computers never tire or get interrupted making the drill and practice more effective and fun. It is important to allow the student time to get out of his/her seat to let off energy and relieve a little stress. A classroom that utilizes centers is good for this. In giving instructions you should say the child's name or touch them before giving the direction, write the directions on the board or paper for each child to keep, and ask that the student repeat the direction orally. This helps to reinforce the direction and gives them something to refer back to if they forget.

Once the student turns in the work or answers orally, provide immediate feedback. This assures the student of their answer or allows them to correct the answer and keeps them on task. The most important, strategies is to provide three or four hours of academic work. Slow learners are not efficient learners and therefore require more hours of academic instruction to keep pace. A very big problem that every school faces, i.e. the difficulty to deal with the slow learners.

The teachers have their big headache over these children. Handle them in homework & class work, understanding the topic, etc are the areas concerned with the slow learners. We try to advise them or we try to get result by hook or crook through putting negative enforcement by punishing them. It is estimated that due to that problem many slow learners or dropout students are being termed as weak students & thrown out of the school. But that is not the solution. The result of the action of the throwing out the child out of the school paves the way to create a dark spot in the life of the victim child.

Then, where are the solutions? If the teachers will give time to think over those children, definitely the solution comes in their hand. It is also the proof in history that many slow learners have become qualified themselves as the scientists & writers in their life. So, why not we experiment with these slow learners who are with us? Have we thought over it? Have we tried to understand the life of a slow learner? The following discussion may help the teachers to improve the skill of the slow learners.

Psychological Analysis & Problem Solution

The more & more we think about the child the more we get the solution. Firstly, we have to search the problem area of the child. The problem of the child may be his family or friends or his personal condition. If we go for personal asking questions as a relative of his own, then we can be assured about getting some difficulties for which the child is not reading. Them we, from our level will try to get solution of this problem.

Guidance from his Level

Child has a level of his own. Level of understanding is different from one child to another. The weak child more often can't understand the studies because he has not understood the previous formula / concept in the previous classes. How can he understand the concept of class IX if he has not understood the simple concept of class VII & VIII? That's why the child should be personally taught from his understanding level.

Encouragement in Small Success

The greatest factor for the success of the life of the child is his encouragement. If we try to find out the strengths of the weak child then we come across some of them. If we try to applaud him with encouraging words & give confidence he definitely feels his importance & worth. Once the child has grown his confidence means he will definitely improve. The most important cause of his weakness is we; the teachers always give importance to the good children & neglect the weaker in the class. Encouragement can change the whole personality of a child.

Fixing the Goal & Prescribing a Time Table

The child should be persuaded to make a time table for the study purpose. Sometimes some children have no goal regarding study. The teacher should observe those children & inspire them to fix the goal for the life & help him to make a time table for every day work so that the child will be captured through the time table to do the things at write time.

Giving Memory Tips

More often the child forgets what ever he learns. That's why he loses his confidence on him & differentiates between him & the good students. The teacher's role is to give the tips such as how to recall, in which way to write systematically, when to learn, how to learn etc.

Giving Importance in the Class

It's always seen that the class room teaching goes on with the direction & understanding of the strong children. But if the average children do not understand your teaching & you are just running towards the completion of syllabus then the whole teaching is a futile one. Some times it's very urgent to go near the weak child & ask personally whether he has understood or not. Here the teacher's asking approach should be very polite & sweet, not rude.

Self Reading Method

Most of the weak children are found that they neglect self reading. They may have the language understanding problem for which they do not take interest to read. If the teacher freely tells the child to come at home or to him in extra time for understanding the key words then little the child will take interest to self reading. Then definitely he improves himself slowly.

Questions for Practice

Some questions can be given time to time to engage the learner in the habit of study. That is a practice which can enable the student to come across the learning point at a regular basis.

Special Guidance beyond School Hour

Basically we the teachers now have become very professional. After school hour we hesitate to give even a single minute to the children which reduce our rapport. The weak children, they need special attention beyond school hour that is personally to take up the child's difficulty. We the teachers, beyond school hour, either we waste time in gossiping or earn money in tuition. If we give 1 hour extra time for the weak children then definitely they will improve. Because it is very difficult to give time to the weak ones in the classroom itself.

Seating Arrangement

More often we see that the strong children in the class room don't wish to sit with the weak children. The weak ones always sit with the weak. This is another cause for the no improvement of the weak children. If the class teacher prepares seating arrangements properly to benefit the weak children-to make arrangement to sit the strong one with the weak one & instruct to the strong one to help the weak one in studies then the weak ones may be improved in studies.

Search Physical or Mental Problem

The teacher should find out any physical or mental problem of the child. A child is not writing anything from the black board means may be some eye defect. A child is not obeying the words of the teacher, may be some mental problem is there. Some children are severely affected by the physical problems which made them lazy to read & write. Firstly the teacher/parent should find out the problems then treat them accordingly.

Creating Confidence Level in his Interest Areas

The teacher should observe the child & secretly know the interest areas of the child. Even if the child plays, act, does some work the teacher / parent should find out his interest / specialty. Because every child is special. The encouragement can be started from the child's interest areas. When the child builds his confidence in his interest area then we can expand & inspire the same confidence in other areas also.

Be a Friend to him

Be a friend to the weak child. Teacher should try to knowingly mix with the child more & more with him. Unknowingly when the friendship is build with that child then the child starts loving the teacher. The starting of love starts the surrender of the child towards the same teacher. Then the teacher, whatever he tells the child obeys it. The mystery of all success is the love, understanding & friendship. Oh teacher! Many more children are waiting to catch your lovable hand. They are searching you as a friend. They are so called by the society as slow learners or weak ones but actually they are not. May be some unfortunate moment misguided them. Is it not noble to improve them, support them to develop in their own pace? Is it not wise to take care of them? The history has proved the slow learners such as Thomas Edison & Gandhi as the world class Scientist & Leader respectively. Every child is special. As every child has a soul, there is every possibility of improvement, sooner or later. The goal of the soul is to develop. The source of energy is lying within them but the only thing is to stretch the hand of confidence towards them which will solve their problem & improve their quality.

MENTAL RETARDATION

A developmental disability characterized by significantly sub average general intellectual functioning, with concurrent deficits in adaptive behavior. The causes are many and include both genetic and environmental factors as well as interactions between the two. In most cases the diagnosis is not formally made until children have entered into school settings. In the preschool years, the diagnosis is more likely to be established by evidence of delayed maturation in the areas of sensory-motor, adaptive, cognitive, social, and verbal behaviors. By definition, evidence of mental retardation must exist prior to adulthood, where vocational limitation may be evident, but the need for supervision or support may persist beyond the usual age of social emancipation.

Definition

Mental retardation is a developmental disability that first appears in children under the age of 18. It is defined as an intellectual functioning level that is well below average and significant limitations in daily living skills. Limitations in adaptive behavior must also be demonstrable in order to satisfy diagnostic criteria for mental retardation. This criterion is important because certain artistic or other gifts may not be revealed by formal IQ testing, and different levels of learning difficulty may be accentuated by the demands of specific environments. Outside such environments, an individual may navigate a normal course in life.

Levels of Mental Retardation

Mental retardation varies in severity. There are four different degrees of mental retardation: mild, moderate, severe, and profound. These categories are based on the functioning level of the individual. Individuals with mental retardation are typically sub classified in terms of the manifest severity of cognitive disability as reflected by the ratio of mental age to chronological age, or *intelligence quotient* (IQ). Sub average intellectual functioning is defined as an IQ score of at least two standard deviations below the mean, or approximately 70 to 75 or below. Mild, moderate, severe, and profound degrees of mental retardation refer to below the normal IQ for the general population.

Class	IQ
Profound mental retardation	Below 20
Severe mental retardation	20–34
Moderate mental retardation	35-49
Mild mental retardation	50–69
Borderline intellectual functioning	70–84

Mild Mental Retardation

Approximately 85 percent of the mentally retarded population is in the mildly retarded category. Their IQ score ranges from 50 to 75, and they can often acquire academic skills up to the sixth grade level. They can become fairly self-sufficient and in some cases live independently, with community and social support.

Moderate Mental Retardation

About 10 percent of the mentally retarded population is considered moderately retarded. Moderately retarded individuals have IQ scores ranging from 35 to 55. They can carry out work and self-care tasks with moderate supervision. They typically acquire communication skills in childhood and are able to live and function successfully within the community in a supervised environment such as a group home.

Severe Mental Retardation

About 3 to 4 percent of the mentally retarded population is severely retarded. Severely retarded individuals have IQ scores of 20 to 40. They may master very basic self-care skills and some communication skills. Many severely retarded individuals are able to live in a group home.

Profound Mental Retardation

Only 1 to 2 percent of the mentally retarded population is classified as profoundly retarded. Profoundly retarded individuals have IQ scores under 20 to 25. They may be able to develop basic self-care and communication skills with appropriate support and training. Their retardation is often caused by an accompanying neurological disorder. The profoundly retarded need a high level of structure and supervision. The *American Association on Mental Retardation* (AAMR) has developed another widely accepted diagnostic classification system for mental retardation. The AAMR classification system focuses on the capabilities of the retarded individual rather than on the limitations. The categories describe the level of support required. They are: intermittent support, limited support, extensive support, and pervasive support. Intermittent support, for example, is support needed only occasionally, perhaps during times of stress or crisis. It is the type of support typically required for most mildly retarded individuals. At the other end of the spectrum, pervasive support, or life-long, daily support for most adaptive areas, would be required for profoundly retarded individuals.

Causes

Low IQ scores and limitations in adaptive skills are the hallmarks of mental retardation. Aggression, self-injury, and mood disorders are sometimes associated with the disability. The severity of the symptoms and the age at which they first appear depend on the cause. Children who are mentally retarded reach developmental milestones significantly later than expected, if at all. If retardation is caused by chromosomal or other genetic disorders, it is often apparent from infancy. If retardation is caused by childhood illnesses or injuries, learning and adaptive skills that were once easy may suddenly become difficult or impossible to master. In about 35 percent of cases, the cause of mental retardation cannot be found. Biological and environmental factors that can cause mental retardation include genetics, prenatal illnesses and issues, childhood illnesses and injuries, and environmental factors.

Genetics

About 5 percent of mental retardation is caused by hereditary factors. Mental retardation may be caused by an inherited abnormality of the genes, such as fragile X syndrome. Fragile X, a defect in the chromosome that determines sex, is the most common inherited cause of mental retardation. Single gene defects such as phenylketonuria (PKU) and other inborn errors of metabolism may also cause mental retardation if they are not found and treated early. An accident or mutation in genetic development may also cause retardation. Examples of such accidents are development of an extra chromosome 18 and Down syndrome. Down syndrome is caused by an abnormality in the development of chromosome 21. It is the most common genetic cause of mental retardation.

Prenatal Illnesses and Issues

Fetal alcohol syndrome affects one in 600 children in the United States. It is caused by excessive alcohol intake in the first twelve weeks of pregnancy. Some studies have shown that even moderate alcohol use during pregnancy may cause learning disabilities in children. Drug abuse and cigarette smoking during pregnancy have also been linked to mental retardation. Maternal infections and illnesses such as glandular disorders, rubella, toxoplasmosis, and cytomegalovirus infection may cause mental retardation. When the mother has high blood pressure or blood poisoning, the flow of oxygen to the fetus may be reduced, causing brain damage and mental retardation.

Birth defects that cause physical deformities of the head, brain, and central nervous system frequently cause mental retardation. Neural tube defect, for example, is a birth defect in which the neural tube that forms the spinal cord does not close completely. This defect may cause children to develop an accumulation of cerebrospinal fluid on the brain. By putting pressure on the brain hydrocephalus can cause learning impairment.

Childhood Illnesses and Injuries

Hyperthyroidism, whooping cough, chickenpox, measles, and Hib disease may cause mental retardation if they are not treated adequately. An infection of the membrane covering the brain or an inflammation of the brain itself cause swelling that in turn may cause brain damage and mental retardation. Traumatic brain injury caused by a blow or a violent shake to the head may also cause brain damage and mental retardation in children.

Environmental Factors

Ignored or neglected infants who are not provided the mental and physical stimulation required for normal development may suffer irreversible learning impairments. Children who live in poverty and suffer from malnutrition, unhealthy living conditions, and improper or inadequate medical care are at a higher risk. Exposure to lead can also cause mental retardation. Many children develop lead poisoning by eating the flaking lead-based paint often found in older buildings.

Diagnosis

A complete medical, family, social, and educational history is compiled from existing medical and school records and from interviews with parents. Children are given intelligence tests to measure their learning abilities and intellectual functioning. Such tests include the Stanford-Binet Intelligence Scale, the Wechsler Intelligence Scales, the Wechsler Preschool and Primary Scale of Intelligence, and the Kaufmann Assessment Battery for Children. For infants, the Bayley Scales of Infant Development may be used to assess motor, language, and problem-solving skills. Interviews with parents or other caregivers are used to assess the child's daily living, muscle control, communication, and social skills. The Woodcock-Johnson Scales of Independent Behavior and the *Vineland Adaptive Behavior Scale* (VABS) are frequently used to test these skills.

Treatment

Training in independent living and job skills is often begun in early adulthood. The level of training depends on the degree of retardation. Mildly retarded individuals can often acquire the skills needed to live independently and hold an outside job. Moderate to profoundly retarded individuals usually require supervised community living. Family therapy can help relatives of the mentally retarded develop coping skills. It can also help parents deal with feelings of guilt or anger. A supportive, warm home environment is essential to help the mentally retarded reach their full potential.

Prognosis

Individuals with mild to moderate mental retardation are frequently able to achieve some self-sufficiency and to lead happy and fulfilling lives. To reach these goals, they need appropriate and consistent educational, community, social, family, and vocational supports. The outlook is less promising for those with severe to profound retardation. Studies have shown that these individuals have a shortened life expectancy. The diseases that are usually associated with severe retardation may cause the shorter life span. People with Down syndrome develop in later life the brain changes that characterize Alzheimer's disease and may develop the clinical symptoms of this disease as well.

Prevention

Immunization against diseases such as measles and HIV prevents many of the illnesses that can cause mental retardation. In addition, all children should undergo routine developmental screening as part of their pediatric care. Screening is particularly critical for those children who may be neglected or undernourished or may live in disease-producing conditions. Newborn screening and immediate treatment for PKU and hyperthyroidism can usually catch these disorders early enough to prevent retardation. Good prenatal care can also help prevent retardation. Pregnant women should be educated about the risks of drinking and the need to maintain good nutrition during pregnancy. Tests such as amniocentesis and ultra sonography can determine whether a fetus is developing normally in the womb.

Strategies

- Activities should be divided into manageable parts and carefully sequenced to offer a progression of skills.
- Repetition of important tasks may also facilitate learning.
- Whenever possible, it is helpful to provide a demonstration so participants can model the desired behavior.
- Use verbal instructions that are clear and easy to understand.
- Provide careful supervision of all activities especially those in which accidents or injuries are possible, but be careful not to overprotect participants.
- Explain required learning tasks in terms of concrete concepts.
- Stress real life applications.
- Plan activities that are age appropriate.
- Plan activities that require skills useful in community living, job training, etc.
- Try to ensure that the challenges of an activity correspond with the skills of the participants.
- When possible start an activity at the participant's current skill level rather than the lowest possible level.
- Small group and cooperative activities may facilitate social development for those with deficiencies in adaptive behavior.
- Establish necessary rules for appropriate behavior, and use consistent consequences.

Parental Concerns

All states are required by law to offer early intervention programs for mentally retarded children from the time they are born. The sooner the diagnosis of mental retardation is made, the more the child can be helped. With mentally retarded infants, the treatment emphasis is on sensori motor development, which can be stimulated by exercises and special types of play.

It is required that special education programs be available for retarded children starting at three years of age. These programs concentrate on essential self-care, such as feeding, dressing, and toilet training.

There is also specialized help available for language and communication difficulties and physical disabilities. As children grow older, training in daily living skills, as well as academic subjects, is offered. Counseling and therapy are another important type of treatment for the mentally retarded.

Retarded children are prone to behavioral problems caused by short attention span, low tolerance for frustration, and poor impulse control. Behavior therapy with a mental health professional can help combat negative behavior patterns and replace them with more functional ones. A counselor or therapist can also help retarded children cope with the low self-esteem that often results from the realization that they are different from other children, including siblings.

Counseling can also be valuable for the family of a retarded child to help parents cope with painful feelings about the child's condition and with the extra time and patience needed for the care and education of a special-needs child. Siblings may need to talk about the pressures they face, such as accepting the extra time and attention their parents must devote to a retarded brother or sister. Sometimes parents have trouble bonding with an infant who is retarded and need professional help and reassurance to establish a close and loving relationship.

GIFTED CHILDREN

Meaning

Someone who shows, or has the potential for showing, an exceptional level of performance in one or more areas of expression.

Characteristics of Gifted Students

- Learn Quickly and Easily
- Able to use abstract thought and critical reasoning
- Exhibit Verbal Proficiency
- Have a high energy level
- Become bored and frustrated
- Dislike repetition

- Receive negative adult attitudes to smartness
- Dominate Discussions
- Difficulty with listening skills
- Become frustrated with inactivity and lack of challenge
- Be extremely persistent
- Concentrate on tasks of high interest for extended periods of time
- Exhibit unusual emotional depth and intensity
- Be highly sensitive
- Be acutely perceptive
- Disrupt class routine
- Resist interruptions or schedules
- Perceived as stubborn or uncooperative
- Be unusually vulnerable
- Perceived as immature
- Be confused if thoughts and feelings not taken seriously
- Aim at perfection
- Exhibit independence and nonconformity
- Heightened self-awareness
- Relate more to older children and adults
- Feel frustrated
- Fear failure
- Challenge and question indiscreetly
- Exhibit rebellious behavior
- Social isolation
- Low self-esteem due to seeing differences from peers as bad
- Seen as a "show off"
- Keen sense of humor
- Possess unusual imagination Causes
- Experience
- Biological Factors
- Social Factors
- No single factor that "causes" giftedness

Difficulties for Gifted Children

- Perfectionism
- Isolation
- Underachievement– vs. Selective Achievement v Selective
- Impostor Syndrome Impostor Syndrome
- Masking Abilities Masking Abilities
- Delinquency
- Depression
- Anxiety
- Suicide

Strategies for Teaching Gifted Students

Create alternative activities that go beyond the regular curriculum. Work with students to design an independent project that they would be interested in completing for credit If possible, involve students in academic competitions in your area. Create tiered assignments, which have different expectations for different levels of learners. Computers can be used to complete alternative activities and independent projects. Program For Gifted

Acceleration and Enrichment

Acceleration refers to the speeding up of instruction. Gifted children are fast learners and require little repetition of information. Enrichment refers to the increased depth of study of a particular topic. It extends the regular curriculum.

Both are needed in some form:

- *Multiple Options*: Is the program a "one size fits all" program or are there various options for the different needs of the different types of gifted children? A profoundly gifted child has significantly different educational needs than does a mildly gifted child, for example. In addition, a child may be exceptionally gifted in math, but not in language arts. Multiple options are essential.
- *Student Learning Expectations*: Learning outcomes must be clear. The students may have fun, but they must also learn something new.
- *Challenging Curriculum*: Gifted children need a stimulating curriculum. Without it, they can "tune out," losing interest in school. A curriculum for gifted children should require them to stretch their minds.
- *Flexibility*: Flexibility is needed in order to respond to the needs of individual gifted children. Rigid adherence to the system often prevents some gifted children from appropriate challenges.
- *Staff Development Plan*: Teachers who have been trained to work with gifted children are much more effective than those who have not.
- *Guidance Component*: Gifted children often feel isolated or "different." They sometimes don't feel like they fit in socially with the other children. They also can be very sensitive and have a harder time than other children dealing with the day-to-day stress of school or growing up. The guidance can be individual or group guidance.
- *Honoring Academic Talent*: Schools must honor all talent areas in the same way athletic talent is honored Names of achievers can be listed or announced in the same way sports heroes are listed and announced.

TIPS FOR NURTURING GIFTED CHILDREN

- Appreciate gifted learners as children.
- Interact with families with gifted children.

- Recognize how the personal and instructional needs of a gifted child differ from others.
- Appreciate the differences among high achievers, gifted learners, and creative thinkers.
- Understand the developmental crises for gifted students.
- Assure your child that being different is okay.
- Be an encourager.
- Emphasize that what is learned is more important than any grade.
- Be an active listener and elicit children's perceptions.
- Follow their interests and leads in learning situations rather than pressure them with your agenda.
- Talk up to them.
- Enjoy music, plays, museums, art, sports, and historical places together and discuss the experience.
- Model life-long learning habits
- Facilitate real-life reading, writing, science, and math experiences.
- Give books and learning games as presents, and then spend time together reading and playing those games.
- Recognize that gifted children need to question and respond critically.
- Maintain a sense of humor!

LEARNING DISABILITIES

WHAT IS A LEARNING DISABILITY

A child with a learning disability cannot try harder, pay closer attention, or improve motivation on their own; they need help to learn how to do those things. A learning disability, or learning disorder, is not a problem with intelligence. Learning disorders are caused by a difference in the brain that affects how information is received, processed, or communicated. Children and adults with learning disabilities have trouble processing sensory information because they see, hear, and understand things differently. Symptoms and types of learning disabilities and disorders

Motor Difficulties and Learning Disabilities

Motor difficulty refers to problems with movement and coordination whether it is with fine motor skills or gross motor skills. A motor disability is sometimes referred to as an "output" activity meaning that it relates to the output of information from the brain. In order to run, jump, write or cut something, the brain must be able to communicate with the necessary limbs to complete the action. Signs that your child might have a motor coordination disability include problems with physical abilities that require hand–eye coordination, like holding a pencil or buttoning a shirt.

Math Difficulties and Learning Disabilities

Learning disabilities in math vary greatly depending on the child's other strengths and weaknesses. A child's ability to do math will be affected differently by a language learning disability, or a visual disorder or a difficulty with sequencing, memory or organization. A child with a math–based learning disorder may struggle with memorization and organization of numbers, operation signs, and number facts.

Language Difficulties and Learning Disabilities

Language and communication learning disabilities involve the ability to understand or produce spoken language. Language is also considered an output activity because it requires organizing thoughts in the brain and calling upon the right words to verbally explain something or communicate with someone else. Signs of a language–based learning disorder involve problems with verbal language skills, such as the ability to retell a story and the fluency of speech, as well as the ability to understand the meaning of words, parts of speech, directions, etc.

Reading Difficulties and Learning Disabilities

There are two types of learning disabilities in reading. Basic reading problems occur when there is difficulty understanding the relationship between sounds, letters and words. Reading comprehension problems occur when there is an inability to grasp the meaning of words, phrases, and paragraphs. Signs of reading difficulty include problems with: letter and word recognition, understanding words and ideas. reading speed and fluency, general vocabulary skills.

Writing Difficulties and Learning Disabilities

Learning disabilities in writing can involve the physical act of writing or the mental activity of comprehending and synthesizing information. Basic writing disorder refers to physical difficulty forming words and letters. Expressive writing disability indicates a struggle to organize thoughts on paper. Symptoms of a written language learning disability revolve around the act of writing and include. They include problems with: neatness and consistency of writing, accurately copying letters and words, spelling consistency, writing organization and coherence.

Auditory and Visual Processing: The Importance of the Ears and the Eyes

The eyes and the ears are the primary means of delivering information to the brain, a process sometimes called "input." If either the eyes or the ears aren't working properly, learning can suffer and there is a greater likelihood of a learning disability or disorder. Professionals may refer to the ability to hear well as "auditory processing skills" or "receptive language." The ability to hear things correctly greatly impacts the ability to read, write and spell. An inability to distinguish subtle differences in sound, or hearing sounds at the wrong speed make it difficult to sound out words and understand the basic concepts of reading and writing.

Problems in visual perception include missing subtle differences in shapes, reversing letters or numbers, skipping words, skipping lines, misperceiving depth or distance, or having problems with eye–hand coordination. Professionals may refer to the work of the eyes as "visual processing." Visual perception can affect gross and fine motor skills, reading comprehension, and math.

Common Types of Learning Disabilities		
Dyslexia	Difficulty processing language	Problems reading, writing, spelling, speaking
Dyscalculia	Difficulty with math	Problems doing math problems, understanding time, using money
Dysgraphia	Difficulty with writing	Problems with handwriting, spelling, organizing ideas
Dyspraxia (Sensory Integration Disorder)	Difficulty with fine motor skills	Problems with hand–eye coordination, balance, manual dexterity
Auditory Processing Disorder	Difficulty hearing differences between sounds	Problems with reading, comprehension, language
Visual Processing Disorder	Difficulty interpreting visual information	Problems with reading, math, maps, charts, symbols, pictures

Diagnosis and Testing for Learning Disabilities and Disorders Specialists Trained to do Psychological Testing and Result Interpretation

- Clinical psychologist
- School psychologist
- Educational psychologist
- Developmental psychologist
- Neuropsychologist
- Psychometrist
- Occupational therapist
- Speech and language therapist

Sometimes several professionals coordinate services as a team to obtain an accurate diagnosis, including input from your child's teachers. Recommendations can then be made for special education services or speech–language therapy school system.

DYSLEXIA

Definition

The term "Dyslexia" is used to cover a wide range of learning problems. It refers to a specific difficulty in learning, either inborn or acquired, in reading, spelling and written language. This may also be accompanied by difficulty in number work. It is a neurological condition in which the child has tremendous difficulty acquiring language skills, even though she may be intellectually bright, with oral skills so good that she is able to bluff her way through the early classes.

Dyslexia is a broad term defining a learning disability that impairs a person's fluency or accuracy in being able to read, write, and spell, and which can manifest itself as a difficulty with phonological awareness, phonological decoding, orthographic coding, auditory short-term memory, and/or rapid naming. Dyslexia is separate and distinct from reading difficulties resulting from other causes, such as a non-neurological deficiency with vision or hearing, or from poor or inadequate reading instruction. There are three proposed cognitive subtypes of dyslexia: auditory, visual and attentional. Although dyslexia is not an intellectual disability, it is considered both a learning disability and a reading disability. Dyslexia and IQ are not interrelated, since reading and cognition develop independently in individuals who have dyslexia.

The National Institute of Neurological Disorders and Stroke gives the following Definition for Dyslexia

"Dyslexia is a brain-based type of learning disability that specifically impairs a person's ability to read. These individuals typically read at levels significantly lower than expected despite having normal intelligence. Although the disorder varies from person to person, common characteristics among people with dyslexia are difficulty with spelling, phonological processing, and/or rapid visual-verbal responding. In adults, dyslexia usually occurs after a brain injury or in the context of dementia. It can also be inherited in some families, and recent studies have identified a number of genes that may predispose an individual to developing dyslexia".

Signs and Symptoms

The symptoms of dyslexia vary according to the severity of the disorder as well as the age of the individual.

The chronological sequence of events:

- In the first year the child may be a bit slow in acquiring the alphabet and some aspects of sight vocabulary.
- By about 7 years of age, the child may begin to have difficulty in reading and spelling and may therefore become demotivated.

- As the child grows older and is not given appropriate help in reading, writing and spelling, these will further lag behind the chronological age.
- The child, faced with his own failure, will show a low self esteem.
- Another feature therefore, is a secondary anxiety problem which manifests itself in many ways. The child may be withdrawn, anxious, aggressive or 'playful '.

Preschool-aged children:

- It is difficult to obtain a certain diagnosis of dyslexia before a child begins school, but many dyslexic individuals have a history of difficulties that began well before kindergarten. Children who exhibit these symptoms early in life have a higher likelihood of being diagnosed as dyslexic than other children. These symptoms include:
  - Delays in speech
  - Slow learning of new words
  - Not crawling
  - Difficulty in rhyming words, as in nursery rhymes
  - Low letter knowledge
  - Letter reversal or mirror writing

Early primary school children:

- Difficulty learning the alphabet or letters order
- Difficulty with associating sounds with the letters that represent them
- Difficulty identifying or generating rhyming words, or counting syllables in words
- Difficulty segmenting words into individual sounds, or blending sounds to make words
- Difficulty with word retrieval or naming problems
- Difficulty learning to decode written words
- Difficulty distinguishing between similar sounds in words; mixing up sounds in polysyllabic words

Older Primary School Children

- Slow or inaccurate reading.
- Very poor spelling which has been called dysorthographia
- Difficulty reading out loud, reading words in the wrong order, skipping words and sometimes saying a word similar to another word
- Difficulty associating individual words with their correct meanings
- Difficulty with time keeping and concept of time when doing a certain task
- Difficulty with organization skills

- Children with dyslexia may fail to see similarities and differences in letters and words, may not recognize the spacing that organizes letters into separate words, and may be unable to sound out the pronunciation of an unfamiliar word.

Dyslexia Symptoms

A discrepancy between the pupil's ability and their actual achievement If you notice that a child who appears to be average or bright when they are talking to you is struggling to read, spell or cope with math/s, this may be the strongest indicator that they may be dyslexic. It is very common for dyslexic children to be quite able, especially in the areas of creativity and physical co-ordination. However, there are differences in the neural links in their brain that makes it hard for them to deal with text without extra support. A reading age or grade level of two years below what you would expect from them is a sign of possible dyslexia. Obviously, this could also be caused by other factors such as lengthy absences from school due to illness.

A Family History of Learning Difficulties

Dyslexia is most often inherited through the genes. It can also be caused by early ear infections. In both cases it is harder for a young child to distinguish the difference between similar sounding words. The numbers of boys and girls who are dyslexic are roughly the same.

Difficulties with Spelling

Spelling is the activity which causes most difficulty for dyslexic children. Noticing spelling errors in short, simple words is the way in which most dyslexic children first come our attention. Examples of words which cause particular difficulty are: *any, many, island, said, they, because, enough,* and *friend*. Other words will sometimes be spelt in the way that you would expect them to be spelt if our spelling system were rational, for example *does/dus, please/ pleeze, knock/nock, search/serch, journey/jerney,* etc. Dyslexic children also experience difficulties with 'jumbled spellings'. These are spelling attempts in which all the correct letters are present, but are written in the wrong order. Examples include *dose/does, freind/friend, siad/said, bule/blue, becuase/because,* and *wores/worse*. 'Jumbled spellings' show that the child is experiencing difficulty with visual memory. Non-dyslexic children and adults often use their visual memory when trying to remember a difficult spelling: they write down two or three possible versions of the word on a spare piece of paper and see which spelling 'looks right'. They are relying on their visual memory to help them, but the visual memory of a dyslexic child may not be adequate for this task.

Confusion Over Left and Right

A fairly quick way to establish this type of confusion is to ask a child to point to your left foot with his or her right hand. If you try similar instructions - in a non-threatening environment - you will soon be able to see if this causes difficulties or not. You may also notice difficulties with east and west, or in following directions like 'Go to the end of the road and turn left, then right, etc'.

Writing Letters or Numbers Backwards

You will have noticed some children who mix up 'b' and 'd', or even 'p' and the number 9. These letters are the same in their mirror image, and cause regular confusion for a dyslexic person. Some pupils make a point of always writing the letter 'b' as au upper-case or capital 'B', as they find this much easier to remember in terms of the direction it faces.

Difficulties with Math/s

One feature of dyslexia is difficulties with sequencing - getting things in the right order. Math/s depends on sequences of numbers - 2. 4. 6. 8. etc. Whilst many people are aware that dyslexic children and students have problems with reading and spelling, they do not know that math/s can also be a real challenge.

Difficulties Organizing Themselves

Whilst you may quite reasonably think that all children live their lives in a mess, this is particularly so for dyslexic children and students, who may have genuine difficulties with planning and thinking ahead to when a book or pen might be needed next. They can really benefit from help with organizing papers and folders under a simple color-coded system.

Difficulty Following 2- or 3-step Instructions

'Go to Mrs. Brown and ask her if Peter Smith is in school today. Oh, yes, and ask if I can borrow her dictionary' - such an instruction is just too much! It involves both sequencing and memory skills, and you would be very surprised to see a dyslexic child return with the dictionary and information about Peter Smith! Dyslexic children love to take messages as much as any other child, but it has to be a less complicated instruction, e.g. 'Ask Mrs. Brown if I can borrow her stapler'.

Causes

- Research shows that dyslexia is unrelated to home environment, intellect or social class. Dyslexics usually follow the normal distribution curve of IQ pattern, and several dyslexics have average to above average IQ.
- Birth traumas such as oxygen deprivation, head injuries and certain medications such as those for seizures are also one of the factors.

- Recent research also indicates that the brains of dyslexics differ structurally from brains of others. Their information processing system also differs in a distinctive manner.
- There is also some evidence to suggest that dyslexia is largely inherited.

Main Characteristics

- Adequate and sometimes above average ability to understand and comprehend.
- Poor development of written language skills
- Lack of ability to differentiate between letters of similar shape, such as 'b' and 'd', 'p' and 'q'. Mirror image reversal of these letters.
- Lack of strong preference for either right-handedness or left-handedness.
- Tendency to transpose word images: to read 'saw' as 'was', 'on' as 'no', etc.
- Serious inability to spell and learn things in sequence, such as months of the year.
- Difficulty in spelling, reading and writing. Some children have difficulty in spatial orientation too.
- Difficulty in copying notes and answering examination questions.

Diagnosis

There is a grave danger of classifying a slow learner as dyslexic. A child can be considered a dyslexic, if: her intelligence is high but her academic achievements are low and she demonstrates a few of the recognised dyslexic symptoms including:

- A disparity between her actual reading ability and listening comprehension ability
- Sequencing and visual memory deficit and
- Problems in spelling.

Treatment

- Dyslexics learn best in highly structured environment.
- They have a poor visual memory for words and must go back to basic phonics and phonetic techniques in a multi-sensory teaching approach.
- The magic formula is: drill, practice and repetition
- There is no medicine or drug that can cure dyslexia, only remedial teaching can.

Assessment

Assessment of children with learning problems provides the basis for remediation.

Assessment information is of two types:

- *General information*: This includes case history material, general abilities of the child, observational data, etc. It gives an overall picture of the child and suggests a beginning point for remediation.
- *Specific information*: This gives results of direct measurement of the students performance in language, arithmetic and other areas that provides the basis for further instruction.

Assessment of General Abilities

This is done to determine whether the child functions at a lower or higher level of intelligence for her age. This cannot be done only on the basis of academic records. A child may be intelligent but due to lack of motivation or other factors perform poorly in academics.

Some of the other ways of judging the child's general abilities are as follows:

- Observing the child's general capacity in areas other than academics compared to other children her age, such as, comprehension, ability to go out and buy things, counting, understanding TV programmes, etc.
- Observing the child when she plays with other children of her age group

A Dyslexic Child in the Classroom

A Guide for Teachers

Much can be done by integrating the child into the class environment where he/she can feel comfortable and develop confidence and self esteem. Class teachers may be particularly confused by the student whose consistent underachievement seems due to what may look like carelessness or lack of effort. These children can be made to feel very different from their peers simply because they may be unable to follow simple instructions, which for others seem easy. It is a class teacher's responsibility to provide an atmosphere conducive to learning for all pupils within their class.

Class teachers need to have an understanding of the problems that the dyslexic child may have within the classroom situation. Hopefully, with this knowledge, a great deal of misunderstanding of a child's behaviour can be prevented. In a positive and encouraging environment, a dyslexic child will experience the feeling of success and self-value. Of particular importance is an understanding of the problems that poor auditory short term memory can cause, in terms of retaining input from the teacher. Examples of poor auditory short term memory can be a difficulty in remembering the sounds in spoken words long enough to match these, in sequence, with letters for spelling. Often children with poor auditory short term memory cannot remember even a short list of instructions.

The following items should provide useful guidelines for teachers and parents to follow and support:

In the class:

- Of value to all children in the class is an outline of what is going to be taught in the lesson, ending the lesson with a resume of what has been taught. In this way information is more likely to go from short term memory to long term memory.
- When homework is set, it is important to check that the child correctly writes down exactly what is required. Try to ensure that the appropriate worksheets and books are with the child to take home.
- In the front of the pupils' homework book get them to write down the telephone numbers of a couple of friends. Then, if there is any doubt over homework, they can ring up and check, rather than worry or spend time doing the wrong work.
- Make sure that messages and day to day classroom activities are written down, and never sent verbally. i.e. music, P. E. swimming etc.
- Make a daily check list for the pupil to refer to each evening. Encourage a daily routine to help develop the child's own self-reliance and responsibilities.
- Encourage good organizational skills by the use of folders and dividers to keep work easily accessible and in an orderly fashion.
- Break tasks down into small easily remembered pieces of information.
- If visual memory is poor, copying must be kept to a minimum. Notes or handouts are far more useful.
- Seat the child fairly near the class teacher so that the teacher is available to help if necessary, or he can be supported by a well-motivated and sympathetic classmate.

Copying from the Blackboard

Use different colour chalks for each line if there is a lot of written information on the board, or underline every second line with a different coloured chalk.

Ensure that the Writing is Well Spaced

Leave the writing on the blackboard long enough to ensure the child doesn't rush, or that the work is not erased from the board before the child has finished copying.

Reading

- A structured reading scheme that involves repetition and introduces new words slowly is extremely important. This allows the child to develop confidence and self esteem when reading.

- Don't ask pupils to read a book at a level beyond their current skills, this will instantly demotivate them. Motivation is far better when demands are not too high, and the child can actually enjoy the book. If he has to labour over every word he will forget the meaning of what he is reading.
- Save the dyslexic child the ordeal of having to 'read aloud in class'. Reserve this for a quiet time with the class teacher. Alternatively, perhaps give the child advanced time to read pre-selected reading material, to be practiced at home the day before. This will help ensure that the child is seen to be able to read out loud, along with other children
- Real books should also be available for paired reading with an adult, which will often generate enthusiasm for books. Story tapes can be of great benefit for the enjoyment and enhancement of vocabulary. No child should be denied the pleasure of gaining access to the meaning of print even if he cannot decode it fully.
- Remember reading should be fun.

Spelling:

- Many of the normal classroom techniques used to teach spellings do not help the dyslexic child. All pupils in the class can benefit from structured and systematic exposure to rules and patterns that underpin a language.
- Spelling rules can be given to the whole class. Words for class spelling tests are often topic based rather than grouped for structure. If there are one or two dyslexics in the class, a short list of structure-based words for their weekly spelling test, will be far more helpful than random words. Three or four irregular words can be included each week, eventually this should be seen to improve their free-writing skills.
- All children should be encouraged to proof read, which can be useful for initial correction of spellings. Dyslexics seem to be unable to correct their spellings spontaneously as they write, but they can be trained to look out for errors that are particular to them.

Remember, poor spelling is not an indication of low intelligence.

Dyscalculia:

- "Dyscalculia" is a lesser-known learning disability that affects mathematical calculations. It is derived from the generic name "mathematics difficulty".
- A student with any degree of mathematics difficulty may be considered to have "dyscalculia" by some educational specialists.

UNDERLYING CAUSES

Dyscalculia has several underlying causes. One of the most prominent is a weakness in visual processing. To be successful in mathematics, one needs to be able to visualize numbers and mathematics situations. Students with dyscalculia have a very difficult time visualizing numbers and often mentally mix up the numbers, resulting in what appear to be "stupid mistakes." Another problem is with sequencing. Students who have difficulty sequencing or organizing detailed information often have difficulty remembering specific facts and formulas for completing their mathematical calculations.

SYMPTOMS

- Many students with disabilities have histories of academic failure that contribute to the development of learned helplessness in mathematics. It is important that mathematics instructors recognize the symptoms of dyscalculia and take the necessary measures to help students that are affected. Some of the symptoms are:
- Students might have spatial problems and difficulty aligning numbers into proper columns.
- Have trouble with sequence, including left/right orientation. They will read numbers out of sequence and sometimes do operations backwards. They also become confused on the sequences of past or future events
- Students typically have problems with mathematics concepts in word problems, confuse similar numbers and have difficulty using a calculator.
- It is common for students with dyscalculia to have normal or accelerated language acquisition: verbal, reading, writing, and good visual memory for the printed word. They are typically good in the areas of science, geometry, and creative arts.
- Students have difficulty with the abstract concepts of time and direction. They may be chronically late.
- Mistaken recollection of names. Poor name/face retrieval. Substitute names beginning with same letter.
- Students have inconsistent results in addition, subtraction, multiplication and division. Students have poor mental
- mathematics ability. They are poor with money and credit and cannot do financial planning or budgeting. Short term, not long term financial thinking. May have fear of money and cash transactions. May be unable to mentally figure change due back, the amounts to pay for tips, taxes, etc
- When writing, reading and recalling numbers, these common mistakes are made: number additions, substitutions, transpositions, omissions, and reversals.
- Inability to grasp and remember mathematics concepts, rules formulas, sequence and basic addition, subtraction, multiplication and division facts. Poor long-term memory of concept mastery.

Students understand material as they are being shown it, but when they must retrieve the information they become confused and are unable to do so. They may be able to perform mathematics operations one day, but draw a blank the next. May be able to do book work but can fails all tests and quizzes.

- May be unable to comprehend or "picture" mechanical processes. Lack "big picture/ whole picture" thinking. Poor ability to "visualize or picture" the location of the numbers on the face of a clock, the geographical locations of states, countries, oceans, streets, etc.
- Poor memory for the "layout" of things. Gets lost or disoriented easily. May have a poor sense of direction, loose things often, and seem absent minded. May have difficulty grasping concepts of formal music education. Difficulty sight-reading music, learning fingering to play an instrument, etc.
- May have poor athletic coordination, difficulty keeping up with rapidly changing physical directions like in aerobic, dance, and exercise classes. Difficulty remembering dance step sequences rules for playing sports.
- Difficulty keeping score during games, or difficulty remembering how to keep score in games, like bowling, etc. Often looses track of whose turn it is during games, like cards and board games. Limited strategic planning ability for games, like chess.

MITIGATIVE STRATEGIES

Although dyscalculia may be difficult to diagnose, there are strategies that teachers and parents should know about to aid students in learning mathematics.

- Encourage students to work extra hard to "visualize" mathematics problems. Draw them or have them draw a picture to help understand the problem, and make sure that they take the time to look at any visual information that is provided
- Have the student read problems out loud and listen very carefully. This allows them to use their auditory skills.
- Provide examples and try to relate problems to real-life situations.
- Provide younger students with graph paper and encourage them to use it in order to keep the numbers in line.
- Provide uncluttered worksheets so that the student is not overwhelmed by too much visual information. Especially on tests, allow scrap paper with lines and ample room for uncluttered computation.
- Discalculia students must spend extra time memorizing mathematics facts. Repetition is very important. Use rhythm or music to help memorize.

- Many students need one-on-one attention to fully grasp certain concepts. Have students work with a tutor, a parent, or a teacher after school hours in a one-on-one environment.
- If possible, allow the student to take the exam on a one-to-one basis in the teacher's presence.
- The student might like instant answers and a chance to do the problem over once s/he is wrong. Often their mistakes are the result of "seeing" the problem wrong.
- In early stages, design the test problems "pure," testing only the required skills. In their early learning, they must be free of large numbers and unnecessary destructive calculations.
- Allow more than the "common" time to complete problems and check to see that student is not panicking.
- Most importantly, be PATIENT! Never forget that the student WANTS to learn and retain. Realize that mathematics can be a traumatic experience and is highly emotional because of past failures. The slightest misunderstanding or break in logic can overwhelm the student and cause emotional distress. Pity will not help, but patience and individual attention will. It is typical for students to work with until they know the material well and then get every problem wrong on the test. Then 5 minutes later, they can perform the test with just the teacher, on the chalkboard, and many times get all problems correct. Remember that this is very frustrating for the teacher/parent as well as the student. Patience is essential.
- Assign extra problems for practice and maybe a special TA or special education is assigned to assist the affected student.
- When presenting new material, make sure the student with discalculia is able to write each step down and talk it through until they understand it well enough to teach it back to you.
- Go over the upcoming lesson with so that the lecture is more of a review.
- Computer-assisted instruction mathematics courses can be developed.

DYSGRAPHIA

"Dysgraphia" is a learning disability resulting from the difficulty in expressing thoughts in writing and graphing. It generally refers to extremely poor handwriting. Most learning disabled students experience difficulty with handwriting and probably could be considered "dysgraphic".

Underlying Causes

Students with dysgraphia often have sequencing problems. Studies indicate that what usually appears to be a perceptual problem usually seems to be directly related to sequential/rational information processing. These students often have difficulty with the sequence of letters and words as they write. As a result, the student either needs to slow down in order to write accurately, or experiences extreme difficulty with the "mechanics" of writing. They also tend to intermix letters and numbers in formulas. Usually they have difficulty even when they do their work more slowly. And by slowing down or getting "stuck" with the details of writing they often lose the thoughts that they are trying to write about. Students with an attention deficit disorder often experience rather significant difficulty with writing and formulas in general and handwriting in particular. This is because ADHD students also have difficulty organizing and sequencing detailed information. In addition, ADHD students are often processing information at a very rapid rate and simply don't have the fine-motor coordination needed to "keep up" with their thoughts.

Some students can also experience writing difficulty because of a general auditory or language processing weakness. Because of their difficulty learning and understanding language in general, they obviously have difficulty with language expression. Recall that written language is the most difficult form of language expression. Although most students with dysgraphia do not have visual or perceptual processing problems, some students with a visual processing weakness will experience difficulty with writing speed and clarity simply because they aren't able to fully process the visual information as they are placing it on the page.

SYMPTOMS

- Students may exhibit strong verbal but particularly poor writing skills.
- Random punctuation. Spelling errors; reversals; phonic approximations; syllable omissions; errors in common suffixes. Clumsiness and disordering of syntax; an impression of illiteracy. Misinterpretation of questions and questionnaire items. Disordered numbering and written number reversals.
- Generally illegible writing.
- Inconsistencies: mixtures of print and cursive, upper and lower case, or irregular sizes, shapes, or slant of letters.
- Unfinished words or letters, omitted words.
- Inconsistent position on page with respect to lines and margins and inconsistent spaces between words and letters.
- Cramped or unusual grip, especially holding the writing instrument very close to the paper, or holding thumb over two fingers and writing from the wrist.
- Talking to self while writing, or carefully watching the hand that is writing.
- Slow or labored copying or writing - even if it is neat and legible.

STRATEGIES

- Encourage students to outline their thoughts. It is important to get the main ideas down on paper without having to struggle with the details of spelling, punctuation, etc
- Have students draw a picture of a thought for each paragraph.
- Have students dictate their ideas into a tape recorder and then listen and write them down later.
- Have them practice keyboarding skills. It may be difficult at first, but after they have learned the pattern of the keys, typing will be faster and clearer than handwriting.
- Have a computer available for them to organize information and check spelling. Even if their keyboarding skills aren't great, a computer can help with the details.
- Have them continue practicing handwriting. There will be times throughout a student's life that they will need to be able to write things down and maybe even share their handwriting with others. It will continue to improve as long as the student keeps working at it.
- Encourage student to talk aloud as they write. This may provide valuable auditory feedback.
- Allow more time for written tasks including note-taking, copying, and tests.
- Outline the particular demands of the course assignments/continuous assessment; exams, computer literacy etc. so that likely problems can be foreseen.
- Give and allow students to begin projects or assignments early.
- Include time in the student's schedule for being a 'library assistant' or 'office assistant' that could also be used for catching up or getting ahead on written work, or doing alternative activities related to the material being learned.
- Instead of having the student write a complete set of notes, provide a partially completed outline so the student can fill in the details under major headings.
- Allow the student to dictate some assignments or tests a 'scribe'. Train the 'scribe' to write what the student says verbatim and then allow the student to make changes, without assistance from the scribe.
- Remove 'neatness' or 'spelling' as grading criteria for some assignments, or design assignments to be evaluated on specific parts of the writing process.
- With the students, allow abbreviations in some writing. Have the student develop a repertoire of abbreviations in a notebook. These will come in handy in future note-taking situations.

- Reduce copying aspects of work; for example, in Math, provide a worksheet with the problems already on it instead of having the student copy the problems.
- Separate the writing into stages and then teach students to do the same. Teach the stages of the writing process. Consider grading these stages even on some 'one-sitting' written exercises, so that points are awarded on a short essay for brainstorming and a rough draft, as well as the final product.
- On a computer, the student can produce a rough draft, copy it, and then revise the copy, so that both the rough draft and final product can be evaluated without extra typing.
- Encourage the student to use a spellchecker and, if possible, have someone else proofread his work, too. Speaking spellcheckers are recommended, especially if the student may not be able to recognize the correct word.
- Allow the student to use cursive or manuscript, whichever is most legible
- Encourage primary students to use paper with the raised lines to keep writing on the line.
- Allow older students to use the line width of their choice. Keep in mind that some students use small writing to disguise its messiness or spelling.
- Allow students to use paper or writing instruments of different colors.
- Allow student to use graph paper for math, or to turn lined paper sideways, to help with lining up columns of numbers.
- Allow the student to use the writing instrument that is most comfortable for them.
- If copying is laborious, allow the student to make some editing marks rather than recopying the whole thing.
- Consider whether use of speech recognition software will be helpful. If the student and teacher are willing to invest time and effort in 'training' the software to the student's voice and learning to use it, the student can be freed from the motor processes of writing or keyboarding.
- Develop cooperative writing projects where different students can take on roles such as the 'brainstormer,' 'organizer of information,' 'writer,' 'proofreader,' and 'illustrator.'
- Provide extra structure and use intermittent deadlines for long-term assignments. Discuss with the student and parents the possibility of enforcing the due dates by working after school with the teacher in the event a deadline arrives and the work is not up-to-date.
- Build handwriting instruction into the student's schedule. The details and degree of independence will depend on the student's age and attitude, but many students would like to have better handwriting.

- Keep in mind that handwriting habits are entrenched early. Before engaging in a battle over a student's grip or whether they should be writing in cursive or print, consider whether enforcing a change in habits will eventually make the writing task a lot easier for the student, or whether this is a chance for the student to make his or her own choices. Beware of overload, the student has other tasks and courses.
- Teach alternative handwriting methods such as "Handwriting Without Tears." <www.hwtears.com/inro.htm>
- Writing just one key word or phrase for each paragraph, and then going back later to fill in the details may be effective.
- Multisensory techniques should be utilized for teaching both manuscript and cursive writing. The techniques need to be practiced substantially so that the letters are fairly automatic before the student is asked to use these skills to communicate ideas.
- Have the students use visual graphic organizers. For example, you can create a mind map so that the main idea is placed in a circle in the center of the page and supporting facts are written on lines coming out of the main circle, similar to the arms of a spider or spokes on a wheel.
- Do papers and assignments in a logical step-wise sequence. An easy way to remember these steps is to think of the word POWER.
  - *P*: Plan your paper
  - *O*: Organize your thoughts and ideas
  - *W*: Write your draft E - edit your work
  - *R*: Revise your work, producing a final draft
- If a student becomes fatigued have them try the following: Shake hands fast, but not violently.
  - Rub hands together and focus on the feeling of warmth.
  - Rub hands on the carpet in circles
  - Use the thumb of the dominant hand to click the top of a ballpoint pen while holding it in that hand. Repeat using the index finger.
  - Perform *sitting pushups* by placing each palm on the chair with fingers facing forward. Students push down on their hands, lifting their body slightly off the chair.
- Allow student to tape record important assignments and/or take oral tests.
- Prioritize certain task components during a complex activity. For example, students can focus on using descriptive words in one assignment, and in another, focus on using compound sentences.
- Reinforce the positive aspects of student's efforts.
- Be patient and encourage student to be patient with himself.

Strategies For Spelling Difficulties

- Encourage consistent use of spell checker to decrease the overall demands of the writing task and encourage students to wait until the end to worry about spelling.
- Encourage use of an electronic resource such as the spell check component in a Franklin Language Master to further decrease the demands. If student has concurrent reading problems, a Language Master with a speaking component is most helpful because it will read/say the words.
- Have the student look at each word, then close their eyes and visualize how it looks, letter by letter.
- Have the student spell each word out loud while looking at it, then look away and spell it out loud again several times before writing it down.
- Have the students break the spelling list down into manageable sections of only 3 to 5 words. Then take a break after mastering each section.
- Have a scrabble board and computer accessible for affected students.

DISADVANTAGED GROUPS: SOCIAL, ECONOMICAL AND EDUCATIONAL (OVER ACHIEVERS AND UNDER ACHIEVERS)

Overachieving and underachieving are two conditions which are experienced by many people. These are most commonly noticed in children, in terms of academics, sports and other activities which they take part in. Over-and-underachieving are issues that must be addressed by confidence building. There are various ways helping a child become more confident, and these should be seriously considered if parents hope to see him or her grow into well-balanced adulthood.

THE UNDERACHIEVERS: MEANING

'Under achieving' implies that children should be achieving a certain norm at the certain age or time, and they currently are not. The Underachievers are often termed as the mistaken identity of low-ability students. They are endowed with high intellectual potential but suffer from the crisis of low scholastic performance. Certain traits such as rebellious attitude, frequently lying, fear phobia with regard to success, day dreaming, inattentiveness, etc may be either one reason in isolation or multiple reasons in combination with another. It may also occur due to physical deformities. Underachieving is the state in which a person performs significantly below his or her obvious potential. Parents can more readily relate to the problems faced by an underachieving child, because they tend to focus heavily on reversing this trend for most of the child's life.

CONCEPT OF UNDERACHIEVERS

Underachievers are kids who have a lot of potential but don't live up to that potential in school. Underachievers span all social, economic, and ability levels. Many underachievers have very high IQ's. Teachers and parents often accuse underachievers of being lazy, of having attitude problems, or of not caring about themselves. Sometimes these kids get into trouble at school and at home. Nobody realizes that underachievement is the issue.

An underachiever child tends to have little interest in school work and related activities, invariably blames others for mistakes, is generally disorganized and either socializes too much or too little. The fact is that though they seem to be opposite syndromes, overachieving and underachieving are really related conditions that stem from low self esteem.

Children who focus on achieving too much actually consider their academic grades as barometers of their personal worth. Underachievers are scared to perform well and may even be averse to trying – simply because they lack sufficient self esteem. For reasons that may well lie in problematic parenting styles, such kids assume that they are not good enough to succeed at anything. Two types of under achievement have been identified. The first is where children only achieve on occasions, apparently when the mood takes them. More likely, their refusal to work or put themselves forward for selection in a team can be linked with some emotional crisis that suddenly erupts: a relationship may break up; a family problem may arise; a personality clash may develop with a specific teacher. Generally, these children have few long-term problems if they can get immediate help to overcome their difficulty and their progress at school is closely monitored. These children are known as situational underachievers.

The second type of underachiever is a much more serious problem for the school, the home and particularly for themselves. The chronic underachiever has many characteristics that give him a label hard to remove. Over 80 percent of identified underachievers are boys! They may become aggressive, giving vent to their frustration by causing trouble or they may become sulky and withdrawn and refuse to develop their talent.

SIGNS AND SYMPTOMS OF UNDERACHIEVERS

Commonly encountered characteristics of underachievers may include the following:

- Often impulsive with poor personal judgment and adjustment abilities;
- Poor test results at school and no hobbies or interests at home;
- A low self-image, often displaying distrust, indifference, lack of concern and/or hostility;
- Feel victimized or helpless and may not accept any responsibility for themselves or their actions;

- Feel rejected by their family and resist attempts to help by parents or teachers
- Choose friends with similar negative attitudes to school, show no leadership qualities and may be less mature than their peers;
- Have little motivation with poor study habits; may refuse to do homework or leave much work incomplete;
- Either cannot plan for the future or set goals well below their true ability or potential.

The Causes

The underachievers are made and not born. It is the child's choice to underachieve. We have to look at both sides of the education coin: the school and the home. The pressure on children, especially at secondary school, to conform to the mediocre often has more influence than anything parents or teachers can say. Fortunately, negative peer pressure is usually a passing phase. As the pressure to succeed at the Higher School Certificate increases, so too does the realization that one way to a happy and successful future is to work hard to obtain a particular job or to gain a place at university or college. Another cause of under achievement can be family background. There can be difficulties when some members of the family perceive a bright child is showing off.

If a child is frequently on the move, for one reason or another, it can mean that he is never in a school long enough for any talent to be recognized by himself or his teachers, let alone developed and nurtured. It's quite possible for people with the potential to do exceptionally well, to go through life without realizing that they have a gift which can, and should, be developed. The major cause of under achievement among the talented is emotional disturbance between parent and child. Children like this are angry at the parents for some reason and vent their anger and frustration in many ways. They feel they must hurt their parents by failing at school and not allowing them to take pride in their achievements.

When conflict exists between the parents when one parent is a stern perfectionist and the other tries to compensate for this, the child starts to achieve to please dad, but then feels pressure from mum which carries the message: 'You don't need to work so hard!'. The child becomes confused trying to please both parents. Sometimes the family has unrealistic, perfectionist expectations and the child equates his/her own worth with doing well at school rather than simply being an individual. There might be a negative relationship with a father who feels threatened by his son surpassing him and being more successful at school than he was.

Some parents are 'pushy' and try to relive their own lives through their children and force them along at too fast a pace, causing stress and unhappiness. Such pushy parents cannot accept that their children are only children. The child's only defense is to deliberately fail at school. A vicious circle like this can only be broken if the parents learn to understand what is happening. The role model that a parent displays might not be acceptable to the child and lead to his being constantly embarrassed and having a poor self esteem. Any of these problems is likely to create a poor self-image. Fearing success so much, the child creates failure. Such a child prefers not to complete work rather than be awarded a grade that he or she feels will not reach the parents' expectations.

- Home origins of underachievement:
  - The over welcome child
  - Early illness
  - Birth order
  - Marital discord
  - Conflicting parenting styles
  - Kind mom/ogre dad
  - Wonderful dad/ogre mom
  - Dummy dad
  - Mousy mom

Characteristics

- All underachievers, whether dependent or dominant in their behaviour exhibit:
  - Forgetfulness
  - Disorganisation
  - Carelessness and superficiality on tasks
  - Non-academic interests
  - Manipulation of relations with parents and teachers
  - Loneliness and social withdrawal
- Personal:
  - Low self-concept, negative self-evaluation
  - Social immaturity, unpopular with peers
  - Choose companions who do not like school
  - Feelings of rejection, helplessness, feeling victimized
  - Hostile toward adult authority figures
  - Low aspirations for future, career, less persistent and assertive
  - Externalization of conflicts, problems
- School:
  - Lack of discipline in tasks, high distractibility
  - Don't see connection between effort and achievement outcomes
  - Few strong hobbies or interests
  - Resistant to influence from teachers, parents
  - Withdraw in classroom situations
  - Lack of study skills,

- Weak academic motivation
- Leave schoolwork incomplete, nap during study times
- Perform well on synthesis tasks but not on tasks requiring precise, analytic processing

Suggestions

It is essential to build the child's self-confidence and independence. Encourage the child to see him or herself as a unique individual with a valuable contribution to make to family and society. Never take away the thing or things that a child loves and succeeds in. Don't lecture or nag a child. Reason is always preferable. Don't pressure the child into doing something because you think it's a good idea. Don't set artificial times for work to be done at all costs and make the child feel that you are being a martyr. This reinforces the idea of failure, not only at school but at home as well. Be more natural in your interest and enthusiasm. Don't keep checking up on the child's progress. This seems to the child that her or she is irresponsible and not in control of life. It also implies a damaging lack of trust.

Learn to Trust the Child's Judgment

Get used to saying things which make it clear that the child's feelings are important and that you value his or her opinions. Explain that it's all right to feel angry but that it must be expressed in acceptable ways. Your relationship with your child must be based on mutual respect. It often helps an underachieving child to point out achievable goals for them. Put the goals in some priority order, but be flexible. Guide, don't push. Give underachievers the opportunity to work at their area of ability and make sure someone the child respects is available when help is needed. Isolation is a fine fertilizer for under achievement.

STRATEGIES

- Single-sided interests:
  - Identify "acceptable minimums for tasks
  - Pick up pace of instruction
  - Identify "have to have" skills and focus on these
  - Help child focus on their single-sided interests
- Claims of boredom:
  - Develop diagnostic- prescriptive instruction
  - Compact the regular curriculum
  - Use continuous progress for learning
  - Fast paced content presentations
  - Subject acceleration
  - Find "cause" of boredom
- Perfectionism:

- Teach strategies for when to quit, how to match effort to tasks, setting goals, focusing on successes not failures, and separating self-concept from products
- Role model mistake making

- Peer Pressure to Underachieve:
  - Selectively encourage certain friendships
  - Take interest in child's friends
  - Encourage extra- curriculars
  - Teach strategies for resisting peer pressure
- Lack of Organizational Skills:
  - Study habits training
  - Strategies for developing work plans, priorities, balance, flexibility
  - Provide consistent space and schedule for study at home
- Stress:
  - Teach time management techniques
  - Relaxation exercises
  - Exercise routines
  - Socialization opportunities

STRATEGIES FOR IMPROVING ACADEMIC PERFORMANCE

Supportive Strategies

Behaviors that affirm the worth of the child in the classroom and convey the promise of greater potential and success yet to be discovered and enjoyed:

- Daily class meetings to discuss student's concerns
- Directive atmosphere to show who is in charge
- Daily written contracts of work to be done
- Free time scheduled each day to show import of relaxation, free choice
- Use of concrete, predictable teaching methods
- Eliminate work already mastered
- Allow independent study on topics of personal interest
- Non authoritarian atmosphere
- Permit students to prove competence via multiple methods
- Teach through problem solving rather than rote drill

Intrinsic Strategies

Behaviors that are designed to develop intrinsic achievement motivation through the child's discovery of the rewards available as a result of efforts to learn, achieve, and contribute to the group:

- Daily review of/reward for small successes
- Allow students to evaluate work prior to teacher marking

- Frequent, positive contact with family about child's progress
- Verbal praise for any self-initiating behaviors
- Assign specific responsibilities for classroom maintenance, management
- Practice reflective listening, comment to clarify student statements
- Student sets daily/weekly/monthly goals with teacher approval

Remedial Strategies

Behaviors that are used to improve the student's academic performance in an area of learning difficulty which led to experience of failure and loss of motivation to engage in learning tasks:

- Programmed instruction materials, students grade own papers upon completion
- Peer tutoring of younger students in areas of strength
- Small group instruction in common areas of weakness
- Encourage students to work on projects not involving marks or external evaluation
- Self-selected weekly goals for improvement
- Private instruction in areas of weakness
- Use of humor and personal example to approach academic weakness areas
- Familiarize students with learning styles and personal implications for performance

OVERACHIEVER: MEANING

Overachieving can be defined as performing far better than what is expected. In academics, it is defined as one's academic performance which is way higher than one's performance in standardized tests such as intelligence quotient tests. A child may be an overachiever if he feels an impulsive need to get perfect grades and be on top of everybody else in his class. Overachieving – and the diametric opposite trait of underachieving – are two rather common conditions in today's times. The seed for either trait is often planted in childhood, when many children fall into these categories in terms of academic performance, sports and many other activities. We define overachieving as a state in which a person performs far better than what is expected – or even necessary.

An overachieving child, for instance, feels prevailed upon to obtain very high grades, with the objective being to top the class. Most parents would not find anything wrong with this. After all, which parents do not want their children to be the best among their peers? This is precisely where the problem lies – children take their cue from their parents in most things, and in this case the stage is being set for some significant mental, physical, emotional and social problems in later life. Overachieving kids tend to skip meals, sleep less than required and refrain from social interactions and informal conversations. All that matters is getting A's. If such tendencies percolate over into adulthood – which they invariably do – such a person is a prime candidate for some rather large social and health issues.

CONCEPT OF OVERACHIEVER

Overachieves are used to setting impossible goals and then meeting them, but they can melt down when their extraordinary efforts fail. They can also develop unhealthy habits, like working long hours and skipping meals and sleep. Few overachievers become truly dysfunctional, but it's important to recognize the warning signs before behaviour become destructive.

Work Addiction

- *Symptoms*: Some overachievers use work to avoid negative feelings. They constantly think and talk about work, can't "turn it off" at the end of the day, and don't take vacations or lunch breaks.
- *What to do*: Workaholics tend to drag out a task with unnecessary attention to detail, so you need to establish their priorities for them and monitor progress closely. Reward the results of their work, not the amount of time they spend, and insist that they take lunch breaks and leave at a decent hour.

Depression and Self-Criticism

Symptoms

Inability to cope with failure is another warning sign. If a colleague is Unusually quiet or low-energy, taking lots of sick days, or skipping meetings and Company functions — particularly after a setback at work — take note. "Everyone fails now and then, but it's difficult for overachievers to deal with that," "On occasion, you will see dysfunctional behaviour that drives the person to the point of suicide when they've set a goal they can never, ever meet."

What to do

Tread carefully. "Managers need to refer the person to a professional psychologist for help and not try and deal with it on their own," Address the issue directly with the employee, but don't tell them, Instead, refer anyone with an emotional problem to a mental health professional.

Unethical Behavior

- *Symptoms*: Most overachievers don't fall into this category, but some can cross legal and ethical boundaries in order to reach their goals. If someone on consistently breaks rules to get ahead — for example, neglecting to fill out Paper work because it takes too much time and they can't be bothered,don't ignore the problem. It could lead to serious legal issues.

- *What to do*: If an Overachiever has acted unethically, keep an eye on the situation and record your observations. When you've gathered sufficient evidence, approach the person with someone to serve as a witness. At this point, they will realize they've crossed a serious line and will shape up or get professional help.

Hypercriticism

- *Symptoms*: If an overachiever shows blatant disregard for other opinions or actively looks for faults in others, it can cause a serious rift with colleagues. Sometimes criticism is necessary to improve performance and get work done, but it becomes destructive when negative comments far outweigh the positive ones.
- *What to do*: A counsellor, can provide guidance without the overachiever becoming alarmed at the stigma of professional help. Mentoring programs that pair experienced members can also assist in putting hypercritical overachiever back on the right track. Mentors can provide wise counsel on tough workplace challenges and give feedback to develop new skills and competencies.

Physical or Emotional Abuse

- *Symptoms*: Most warning signs are difficult for the overachiever to recognize in himself. The biggest is a quick loss of temper, such as swearing, yelling, huffing out of a room, or pounding on the table. Sometimes an overachiever will tease other team members in order to motivate them without realizing that it causes undue stress.
- *What to do*: Set guidelines and clear boundaries. Make a list of contingency plans.

THE NEGATIVE ASPECTS OF OVERACHIEVING

Loss of Focus or Passion

Overachievers are often spread quite thin. With only so many hours in the day and so much energy and effort to give, you have to divide your attention among a number of endeavors if you over schedule your time. When you feel pressure to excel in every area, you may lose the chance to discover a genuine personal interest or talent as you attempt to master all your activities. Consequently, you are likely to lose sight of what you truly like and to get less enjoyment from the things you do.

Poor Physical Health

The workload and time constraints of the typical overachiever leave relatively little time for sleep. In fact, sleep deprivation is common among overscheduled students, with many of them sleeping less than six hours per night. Excessively busy kids tend to suffer from poor eating habits, as well. If you don't have the time to sit down to three solid meals per day, you may have to grab food on the go, and such diets are often full of fats and sugar. Teens need sufficient sleep and nourishment to stay physically and mentally strong, so if you have too much to do, you may end up sacrificing your health.

Poor Mental Health

"School demands and frustrations" and "taking on too many activities or having too high expectations" are the leading causes of teenage stress. The desire to please others, as well as our culture's clear emphasis on success, is creating a generation of workaholics who are draining themselves mentally and emotionally.

Unhealthy Self-image

Overachievers often bases their feelings of self-worth on their accomplishments. The more they do, and the more they do well, the better they feel about themselves. Reliance on external validation, though, can be extremely harmful. If you focus on grades, test scores, awards, and other external markers of success, you can lose sight of your inner identity. Overachieving frequently causes students to forget that self-worth is measured from within rather than by what others think or say.

Problems Getting into College

The majority of colleges indicate that they are looking for all-round students. Essentially, they prefer applicants who achieve balance among their academic pursuits, their extracurricular activities, and their personal lives. When admissions officers look at resumes, they are attempting to assess leadership, commitment, and integrity. If you're an overachiever, beware. More is not necessarily better.

MAINTAINING BALANCE

Do what you Like

Sit down and make a list of your commitments. Then, rank them according to how much you enjoy each one. Weed out the activities from which you gain little or no pleasure. Instead, create a schedule of activities that reflects your true interests and passions, and don't be afraid to cut something out or to say no if you're being pressured to stay involved. In the end, you'll be a happier person.

Schedule Time to Relax

If you never have a minute to rest or have fun, you are doing too much.

Take a look at your calendar and carve out specific times to ease off your usually hectic pace. All work and no play will end up stressing you out.

Take care of yourself, Inside and Out

Make sure that you eat healthy foods and that you get a sufficient amount of sleep each night. Also, remember that exercise is a necessary ingredient for both a strong body and a strong mind. And when you're feeling overwhelmed or stressed, take a break. Most importantly, ask for help when you need it. Parents, friends, teachers, and counselors are all people to turn to if you start to experience burnout.

WOMEN: EXPLOITATION AT HOME AND WORK

Although, there are many groups of women who defend women s rights they are still exploited. That is to say women are easier to be exploited than men. women usually have law salaries.For example, women work long hours in factories but they are given low salaries in comparison to men Hence, women contribute themselves to their fact of being exploited by accepting to work for minor wage.

In addition, women are exploited in media broadly. So, they become like goods which are sold and bought. For instance, in advertisements we usually see women presenting products or an idea about products, but unfortunately, they use their bodies to attract consumers. However, the consumers do not focus on the quality of the product being advertised but they focus on the quality of the women who advertise the product. In fact, this is the purpose of the advertisement agencies where very skilled people work on those advertisements.

SEXUAL HARASSMENT AT THE WORKPLACE

There is a pressing need to examine the aspect of sexual harassment at workplace from the perspective of emancipation of women as well as the abuse of the image in which a woman is cast. India doesn't have any legislation to deal with sexual harassment at work places at the moment. The sexual harassment of women at work place bill, 2006 is still under consideration. Various women's groups have been lobbying with Parliamentarians to get it passed at the earliest. However, only time will reveal as to when it shall actually come into force. Till then, the guidelines that the Supreme Court has laid down in the *Vishaka case* are to be followed. These guidelines encompass a comprehensive definition of sexual harassment, directions for establishment of a complaint mechanism and the duty under which employers are obligated to obviate any such act.

It also directs the legislators to formulate law on the basis of these guidelines. Abstract guidelines by the Supreme Court without any established mechanism to protect women in form of legislation mean that the only legal remedy available to fight this evil is approaching the Court under Art. 32 for violations of gender equality, right to life and liberty and right to profession which is subject to the condition of a safe environment safeguarded as fundamental rights under the constitution under Art. 14, 15 and 21. In light of the legal scenario that surrounds sexual harassment, working women need to follow a code to protect them.

SUGGESTIONS

Be Aware

It's the simplest thing for safety that one can pursue, rigorously and consciously. By being alert and detecting any signs of this heinous evil in your immediate surroundings, one can prevent such events from taking place. Precautions like dressing appropriately, compliment the need for awareness.

- *Trust your gut*: No definition can comprehensively include all aspects of sexual harassment and it is subjective as well. There is no bracket formula to determine whether an act, perhaps bordering on somewhat friendly', constitutes an act of sexual harassment or not. But, for you, anything that puts you in a discomfort zone, some place that you'd want to extricate yourself from is sexual harassment.
- *Say no*: The thin line of demarcation between sexual interest and sexual harassment shouldn't be disregarded. A sexual interest can be doused by a negative reply. Also, just because the person concerned is a senior, does not mean you cannot say no. Sometimes, a stinging retort may work wonders; however, it can worsen the attention-craving situation of the perpetrator at times.

It is essential to remember that these are only the basic things that one can do to prevent such events from taking place and the first sign of any kind of serious trouble, should necessitate a proper complaint at an official level; either within the organization or before the police under section 354 of the Indian Penal Code dealing with assault or criminal force to a woman with the intent to outrage her modesty, section 509 dealing with word, gesture or act intended to insult the modesty of a woman or section 209 which deals with obscene acts or songs.

Bullying

Bullying is the common denominator of harassment, discrimination, prejudice, abuse, persecution, conflict and violence. When the bullying has a focus it is expressed as racial prejudice or harassment, or sexual discrimination and harassment, and so on. Although bullying often lacks a focus, bullies are deeply prejudiced but at the same time sufficiently devious to not reveal their prejudices to the extent that they contravene laws on harassment and discrimination.

Dealing with Workplace Bullying

Step 1: Regain control:

- Recognise what is happening to you as *bullying*
- Criticisms and allegations, which are ostensibly about you or your performance and which sometimes contain a grain of truth, are not about you or your performance. Do not be fooled by that grain of truth into believing the criticisms and allegations have any validity - they do not. The purpose of criticism is *control*; it has nothing to do with performance enhancement.
- Criticisms and allegations are a projection of the bully's own weaknesses, shortcomings, failings and incompetence; every criticism or allegation is an admission by the bully of their misdeeds and wrongdoing, something *they* have said or done - or failed to do.
- You may be encouraged to feel shame, embarrassment, guilt and fear - this is a normal reaction, but misplaced and inappropriate. Guilt and fear are well-known as tactics of control. This is how all abusers, including child sex abusers, control and silences their victims.
- You cannot handle bullying by yourself - bullies use deception, amoral behaviour and abuse of power. Get help. There is no shame or failure in this - the bully is devious, deceptive, evasive and manipulative - and cheats.

Step 2: plan for action:

- Find out everything you can about bullying.
- Overcome all the misperceptions about bullying.

Step 3: Take action:

- Keep a log of everything - it's not each incident that counts, it's the *number, regularity* and especially the *patterns* that reveal bullying. With most forms of mystery, deception, etc it's the *patterns* that are important. The bully can explain individual incidents but cannot explain away the pattern. It's the *pattern* which reveals *intent.*
- Keep your diary in a safe place, not at work where others can and will steal it; keep it at home, and keep photocopies of important documents in a separate location; in several cases the bully has rifled the desk drawers of their target, stolen the diary and then used it as "evidence" of misconduct.
- Keep copies of all letters, memos, emails, etc. Get and keep everything in writing otherwise the bully will deny everything later.
- Carry a notepad and pen with you and record everything that the bully says and does. Also make a note of every interaction with personnel, management, and anyone else connected with the bullying. Expect to be accused of "misconduct" and "unprofessional behaviour" and a few other things when you do this.

- Record everything in writing; when criticisms or allegations are made, write and ask the bully to substantiate their criticisms and allegations in writing by providing *substantive and quantifiable evidence..*
- Denial is everywhere. The person who asserts their right not to be bullied is often blowing the whistle on another's incompetence. Expect the bully to deny everything, expect the bully's superiors to deny and disbelieve everything, and - as evidenced by thousands of cases reported to my Advice Line - expect personnel/human resources to disbelieve you and deny the bullying, for they will already have been deceived by the bully into joining in with the bully and getting rid of you. Click here for more on how and why Human Resources often don't support targets of bullying.
- The serial bully likes to play people off against each other so try to reunite yourself with your employer against the bully. Point out professionally to your HR people that the serial bully is encouraging the employer and employee to engage in adversarial interaction and destructive conflict in which there are no winners, only losers.

Night Shifts for Women

Before the amendment in the Factories Act, under s.66 women were not allowed to work night shifts. However after the amendment was approved, women are permitted to work between 10 p.m. to 6 a.m. in sectors including the Special Economic Zone, IT sector and Textiles subject to the condition that the employers shall be obligated to perform the duty to protect them.

This is clearly given in the proviso to the section which is as following: "provided adequate safeguards in the factory as regards occupational safety and health, equal opportunity for women workers, adequate protection of their dignity, honour and safety and their transportation from the factory premises to the nearest point of their residence". Hence, women can now work night shifts in these sectors.

If you work the night shift, here are some things you have the right to expect, along with some tips for you:

- You can demand that your employer have any or all of the following: female wardens, proper lighting, secure transport facility, security at entry and exit points etc.
- Be extra careful to prevent any mishap by staying alert.
- Always ensure you have company while going to and from work.
- Keep the contacts of family, friends or relatives who can quickly be contacted in case of emergency.
- If possible taking self defense classes.

Equal Opportunities for Women

Not getting equal pay, being denied opportunities for growth and promotion are some examples of the kind of economic exploitation that women are subjected to in certain sectors. In spite of legislation in place it is widely observed that women are usually underpaid as compared to their male counterparts performing the same job.

Delhi High Court in 2005 in its ruling in The Cooperative Store Ltd. v. Bimla Devi and other laid down that unequal pay is not only a violation of the said act but also, of Article 14 of the Constitution, Right to Equality. Furthermore, India is a signatory to the International Labour Organisation Convention for the Elimination of All Forms of Discrimination against Women, to which India is a signatory, specifically to Article 11 that deals with the elimination of discrimination in the field of employment.

However, in spite of allegiance to an International Convention, having a specific legislation in force and a High Court ruling declaring equal pay to be incorporated in fundamental rights, the stark reality of the situation is different. Women still get underpaid. What women can do in similarly placed situations?

Here are some tips:

- Be Aware and Assertive: when one is aware of her rights, can one assert the same by approaching the immediate head of the organization or the concerned authority.
- Be an efficient and a good worker: The organization will be reluctant to lose an employee if you have carved out a niche for yourself and are in the least indispensable.
- Form a Group: Collective bargaining is powerful, so by rounding up all the women in the organization who shall in most probability be facing the same or similar problem and dealing with the situation collectively is quite effective as well.
- Seek Help: If things get out of hand, the only solution remaining is to approach the Courts.

Forms of Violence against Women

Violence against women manifests itself as physical, sexual and/or psychological harm. These categories of violence are not mutually exclusive, and forms of Violence against women should be understood broadly to encompass a range of behaviors designed to exert power and control over women. The UN Declaration on the Elimination of Violence against Women classifies three primary forms based on where the acts occur and the relationship between victim and executor:

- Violence in the family;
- Violence in the community; and
- Violence carried out by the State.

Violence carried out in the family includes domestic violence, also referred to as intimate-partner violence or spousal abuse to clarify that the executor and victim have a long-term relationship. Marital rape and child sexual abuse are also types of Violence against women occurring in the home. Community-based violence includes rape and sexual assault, sexual harassment in the workplace and in educational institutions, as well as the exploitation of women and girls through human trafficking and prostitution.

Violence carried out by the State includes the use of rape during war or by law enforcement, security or military forces both during armed conflict and in peacetime or by peacekeeping personnel in non-conflict settings as well as abuse of women in State custody or under State control. These categories serve as guidance to understand the scope of Violence against women, but they should not be adhered to rigidly.

Service-providers and advocates who work with Violence against women survivors often encounter forms of Violence against women that are not yet well-recognized by law enforcement and legal systems, such as stalking or the use of new technologies, the Internet and electronic mail, to execute cyber violence against women. This compilation sometimes makes use of the term gender-based violence.

Gender-based violence (GBV) refers to harm that is executed against a person as a result of power inequalities that are themselves based on gender roles. Due to gender discrimination, which places women in vulnerable and disempowered positions, female victims "suffer exacerbated consequences as compared with what men endure."

KINDS OF VIOLENCE AGAINST WOMEN

Domestic Violence

Violence against women in the family occurs in developed and developing countries alike. It has long been considered a private matter by bystanders — including neighbors, the community and government. But such private matters have a tendency to become public tragedies.

Traditional Practices

In India women fall victim to traditional practices that violate their human rights. The persistence of the problem has much to do with the fact that most of these physically and psychologically harmful customs are deeply rooted in the tradition and culture of society.

Female Genital Mutilation

According to the World Health Organization, 85 million to 115 million girls and women in the population have undergone some form of female genital mutilation and suffer from its adverse health effects. There is a growing consensus that the best way to eliminate these practices is through educational campaigns that emphasize their dangerous health consequences. Several Governments have been actively promoting such campaigns in their countries.

Son Preference

Son preference affects women in India. Its consequences can be anything from foetal or female infanticide to neglect of the girl child over her brother in terms of such essential needs as nutrition, basic health care and education.

Dowry-related Violence and Early Marriage

In India, weddings are preceded by the payment of an agreed-upon dowry by the bride's family. Failure to pay the dowry can lead to violence. Early marriage, especially without the consent of the girl, is another form of human rights violation. Early marriage followed by multiple pregnancies can affect the health of women for life.

VIOLENCE IN THE COMMUNITY

Rape

Rape can occur anywhere, even in the family, where it can take the form of marital rape or incest. It occurs in the community, where a woman can fall prey to any abuser. It also occurs in situations of armed conflict and in refugee camps.

Sexual Assault within Marriage

In India sexual assault by a husband on his wife is not considered to be a crime: a wife is expected to submit. It is thus very difficult in practice for a woman to prove that sexual assault has occurred unless she can demonstrate serious injury.

Sexual Harassment

Sexual harassment in the workplace is a growing concern for women. Employers abuse their authority to seek sexual favours from their female co-workers or subordinates, sometimes promising promotions or other forms of career advancement or simply creating an untenable and hostile work environment. Women who refuse to give in to such unwanted sexual advances often run the risk of anything from demotion to dismissal. But in recent years more women have been coming forward to report such practices — some taking their cases to court.

Prostitution and Trafficking

Many women are forced into prostitution either by their parents, husbands or boyfriends — or as a result of the difficult economic and social conditions in which they find themselves. They are also lured into prostitution, sometimes by "mail-order bride" agencies that promise to find them a husband or a job in a foreign country. As a result, they very often find themselves illegally confined in brothels in slavery-like conditions where they are physically abused and their passports withheld.

VIOLENCE AGAINST WOMEN MIGRANT WORKERS

Female migrant workers typically leave their countries for better living conditions and better pay — but the real benefits accrue to both the host countries and the countries of origin. But migrant workers themselves fare badly, and sometimes tragically. Many become virtual slaves, subject to abuse and rape by their employers. Working conditions are often appalling, and employers prevent women from escaping by seizing their passports or identity papers.

Pornography

Another concern highlighted is pornography, which represents a form of violence against women that "glamorizes the degradation and maltreatment of women and asserts their subordinate function as mere receptacles for male lust".

Violence Against Refugee and Displaced Women

Women and children form the great majority of refugee populations all over the world and are especially vulnerable to violence and exploitation. In refugee camps, they are raped and abused by military and immigration personnel, bandit groups, male refugees and rival ethnic groups. They are also forced into prostitution.

CHALLENGING TRADITIONAL ATTITUDES

The meaning of gender and sexuality and the balance of power between women and men at all levels of society must be reviewed. Combating violence against women requires challenging the way that gender roles and power relations are articulated in society. In many countries women have a low status. They are considered as inferior and there is a strong belief that men are superior to them and even own them. Changing people's attitude and mentality towards women will take a long time — at least a generation, many believe, and perhaps longer. Nevertheless, raising awareness of the issue of violence against women, and educating boys and men to view women as valuable partners in life, in the development of a society and in the attainment of peace are just as important as taking legal steps to protect women's human rights.

It is also important in order to prevent violence that non-violent means be used to resolve conflict between all members of society. Breaking the cycle of abuse will require concerted collaboration and action between governmental and non-governmental actors, including educators, health-care authorities, legislators, the judiciary and the mass media The Declaration provides a definition of gender-based abuse, calling it "any act of gender-based violence that results in, or is likely to result in, physical, sexual or psychological harm or suffering to women, including threats of such acts, coercion or arbitrary deprivation of liberty, whether occurring in public or in private life".

The definition is amplified in article 2 of the Declaration, which identifies three areas in which violence commonly takes place:

- Physical, sexual and psychological violence that occurs in the family, including battering; sexual abuse of female children in the household; dowry-related violence; marital rape; female genital mutilation and other traditional practices harmful to women; non-spousal violence; and violence related to exploitation;
- Physical, sexual and psychological violence that occurs within the general community, including rape; sexual abuse; sexual harassment and intimidation at work, in educational institutions and elsewhere; trafficking in women; and forced prostitution;
- Physical, sexual and psychological violence perpetrated or condoned by the State, wherever it occurs.

Finally, women are exploited everywhere even in developed countries. Women's exploitation makes them lose their morality and responsibility towards their sons and their daughter. Women should be aware of themselves to avoid this kind of exploitation which invades the societies.

FRAMEWORK OF GUIDING PRINCIPLES TO COMBAT VIOLENCE AGAINST WOMEN

- *Women's rights as human rights*: A critical strategy for all advocacy work is to clearly demonstrate that violence against women is linked to other human rights violations and therefore States have commitments to exercise due diligence. An important related principle behind all good practices is that they address the *root causes* of violence against women, such as structural inequalities between men and women, issues of power and control and gender discrimination.
- *Women themselves at the center*: Essential characteristics of all good practices is that they empower women, economically, politically or in other ways, to make changes in their lives and in society. Women survivors, particularly service users, should be participants in program design, implementation and evaluation. Effective interventions are those that are based on understanding the needs articulated by women themselves and not on behalf of women.

- *Men are responsible and also engaged*: A guiding principle of practices addressing violence against women is that they target men. Programs that address men range from those that acknowledge men's responsibility as executors of violence and establish appropriate prosecution and treatment measures, to others that engage non-violent men as positive role models, as activists in preventing violence against women and as advocates for gender equality in all spheres.
- *Political commitment and leadership*: Good practices are those that are based on and supported by a clear political will from national authorities. Leaders at all levels, in political office, representing religious authorities, from the local community and even recognized sports figures or celebrities, can influence how violence against women is perceived and can play a role in changing societal tolerance for this problem.
- *Evidence-based approaches*: All effective interventions are underpinned by accurate empirical data about the scope of violence against women, its causes and its consequences for individual women survivors but also for family members and society at large. Many interventions may have some positive effect on alleviating violence in general e.g. limiting the depiction of violent acts on television or in film,but an essential strategy to address violence against women is acknowledgment and awareness raising of the specific and underlying causes of this form of violence.

IDENTIFYING GOOD PRACTICES AND APPROACHES

- *Coordination, co-operation and partnerships*: A multi sectoral approach that coordinates and integrates a wide range of actors is a principle that guides any work on improving overall response to violence against women. The specific actors or stakeholders involved may vary depending on the type of VAW addressed, but the strategy is the same – to work with a broad range of professionals and services from the national to the community and grass-roots level and to forge partnerships across sectors.
- *Sharing of knowledge, skill building and training*: The use of knowledge-exchange and educational programs is a tactic, rather than a strategy. Nevertheless, it is included here to illustrate the guiding principle that practitioners who are working on VAW should regularly and routinely share information and participate in skill building. As a corollary, training for service providers, law enforcement, the legal and health sectors, policy makers and any other key stakeholders should be integrated into routine staff development and be informed by agreed-upon standards and guidelines.

STRATEGIES THAT UNDERLIE GOOD PRACTICES

Real change toward ending violence against women requires "a coordinated and sustained effort on many levels."Good practices are supported by various strategies that determine on which level a project operates and how it interacts with other programming. Interventions can be viewed along a spectrum from "micro level," those that provide for the needs of victims, change societal attitudes, build awareness of women and men, to "meso level," those that target local institutions, and lastly "macro-level," those that address higher-level policy or legislative change.

Put another way, some interventions can be characterized as short-term, those that aim for immediate improvement of the situation and others take a long-term approach; they strive for system change. Determining how short-term and long-term advocacy interact is an important part of strategy development that underpins good practices.

Although violence against women is a distinct social problem that should be addressed through targeted initiatives, it also has important links to other issues of women's human rights, health and development. Therefore, an effective strategy behind good practices is to approach violence against women not as an isolated problem. It is an effective practice overall to integrate anti-VAW messages into programs where there are significant intersections, for example on HIV/AIDS prevention, reproductive health, family planning, law reform, micro-enterprise development or land access and use programs.

Prevention

The World Health Organization recommends that the prevention of violence against women be considered a high priority for national health, social and legal agendas of both industrialized and developing countries. The WHO also defines prevention activities at three levels: primary prevention; secondary and tertiary.

Despite the recognized value of primary prevention, experts note that there is a significant lack of sustained and long-term investment in such efforts. Primary prevention can take a number of forms but at their core they focus on changing gender-related attitudes and stereotypes at the individual level, among both men and women, and at the societal level.

Awareness Raising Campaigns

Awareness raising is at the core of prevention efforts and can include working with the general public to change societal attitudes and tolerance of violence against women, to expose the public to the magnitude of this problem, to end secrecy about violence against women and to send a clear message that it should not be tolerated. Awareness raising activities can also target specific groups with narrow messages. Included in this resource are examples of innovative communication methods specific to domestic violence, sexual assault and harassment, harmful traditional practices, trafficking and commercial sexual exploitation, mainly in the form of posters and video clips.

Public Awareness

Public awareness raising campaigns can be used to initiate public debate about violence against women and challenge social norms. Indeed, some of the more promising awareness campaigns are those that use mainstream media and common technology to promote seldom-heard or thought-provoking messages about violence against women. For example, NGOs have partnered with mobile phone providers to send anti-violence text messages to their customers.75 The term "social marketing" describes the use of techniques from the advertising world used to promote messages of social significance.

Global Campaigns

The UN is currently running several global campaigns to raise awareness of specific aspects of violence against women and to call for further action. UNITE to End Violence Against Women focuses on global advocacy; strengthened efforts and partnerships at the national and regional levels; and UN leadership by example. States are urged to enact or strengthen laws and enforce such laws to end impunity. The Secretary-General will form a global network of male leaders to assist in mobilizing men and boys to become involved in the struggle to end violence against women.

Empowering Women

Women themselves are a critical focus of any initiative to eliminate violence against women. While there are, of course myriad projects directed to women specifically, many, such as self-help groups or telephone hotlines, these are services to assist women who have already in some way identified themselves as experiencing or having survived violence. Activists against VAW point to the fact that some women lack awareness that gender-based violence is not simply an inevitable part of being female but are a human rights violation and mechanisms exist for redress. Thus, awareness raising that targets women may have some of the features of awareness rising for the general public, such as promoting the unacceptability of violence against women.

Most often, however, awareness raising for women takes the form of outreach which can be directed to women in risk groups, such as women who are preparing to travel abroad for work or commercial sex workers, or to specific groups who may have limited access to information, such as rural women, women who lack education, women with disabilities, migrant or refugee women. Legal literacy is a specific form of outreach to provide women with information about local laws with an aim to improve their understanding of how to access the legal system to protect one's rights. An important principle behind all awareness raising materials for women is that they contain messages of empowerment and give women concrete alternatives to either avoid violence or escape it if it has already occurred.81 Economic empowerment programs are often characterized as prevention work, but because they are also effective components of assistance services for women survivors of violence.

Key Actions

- Designate appropriately trained, knowledgeable, and accountable personnel to be responsible for recruitment and hiring of employees and consultants. These personnel should be trained in human resources, knowledgeable about the risks of staff misconduct with regard to sexual violence, including sexual exploitation, and must be held accountable for implementing internationally recognised standards in hiring practices.
- When recruiting local/national and international staff, including short-term consultants, interns, and volunteers, careful hiring practices should include reference checks for all categories of employee. Reference checks should specifically include questions seeking information about the candidate related to any prior acts, personnel actions, or criminal history. Careful reference checks can filter out those candidates with a history of exploitative behaviour, particularly those who move from one emergency situation to the next, or who have criminal records for sexual violence.
- Do not hire any person with a history of perpetrating any type of gender-based violence, including sexual exploitation, sexual abuse, or domestic violence.
- Coordinate with other organisations to establish systems for sharing information about employees terminated for engaging in sexual exploitation or abuse. Any such system must be established in accordance with relevant laws governing employers and employees.
- Recruit more women employees at all levels.
  - Sexual exploitation and abuse are grounded in gender inequality; therefore, activities in emergency situations must be conducted in a gender-sensitive manner and the views and perspectives of women and girls must be adequately considered.
  - Human Resources must endeavour to increase the numbers of local/national and international women staff hired to work in emergencies.
  - Identify, understand, and address obstacles to employing women. Recognise that women, especially if they are local/

national, may have some limits on their access to and availability for work. There may be low literacy rates among adult females in the population, or cultural beliefs that limit opportunities for women to work. Implement strategies and employment schemes to accommodate women and remove obstacles.

SENIOR CITIZENS: EMOTIONAL, SOCIAL AND PHYSICAL PROBLEMS

Senior citizens provide much needed comfort and wisdom to their families and communities, but there are also times when they need assistance. The guidance center can help them with certain needs. If a senior citizen is struggling to pay his or her rent, a worker at the guidance center can point him or her to local non-profit groups that may offer utility vouchers

CONCEPT OF SENIOR CITIZENS

As we age, a great number of changes occur in our body. Such changes are the root cause for various diseases. Heart disease is more commonly seen in senior citizens. Most of the senior citizens do not even know that they are at the risk of heart disease. As we age, our general activities get reduced. As the body needs have reduced, the cholesterol or the bad fat gets deposited in various tissues and even in arteries blocking them or narrowing them resulting in decreased blood flow to the heart. This situation finally leads to heart attack due to blockage of blood supply to the heart. Senior citizens with diabetes are at increased risk for myocardial infarction. Hence, it is essential to maintain appropriate sugar levels by regular usage of medications. To avoid the risk of heart attack it is essential to follow certain practices. They include consuming low fat or zero cholesterol foods, involving in some sort simple exercises regularly, quit habits such as smoking and consumption of alcohol. It is essential to take a healthy nutritious diet rich in fresh fruits and vegetable. Thus, by knowing the facts of heart disease in senior citizens, they can easily combat heart attack.

PROBLEMS AND ISSUES

Senior citizens who are living alone have been found abused, robbed, humiliated, and, in many cities in India, they have been found murdered. The most important problem senior citizens face today is loss of independence. All other issues fall under this umbrella of inconvenience and distress. Whether older persons have financial hardships, failing health or isolation

Deteriorating health, malnutrition, lack of shelter, fear, depression, senility, isolation, boredom, non-productivity, and financial incapacity are the most common problems that senior citizens all over the world face today. These problems can be grouped into two categories that relate to the physical and mental health and the financial capacity of the senior citizen. The rise in the number of those who are non-productive' and who do not generate any hope' immediately raises an economic problem. It is also a social problem: Who is going to provide support to them and how? Apart from food and shelter, the old need care and medicines. They also crave love and tender care. They would like to interact, be heard, be visible, and would like a bit of space of their own and have a constructive and creative role to play in society. Among the old, the problems of old women, single, divorced and widowed, are different from those of old men.

- Physical and mental health: Stability of physical and mental health is a key concern that senior citizens have to contend with as they go through their twilight years. The human body is a system that wears out with long and repetitive use; and quite easily, with neglect and abuse. Aging is a life-cycle stage where the human capacity to think, act, relate, and learn starts to falter and deteriorate. Aging breeds illnesses such as loss of memory, immobility, organ failure, and poor vision. These are critical dysfunctions that could sideline a senior citizen to a lonely and miserable life. While a clean and discreet lifestyle in his or her prime could reduce the susceptibility of a senior citizen to dreaded post-retirement illnesses, the onset of any dysfunction is one unpredictable happening even if the person might have had robust financial health..
- Financial capacity: Possessing sustainable financial capacity before, during, and after the inception of a senior status is both a basic problem and an elusive dream for most people. This financial dilemma is common among senior citizens who are usually relegated to an abject position of economic inactivity. Lack or absence of financial capacity creates a stressful life and invites the entry of problems other than physical and mental health issues. For instance, domestic problems in an extended family system can aggravate the problem of a financially-destitute senior citizen.

A financially secure senior citizen with the same illness, however, may have a longer life to live because money can give quick and convenient access to life-giving remedies. Even with state-of-mind dysfunctions like severe depression, boredom, nervous breakdown, and self-pity, financial capacity can buy options to rejuvenate and refresh a financially-capable senior citizen, through travels, elderly recreation, social renewal, and continuing education. A poor senior citizen in the same state of mental degradation cannot afford to do the same; and more so, be back into the mainstream of society.

Ageing Marginalized

An overwhelming number of people live in rural areas but migration from rural to urban areas is substantial, which creates problems for the ageing at both ends. If children go to urban areas leaving behind the aged in the rural areas, that creates one set of problems, and if the old are taken along, it creates another set of problems. The growth of the urban population has been haphazard, and there are acute shortages of housing and other facilities. The health care system is woefully inadequate and there is hardly any specialised agency focusing on the old. There are no programmes available to train people taking care of the aged. In other words, the entire responsibility of taking care of the old continues to be with the traditional institution of the family.

Ageing in Urban Areas

The entire responsibility of support and care of the ageing falls on the male children with whom the ageing live. The composition of the family in urban areas is becoming nuclear and smaller, as a result of which there are fewer people available in the house to provide care and comfort to the ageing. Those who are available are torn apart by the stresses of urban living. Women too in the urban areas are now working outside the family. They have fixed schedules of work and have other pressures on them. Children are loaded with their studies, competitive examinations and concerns for making their careers.

The authority that the ageing exercised on their children in the past as a result of greater experience has almost vanished, and the aged are now told, You don't know'. There are several reasons for this admonishment. First, the children of the ageing are not in the same profession. Second, the quantum of information which their children claim to have makes the ageing look almost primitive. Third, the whole techno-economic situation has now completely changed, which leaves the ageing bewildered and redundant. When paucity of accommodation, high cost of living, general stress and tensions at all levels are added to these, the problems of the aged are extremely serious.

Discussion

In the past, ageing was not a serious issue and societies did not give it priority. They dealt with it as a natural phenomenon. Family members were responsible for the care and management of the old. But now the situation is different. The size of the people in the ageing category is already bulging and it is growing very fast. The problems posed by ageing are by no means accidental and isolated. They have grown as a result of the development process itself. At family, community and government levels the problems of the ageing get no or very low priority. It is taken for granted that the problem will get solved on its own or that it is a problem of individual families, with communities and governments having nothing to do with it.

The family, where the ageing is supposed to get care and comfort, is on the rocks and in any case shrinking. The members of the family are spread around in pursuit of their careers. The old, on their part, are not getting detached either. They think that they are going to live for ever and that in any case this is not the time to quit. They are bored looking after grandchildren, listening to religious discourses and devotional music, making rounds of holy places or just sitting before the small screen. They seek companionship, appropriate creative and constructive roles. In India even systematic thinking as to what should be the policy towards the ageing has not begun. At this stage the country is caught up in the whirlpool of market forces and resultant consumerism. A shift from consumption to conservation, from individual to community, is bound to take place, which will be in keeping with the Indian ethos. It is possible to be modern with the emphasis on conservation and focus on the community.

Taking care of the aged means highlighting the importance of conservation and humanitarianism. It will also strengthen the community, for the aged can be best taken care of within the fold of the family, bound by filial rights, duties and obligations. There is no institution that can replace the family but there is room to build into it the ideas of equality, justice and freedom. All this will not happen automatically. The focus has to be human development. That will provide new strength to the family and further support from the community. Thus a combination of modern knowledge and intense feeling for those who are non-productive can provide physical and emotional comfort to the old.

FACILITIES FOR THE SENIOR CITIZENS

The facilities for the Seniors citizens like retirement homes, medical aid, free meals, Indoor games and outdoor games transportation, nursing, healthy, environment,domestic help Books & magazines etc. to be provided by the government.

Senior Citizens Discounts

Our governments are announcing many schemes every year for the senior citizens. The Indian Railways and Indian Airlines give some senior citizen discounts up to 30 per cent but most of the senior citizens are not in a position to avail the available facilities. All the Public Sector banks give 0.5 per cent interest to senior citizens.

Senior Citizens Retirement

The activities of senior citizens increase after the retirement. All the market and government related work has to be done by these elderly persons after retirement. There are no senior citizen jobs available for them., They have social problems &, housing problems. The government should find some jobs for seniors citizens.. There are groups of aging Senior citizens. These seniors have no activity to do whole day. These senior people find difficult to spend the whole day honourably. They need elder care by their own family members. There are very few Retirement homes. They need assisted living facilities.

These old people have all type of problems after retirement. They have family problems. Their children do not want to live with them.. They have to travel long distance to collect their pension or pay the electricity, telephone, water bills. They are living in the houses bought against home loans, and paying back the home loans out of pension.

Senior Citizen's Medical Insurance

Senior citizens have health problems. They are getting injuries every day due to uneven surface of bad roads. No one is ready to help them.The senior citizens health insurance required is not affordable.

TIPS FOR HELPING A DEPRESSED ELDERLY

- *Invite your loved one out*: Depression is less likely when people's bodies and minds remain active. Suggest activities to do together that your loved one used to enjoy: walks, an art class, a trip to the museum or the movies—anything that provides mental or physical stimulation.
- *Schedule regular social activities*: Group outings, visits from friends and family members, or trips to the local senior or community center can help combat isolation and loneliness. Be gently insistent if your plans are refused: depressed people often feel better when they're around others.
- *Plan and prepare healthy meals*: A poor diet can make depression worse, so make sure your loved one is eating right, with plenty of fruit, vegetables, whole grains, and some protein at every meal.
- *Encourage the person to follow through with treatment*: Depression usually recurs when treatment is stopped too soon, so help your loved one keep up with his or her treatment plan. If it isn't helping, look into other medications and therapies.
- *Make sure all medications are taken as instructed*: Remind the person to obey doctor's orders about the use of alcohol while on medication. Help them remember when to take their dose.
- *Watch for suicide warning signs*: Seek immediate professional help if you suspect that your loved one is thinking about suicide.

WAYS TO COMBAT AND PREVENT DEPRESSION

- *Getting out in to the world*: Try not to stay cooped up at home all day.
- *Connecting to others*: Limit the time you're alone.
- *Participating in activities you enjoy*: Pursue whatever hobbies or pastimes bring or used to bring you joy.
- *Volunteering your time*: Helping others is one of the best ways to feel better about yourself and regain perspective.

- *Taking care of a pet*: Get a pet to keep you company.
- *Learning a new skill*: Pick something that you've always wanted to learn, or that sparks your imagination and creativity.
- *Enjoying jokes and stories*: Laughter provides a mood boost.
- *Maintaining a healthy diet*: Avoid eating too much sugar and junk food. Choose healthy foods that provide nourishment and energy, and take a daily multivitamin.
- *Exercising*: Even if you're ill, frail, or disabled, there are many safe exercises you can do to build your strength and boost your mood—even from a chair or wheelchair.

COUNSELING AND THERAPY

Studies have found that therapy works just as well as medication in relieving mild to moderate depression. And unlike antidepressants, therapy also addresses the underlying causes of the depression.

- Supportive counseling includes religious and peer counseling. It can help ease loneliness and the hopelessness of depression.
- Psychotherapy helps people work through stressful life changes, heal from losses, and process difficult emotions.
- Cognitive behavioral therapy helps people change negative thinking patterns, deal with problems in healthy ways, and develop better coping skills.
- Support groups for depression, illness, or bereavement connect people with others who are going through the same challenges. They are a safe place to share experiences, advice, and encouragement.

CURRENT SITUATION OF THE HEALTH ISSUES OF SENIOR CITIZENS

Every Senior Citizen has to cope up with his health and associated problems by taking special care by way of proper life style, exercises, regular walking without talking, yoga-pranayam, proper diet and keeping busy physically and mentally by keeping in view the dictum -"Use it or Lose it. ' Number of Senior Citizens suffering from Hyper Tension, Heart Problems, Diabetes, Arthritis etc is very large. Facilities to diagnose and treat old age ailments are very much limited and treatments, whether surgical or by medicines are very very costly. With limited income and no affordable health security schemes available to Senior Citizens, most of the Senior Citizens do not dare to go for any treatment and leave everything to God's grace!

Many are not able to travel independently to Govt./Municipal hospitals, where they have to wait in long queues and treatment mooted out to them is almost inhuman! Apart from ward boys, even well educated Doctors taught to serve all with missionary zeal misbehave with elders and even insult them. They are not available on their seats for a long time or remain busy chitchatting! They along with all medical and para medical staff in all Public & Private Hospitals should be given periodical orientation course for treating Senior Citizens in a proper way. This is envisaged in para 40 of National Policy on Older Persons, 1999.

ACTION PLAN BY THE HEALTH MINISTRY

- Implement all the provisions of NPOP, 99 in para 33 to 48 by 31-3-2008.
- Increase Govt/Municipal Hospitals and provide free treatment to all Senior Citizens, as done by Maharashtra Govt. Provide specific number of earmarked beds in each hospital. Raise the image of the Public hospitals by giving better and humane service.
- Make it statutorily compulsory to provide separate departments for Geriatric, Alzheimer, and Hospice Care in each Hospital in Public as well as Private sector.
- Fix outer limit of fees by Private Hospitals for treatment, pathological examination, and consultations of Senior Citizens.
- As many Senior Citizens are not mobile, provide Mobile Hospitals and make compulsory for each Doctor to visit certain number of such Senior Citizens at their residence regularly.
- Provide free medicines to needy Senior Citizens for common ailments like hyper tension, heart, diabetics, arthritics etc by special budget provisions, donors etc
- Provide user-friendly Medical Security Insurance on lines of Arogya Kavach of Pimpri, Sahyadri Scheme of Pune, Yasashvini of Karnataka.
- A simple directive of separate queues, which is not implemented by most of the Hospitals should be monitored.
- Create a Health Welfare Fund. Provide Convalescent Homes, Holiday Homes, Day Care Centres etc. Provide health care facilities in Vrudhashrams.
- Provide opportunities for second careers, activity centres to keep them active to utilize and maintain their mental health by holding competitions by way of Essay writing, Quiz, Brain Storming Sessions etc at District, State & Centre level periodically on subjects of social & national interest to get views & guidance from Think-Tank of the Nation
- Crate health awareness literature for preventive measures & healthy life style and make easily available.
- Health Ministry must, if necessary by legislation, make it compulsory for every Corporate Body, Businessman and if possible, every Employer to provide health facilities to all their surviving retired employees and their spouses on par with serving employees.

They must be made to raise the pension, where it is paid, on every revision of pay-scale of the post on which the employee had retired on the same principle, as envisaged by Supreme Court.

Long lasting proper solution may lie in declaring the Health Care as a fundamental right for every citizen right from the birth and insuring everyone

ARE SENIOR CITIZENS AN ASSET OR LIABILITY

The tag senior citizen is generally given to a person who is between 58 and 65 years of age and has superannuated from active service. This age band fixed for retirement was based on the old system followed decades ago when longevity was lower than 60 years. With the advance in medical sciences and health supporting systems, longevity now goes up to 75. Perhaps, the retirement age needs revision to make use of the services of experienced people for some more time in the interest of national development.

Some senior citizens have the right attitude, take things in their stride, plan well their post-retirement life and keep their body and mind in reasonable good trim. They largely have a positive approach. There are others who take a dim view of life and think of retirement as something of a punishment. While the optimists keep themselves busy with productive work, the pessimists become dejected, feel neglected and find fault with everyone.

Family situations and financial position do play a part in influencing the lives of elders. Some are fortunate to live with their children or within their reach in the same city/town. They lead a relatively satisfied life. The longer the distance, the greater their feeling of insecurity and loneliness. If the children are within the country, the parents are fairly satisfied — they can visit them or the children can come home for occasions like marriages and festivals. The pangs of separation and the fear of loneliness, on the other hand, increase if the children live abroad. Thus the elders' lives are situation-dependent. The presence of relatives and old-age homes, however comfortable, cannot provide for emotional needs.

Some people overcome the blues by taking recourse to cultural and social activities but others suffer silently. Low income and poor health aggravate the misery. Thus arises the question whether senior citizens are an asset or liability to the families and society at large. The answer is they are undoubtedly an asset if they have the right attitude to life. The present-day elders truly represent the generation of the pre-Independence era known for a value-based life. They were accomplished, humble and honest and practiced to a large extent what was taught.

As most senior citizens are highly experienced, they can contribute tremendously The present time society needs to give senior citizens, a life of dignity in their twilight years. Urbanization, migration, industrialization, women entering in the labor force and many such social changes has steadily chipped away the joint family system. The result is that senior citizens are now forced to face a life of despair and loneliness. There are very few mechanisms to look into the problems of senior citizens. We can solve social problem by the change in social reality and application of knowledge. Because the root of this problem is lack of education, so we should provide education to this particular social group. Educated senior citizen can deal with the problem in a better way. And finally the family member of these people must understand that the old person in their home is an asset not liability. The education and the mindset of family member can reduce this problem form the society.

4

Policy Options and Future Population Growth

INTRODUCTION

The modern expansion of human numbers started in the late 18th century with a long-term decline in the death rate in Europe and Northern America. This reduction in mortality was the consequence of a lower incidence of epidemics and famines and improvements in standards of living, levels of nutrition and basic public health measures.

By the year 1900 the world's population had risen to about 1.6 billion, and in 1950 the total stood at 2.5 billion. Since the middle of this century, a huge new spurt of growth has occurred in Africa, Asia, and Latin America, again the consequence of a rapid decline in mortality. As a result, more people have been added since 1950 than were alive in that year, and in 1995 the world's population reached 5.7 billion. The acceleration in growth is well demonstrated by the shortening of time intervals to add successive billions to the world's population.

The first billion was reached around 1800, the second billion took 125 years, the third 35 years, the fourth 14 years, and the fifth just 13 years. If current projections turn out to be accurate, the next few billions will be added at the same rapid pace. This document reviews population projections for the world and its major regions until the year 2050. A brief summary of the latest United Nations projections and their underlying assumptions is presented first. This is followed by a discussion of the implications of the changes in the age composition that accompanies the demographic transition. The concluding section outlines policy options for slowing population growth.

FUTURE POPULATION TRENDS

According to the most recent UN medium projections, the population of the world will continue to grow at least until 2050, when the total is expected to reach 9.4 billion. This represents an increase of 3.7 billion over the 1995 population of 5.7 billion.

Table. Total Population Estimates (1950-1995) and Projections (1995-2050), by Region

	Population (billions)					Percent Distribution			Percent Increase	
	1950	1995	2000	2025	2050	1950	1995	2050	1950-1995	1995-2050
Africa	0.22	0.72	0.82	1.45	2.05	8.9	12.7	21.8	221	184
Asia	1.32	3.47	3.57	4.68	5.35	56.0	60.9	58.6	145	58
Latin America	0.17	0.48	0.51	0.69	0.81	6.6	8.4	8.7	187	70
Europe	0.55	0.73	0.73	0.70	0.64	21.7	12.8	6.8	33	–12
Northern America	0.17	0.30	0.31	0.37	0.38	6.8	5.2	4.1	73	29
South	1.71	4.52	4.90	6.82	8.21	67.8	79.4	87.6	164	82
North	0.81	1.17	1.19	1.22	1.16	32.2	20.6	12.4	44	–0.8
World	2.52	5.69	6.09	8.04	9.37	100.0	100.0	100.0	125	65

[a] includes Oceania

Nearly all of this future growth will occur in the "South"—*i.e.*, Africa, Asia, and Latin America—where population size is projected to increase from 4.5 to 8.2 billion between 1995 and 2050. In contrast, in the "North", population size is forecast to remain virtually stable, growing very slowly from 1.17 to 1.22 billion between 1995 and 2025, followed by a modest decline to 1.16 in 2050.

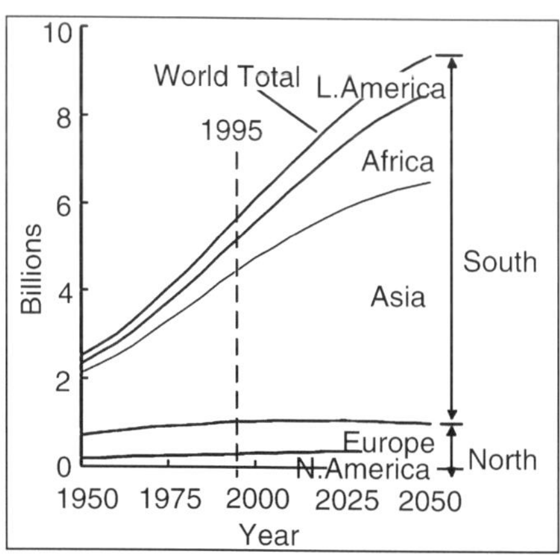

Fig. Total Population by Major Region, Estimates, (1950-1995) and Projections (1995 to 2050)

The plot of world population size over time in Figure indicates that we are now at the steepest part of this curve. Figure presents the trend in annual increments in population size.

After rising steadily over the past several decades, annual increments in the world's population peaked at 87 million per year in the late 1980s and since then they have dropped slightly to 81 million per year in 1995–2000. This high level of growth will remain virtually unchanged through the first two decades of the 21st century before beginning a significant decline. After the year 2025, additions to the South will exceed those of the world as a whole because the North's population is projected to experience an absolute decline.

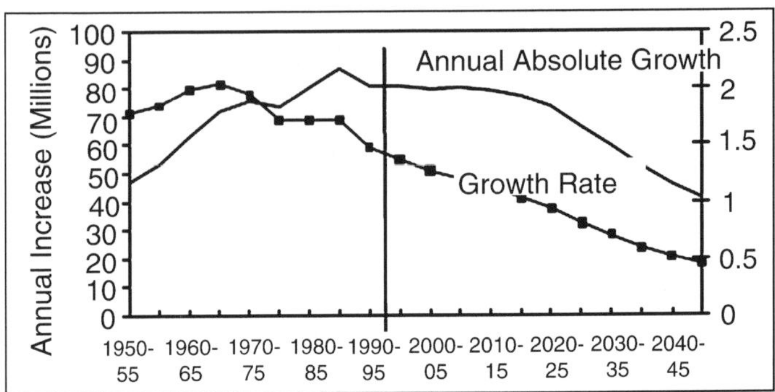

Fig. Annual Absolute Population Growth and Population Growth Rate for the World, Estimated (1950-1995) and Projected (1995-2050)

The trend in the world's annual growth rate (measured in per cent per year) also rises and falls over the one-century period from 1950 to 2050. However, its peak occurred in the late 1960s, before the maximum in the annual absolute growth. Between the late 1960s and the late 1980s, the world's growth rate declined while absolute annual growth rose. These trends are consistent with each other because the growth rate is applied to a rapidly expanding population base to yield the annual increments. The growth rate of the South exceeds that of the world as a whole and that of the North throughout the period 1950 to 2050. Projected population trends vary widely among world regions. In 1995, Asia had a population of 3.47 billion, more than half of the world total, and its population is expected to grow by more than half to 5.35 billion by 2050. Africa, with 0.72 billion inhabitants in 1995, is likely to experience by far the most rapid expansion, nearly tripling in size by 2050. Latin America, with 0.48 billion in 1995, was the smallest of the regions of the South; this is expected to continue with a growth pattern similar to Asia's.

Trends for the two principal regions in the North are expected to diverge between 1995 and 2050: an increase from 0.30 to 0.38 billion in Northern America, but a decline from 0.73 to 0.64 billion in Europe. One consequence of the wide diversity of regional growth rates is that the regional distribution of population will shift significantly over time. While Asia's and Latin America's (8.4 per cent) shares of the world total remain virtually unchanged, Europe's declines by half (from 12.8 to 6.8 per cent) and Africa's rises (from 12.7 to 21.8 per cent). Between 1995 and 2050, the North's share is expected to decline from 20.6 to 12.4 per cent. Population sizes for the ten largest countries in 1995 and in 2050 are presented in Table.

Table Ten Largest Countries by Population Size in 1995 (Estimate) and 2050 (Medium Projection)

Rank	1995		2050	
	Country	Population size (millions)	Country	Projected population size (millions)
1	China	1,220	India	1,533
2	India	929	China	1,517
3	United States	267	Pakistan	357
4	Indonesia	197	United	States
5	Brazil	159	Nigeria	339
6	Russian Federation	148	Indonesia	318
7	Japan	125	Brazil	243
8	Pakistan	136	Bangladesh	218
9	Bangladesh	118	Ethiopia	213
10	Nigeria	112	Zaire	165

In 1995, China (1.22 billion) and India (0.93 billion) were by far the largest countries, together accounting for about half the South's total. The top ten included six Asian countries and only one country each in Latin America and Africa. By 2050, the ranking is expected to have shifted substantially: India's population will exceed China's, and Ethiopia and Zaire will have risen into the top ten, replacing Japan and the Russian Federation.

ASSUMPTIONS UNDERLYING THE PROJECTIONS

The population of the world now increases every year because the global birth rate exceeds the death rate. For example, in the early 1990s population size increased at a rate of 1.5 per cent per year, the difference between a birth rate of 2.4 per cent and a death rate of 0.9 per cent. At the country level, population growth is also affected by migration, but for the regional aggregates of population used in this analysis, migration is usually a minor factor.

The annual birth and death rates of populations are in turn primarily determined by levels of fertility and mortality experienced by individuals. The most widely used fertility indicator is the total fertility rate (TFR), which equals the number of births a woman would have by the end of her reproductive years if she experienced the age-specific fertility rates prevailing in a give year.

Mortality is usually measured by the life expectancy at birth (LE), which equals the average number of years a newborn would live if subjected to a given set of age-specific mortality rates. In order to make longrange population projections, assumptions have to be made about the future trajectories of fertility and mortality. The UN's past estimates and projected future levels of fertility for the period from 1950 to 2050 are presented in Figure.

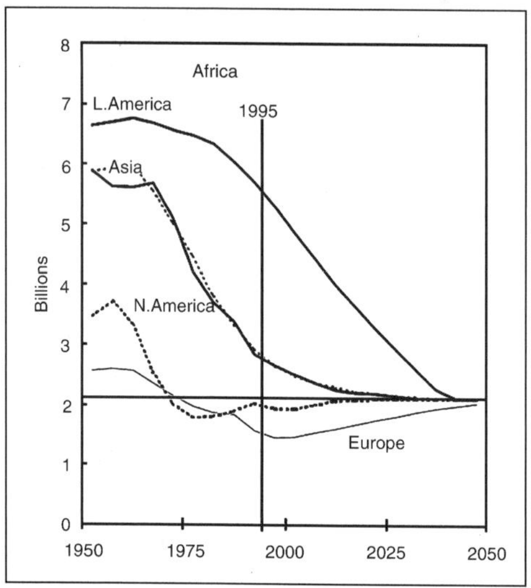

Fig. Total Fertility Rate by Region,
Estimates (1950-1995) and Projections (1995-2050)

The total fertility rate in the South was high and virtually stable at around 6 births per woman on average in the 1950s (the slight temporary decline in the late 1950s in Asia was due to a large famine in China). This level of fertility reflects a near absence of birth control, a condition that has prevailed for centuries before the middle of this century. In the late 1960s, a decline in fertility started nearly simultaneously in Asia and Latin America.

The rate of decline since 1970 was most rapid in Asia, in large part due to an exceptionally sharp reduction in China. Africa has experienced only limited reproductive change, although Northern Africa has seen significant declines in fertility, and there are a few countries in sub-Saharan Africa (for example, Botswana, Kenya, Zimbabwe, and South Africa) where a fertility decline has begun. As a result of these divergent past trends, fertility levels in 1990-1995 differed widely among regions from a high of 5.7 births per woman (bpw) in Africa, to 2.8, and 2.9 bpw in Asia and Latin America, respectively.

The average for the South in 1990-95 stood at 3.3 bpw. In contrast, the average in the North was already low (2.8 bpw) in the early 1950s and has since declined to 1.7 bpw in the early 1990s. Except in the 1970s, fertility levels in Europe have on average been below those of Northern America. Future trends in fertility in the South are based on the assumption that the total fertility rate will eventually reach and then remain at the so-called "replacement" level in all regions. Replacement fertility is just above 2 bpw and it represents the level at which each generation just replaces the previous one, thus leading to zero population growth. Below-replacement fertility produces, in the long run, population decline. As is evident from Figure, the total fertility rates in Asia and Latin America are expected to reach the replacement level around 2025.

Africa is assumed to be on a trajectory towards replacement fertility, but this level is not expected to be reached until the middle of the next century. Europe now has below-replacement fertility and this is expected to remain so until 2050. Africa is the only region in which the future trend in fertility is sharply different from the past, and for this reason its projection must be considered the most speculative. Mortality levels have also changed rapidly over the past few decades.

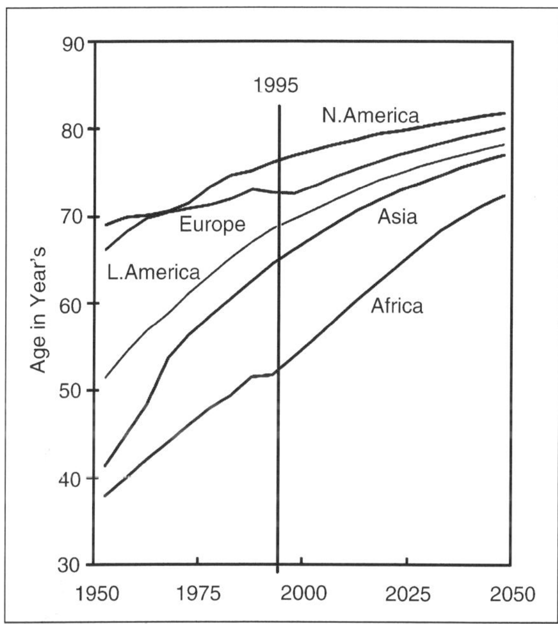

Fig. Life Expectancy by Region, Past Estimates and Projections

The South has experienced exceptional improvements in life expectancy from an average of 41 years in 1950-55 to 62 years today. By the early 1990s, Latin America had reached mortality levels similar to those prevailing in the North in the 1950s, and Asia was not far behind. Africa has had the highest mortality levels and the slowest rate of improvement. As a result its life expectancy, at 52 years in 1990-95, is still substantially below that of the other regions of the South.

As expected, Europe and Northern America already had achieved relatively low levels of mortality by 1950, but they have nevertheless seen significant further improvements since then. Life expectancy in the North now stands at 74 years. Projections of future life expectancies by the UN assume continued improvements over time in all regions. However, increments will be increasingly difficult to achieve as countries reach ever higher levels of life expectancy. Its maximum, to be reached in the 22nd century, is assumed to be 85 years. By 2025, mortality conditions in Asia and Latin America are expected to be similar to those that prevailed in the North in the 1970s. Africa will continue to lag, in part because the continent is most heavily affected by the AIDS epidemic. It should be noted that the assumptions made by the UN about future trends in fertility and mortality are not based on a firm theoretical basis. Instead, the UN relies on empirical regularities in past trends in the now-developed countries, mostly in the North, where fertility declined to around the replacement level, and increases in life expectancy became smaller over time. This is a plausible approach that unfortunately leaves room for potential inaccuracies in projection results.

THE CHANGING AGE COMPOSITION

The declines in fertility and mortality that occur over the course of the demographic transition are accompanied by important changes in the composition of the population by age. In general, countries in the early stages of the transition (when fertility is high and population growth rapid) have a younger age structure than countries that have reached the end of the transition. In the South this trend over time is illustrated in Figure which presents the estimated distribution by age in 1975 and the projected distribution for 2000, 2025 and 2050.

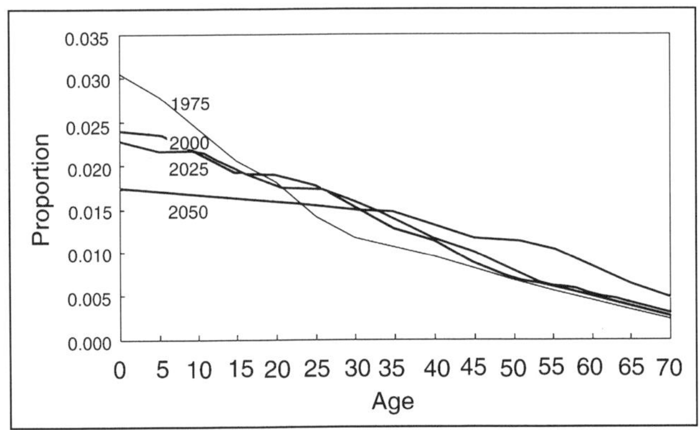

Fig. Distribution by Age of the Population of the Developing World, Estimated 1975, Projected 2000-2050

The proportion of the population under age 15 is expected to decline from 44.9 per cent in 1975 to 24.3 per cent in 2050, while the population over age 65 is projected to rise from 3.1 per cent to 7.7 per cent in 2050. These changes will have important social and economic consequences *e.g.* for the allocation of resources to education, health and social security. Here I comment briefly on two significant demographic consequences of this variation in the age structure.

THE AGE DEPENDENCY RATIO

The age dependency ratio (ADR) of a population at a given point in time is defined as the ratio of the population in the ages below 15 (P15)and over 65 (P65) to the population between ages 15 and 65 (P15-65):

- ADR=(P15+P65)/P15-65

This ratio aims to measure how many "dependents" there are for each person in the "productive" age group. Obviously, not every person below 15 and over 65 is a dependent and not every person between ages 15 and 65 is productive, but despite the crudeness of this indicator it is widely used to document broad trends in the age composition. Over the course of a demographic transition the ADR shows a characteristic pattern of change. Figure presents this pattern as estimated from 1950 to 1995 and projected from 1995 to 2050 for the South.

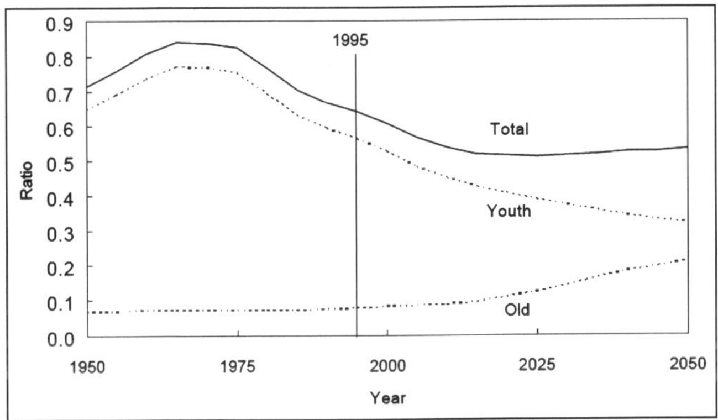

Fig. Age Dependency Ratio for the Developing World, Estimated (1950-1995), and Projected (1950-2050)

Early in the transition the ADR typically first rises slightly as mortality declines and more births survive infancy and childhood. Next, the ADR falls sharply as the decline in fertility reduces the proportion of the population under age 15. Finally, at the end of the transition the ADR rises again as the proportion of the population over age 65 rises. These changes are clearly reflected in the corresponding trends in the youth dependency ratio (P15/P15-65) and the old age dependency ratio(P65/P15-65) which are also plotted in Figure.

POPULATION MOMENTUM

At the end of the demographic transition natural population growth reaches zero once three conditions are met:

- Fertility levels off at the replacement level of 2.1 births per woman (more precisely, the net reproduction rate should be 1). If fertility remains above replacement, population growth continues; if it is lower, population growth will turn negative.

- Mortality stops declining. This in practice is not likely to happen because improvements in medical technology and health care as well as changes in lifestyles etc. will probably insure continued increases in life-expectancy.
- The age-structure has adjusted to the post transitional levels of fertility and mortality.

The adjustment in the age structure at the end of the transition takes many decades to complete. A key implication of this slow adjustment process is that in countries with a young age structure population growth will continue for many years, even if fertility could immediately be brought down to the replacement level of two children per woman.

The tendency of population size to increase for some time after a two-child family has been reached is referred to as population momentum; it is the consequence of a young population age structure. The population momentum inherent in the age structure of a particular population at a given point in time can be estimated with a simple population projection. Specifically, a population projection is carried out in which future fertility is set to the replacement level, mortality is held constant and net migration is zero. The momentum is estimated as the increase in population size that occurs under these conditions, which in the long run lead to zero growth. Results of the application of this procedure are summarized for groups of countries in Table.

Table. Estimates of Population Momentum in 1995 by Region Per cent Increase

	Percent increase 1995 to 2100
South (Low and middle-income countries)	40
East Asia & Pacific	35
Latin America & Caribbean	54
Middle East & North Africa	62
South Asia	44
Sub-Saharan Africa	54
North (High-income)	09

As expected, population momentum in 1995 is much higher in the low and middle income countries in the South (40 per cent) than in the high income countries in the North (9 per cent). This finding implies that momentum is responsible for nearly half of the projected future population growth in the developing world. In the South the highest momentum is found in the Middle East (62 per cent) and in sub-Saharan Africa (54 per cent).

POLICY OPTIONS FOR REDUCING FUTURE POPULATION GROWTH

The already difficult task of reducing poverty and bringing about sustainable development in the developing world will, of course, be made even harder by the expected addition of several billion people by the middle of the next century. Efforts to slow this population expansion cannot include increases in mortality, and they therefore have to focus on reducing fertility. Three broad policy options for accelerating fertility decline can be pursued.

REDUCE UNWANTED FERTILITY AND THE UNMET NEED FOR CONTRACEPTION BY STRENGTHENING FAMILY PLANNING PROGRAMMES

Approximately one in four births in the developing world (excluding China) is unwanted, and a larger proportion is unplanned. In addition, an estimated 25 million abortions are performed each year in less developed countries—many of them under unsafe conditions. The main reason for this high rate of unwanted pregnancy is the existence of a partially unsatisfied demand for contraception. When questioned in recent surveys, a majority of married women in the developing world said that they did not want a pregnancy soon. Some of these women did not want any more children because they had already achieved their desired family size, while others wanted to wait before having the next wanted pregnancy.

The proportion of married women who want to avoid an immediate pregnancy varies widely among countries and regions. It is lowest in sub-Saharan Africa (39 per cent), where desired family size is relatively high, and it is highest in Asia (61 per cent) and Latin America (67 per cent), where the small-family norm has spread. These numbers are growing over time as desired family size declines. Ideally, all these women should be protected from the risk of pregnancy by practicing contraception (including sterilization). Unfortunately, this is not the case. Among women with a potential demand for contraception, the proportion that is actually using a method ranges from a low of 41 per cent in sub-Saharan Africa to a high of 77 per cent in Asia.

The remaining women have a so-called unmet need or latent demand for contraception: they do not want to become pregnant but are not protected by contraception. On average, about one in six married women in the developing world (excluding China) has an unmet need for contraception; it is higher than average in sub-Saharan Africa (23 per cent) and lower in Asia (14 per cent). Among married women who are not seeking pregnancy, about 120 million have an unmet need for contraception. If sexually active unmarried women as well as unsatisfied users were added, these figures would rise considerably.

The existence of this unmet need was first documented in the 1960s, and it convinced policy makers that family planning programmes were needed and would be acceptable. Why do apparently motivated individuals fail to practice contraception? The answer lies in a mixture of social and health service–related reasons.

Lack of access to services or information was and remains a key obstacle. In addition, other factors—such as fear of side effects of contraceptive methods and overt or suspected disapproval of husbands/partners and other family members—are significant barriers to use in many societies. To be effective, programmes must therefore go beyond the simple provision of services to address social and health concerns as well. Despite considerable progress over the last several decades, the coverage and quality of family planning services remain less than satisfactory in many countries. In addition, some countries have imposed demographic and provider targets on family planning programmes, thus actively interfering with trust between clients and providers.

To ensure that family planning programmes appropriately assist individuals in reaching personal fertility goals, governments should offer family planning as a strictly voluntary service embedded within or linked with other reproductive health services. The quality of these programmes can be improved by extending services to underserved populations, broadening the choice of methods available, assuring the technical competence of providers, emphasizing the shared responsibility of men for protection from unwanted fertility and disease and increasing public awareness of the value of and the means to fertility regulation. The most direct and convincing evidence of the value of well-designed family planning services attentive to related child and reproductive health needs is provided by an extensive experiment conducted in the Matlab district of rural Bangladesh since the mid-1970s.

When the Matlab experiment began, Bangladesh was one of the poorest and least developed countries, and there was considerable skepticism that in such a setting reproductive behaviour could be changed. The Matlab experiment's initial phase relied on a very simple design: traditional birth attendants were hired to visit households every three months to provide oral pills and condoms to couples who expressed an interest.

By the second year of this intervention, contraceptive use was a modest 6 per cent higher in the treatment than in the comparison area. This result demonstrated the existence of some demand, but its fragile nature clearly called for a more comprehensive approach to services, one which took into account in its design social, psychological, and health concerns limiting adoption of fertility regulation.

In the second phase of the project, started in 1977, the choice of methods was expanded; the quality of backstopping, referral, and follow-up was greatly improved; a new cadre of better-trained and relatively well-educated younger women replaced the traditional birth attendants as service providers; and extensive management changes were undertaken to ensure that visitation was dependable and client problems were addressed promptly.

The results of these improvements in the quality of services were immediate and pronounced. In the treatment area, contraceptive use rose to one-third of all married women within a year, while no such change was observed in the comparison area. The difference between these two areas has been maintained over time. The success of the Matlab experiment not only demonstrated that appropriately designed services could reduce latent demand even in very traditional settings, but it also provided an impetus to the national family planning programme of Bangladesh. Sessions learned from the experiment were used to redesign government services, and these changes were in turn instrumental in raising contraceptive use nationwide from a negligible level in the 1960s to nearly 50 per cent in the early 1990s.

REDUCE THE DEMAND FOR LARGE FAMILIES THROUGH INVESTMENTS IN HUMAN DEVELOPMENT

Although family planning programmes claim most of the attention of population policy makers and of the resources at their disposal, their potential effect is largely limited to reducing the unmet need for contraception. Since such programmes are voluntary, they cannot reduce fertility below the level wanted by couples and they cannot bring about population stabilization in countries where on average the desired number of children still exceeds two. Many individuals and couples continue to want and have large families, in part because of fears of infant and child mortality as well as the need for children to assist them in family enterprises and to support them in old age.

In most of the developing world, desired fertility still exceeds two surviving children; in some areas, such as sub-Saharan Africa, desired family size is typically above five children. In many societies, sons are valued more than daughters because families feel they cannot rely on daughters for their future security; larger numbers of births are therefore needed to ensure the survival of sons. Since population stabilization cannot occur until well after fertility has reached a level of just two surviving children per couple, high demand for children remains a fundamental cause of population growth.

Early population stabilization therefore requires measures that reduce the demand for large families through affirmative social and economic policies. Their objective is to change the costs and benefits of child rearing so that more parents will recognize the value of smaller families, while simultaneously increasing the investment in children.

The following variables have substantial effects on desired family size, as well as on the ability of individuals to regulate their fertility:

- *Education:* Among the socioeconomic variables that have been studied for their potential effect on fertility and desired family size, education stands out as the most consistent. Compared with their uneducated counterparts, educated parents rely less on children for income and social survival, in particular in old age, and their childrearing costs—both economic and time—are higher. Educated women are more able to make independent reproductive decisions and to engage in innovative contraceptive behaviour. Mass education lowers the labour value of children by requiring attendance in school, and raises the costs of children, thus leading to smaller desired families. It also lowers fertility by promoting and facilitating the spread of nontraditional behaviours, roles, and values.

- *Child survival*: A high death rate among children encourages high fertility in several ways:
  - It requires excess births to insure that at least the desired number of children will survive to adulthood;
  - It discourages investments in children's health and education; and
  - It makes the planning of families difficult because the number and timing of future deaths are unpredictable; it thus contributes to fatalism.

All these effects can be counteracted by implementing public health measures to reduce infant and child mortality. The potentially important role of this variable has been demonstrated empirically in different societies, and no population in the developing world has experienced a sustained fertility reduction without first having gone through a major decline in infant and child mortality.

- *Investments in women*: Improvements in the economic, social, and legal status of girls and women can reduce desired fertility in several ways. Increasing women's educational levels and economic prospects decrease their reliance on children for status and security. Empowering women is also likely to lead to reductions in the dominance of husbands (or other household members) over women, the societal preference for male offspring, and the value of (and thus need for) children as insurance against adversity (for example in old age) and as securers of women's positions in families. Although the precise role of each of these effects varies among and within societies, there is little doubt that the overall effect of increasing gender equality significantly influences reproductive behaviour.

Most governments already pursue these socially desirable objectives independent of their potential role in lowering the rate of childbearing. The demographic benefits simply strengthen the rationale for intensifying these social policies.

ADDRESS THE MOMENTUM OF POPULATION GROWTH

While a young age structure—the key force behind population momentum—is not amenable to modification, an option to reduce momentum is available that has received little attention in past policy debates. Further reductions in population growth can be achieved if the average age at which women begin childbearing rises (by delaying the first birth) and through wider spacing between births. Previous research has clearly demonstrated that fertility levels in any given year are significantly affected by shifts in the timing of births. If successive age cohorts of women start their childbearing earlier and space their births closer together, for example, fertility for that period rises temporarily.

Conversely, a delay in the onset of childbearing and wider spacing of births leads to a decline in fertility and hence in the population growth rate. Young women often have little choice about whether or not to have sexual relations, when or whom to marry, and whether to defer childbearing. Short intervals between generations are often a result of the pressures on young women to marry and to bear children early as a means of finding social acceptance and long-term economic security.

The early onset of fertility and the close spacing of births present health risks to girls and young women, limit their education and livelihood possibilities, Delaying the onset of childbearing will therefore not only reduce population growth, it also significantly improves personal well being and the quality of family life, especially for women. Governments that wish to encourage later childbearing have several options at their disposal. National legislation to raise the age at marriage has been moderately effective in a few countries, such as Tunisia and China. However, legislation has the drawback that it attempts to force rather than encourage changes in social customs that involve not only the young people but also their families. Indirect approaches are likely to be more effective. A greater investment in the education of girls, particularly at the secondary level, is the most obvious example. The longer girls stay in school, the later they marry and the greater the delay in childbearing. In general, supportive measures that enhance adolescents reproductive health, educational levels, and income-generating potential will lead to more rapid human capital development, to increased productivity, and it offsets population momentum.

CONCLUSION

The unprecedented speed with which the world's population has grown over the last four decades has resulted in a more than doubling of the number of inhabitants, bringing the total to 5.7 billion by 1995. Despite substantial and partially successful efforts to reduce growth in the less developed countries, this expansion of human members is expected to continue at a rapid pace over the next decades. Current projections suggest that the world population will continue to grow, reaching 9.4 billion in 2050, with nearly all of this growth occurring in Africa, Asia, and Latin America. Longer-range projections to the end of the next century estimate totals of over 10 billion.

Three strategies are available to governments that consider current and expected future population growth rates higher than desirable:

- Strengthen family planning programmes to provide women with the knowledge and means to regulate their fertility. These programmes can lower fertility if they successfully provide a broad clientele with high quality services, because there is still a substantial unmet need for contraception and abortion. Meeting this need will reduce unwanted pregnancies which now account for about one in four births (outside China).

- Emphasize "human development," in particular education, gender equality and child health. Improvements in these areas are instrumental in reducing desired family size. Since desired family size is still above two in much of the developing world, population stabilization cannot be achieved until fertility preferences decline further.
- Encourage delays in childbearing. This is a relatively new but potentially effective population policy option aimed at reducing population momentum. One of the more desirable ways to achieve childbearing delays is by raising investments in education, especially of girls, because it is associated with later marriage and onset of childbearing.

To be effective in addressing the expected population expansion policies should include but also go beyond the provision of services. Voluntary fertility reduction as a societal development goal is best achieved through mutually reinforcing investments in family planning, reproductive health, and a range of socioeconomic measures. Such policies operate beneficially at both the macro and micro levels; the same measures that slow population growth improve individual health and welfare.

5

Features of Sex-Ratio Imbalance

For multiple reasons, India's experience is crucial to understanding the current increase in the proportion of males versus females in populations across Asia. First, rising sex ratios in India have been recorded since the early 1980s, and have since continued increasing with no sign, so far, of reversing course. The impact of this early rise is already visible among the adult population of several Indian districts. Second, even if sex-ratio values in India are still beneath those of China, its potential contribution to the overall "masculinization" of Asia is particularly formidable in view of India's demographic weight. The prospect of further worsening of India's sex composition requires close monitoring of current sex-ratio trends in the country. Lastly, the Indian scenario of female discrimination is extremely complex in view of India's social and economic diversity: the interplay of cultural and economic factors, along with the impact of policy initiatives, has produced a heterogeneous situation; in turn, this complexity offers ways to better understand the mechanisms at work, and to inform the policy debate on the struggle against gender discrimination.

A vast amount of knowledge on sex discrimination in India has been accumulated over the last twenty years. Moreover, detailed statistics from various sources exist that describe several aspects of sex discrimination–such as sex ratio at birth, child sex ratio, female excess mortality and abortion practices–at various scales of analyses and for many different subpopulations.

This document will therefore summarize the available literature and statistical sources, in order to propose a comprehensive review of the main dimensions of the recent sex-ratio degradation in India: its origin, its mechanisms and social characteristics, its implications in the long run and its major causes. This will then lead us to a discussion of the recent policy experience and its future prospects. The first section focuses on the recent demographic trends observed in India. We examine the evolution of the sex ratio over the last decades, and the variations observed within the country.

In the next section, we present some results of demographic projections up to 2050, and examine the future consequences of skewed SRBs over India's age and sex distribution, as well as their potential implications on social and economic organization. The next section examines the underlying factors behind the recent reduction in the proportion of female children, distinguishing in particular between the supply-and demand-side factors. The last section is devoted to policy responses and future prospects, opening up the discussion on potential avenues for confronting the current challenges.

SEX-RATIO TRANSITION IN INDIA

Sex discrimination has long had visible demographic repercussions on India's population. In view of this historical dimension, it may be useful to discuss the discriminatory regimes that characterize the social and demographic systems that have prevailed in India at different periods. As suggested, therefore emphasize both their relative stability over time, as well as their gradual transition to the demographic system present today. As suggested, first depict a few elements of the old regime that characterized most of India till the 1970s.

OLD REGIME: NEGLECT AND INFANTICIDE

The first censuses conducted by the British administration in colonial India had already stressed the unusually male-heavy character of the Indian population. Boys predominated among Indian children, and high sex ratios were even recorded among older age groups. However, in the absence of reliable statistics, it took decades for statisticians to make sense of this apparent oddity, and to establish that the inflated sex ratios observed in many parts of India since the 19 century were not the artificial offshoot of poor registration or female under-enumeration. Rather, they were directly related to unusually high mortality levels among women of all ages.

Unfavourable death rates were indeed common amongst Indian women of all ages. The practice of female infanticide had been detected early on in some provinces of West India, where a few caste groups chose to limit the number of daughters by killing them immediately after birth. But the real culprit was the less visible impact of excess female mortality among infants and children. Extremely high death rates observed during the colonial period meant that more than a quarter of children born would not reach the age of 5; a slight level of female excess mortality could thus translate into a significantly reduced number of girls. As a result, the sex ratio did not decrease with age in India, as observed elsewhere. Higher mortality conditions were also at work among young adult women and even among some older groups.

While largely applicable to South Asia, this pattern was more pronounced in the Northern provinces and regions encompassing the contemporary states of Punjab to Gujarat, which already had the distinction of having the highest child sex ratio in the country. While life expectancy started to increase regularly in India after 1920, it appears that men reaped more benefits from this progress than did women. On the whole, health facilities, improved nutrition and better protection against epidemics or death were geared more towards enhancing survival conditions for boys and men, which was considered a prime objective for many households and communities. As pointed out previously, this demographic system was based on the overall impact of excess female mortality.

With the exception of cases of infanticide, limited to small regions and specific communities, higher mortality could hardly be construed as a deliberate attempt to reduce the lifespan of girls and women. Rather, it was the prevalence of systematic differential treatment that caused these lower survival rates: poorer food intake, lesser access to medical care, etc. These various factors–usually labelled as "female neglect"–exacerbated mortality rates among women, even though the difference, for lack of reliable vital statistics, remained invisible. In fact, because of the mortality risks, having more children was the first demographic imperative, and less importance was therefore given to the actual sex composition of the offspring.

Consequently, the old regime can be said to have been characterized by archaic and crude discriminatory methods, such as neglect or infanticide. The latter, due to its overall threat to human values, could never spread beyond a handful of communities. Along with abortion, infanticide was also sporadically practiced as a last-resort technique to eliminate unwanted births, such as out-of-wedlock pregnancies, but was also often gender-blind. In spite of its overall toll on Indian girls and women, excess female mortality was the outcome of a passive strategy aimed at better resource allocation for boys and men from birth. Its local impact on given families was somewhat erratic, however, and many girls and women did in fact survive the hard conditions meted out to them. In a way, mortality differential reflects a rather ineffective modus operandi to alter the sex composition, due to its reliance on crude and low-tech methods.

THE NEW REGIME AND SEX-SELECTIVE ABORTIONS FROM THE 1980S

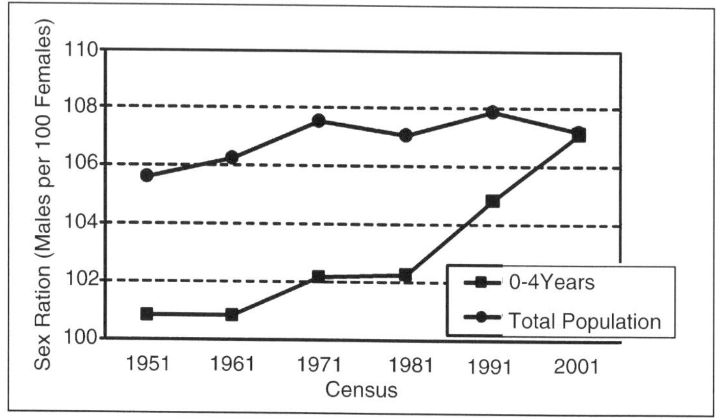

Fig. Sex Ratio of the Child and Overall Population, India, 1951-2000

Mortality conditions rapidly improved after Independence in 1947. The survival environment likewise began to improve for women, who increasingly benefited from improvements in child and adult mortality. However, the sex-discrimination regime started to undergo a deep change during the late 1970s, as summarized by Figure, showing the rapid increase in the child sex ratio after 1981.

The reason for this dramatic shift stems from the introduction into India of methods of prenatal sex determination, such as amniocentesis and ultrasound technology.

While part of an overall effort to improve health conditions for both mothers and children, these new technologies had the unexpected option of offering couples advanced information on the sex of their future children. Some years earlier, India had also established a new and rather liberal law on abortion, which in many cases rendered the termination of a pregnancy considerably easier, for reasons ranging from foetal physical defect to contraception failure.

As such, the change in abortion regulations was an offshoot of a government endeavour unrelated to sex discrimination. The law was primarily meant to address the issue of unwanted pregnancies, as part of a comprehensive family-planning strategy that encompassed many contraceptive options, as well. But the combination of new technologies for pre-natal sex determination and abortion proved to be a dramatic cocktail, which would quickly become an efficient sex-selection device. From the 1980s, sex-selective abortions became the primary method used to alter the sex composition of children. The emergence of sex-identification techniques heralded a new discriminatory regime in India, which is responsible today for the dramatic sex-ratio situation in many of its regions.

What primarily distinguishes the combination of scan and abortion from older methods is its high level of efficiency in terms of outcome. Moreover, these services were provided by the medical community, and thus inspired much more trust than the traditional methods implemented by local specialists. A further advantage lay in the shortened duration of the process of sex selection, as families did not have to wait until delivery. While still traumatic for many women, abortion was considered far less physically or psychologically painful than a pregnancy followed by infanticide, or later infant or child deaths. Compared to the older methods, this new technique also spares women months of pregnancy and final delivery, or of raising an "unwanted" girl child; it also appears to be a modern way to go about sex selection. Another advantage over the techniques of the old regime relates to the fact that an early abortion allows women to avoid exposure from others outside their immediate family members. Many couples could therefore conceal their pregnancy, and implement their sex-discrimination strategy, with little scrutiny from the community at large.

Modern techniques therefore set the new regime apart from older discrimination strategies. In addition, the immediate entourage now plays a much larger role in the decision-making than in the past, when community values and preferences–at the village or caste level–could be more strictly implemented. Modernization reduced the role of many traditional institutions operating at a larger scale, and the new regime penetrated households at a time when the small-family norm was also making rapid progress.

In particular, fertility reduction meant that parents could decide the number of offspring they had according to their available resources, rather than by following traditional values. In addition to the quantity of children, this new demographic perception also resulted in efforts to adjust the "quality" of the offspring, through better health care and education. However, gender composition also emerged as a crucial dimension of this new strategy, for reasons as suggested, enumerate later.

It may not come as a surprise to learn that, from the trial period when pre-natal monitoring techniques were first tested in India, women expressed great interest in knowing the sex of their foetus. Other family members, such as the father or his parents, also understood its potential for sex selection, and encouraged women to overcome their physical or psychological reservations on abortion if they wanted to avoid the birth of a girl.

While some see the spread of sex selection mainly as supply-driven, there is no denying that son preference had nearly always prevailed, and preceded introduction of modern technology. Present-day economists might say that the "markets" in the old regime were somewhat inefficient, as they had offered little by way of effective technical solutions to respond to this unmet demand.

DEMOGRAPHIC OUTCOME AND MECHANISMS

The demographic outcome of these changes in the discriminatory regime is now better known, especially since the 2001 census has provided detailed figures on child sex ratio for various components of the population. For instance, Table shows the gradual increase in the proportion of boys (per 100 girls) from 1981 to 2001, a rise that was significantly faster in urban areas. A ratio favourable to boys and adverse to girls coincides with the introduction of modern prenatal sex-determination methods.

Table. Child Sex Ration in Urban and Rural Areas, India, 1981-2001

Year	Total	Rural	Urban
1981	104.0	103.8	107.4
1991	105.8	105.5	107.0
2001	107.9	107.1	110.4

This increase was more pronounced in cities, as well as in the Northern and Western parts of India. Child sex ratio further deteriorated between 1991 and 2001 in these areas, with some district-level values going higher than 115. (Some higher, rather aberrant, figures above 130 were also reported in a few pockets.) Elsewhere in India, there was apparently no large-scale deterioration in sex-ratio figures, which by and large remained below the national average. However, close scrutiny of the district-level data shown in Figure also indicates a small rise in child sex ratio in some areas, such as Kerala, Maharashtra, etc.

His increase, albeit modest, points to a potentially worrying trend, as the child sex ratio in areas long thought to be immune from significant sex discrimination may also be on the rise. Sex selection appears to have played a major role in causing the deterioration observed in child sex ratio. Excess female mortality among infants and children contributes only moderately to the deficit of girls.

For instance, Table shows that mortality is indeed higher for girls one month after birth, but the absolute mortality gap itself is limited. While old techniques have not completely disappeared, they are today more common among lower sections of society.

Table. Neonatal and Post-neonatal Mortality Rates in India, 1998-99

Source/Year	Sex	NN mort (1)	PNN mort (2)
NFHS 1998/1999	Male	50.7	24.2
	Female	44.6	26.6
	F/M ratio	0.880	1.099

1. Neonatal (NN) mortality: probability of dying within the first month of life
2. Post-neonatal (PNN) mortality: probability of dying between the first month and the 1st anniversary of life

Even if reliable data on abortions are missing, the intensity of sex-selective abortions can be gauged by examining the SRB according to the stage in family formation. For a majority of pregnancies, SRB appears close to its normal value. This is the case for first births, for instance, for which sex ratio is often very close to normal values. Most families do cherish diversity, after all, and do not shun the birth of an initial daughter. Similarly, births that follow the birth of a son may not be greatly affected by sex selection.

Rather, it is with regards to later pregnancies among sonless couples that SRB values tend to surge. Parents want to avoid the "worst-case" scenario– *i.e.*, a family without a son. This is reflected in the sex ratio of higher-parity births (meaning, the second, third, etc.), as Table shows for Punjab and Haryana. While the proportion of these amount to less than a quarter of all pregnancies, among these the SRB may jump to values of 130 or more, roughly indicating an excess of 25 (130-105 males versus females) male births out of a total of 230 (130+100). These additional male births have probably followed one or more abortion attempts.

Table. Sex Ratio at Birth by Birth Order, India, 1978-98

Year	India		Haryana		Punjab	
Date	1978-92	1984-98	1978-92	1984-98	1972-98	1984-98
All birth order	106	108	110	114	114	120
1st birth	105	107	109	110	109	101
2nd	107	108	100	114	111	123
3rd	107	108	114	129	117	136
4th+	106	108	116	108	122	134

While the arithmetic of SRB by rank and previous birth is somewhat complicated, simple observation indicates that pregnancies at risk (in which the life of the woman, for instance, is in danger) constitute a minor proportion of all pregnancies. This may have important policy consequences. Nevertheless, the sex ratio for all births may rise above 110, and this is not without consequence. One worse-case scenario would involve cases in which even the first birth of a daughter is avoided, at which point sex ratio could go even higher than 130.

REGION, RELIGION AND ECONOMIC STATUS

One of the main traits of increasing proportion of males within the Indian population corresponds to the wide variations in sex ratio observed within the country, and at times even within regions. Census data have provided a detailed mapping of such differentials across the country, but as suggested, offer here a brief summary of the main distinctive features observed. The first factor is the geographical patterning of differences, to which we have already referred.

The deterioration of child sex ratio has been observed in a limited number of states, particularly those in the West of the country, stretching from Punjab to Maharashtra. On the whole, this spatial clustering has remained steady over the years, as indicated by the maps for 1991 and 2001, even though this stability partly conceals the actual intensification observed in states already affected. Other regions in India appear practically unaffected and, except for isolated pockets in specific states (such as in Tamil Nadu or Orissa), local sex-ratio values are seemingly normal, particularly in view of levels observed in Western India.

The following map shows that regional differences in child sex ratio are also visible on a district level. Another factor observed consists of the socio-cultural composition of the population. Some religious groups, such as Sikhs or Jains, exhibit extreme sex-ratio values on the whole, while such figures tend to be normal or low among other groups, such as tribal communities. It stands to reason that, had the census variables been detailed enough to identify other communities (such as individual caste groups), many more differentials regarding specific communities would also have come to light. An additional dimension that emerges from this analysis springs from socio-economic differentials. We have already seen that higher sex ratio is observed in urban India as compared to the country's villages.

But further analysis also points to the positive linkage between abnormal sex ratio and better socio-economic status and literacy. This contradicts the spontaneous explanation of sex selection being an archaic practice common only among the uneducated. In fact, it can even be shown that, all other things being equal, female literacy and other economic indicators tend to increase the sex ratio of children, at least in India. For instance, the sex ratio of last births in Punjab was 127, according to the 2001 census, but it proved even higher (139) among the most educated women. This finding sits somewhat uncomfortably alongside the assumption that improvement in women's agency–closely related to education, standard of living and modern employment–is a key to social development. Moreover, it is important to understand the active role played by elite households in gender discrimination.

The global picture of sex-ratio variations appears somewhat complex in view of the three distinctions reviewed above–*viz.*, geographical variations across regions, socio-cultural determinants and the positive influence of socio-economic status on child sex ratio. Observers often confuse one with the other, and conclude that higher rates in Punjab are linked to the state's relative economic affluence, to its religious composition or to some unknown local factors (observers have at times even hinted at a mysterious "Bermuda Triangle" effect in Northwest India). In fact, the discriminatory behaviour may be best understood as the combined offshoot of these three factors, playing a cumulative role on sex ratio.

Table. Sex Ratio of Last Birth by Population Characteristics, India, 2001

Background characteristics		**Sex ratio of births during the previous year**
All		110.4
	Residence	
	Rural	110.4
	Urban	110.6
Religion		
	Hindum	107.4
	Christian	103.8
	Sikh	129.8
	Buddhist	108.4
	Jain	118.0
	Caste/Tribe	
	Scheduled Tribe	106.4
	Scheduled Caste	108.6
	Others	111.5

Background characteristics		Sex ratio of births during the previous year
Mother's education level		
	Illiterate	108.7
	Literate but below primary	110.0
	Primary but below middle	111.8
	Middle but below matric/secondary	113.0
	Matric/secondary but below graduate	115.3
	Graduate and above	114.1
Numbers (in millions)		19.9

SEX-RATIO IMBALANCE AND EXCESS MALE POPULATION

Changing sex ratios among children are going to have a lasting impact on population dynamics in India, as most of today's births will survive for more than 60 years. In this section, as suggested, examine some of the most obvious impacts of high SRB in the long term, by examining the characteristics of projected age and sex distribution.

Population characteristics lend themselves quite easily to such forecasting exercises, in view of their strong inertia. While this is true of several demographic features (such as mortality or fertility), it is no longer the case for variables that are far less predictable, such as migration or urbanization. In the case of masculinization, we are hardly in a better position, since increasing SRB is a trend that has never been documented in the past, anywhere in the world. Consequently, our projections' set of hypotheses remains speculative.

OPTIONS AND HYPOTHESES

Demographic projections are already available for Indian states, prepared by the Census of India. However, these projections have two serious limitations. First, they run only up to 2026, while we need to go well beyond this date, as generations born today are likely to reach marriageable age after 2026. We have therefore opted for a longer timeframe, and chosen to project the population until 2050, as done by the UN Population Division. A second drawback of the available census projections relates to their unique SRB scenario.

As suggested, subsequently attempt to explore various options, in order to understand the effects of such SRB variations on age and sex structures. The projections are run for two sets of populations: the total population of India; and the adjacent states of Haryana and Punjab, and Chandigarh Union Territory (referred to hereafter as "Northwest India").

These states form a bulk of almost 50 million people, and have been selected for their extreme situation with regard to current levels of child sex ratio. They are characterized by a relatively high level of sccial and cultural homogeneity, the imprint of Punjabi culture and rapid economic development over the last decades, including in rural areas. Hypotheses for this set of projections have been kept extremely simple.

Mortality and fertility are supposed to follow the United Nations' projected estimates for 2005-2050 at the national level. As for Northwest India, we have simply corrected the UN estimates by assuming the same differentials as are observed today.

Life expectancies are therefore higher in Northwest India than in the country as a whole, but fertility (the average number of children a woman has during her lifetime) is lower in Northwest India. The projection procedure further assumes no migratory exchanges, including between regions, and uses the South Asia mortality models and the Asia model for age-specific fertility rates.

Table. Fertility and Mortality Hypotheses Used for 2001-2050 Projections

	India		Northwest India	
	2001	**2050**	**2001**	**2050**
Fertility rates	3.11	1.85	2.71	1.85
Male life expectancy	61.7	73.4	65.2	76.9
Female life expectancy	64.2	77.9	67.2	80.9

Scenarios related to future SRB constitute a more delicate affair, since we have no historical experience in human history to help us anticipate the course of SRB in Asia. Using the highest observed Asian value of 138 and the standard biological value of 106, we have developed four distinct scenarios:

- *High-Higher*: SRB moves from its current level to 138 in 2030, and stays at this level. To a certain extent, this represents the "worst-case scenario", as we assume that SRB will further increase to the highest value and fail to decrease till 2050. This scenario is probably not plausible, but serves as an upper limit.
- *High-High*: in this "business-as-usual scenario", SRB stays at the 2001 level until 2050. Here we assume that no progress is made in alleviating son preference or the use of sex-selection technology. This scenario indicates what would happen if things were to remain as they were at the beginning of the 21 century. For India, this means an SRB of 111; but for Northwest India, the 2001 value of 126 is probably untenable in the long run.
- *High-Low*: this is a truly "transitional scenario", in which high SRB gradually declines from its actual value in 2001 to 106 in 2030, and

thereafter stays at the same level. This corresponds to a reasonably optimistic scenario, in which the sex-ratio crisis ends completely in less than 25 years.

- *Low-Low*: in this "floor-level scenario", SRB reverts to 106 from 2001 onwards. While implausible (as SRB is unlikely to have come back to normal value immediately after the last census), this estimate will serve as a reference to help us to imagine the population dynamics as if no further sex selection had ever taken place.

Table summarizes the values used to project SRB according to our four scenarios.

Table: Four Scenarios of Evolution of Sex Ratio at Birth, Used for 2001-2050 Projections

	Sex ratio at birth					
	2001	2030	2050	2001	2030	2050
	India			Northwest India		
High-Higher	111	138	138	126	138	138
High-High	111	111	111	126	126	126
High-Low	111	106	106	126	106	106
Low-Low	106	106	106	106	106	106

FINDINGS AND THE MEANING FOR FUTURE POPULATION STRUCTURES

Projections of India's populations subsequently show the impact of these four scenarios on overall population growth. India will have a population of 1.733 billion in 2050 according the Low-Low scenario, but of only 1.694 billion according to the High-Higher scenario. Thus, high SRBs may reduce the overall growth of India's population by several million people, though this can in no way be considered a "just" decline. These differences in the final population for 2050 are quite sizeable, in view of the fact that fertility and mortality conditions are assumed to be identical for all scenarios.

In fact, they reflect the impact that a lack of women would have on fertility potential: fewer women today translates into fewer births after 20 years. The next figures present findings related to the overall sex ratio. As can be expected, the extreme High-Higher and Low-Low scenarios lead to divergent sex-ratio profiles for the next fifty years. In the High-Higher scenario, the overall index reaches 117, but in the High-High scenario, the overall sex ratio will shrink slightly in the next decades.

This reduction is, of course, more pronounced for the next scenarios, in which SRB is declining or already back at a normal level. The change in India is rapid as a result of India's continuous population growth after 2040. In the two intermediary scenarios (High-High and High-Low), which most likely delimit the demographic future of India, the SRB remains within a more reasonable range. But it may also be noted that the sex ratio will remain distinctly in favour of males till 2050. This is even true for the speculative Low-Low scenario, indicating that the combination of past gender imbalances and future age structures will not be enough to turn around the heavily male nature of India's population. These trends translate into wide gaps between the male and female populations: for instance, if SRB remains at 2001 levels (the High-High scenario), there will be 47 million more men than women in 2050. Sex-ratio estimates above 100 may also be compared to the rest of world (Asia excluded), where the sex ratio of 97 in 2005 is not expected to rise in the next several decades.

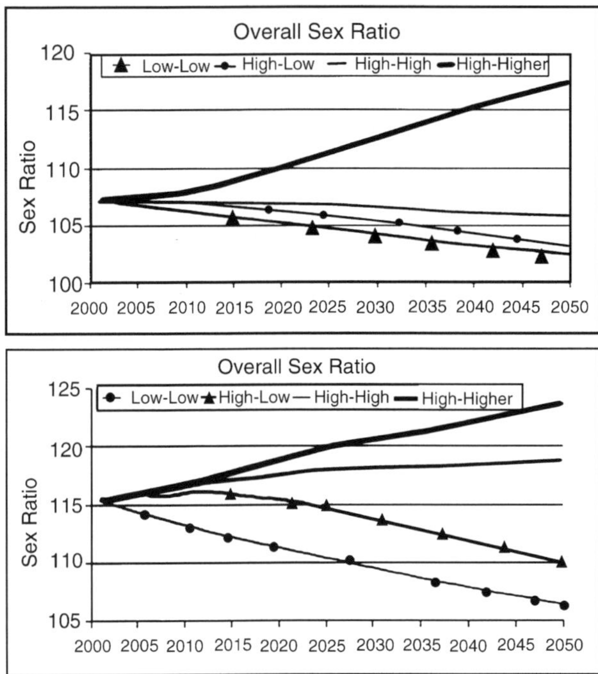

Fig. Overall Sex Ratio, 2001-2050, India (above)and Northwest India (below)

Figure also shows the trend for Northwest India. Starting from a very high level at the beginning of the century, this region is unlikely to witness the kind of improvements that can be envisioned for the rest of the country. In fact, if SRB stays at the same level (the High-High scenario), the process of masculinization will gradually involve all age groups, as younger generations (which are heavily male) age, and the overall indicator will continue to increase to about 119 in 2050.

The transitional scenario will bring about a decline in the overall sex ratio only in the 2010s, but the sex ratio of the entire regional population will remain above 110 by 2050. The widening divergence between those two scenarios (High-High and High-Low) corresponds to the impact of a possible SRB decline between 2000 and 2030. The overall demographic gap between males and females in 2050 represents 14 per cent of the projected female population in the High-Low scenario, compared to 23 per cent in the High-High scenario.

SKEWED SEX RATIOS AND MARRIAGE PATTERNS

Our projections also allow for a more detailed exploration of these data by age group. As suggested, consider here only young adults, in order to examine the impact of skewed SRBs on the population of marriageable age. We have retained here the 20-49 age group for both sexes, a choice dictated chiefly by our comparative regional perspective.

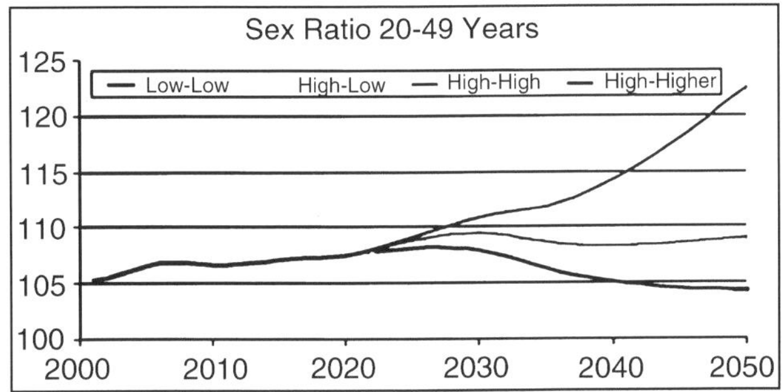

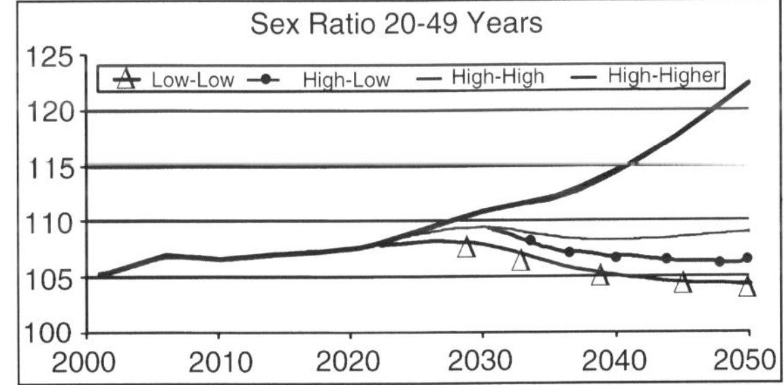

Fig. Sex Ratio of 20-49 Age Group, 2001-2050, India (above) and Northwest India (below)

We first computed the sex ratio of this age group according to the four scenarios. As can be expected, differences will be visible only after 2020, when the consequences of unbalanced SRBs post-2000 will become visible among adults. As our simulation indicates, this sex ratio is already at 105, and will increase slightly till 2025. After this date, trajectories are divergent, but our central scenarios (High-High and High-Low) do not translate into large differences in 2050, as sex ratio among adults will remain in the 106-109 range. Even if SRB were to remain at the normal level of 106 over the whole projection period, the female deficit in the marriageable age group (20-49) would be at least 25 million in India by 2030, as a result of previous skewed sex ratios and dynamics affecting the age structure of a population.

But other scenarios point to a deficit in the range of 29-34 million, with limited possibilities of decline in the following decades. In fact, even in the optimistic transitional scenario, the female deficit in the 20-49 age group would be around 23 million. Figure indicates that the gap between men and women in this broad age group will hover at around 8 per cent of the adult male population if there is no transition. This gap will reduce to 6 per cent if SRB comes back to 106 in 2030.

The different scenarios have a more visible impact in Northwest India, due to the current high level of SRB in that region. In fact, if nothing changes, the sex ratio in the 20-49 age group will climb to 125, as against 115 in case of decline. All scenarios lead to a 15 per cent excess of men by 2020, which may further climb to 20 per cent if SRB stays at its current level. Even in the more optimistic case of a transitional scenario, the surplus will remain above 15 per cent of the adult male population till the 2040s.

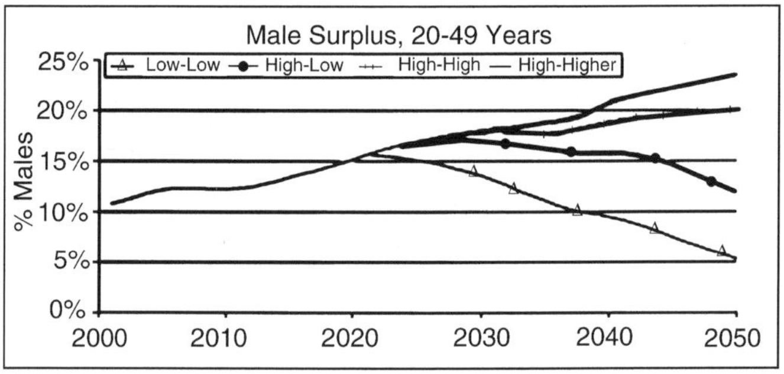

Fig. Male Surplus Among the 20-49 Age Group, 2001-2050, India (above) and Northwest India (Below)

Indeed, this deficit is already being felt in many pockets of Punjab, where young men have difficulties finding brides. Men in such situations are increasingly resorting to unusual solutions, such as non-endogamous unions (involving other caste groups), import of brides from other regions (such as tribal India or Southern states) or trafficking. In terms of marriage patterns, a shortage of potential brides may force men to delay their marriages. Marrying older is the first adjustment to adversely imbalanced sex ratios.

But the effect of delayed marriages for one generation of men will then be felt on the younger generation, as they become adults. As in a queue, unmarried men will accumulate as new cohorts of bachelors reach marriageable age. This growing pool of unmarried men will create a bottleneck that is unlikely to be solved solely by delaying marriages. Single men reaching 25 in 2025 and entering the marriage market will not only exceed the number of young women of corresponding age, but will also have to compete with a larger than expected number of older men who are still single. As a result, many of these men will not be able to marry. This means that not only will a significant share of men above 30 still be single, but also that many will never be able to marry at all. Of course, this assumes that marriage patterns do not undergo highly improbable changes, such as earlier female marriages, generalized polyandry (wherein a woman takes multiple husbands), same-sex arrangements or extremely high levels of divorce and remarriage among women.

While high proportions of unmarried men or women above age 40 have already been observed in many countries (post-war Ireland being a prime example of late marriage and high proportions of people never marrying), these marriage patterns are mostly unrelated to the marriage squeeze, resulting instead from deliberate behaviour. In India, where unmarried persons lack a clear status in traditional society, the proportion of men and women unmarried at age 50 is usually extremely low (less than 1 per cent), indicating that marriage acts as a compulsory institution for almost everyone. As such, rising proportions of unmarried men are obviously at odds with the prevailing custom.

When restricted to specific regions, broadening the marriage radius can, to a large extent, help to solve the marriage squeeze by allowing inter-caste and inter-regional unions, as is seen today in Northwest India. But the sheer magnitude of the projected deficit renders this solution unfeasible when more than a million potential brides are missing, and even migrations from neighbouring countries (most of whose populations are not of the same religion) may not be a workable solution. From a strictly quantitative viewpoint, male migrations out of South Asia would appear to be a more feasible solution, even if current barriers to international mobility would not allow for such demographic transfers.

IMPLICATIONS FOR MEN AND WOMEN

Going beyond marriage itself, the reduced number of women would mean that women's family roles–as wife, daughter-in-law or mother–would become increasingly in demand. These traditional family roles would, therefore, be enhanced at the expense of other life courses, such as decisions regarding celibacy, or opting for a career. Pressure towards early marriage may be detrimental to women's education, training and employment; their permanent or temporary withdrawal from the workforce may be encouraged, in order to give them adequate time to act as (traditional) wives or mothers.

As such, we may foresee a decrease in women's participation rates outside of the home, which may seem difficult when such figures for Indian women are already very low by international standards. At the same time, this would raise the demand for male labour, especially in the low-skilled and low-wage sectors that are currently largely occupied by women. The impact for men of delayed marriage would probably be favourable to longer educational and training periods, resulting in better human capital and skills. But the consequence on participation rates is less clear.

A family life that is bound to start later is likely to require higher income levels and savings, particularly if the competition for brides is severe. But at the same time, we can also envisage unemployment, enhanced job mobility and lower rates of participation and savings among some men who are excluded from or opting out of the marriage system. In fact, the entire Indian family structure would undergo significant changes. Many unmarried men would have to be accommodated within the family structure, but with a reduced share of domestic power due to their marital status.

Some may also live on their own, an unusual arrangement for most Asian countries. Late marriage also means a more fragile status for men. Even while marrying older men, women may have a stronger role in the new family settings, as enhanced possibilities for divorce and remarriage may strengthen their position vis-à-vis their in-laws. In such a context, it is difficult to forecast whether the patrilineal system could survive in its current form. Parents of girls, even in smaller numbers, could benefit from a reversed flow of the dowry system, to encourage new living arrangements and more flexible or symmetrical family solidarity. But at the same time, scarcity of women would probably not enhance their position in society, due to the increased risk of gender-based violence, the rising demand for sex work and the development of trafficking networks.

Lower demographic weight in democratic systems would also translate into a weaker political voice in public decision-making, a trend that could be reinforced by women's lower involvement in nondomestic activities such as employment and civil life. At the same, men would strengthen their control on public and political institutions, and may be able to bend legislation relevant to women in order to accommodate their own needs.

MARRIAGE SQUEEZE AND POTENTIAL LOSERS

These various scenarios refer to an "aggregate" society, as if each family and member were in a similar position vis-à-vis a shortage of women. This is far from being the case, however, and we can easily identify some of the potential winners and losers in the changing demographic equation that would follow a long-term increase in the proportion of male versus female births. The marriage system is basically "hypergamic" in India, with women marrying up into slightly better-off families. Such a system stimulates efforts by potential brides and their family to invest large resources (such as dowry) to marry into families further up the socio-economic or status ladder.

Hypergamy always puts elite women and destitute men at the greatest risk: the former may not find available grooms in the proper stratum, while the latter may not be able to attract even the poorest women, aspiring to marry into better households ("Don't marry me to a ploughman," goes a common wedding song sung by rural Indian brides). The few studies devoted to the impact of past sex-ratio distortions in Northwest India have already shown that men unable to marry locally have resorted to the importation of brides from distant regions, lower economic backgrounds or lower caste groups. While this solution is compatible with hypergamy, strict caste rules may have to be stretched in order to allow marriage with distant communities. Moreover, dowry demands are likely to be reduced in order to facilitate such arrangements. These marriages may also be difficult to organize, thereby creating new networks (of villages, of matchmakers) or, at times, criminal organizations (women traffickers).

Such practices are, of course, bound to intensify in the future, with unmarried men compelled to broaden their search radius even wider in order to reach women from other regions, low-status groups (such as tribal communities), etc. What seems obvious is that dowry will become less relevant, and that money, particularly in prosperous regions like Northwest India, may help to attract potential women from other regions. Hence, we can easily imagine that the poorest men will be affected at disproportionate rates by the marriage squeeze, and that many among them may end up remaining single for lack of resources to marry, as already observed in some Indian regions. These individuals are likely to become the main losers in the new marriage system.

If, on the whole, a tenth of the male population is to be considered as surplus due to the marriage squeeze, this proportion is likely to be much higher among the underprivileged, with the number of men forced to remain single being several times greater. This will most likely act as a strong destabilizing factor for this male population, and may translate into classbased tensions.

SEX SELECTION: HOW AND WHY?

To understand the underlying determinants for sex selection in India, as suggested, use a framework originally devised in 1973 by Ansley Coale for researching fertility decline. According to Coale, three preconditions needed to be met in order for birth rates to fall: birth limitation had to be within the "calculus of conscious choice" for parents; it had to be advantageous to them; and it had to be feasible. As suggested, now adapt these prerequisites (conceivable, advantageous and feasible) to the SRB scenario. These conditions can be translated into a simple matrix: parents should be willing and ready to practice sex selection, and also able to do it. The first condition sounds straightforward, as the availability of the requisite technology is an indispensable ingredient for sex selection. But as we have seen, there are different methods available, and each entails certain costs or limitations.

Legal conditions may also act as a hindrance to sex selection. To a large extent, this latter component refers to supply-side factors, although this also needs to be widened to include non-material elements such as prohibitions or awareness factors. The second condition encompasses two aspects. First, this includes the ethical or religious context. As some of its ingredients (especially abortion) may be repugnant to them, parents may be unable to adopt them as techniques to regulate the sex composition of their offspring.

The second aspect relates to what can be referred to as the rationale framework: parents will engage in sex selection only if they gain distinct benefits from their efforts. Even when sex selection is both acceptable and accessible, it may not be of any interest, as is seen in many parts of India where sexratio levels appear normal. To explore this component, as suggested, review various determinants, including the economic and symbolic, such as prestige.

ABLE

The discussion of feasibility factors for sex selection should start with the technological evolution. Many methods existed in the past to influence the sex composition of one's family. But a major breakthrough occurred when new techniques based on scan-and-abortion emerged.

Methods

We briefly reviewed the basic methods used to influence child sex ratios. But many other folk methods (based on timing, specific diet, rituals, etc.) existed in the past, and are still reported today. These were probably of limited reliability, however, and unlikely to have left any tangible impact on India's sex composition.

Of course, the dramatic technological breakthrough due to the introduction of ultrasound technology is probably the main cause for rising SRBs, but remnants of the old discriminatory regime have not completely disappeared. In fact, the existing sex differentials in infant and child mortality demonstrate that neglect, as an indirect method to eliminate "surplus girls", is still common. Moreover, the influence of new technology is far from complete, though government intervention has blocked the introduction of more "high-tech" methods of sex selection.

As such, supply is somewhat crippled by current legislation, and may tend to lie below the actual level of demand for sex selection. Such a situation, of course, is likely to encourage criminal or other initiatives to circumvent regulations.

Traditional Methods

One of India's oldest means used to alter the gender composition of children is also the crudest, *i.e.*, female infanticide. The method relies on a set of procedures to kill girls within a few days after their birth. Techniques vary locally according to indigenous know-how and available resources (such as local poisonous plants). Such techniques have also evolved spontaneously over the years, incorporating newly available elements (such as pesticide). Infanticide's efficiency is beyond doubt, and its financial cost is also extremely limited because of its reliance on local resources. But this method also presents many drawbacks, especially due to the distress caused to mothers. The huge psychological cost of female infanticide has subsequently made its use exceptional, and often limited to especially unwanted births (*e.g.*, the pregnancy of single or widowed women).

As a result, infanticide as a routine practice (and not as a last-resort solution) has never spread widely in India, as was the case in some East Asian countries, remaining instead restricted to a few communities, such as specific sub-castes in Western India or in Tamil Nadu. Lack of privacy related to matters such as pregnancy and delivery also tended to facilitate knowledge of infanticide, requiring both local tolerance and discretion in case of legal threats. Neglect is a far more common method. It consists of a passive strategy intended to deprive girls of fair access to and share of resources, with a reduced probability of survival as a consequence.

Discrimination may be extremely subtle, and surveys are often unable to capture inequality in resource allocation. Some of the factors most often mentioned include post-natal care, proper clothing, parental surveillance, breastfeeding, food allocation (both quantity and quality), recourse to health facilities (frequency and expenses), immunization, etc. It is also expressed in other attitudes towards girls (such as with regards to schooling) that have no demographic consequences. All discrimination strategies towards girls do not invariably cause mortality, of course, as many Indian girls survive childhood in spite of severe deprivation.

We may therefore conclude that neglect is typically a low-tech technique. While it requires almost no financial or other parental effort, its own reliability as a way to eliminate daughters is limited. It may even be asked whether this constitutes a strategy *per se*, rather than merely being the random, unpredictable outcome of a certain set of practices.

Sex Determination and Selective Abortion

Pre-natal diagnostic techniques involve two main technologies, *viz.* amniocentesis and ultrasonography. In India, pre-natal sex determination relies mostly on the latter, a non-invasive technology that is also easier and cheaper to conduct than amniocentesis, and is reliable after at least 14-16 weeks of gestation. Both of these techniques were first tested in India in 1974, starting with amniocentesis.

By the 1980s, thousands of pre-natal clinics were already in operation. Abortion in India benefited from an early liberal legislation–the MTP Act, discussed since 1964, ratified in 1971 and introduced in 1974 (though not in Jammu and Kashmir). In 1975, the MTP Rules and Regulations defined when (12-20 weeks of pregnancy), by whom (registered allopathic doctors) and where unwanted pregnancies could be legally terminated. The Act was amended in 2002 and 2003, to improve women's access to safe abortion. One peculiar dimension of this Act is that it appears to focus on married women, and can be misconstrued as discriminating against single, divorced or widowed women. Apart from the usual social and health reasons, the most liberal provision of the Act includes contraceptive failure as a reason for abortion, paving the way for the probable use of abortion as a last-resort family-planning method.

The number of abortions that take place in India is poorly known, especially because many terminations take place outside registered centres and are performed by uncertified providers (who may, however, often be medical practitioners). Estimates vary from 13 to 21 per 1000 births, based on large-scale surveys and state statistics, while micro-level studies may provide lower estimates. In absolute terms, estimates are of 4-6 million abortions every year, but some figures go much higher.

In the public health-care system, an abortion in 2006 could be obtained through 11,000 approved clinics, although with a disproportionate share of these being in urban areas. A large number of users in cities choose to go to private clinics, even if costs in public institutions are free or nominal. Only a small proportion of primary health centres provides MTP services. Because of the lack of proper statistics, it is not easy to assess the proportion of abortions conducted for purposes of sex selection in India, and the estimates on this aspect necessarily vary.

Kulkarni has recently produced a set of estimates based on the gap between estimated and expected SRBs, the difference corresponding to the number of sex-selective abortions of female foetuses. When comparing a biological SRB of 106 for India to (adjusted) observed SRB values, the total number of selective abortions in 1981-2005 can be estimated at 8.0 million. This also corresponds to an average of 557,000 abortions per year since 2001, representing a little more than 2 per cent of annual births. It should also be emphasized that most pregnancy terminations conducted in India take place before the second trimester of pregnancy, and are most likely aimed at limiting or spacing births, rather than sex selection.

Latest Sex-selection Technology

There are several sex-selection techniques not known to be widely available in India, even if the Ericsson method (of sperm sorting) may have been at some point available in clinics in Punjab. Some of the characteristics of these techniques are worth mentioning. Two major pre-implantation methods exist that can be used for sex selection: sperm sorting (sperm that is sorted by sex and then used in artificial insemination or in-vitro fertilization–IVF–procedures), and pre-implantation genetic diagnosis (in which IVF embryos are genetically tested to determine sex and then implanted).

These techniques, which are available in industrialized countries, are expensive and require well-equipped labs. For a variety of reasons, including cost and legal prohibition, these methods are not likely to be accessible to

Indian residents in the near future. But to affluent Indians (who are able to travel or who have international connections), these methods may offer an almost undetectable way to carry out sex selection, without resorting to second-trimester abortion. The technology of sex determination has also undergone constant progress since the introduction of amniocentesis and ultrasound.

One of the latest products, of particular relevance to the Indian experience, is "foetal DNA testing". As the blood of the pregnant mother is known to contain the DNA of her baby after six weeks of gestation, a sample of this blood can be tested to identify the sex of the embryo. The test is reported to be 95 per cent accurate and costs less than US$ 300.

The potential of this technique for Indian users is enormous, especially given that testing can be done from a distance: simply send a sample by mail, and lab results are available a few days later through the Internet. (Interestingly, one British company marketing such a product offers worldwide shipping, except for India and China.) Compared to classic scans, this method offers fast and early results with satisfactory reliability. Since the sex of the embryo can subsequently be determined about two months earlier than by ultrasound, this method offers to shorten the gestation period for aborting women. It may also prove more difficult to detect and monitor.

Knowledge and Accessibility

Knowledge

The availability of sex-selection methods is first mediated by awareness of their existence. Traditional methods had long been in place in India, and were therefore well known in certain communities, with local specialists responsible for preserving the most sophisticated methods (such abortion-inducing plants or ways to dispose of infants). New methods, such as sex-selective abortions, were unknown to most of India's population thirty years ago. Ever since, however, they have spread through multiple channels, ranging from interpersonal exchanges among users to aggressive publicity by suppliers. (Small clinics are said to have played a decisive role in accelerating awareness among potential users by advertising the "benefits" of sex-selective abortions with such famous slogans as "Better a thousand rupees now than a lakh in twenty years", meaning that it is better to pay a small amount today for a sex-selective abortion than a larger amount later for your daughter's dowry.)

Because of the proximity of both ingredients of sex-selective abortions–sex identification and pregnancy termination–to family planning and reproductive-health efforts, these two procedures separately benefited from wide publicity, either as a component of modern pre-natal care or as part of fertility-control methods. Amniocentesis and, later, ultrasound received wide publicity as modern instruments for the monitoring of the foetus, and to avoid birth defects. Initially, they were made available to pregnant mothers at a limited cost in well-equipped health centres. In many parts of India, recourse to multiple ultrasound examinations by expectant mothers is still extremely common, though rarely as an instrument to decide the fate of a pregnancy. Surveys have shown that knowledge of modern sex-selection instruments is today widespread, and that their diffusion most likely followed hierarchical channels, spreading from large cities to smaller towns to villages, and from more affluent groups towards the lower strata of local society.

Clinics

As pre-natal care was incorporated into India's reproductive-health efforts during this period, it received wide publicity as an essential tool to monitor the growth of the foetus. While sex determination was initially available through local government facilities, a change in health policy in the 1980s to regulate sex determination stimulated the growth of private-sector sex-selection services. Compared to government institutions, the private health sector offered services that were widespread, numerous and in several ways of better quality, even if less affordable. To many patients, the wide distribution of clinics around the country meant that the necessary equipment to perform sex determination was available in almost all localities (such as market towns frequently visited by villagers).

While considered expensive at the beginning, scanning later benefited from rapidly decreasing costs, largely fuelled by competition as the private health sector developed. Ultrasound is today a relatively easy technique to implement. It does not require a highly trained staff or extra operational expenditure. A machine costs around ₹500,000 and individual ultrasound test cost ₹300-1000. After the amendment of the PC & PNDT (Pre-conception and Pre-natal Diagnostic Techniques) Act in 2003, the total number of registered units two years later was 26,954.

These units were not evenly distributed throughout the country (Delhi had more than Madhya Pradesh, Bihar and Jharkhand put together), and were more numerous in the Southern states, even though sex selection in these areas is almost negligible. The intra-regional picture may be different, as a detailed analysis conducted in Maharashtra has shown registered clinics to be concentrated in districts with high sex ratios. Close examination of the registration data has indicated many discrepancies, however: registered owners with no qualification to operate the ultrasound machine, individual doctors associated with a large number of units, mobile units likely to escape registration, possible under-reporting of customers, etc.

Providers

Enterprising doctors and clinic managers have played an active role in the diffusion of sexselection technology, along with health workers who have publicized the services. Providers acted mostly as advisers to women who wanted to avoid births, while the fact that, in many cases, the births to be avoided happened to be female births was considered irrelevant, at least initially. Familiar with both technologies and their practicalities, health workers and doctors at various levels were thus the first channels for quality information on the feasibility of sex-selective abortions. Today, physicians are largely conscious of the potential perverse effects of this technology, and are opposed to sex selection and its ethical implications.

As early as 1986, the Federation of Obstetric and Gynaecological Societies of India passed a resolution against pre-natal sex determination and sexselective abortions. Since then, many medical practitioners have joined campaigns against the misuse of these technologies, with the support of professional associations. In 2006, the Indian Medical Association took a firm stand against sex selection, and intends to collaborate fully with the implementation of the PC & PNDT Act.

Doctors have, however, been put in a difficult position due to the activities of a small number among them–those who became rich by performing illegal sex diagnoses or sex-selective abortions. Initially, during surveys in the 1980s, many doctors freely acknowledged their role in offering sexselection services; ever since then, however, they have been more careful in their public declarations.

It should also be noted that it is the medical community that often voices the most favourable comments regarding sex selection, including criticism over the legal provisions of the PC & PNDT Act. In particular, some doctors have stressed that sex selection, despite being condemnable, exists only in response to latent demands from women and their families, and therefore is merely fulfilling a need. Many other arguments have also been advanced in favour of sex selection: the freedom and autonomy of patients to decide upon such procedures for themselves, the family-planning aspect of avoiding unwanted births through abortion, deterrence vis-à-vis infanticide, humanitarian attempts to "relieve" women and girl children of their social and economic burdens, etc.

Legislation

Legislation is now a central part of the supply framework for sex selection in India, and as suggested, describe it in a separate section of this document. The major change related to supply in recent years actually relates to the effect of successive legislations, geared towards preventing the misuse of ultrasound technology to detect the sex of a foetus; and, to a far lesser extent, to the stricter implementation of existing criminal laws against infanticide in some areas.

In the eyes of potential users of sex-selection methods, law enforcement has meant increasing difficulties in getting access to new technology and providers, as well as increased monitoring of their equipment and activities. As a result, access to these facilities has become more difficult of late, as well as more expensive. Many providers have been obliged to stop providing information on a foetus's sex to new customers, while illegal abortions are increasingly conducted by untrained and unregistered practitioners, with serious potential health consequences for women.

WILLING

Understanding the rationale behind sex selection is no doubt key to deciphering the dynamics of sex ratio in India. In this section, as suggested, examine whether sex selection is socially acceptable, and why the birth of a son should be perceived as being more advantageous than that of a girl. As suggested, review various domains, oscillating between narrow economic reasoning and a more comprehensive perspective encompassing non-material motives.

Social Acceptability of Sex Selection

As already noted, sex selection needs to be acceptable and conceivable in both principle and procedure. There are very few known philosophical or religious principles that bar individuals or groups in India from envisaging a deliberate choice in the sex composition of their offspring. Some limited sections of the population may be opposed to sex discrimination on a larger plane, but when confronted with individual choices and facing certain constraints, general principles of gender equity may carry little weight. Another factor related to the legitimacy of sex selection may also be the acceptability of using rational reasoning to make a decision about one's offspring. To a large extent, rapid fertility decline itself has shown that people have accepted the principle of controlled fertility, and it may therefore logically follow that manipulating the "contents" of one's fertility is part of this fundamental behavioural change.

A more significant dimension relates to the actual methods used, such as the difference between infanticide and abortion: the latter option is far less repugnant to most Indians, even though in some isolated villages or communities, sex-selective infanticide has been condoned in the relatively recent past. While perceived as progress in moral terms, abortion still remains a very sensitive matter for many mothers. It often goes unreported in surveys, and it is usually carried out on the sly. In some specific religious communities–such as among Christians and Muslims–abortion is condemned, and sex ratios are at near-normal levels.

Economic Rationale

A common explanation for gender discrimination usually boils down to the fact that girls constitute a source of impoverishment for their family. It is therefore appealing to attempt a costbenefit analysis, in order to examine specific "costs" related to girls, as well as "benefits" accruing from boys. It is important to emphasize at the outset that this overview is unavoidably based on "stylized" facts, which may not always fit nicely with the anthropological diversity of India, where marriage and kinship systems are extremely heterogeneous. Readers familiar with this diversity will therefore have to endure what may appear to be generalizations concealing significant exceptions or anomalies.

Cost Factors

According to many Indian parents, raising a girl entails extra costs related to protective efforts extended especially to daughters. Girls are perceived to be particularly vulnerable, as family honour seems, at times, to rest exclusively on women's behaviour, rather than on men's. But apart from this aspect, raising daughters cannot be said to be more expensive than raising sons, especially when they receive care and education of inferior quality compared to their brothers. As such, it is only with reference to costs arising during or after their marriage that daughters appear to be more "expensive" than sons.

In addition, though the "investment" in daughters is essentially the same as sons before marriage, this money is subsequently considered wasted due to the "patrilocal" nature of marriage, meaning that married couples in India generally live near the husband's family, rather than the wife's. Marriage and related expenditures constitute a large category of costs. This includes several sub-categories, such as wedding expenses borne by the bride's family, customary gifts to the groom's side, and especially dowry (paid to the groom's family), or even post-marriage expenses (additional dowry demands, support at time of first pregnancy, etc.).

Dowry encompasses cash, gold and other jewellery, and additional durables, and it constitutes the major bulk of marriage expenses, often exceeding several years' of household income. While the debate on the nature of dowry is still unresolved, it is safe to say that it is more likely to relate to an actual "groom purchase"–through which the bride's family gets the most "suitable" boy–than to a pre-mortem bequest supposed to compensate for the daughters' exclusion from inheritance rights. Indeed, it has been observed that a dowry's amount is more proportional to the "quality" of the groom and his family–education, background, income, etc.–than to the potential share for the bride herself in the family assets.

High dowry will ensure a proper marriage into the best possible family–hypergamy being a tacit norm–and ensures additional prestige and reputation to the bride's family. It is important to stress that the very low status customarily assigned to unmarried daughters in India usually prevents them from opting out of the system by remaining single. Dowry arrangements have long been common among higher-status groups in North India, but since Independence such arrangements have recorded a formidable spread towards both lower castes and South India.

There are today very few communities in which dowry has not been introduced. Another contemporary feature of the dowry system relates to its apparent unending inflation, fuelled by the combined effect of enhanced competition for suitable grooms, growing economic heterogeneity within endogamous caste groups, affluence in time of rapid economic growth and increasing materialism. The resource flow is almost the opposite in the case of boys, as the groom's family will directly receive a large part of the dowry from the bride's family. For that reason, raising and educating boys seem highly profitable, whereas girls could be seen to mean further expenses.

A traditional nickname for a woman within her family is paraya dhan, which means "somebody else's property". Hence, an oftheard saying has it that raising a daughter is like watering your neighbour's garden. Indeed, the traditional Hindu ideal of "giving away" one's daughters (kanyadana) has become economic nonsense. In rural settings, rich peasants–among whom women generally enjoy no secure rights over family land, as daughters or as widows–may have to part with some of their fields in order to cover dowry expenditures. But among the lower classes, the picture is slightly different, owing to the absence of transmissible assets (such as land or jewellery). As such, the women's labour is considered a more decisive contribution to the prosperity of the household. While dowry has been introduced into many poor communities, such as the landless, the amounts transacted have remained moderate, including for poor families.

Economic Support and Other Benefits

In settings characterized by joint family arrangements, resources are usually pooled between parents and children. This is the case for a large part of the dowry transfer, which may not directly reach the newly wed couple. But the later income of married children will also benefit their parents, as is the case of rural households in which sons work on family land or business. Joint family cohabitation also means that parents can enjoy constant financial and emotional support from their sons' families, whereas married daughters are not supposed to contribute to their parents' expenses after marriage.

This is also true for married sons who are not living with their parents, as they are expected to contribute to their parents' well being until the end of their lives. In a country where pension benefits and social security are almost entirely absent, long-time support extended by sons is a major source of security for ageing parents. But this may not be true to the same degree everywhere in India, as some communities or social categories have a more balanced and less patrilineal family structure.

Symbols and Tradition

A comprehensive cost-benefit analysis of children distinguished by sex also needs to be extended to non-financial domains. For instance, sons living in the vicinity represent a source of protection and affection for their parents. In many marriage systems, daughters are supposed to live away from their parents, and therefore have limited interaction with them after marriage.

There are many other more-symbolic advantages in having sons. First of all, as in any patrilineal society, sons are vital to continue the family lineage (gotra), and often the family activities. Since daughters are usually excluded from an equal share of the inheritance, surviving boys are assured to inherit their parents' property, and will carry on the family name.

In fact, in the most common exogamous system in India (in which grooms marry same-caste brides, but from different lineages and localities), women join the gotra of their husband at marriage, thereby losing membership in their original lineage. Sons are subsequently the only legitimate descendants in this patriarchal system, as their married sisters belong to another lineage altogether. One of the most publicized roles for Hindu sons is also to perform the requisite rituals upon the death of their father (such as lighting the funeral fire), a task from which women are customarily excluded.

The prominent role of sons within the patrilineal system has, of course, added prestige to their status, and is a common source of pride for parents. On the other hand, sonless parents may feel permanent anguish in the face of their family's and community's reaction. But this social pressure is to a large extent merely an echo of the social and economic disadvantages experienced by girl-only families in patriarchal societies.

Many dimensions covered in this section relate to status symbols and to purely economic advantages. For that reason, it is fair to say that high-ranking communities (typically high castes among Hindus) and high-income groups (typically the landed peasantry or urban middle classes) will be especially responsive to demands related to ritual, reputation and financial exchange. Lower-status or lower-income groups, such as backward castes or tribal populations, are therefore in a different position, and son preference in these communities is usually less acute than in the rest of society. But the powerful top-down mechanisms at work in contemporary India mean that many high-caste or urban customs are being "borrowed" by other classes and communities, in a bid to improve their overall social status.

LIMITATIONS OF THE UTILITARIAN FRAMEWORK

Limitations of the Utilitarian Framework Arguments in favour of a family having boys rather than girls seem to stem logically from the previous analyses, as investment in sons generally appears to offer more "returns" to families within a kinship system characterized by dowry and patriarchy. It is only among deprived groups that the patrilineal norms have less economic implications, due to households' limited assets and the proportionally larger contribution of women's work to the domestic economy. This also tallies with variations observed in child sex ratio across social categories, and it would therefore appear that the new technologies available have simply met the "latent demand" for sex selection. Nonetheless, it is essential to remember that the rules of the economic game in any society are only partly economic. Profit maximization, for instance, is subject to many other constraints, such as government intervention and social norms. These latter processes are shaped by historical developments (or "path dependency"), and rarely conform to a strictly economic rationale. This may in part explain why infanticide could never become a common birth-control method.

Norms such as those regulating the marriage system clearly influence bargaining positions in a way that is not strictly economic, and act as constraints to a strict socio-economic laissez-faire system. To a large extent, they represent the legacy of a different period and society, rather than being a reflection of current economic necessities. Moreover, normative systems change in ways that are difficult to predict. At times, they may conform more closely to current economic pressures; but changes in the value systems also take place that are likely to undermine the economic rationale of old behaviours.

POLICY RESPONSES AND FUTURE PROSPECTS

To a large extent, the increase in the proportion of males to females in India appears to have been a spontaneous process. It corresponds to the logical consequence of widespread demand for sons in many communities, as well as the appearance of sex-selection technology. Left on its own, the Indian demographic make-up in naturally more male than female.

It is therefore likely to result in skewed SRBs for a long time, before other factors reverse its course towards higher proportions of men in each age group. But apart from the combined effects of longstanding son preference and free markets (exemplified by the buoyant private health sector in India) that are at the base of rising SRBs in the country, there are many other actors in Indian society that might also impact on gender differentials, now and in the future.

In this section, as suggested, examine the role of the state and other organizations in light of the important sex-selection-related changes that have taken place in India, particularly after the publication of the 2001 census results. As suggested, also review structural factors and social mechanisms that can influence future prospects for sex-ratio stabilization or further degradation.

LEGAL RESPONSE

Sex selection in India does not take place in a legal vacuum. In fact, just a few years after the introduction of the new ultrasound and amniocentesis technologies, in 1983 the Indian Parliament banned the practice of sex determination in all public institutions. In 1988, a pioneer law was passed in Maharashtra to prevent sex determination, following pressure from local activists. But the prime legislation at the all-India level remains the Pre-Natal Diagnostic Techniques (Regulation and Prevention of Misuse) Act, the PNDT Act, passed in 1994.

The Law Against Sex Selection

The PNDT Act prohibited doctors and clinics from using pre-natal diagnostic techniques, such as scans, to determine the sex of a foetus. First offenders faced a penalty of up to three years of imprisonment and a fine of ₹10,000 (US$ 230), and repeat offenders risked a five-year imprisonment and a ₹50,000 fine. The act also prohibited any advertising for diagnosis facilities. Another provision of the law established the presumption that women were compelled to perform sex determination by their husband or another relative, who could in turn be similarly subjected to a threeyear imprisonment and a fine of ₹10,000. Until 2003, however, the law was largely ignored by private providers and families. In fact, the country's SRB recorded a rapid increase during this period, due to the large number of sex-selective abortions.

The context changed with the publication of the 2001 census results, which brought starkly to light the country's deteriorating sex-ratio levels. Two years earlier, a public-interest litigation had also been filed by activists and NGOs, questioning the failure of the 1994 law. The Act was subsequently amended in 2003, and renamed the Pre-Conception and Pre-Natal Diagnostic Techniques (Prohibition of Sex Selection) Act, the PC & PNDT Act, in order to include pre-implantation techniques. But it also attempted to strengthen the control of scan providers, by requiring registration and detailed records of scans provided to pregnant women. The law was unsuccessfully challenged in 2005, and further amendments to the PC & PNDT Act are now in the offing.

The amended law bans sex selection before and after conception, and further regulates the use of pre-natal diagnostic techniques for strictly medical purposes. In particular, the law restricts the use of diagnostic techniques to registered institutions and operators, which have to maintain detailed records. It also expressly prohibits persons conducting pre-natal diagnostic procedures from communicating the sex of the foetus by "words, signs, or in any other manner", while also banning the advertisement of such techniques. "District Appropriate Authorities" provide registration for such units, and are in charge of inspection and investigation, as well as the penalizing of defaulters, with quasijudicial power. In addition, the National Inspection and Monitoring Committee assesses the ground realities through field visits, and provides its reports to the concerned state authorities and the Health Ministry at the Centre.

Implementation and Results

Surveys conducted on the implementation of the law have thus far yielded mixed results. The legislation has received wide publicity, both at national and regional levels, especially in areas where sex selection was thought to be widespread. Following the amendment of the law, there has been a formidable increase in the number of registered bodies (clinics, genetic centres, etc.). Many public departments and civil-society organizations have also seized upon the provisions of the law in order to push for stronger implementation. At the same time, many difficulties and loopholes in the provisions of the Act have been identified.

We can only emphasize a few of them here, but they include: lack of resources to carry out inspection and monitoring, lack of corresponding qualified staff, poor performance of advisory committees at various levels, political pressures brought on the "Appropriate Authorities", conflict of interest for doctors charged with the prosecution of other doctors, insufficient understanding of the law and procedural errors, and, in some cases, victimization of pregnant women.

Doctors have also already complained of harassment, with the Indian Radiological and Imaging Association having created a website to document such cases. Indian officials acknowledge that the law is not yet being enforced throughout the country. By 2006, almost 400 doctors had been prosecuted under the Act, most of them for failing to register their facilities or not keeping proper records. About 11 per cent of these cases referred to the actual communication of the foetus. But very few doctors have actually been convicted–the first jail term was awarded only in March 2006, in Haryana.

Enforcing PNDT

So far, governments at various levels in India do not have much political incentive to launch large-scale operations to implement the PC & PNDT Act. As our analysis of sex-ratio variations within India indicated, regional circumstances vary greatly within the country, and require different solutions. Effective strategies should therefore be implemented by state or local authorities, as disparities in discriminatory behaviour between, for instance, rural Kerala and urban Haryana preclude any common strategy. On a larger plane, there are many reasons why governments are reluctant to invest many resources in the implementation of the Act.

Sex-ratio deterioration is not yet perceived as a catastrophe for which strong government intervention is required. The short-term view of the current situation, which overlooks its harmful consequences for gender equity and future demographic equilibrium, is widely shared among politicians and the public, many of whom may not anticipate the after-effects of sustained demographic imbalances.

Sex-selection is typically a crime with neither a known victim nor a complainant. As a result, vigourous enforcement of the Act may at times be perceived as mere bureaucratic harassment of health providers or of pregnant mothers. Moreover, vigourous intervention by the government into families' demographic strategies has long been considered an anathema in democratic

India. A more structural factor relates to the obviously topdown diffusion of new discriminatory behaviour: offenders (doctors, middle-class families, etc.) are more likely to belong to the privileged classes that are politically more problematic to target.

The PC & PNDT Act provides formidable tools to act against the misuse of technology, but also requires a pronounced effort from local authorities to boost the overworked bureaucratic machinery, and to coordinate operations with the medical community and other civil-society organizations. It is therefore not surprising that the levels of success and zeal have varied greatly across regions. Many state or district officials and other local organizations have indeed chosen to use the provisions of the Act to sustain independent and original initiatives to fight sex selection head-on.

But what is most encouraging is that many individuals within the government apparatus have also been able to use the provisions of the Act to launch vigourous drives towards stronger law enforcement. As suggested, now review two such successful experiences. An impressive initiative was launched in Hyderabad in 2004 by the District Collector, based on the application of the PC & PNDT Act. This started with a sensitization campaign aimed at implementers, followed by an informational workshop for all owners of ultrasound centres in the district.

Forms submitted by operators were then examined, with a vast majority among them being found deficient, mostly for lack of proper information on owners, operators, patients, etc. Following further communication with these 389 registered centres, 91 saw their registration suspended, 74 scan machines were seized, and prosecution was launched against three suppliers and 18 centres. The District Collector reported a sizeable downward impact on the SRB following the strict implementation of the PC & PNDT Act.

Another experiment took place in Punjab's Nawanshahr District, an area characterized by one of the highest child sex ratios recorded in the country in 2001. A massive awareness drive was launched there in 2005, with the active cooperation of local NGOs, which especially targeted the area's ultrasound centres. Local authorities also launched a programme offering a computerized record of pregnancies in the district. Records (including telephone numbers, for follow-ups with mothers) were monitored, and all cases of abortion investigated; teachers and girl students were called upon to act as "ambassadors of the drive against female foeticide".

Unconventional measures, such as "mourning the death of unborn girls" in front of the errant parents and clinics, were also adopted. based on birth data will show their actual impact. The programme caught the attention of the media, government institutions and NGOs elsewhere in India, with calls to reproduce the "Nawanshahr Model". One of the sessions of this initiative relates to the combination of enforcement and awareness strategies: monitoring (based on pregnancy records) is part of a larger drive to modernize and disseminate records as part of "e-governance", while advocacy and awareness also include the special targeting of offending clinics and households. Many NGOs have also initially launched sting operations, such as luring doctors into revealing the sex of a foetus. While often receiving wide publicity, these initiatives are proving somewhat less effective for legal reasons, as proof of criminal wrongdoing is often difficult to establish. But they nonetheless have had an unmistakeable impact on clinic operators in some areas, who have come to realise that the Act can be implemented by non-official entities.

ADVOCACY EFFORTS AND GENDER-EQUITY INITIATIVES

The PC & PNDT Act aims to disrupt the supply side of India's discriminatory sex-selection regime, the dimension that is largely responsible for the brutal deterioration recorded in sex-ratio levels since 1980. But irrespective of the law's effectiveness, many questions are left regarding the effect of rampant son preference and undervaluation of girls. Other initiatives in India have, however, focused on this aspect of the sex-ratio predicament, with some even jointly addressing the supply-and demand-side dimensions.

Gender Equity

Demand-orientated policies are still not very common in India's attempts to crack down on sex-selection. There are, however, several important innovations in the related legal apparatus that are worth mentioning. For instance, the formidable change introduced in the Hindu Succession (Amendment) Act of 2005, hailed as a milestone in reversing intra-family gender inequality, in the future may lead to positive changes in women's status.

The deletion of a specific section of the original Hindu Succession law, from 1956, is likely to affect inheritance rules that were highly gender-unequal in rural Northwest India. One of the consequences of this move will hopefully be to economically empower women, and to counteract the ingrained paraya dhan attitude of treating daughters as a transferable asset–and, consequently, sons as the only financial providers.

Another landmark legislation is a law passed in 2006 that seeks to protect women from domestic violence, and bans harassment under the guise of dowry demands. Despite the fact that the scale of violence towards women in India has been extensively documented in recent surveys, there had been no specific legislation to deal with such abuse at home. While conscious of the fact that the law may not change mindsets, many feminist NGOs welcomed the new legislation. Such legal changes may have beneficial consequences for the practice of dowry, against which similar legislation from 1961 has had little impact.

For instance, if women can become equal inheritors, parents may not have to depend only on their sons for security in their old age, because daughters too will be empowered to take care of them. Another strategy of demand-side measures aims to counterbalance the economics of gender inequality, by offering advantages such as cash or pension benefits to girl-only families, or by setting up positive-discrimination measures for daughters.

Several state governments (*e.g.*, Tamil Nadu, Haryana, Andhra Pradesh) have introduced such steps, which often comprise cash or education incentives to families with only girls. However, while attractive on document, these propositions are both expensive and difficult to implement, especially when potential offenders are richer than the rest of population.

Governments should ideally try to tax male births, in order to raise compensation funds for girl-only families and women's upliftment. But such policies would not only be socially unacceptable, but also unfair to the poorest groups.

Advocacy and the Press

Skewed sex ratios constitute a typical "externality", or harmful consequence of opportunistic behaviour, for which there are almost no identifiable victims. It is therefore crucial to reverse the usual attitude, according to which abortions of female foetuses are considered legitimate, as they pertain to rational household decisions that only belong in the private sphere.

Many dimensions of gender discrimination and violence have long been protected from public scrutiny by the sanctity of the family domain, and have for that reason often remained ignored or underplayed. Shaping public opinion towards a greater awareness of the meaning and consequences of sex selection is one of the main objectives of concerted campaigns in newspapers and through NGOs.

Sex Ratio and the Press

There is no question that the press plays an increasingly important role in demographic matters, by relating statistical phenomena to the public's behaviour. The press in India has closely followed actions undertaken as a response to the sex-ratio crisis, and a large number of articles have been published. Initially, the census data of 2001 provided the core of their analysis. Disaggregated findings pertaining to individual cities or districts allowed a careful identification of the worst affected areas. But the interest in sex-ratio matters continued, and the press has subsequently reported widely on the experiments launched at local levels.

Much information and monitoring initiatives received wide coverage thanks in part to the familiarity gained by journalists on sex-ratio issues. While also stressing the role of individuals (women, doctors, bureaucrats, etc.), the press tends to utilize census data in order to place collective blame on entire localities.

The press has also reported in detail some of the most visible aspects of the enforcement of the PC & PNDT Act, such as decoy operations conducted by NGOs or the prosecution of medical doctors. Scandals related to abortions (such as the frequent discovery of foetuses dumped in the open after possible illegal abortions) have also made headlines. The slower and more systematic implementation of the Act, and the ensuing monitoring of the activities of ultrasound clinics, have understandably not received the same coverage. Several articles have also covered issues related to female deficit and its consequences–especially on marriage patterns–as observed in areas where sex-selection practices were introduced during the 1980s.

For instance, journalists now are regularly writing about brides being imported to Punjab and Haryana. But much of this reporting is too often incorrectly associated with issues of women trafficking, which is only a secondary aspect of the emerging crisis. In fact, women's geographical mobility, through marriage or otherwise, remains widely perceived as a threat to patriarchal order, and is often mechanically related to trafficking or prostitution. However, the stress on the new generation of young male adults in regions experiencing a scarcity of marriageable women is an entirely new phenomenon, and the press coverage (along with research by social scientists) will gradually help to unravel the exact ramifications of local male surpluses.

Advocacy

Numerous advocacy programmes have also been conducted at various scales focusing on the issue of pre-natal sex selection. These activities are carried out mostly by civil-society organizations and public bodies, often with support from international agencies such as UNFPA, and target a wide variety of groups, such as women, the youth, the media, medical associations, NGOs, elected representatives, government administration, etc. Religious organizations have also been enlisted in some campaigns.

In going through the various projects that have been launched by NGOs, we have come to realise the wide gamut of stakeholders that have been taken on board in these awareness campaigns, as well as the large number of communication strategies (through local media, schools and colleges, workshops, street theatre, health infrastructure, local panchayats, etc.) devised to reach out to them. While campaigns were often aimed primarily at potential offenders, such as young women and medical personnel, fighting sex-selection in fact requires simultaneously addressing several constituencies beyond individual mothers and health providers.

This process needs also to integrate the central themes carried by these campaigns, two of which were directed towards gender equity and the crime against women manifested in sex selection on one hand, and on the PNDT law and its implementation on the other. The first option focuses on rights and the unequal status of girls. The design of such campaigns looks primarily at the positive aspects of having a girl child, and at examples of successful girls and women. It is also based in part on wider dissemination of information contained in laws that provide for equal opportunities to girls and women. The second message is driven more by fear and shame, by emphasizing the risks associated with skirting the law, from health hazards related to unsafe abortions to fines and even jail terms faced by offenders.

There is also a need to educate the public on the negative effects of the widening demographic gap between girls and boys born in India. These are somewhat divergent orientations, which seem almost impossible to reconcile within a single advocacy platform. As a result, advocacy actions seem to be segmented and lacking in coordination. While there is undoubtedly a pressing need to amplify the current sensitization and advocacy campaigns, the many initiatives are also in great need of streamlining, in order to facilitate the synergy between the main actors.

MONITORING CHANGE

Local statistics have also appeared in the press lately, with an eye to publicizing success stories. These often originate from local authorities who are eager to advertise progress in sex-ratio levels. But these data are often ambiguous or incomplete, as they are based on unreliable sources, with samples that are often too small to allow for significant interpretation. In fact, when more reliable data are made available, the emerging picture is only moderately encouraging, as no real improvement in SRB seems to be discernible. Figure displays the evolution of SRB as measured for Delhi, where the quality of civil registration is among the best in the country.

Although these data, based on civil-registration records, are not yet perfect, they probably do not demonstrate any clear downward trend since 2000, as the SRB remains above 120. When available for other Western or Northwestern regions, such as Gujarat, no clear improvement is discernible thus far. But these statistics nevertheless point to a stabilization of SRB values in these areas. It would be crucial to monitor SRB evaluation in less-affected areas, such as Orissa or Western Uttar Pradesh, where a rapid increase had already been observed before 2001.

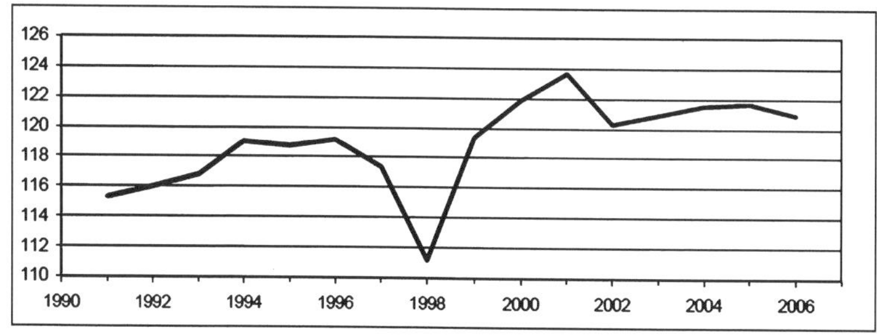

Fig. Sex Ratio at Birth in Delhi, Civil-registration Data, 1991-2006

In fact, throughout this report we have mentioned our imperfect database, and to some extent, we are indeed groping in the dark regarding SRB trends. The last census, in 2001, managed to use data on the child population to send a dramatic picture of sex-ratio degradation in India, but our knowledge has barely improved since then. We are thus unable to monitor adequately the SRB in India since 2001, other than in a few places.

At the same time, better birth registration has been encouraged from various sources, including for urban residents who often need birth certificates for school registration. Several municipalities and state statistical offices, such as that of Delhi, have improved their machinery in order to generate and disseminate more social and economic information on their constituencies. Civil registration is, in fact, a rather straightforward source when it comes to estimating SRB, but there still seems to be no coordinated effort to systematically collate and publish recent available data.

There is no question that sex-ratio data from the 2001 census did provide strong materials for press campaigns and many other advocacy initiatives. These brought wide publicity to affected areas, which often contributed to the public mobilization necessary to eventually reverse trends. Publicity and state-sponsored statistical monitoring has indeed contributed in a significant way to practically banishing female infanticide from Tamil Nadu's countryside. Transparency in matters of demographic change greatly contributes to faster reaction from social and government institutions. In spite of current statistical limitations, the emergence of sex-ratio statistics in the public debate in many Indian states is bound to stay, and to enlarge the discussion, by providing stakeholders new materials with which to monitor policy initiatives and their outcomes.

AGGRAVATION OR IMPROVEMENT IN THE FUTURE

While the projection exercise conducted earlier in this document provides a rather theoretical overview of things to come, it may be useful to show how some of the intervening factors are likely to influence the circumstances of sex selection in India. As suggested, first consider two dimensions–what can be referred to as "intensification" and "diffusion"–and then examine some of the structural factors likely to influence the course of India's sex ratio in the future.

Intensification

"Intensification" refers to households practising more rigorous sex selection. This may in particular concern the first pregnancy, which so far we have seen to be weakly influenced by sexselection strategies implemented by parents. However, a more elaborate discriminatory system may result from lower fertility, when a larger proportion of the population opts for a single child. In fact, if just a few parents were to start targeting the first birth, SRB could easily reach values beyond 130.

Vertical Diffusion

A source of further deterioration of the sex-ratio situation could arise from the "diffusion" of discriminatory regions and social groups–a mechanism that could cause the situation to grow into real epidemic proportions. Diffusion processes can be distinguished as either "vertical" or "horizontal". Vertical diffusion refers to the local spread of a practice from forerunner groups to other, previously unaffected groups. The potential of such a process is tremendous in the Indian context for several reasons. First, we have already noted that socio-economic status is positively associated with sex ratio, which means that the privileged sections of society follow a more discriminatory regime than do others.

Secondly, we have many instances of demographic change spreading in a top-down fashion within local communities, as the upper classes (or castes, etc.) act initially as pioneers in the adoption of new attitudes and behaviours. Fertility decline has been a clear illustration of such top-down diffusion. Thirdly, the so-called "sanskritization" processes of social change, in which lower-status groups imitate the behaviour of the elite, are common in India. Lastly, the extent of the changes observed in Northwest India since 1991 clearly demonstrates that all communities and economic classes are now involved in this process, and not just specific privileged sections. Underprivileged groups, which had long refrained from any active discriminatory practices towards women, may thus start emulating higher-status groups.

Horizontal Diffusion

What has been said previously can to a large extent be repeated about horizontal diffusion–*i.e.*, the propagation of innovative behaviour towards new localities and areas. Demographic behaviour is, on the whole, extremely clustered in India, and examples abound of pockets or entire regions with specific social or demographic features (migration pockets, low-or high-fertility areas, etc.). In times of change, innovation tends to spill over adjacent areas, and the regular spatial distribution of sex ratio in India suggests precisely that modern discrimination has spread from core areas to surrounding zones.

The immediate implication of this observation is that further sex-ratio degradation is likely to be influenced by the geographical position of localities. Already, regions close to Haryana and Punjab, such as Jammu, North Rajasthan, lower Himachal Pradesh or Western Uttar Pradesh, have recorded significant increases in sex ratio. This reinforces the feeling that the scope for geographical progression of imbalanced sex ratio is significant in India.

STRUCTURAL CHANGES, NEGATIVE AND POSITIVE

Many potential factors in the aggravation or improvement of the sex-ratio situation in the country also relate to structural change, such as the forceful economic and social development that has taken place at an accelerated pace since the 1990s. Socio-economic status tends to be associated with more intense discriminatory practices, which means that economic development *per se* may be seen as a factor for further sex-ratio degradation. The same reasoning would also apply to the rapid progress in education, and to the trends towards increased urbanization and suburbanization in India.

Many of the briefly reviewed fundamentals of sex-selection behaviour point in the same direction: conditions are ripe for further rise in sex-ratio values in India. But there are other possible scenarios that are less pessimistic. The economic case of gender discrimination may in fact decrease over time, for a different set of reasons. First of all, norms of all type are not immutable in India, and many have been seen to change in the recent past. Some women have, for instance, recently insisted on lighting the pyre of a parent, a task traditionally reserved for sons.

The growth of human capital among women in India may also, at some point, grant some of them increased autonomy and economic self-reliance, while undermining the foundations of a patriarchal system based on women's submission and exploitation. The joint family system at the basis of the patrilineal system is probably weakening, and improvements in inheritance legislations may undermine it even more. New laws promulgated in India in recent years may prove to have a direct impact on both women's status and dowry in general.

Furthermore, unexpected consequences, such as a possible shortage of brides, may eventually change several factors related to the relative value of girls, starting with dowry and, perhaps, a community's need to stop sex selection for its own sake. There are also many aspects of government interventions that require closer examination. This is especially true for programmes that tend to correct some of the obvious economic bases of gender inequity through cash or other incentives. Increasing the "cost" of sex-selection (through repression and other steps) is obviously a strategy bound to yield results if implemented vigourously. But direct government intervention on the economic side of gender inequity may concern some of the issues reviewed here–the cost of raising a daughter, support for the aged population–and change the terms of this equation by making boys comparatively less "profitable".

LOOKING FORWARD: POSSIBILITIES AND NEEDS

India finds itself today at a crossroad. On the one hand, the overall sex-ratio degradation in the country appears moderate in comparison to the experience of China or South Korea, where SRB has approached values as high as 120. India has also witnessed a real mobilization from civil-society organizations and government agencies, and the legal system has been strengthened to allow for stricter regulations over technology misuse and illegal abortions. But on the other hand, sex-ratio degradation has been concentrated in a few regions of India, and the possibility of wider diffusion to new states is very real. This appears especially worrying as the overall national context is characterized by rapid social and economic development and further fertility decline, factors that could exacerbate the demand for sex selection.

Comprehensive Approach, Two Focuses

The strategy to fight sex selection is still an ambiguous mix of various and, at times, conflicting initiatives. At the moment, there is to be no unifying formula or slogan bringing together all efforts to combat the harmful effects of sex selection. A short message should be devised and directed towards the largest number of current and would-be users, as well as all providers and facilitators of sex selection. There are two main lines of argument against sex selection: one based on elementary gender-equity principles, while the other derives from the threat of future gender imbalances.

Fighting Discrimination

The first option consists in fighting against gender violence or discrimination as expressed by sex selection. Other recent laws on gender-based violence may in fact reinforce the message, and contribute to changing mindsets and attitudes. The current increasing participation of women in processes of social and economic change, if sustained, could also undermine age-old images of women as dependent and home-centred. But combating gender discrimination remains challenging and somewhat at odds with many other aspects of social life, in which gender discrimination is routinely practiced against girls and adult women, while their mobility is severely curtailed.

Moreover, the message against illegal (and therefore unsafe) abortions needs to avoid contradicting the current efforts towards safer pre-natal care and legal abortion facilities. These are not easy tasks. But the idea that sex-selective abortions are a shameful discriminatory act towards girls seems to have left its mark on a broad cross-section of Indian society, and targeting offending groups or localities may be one way to capitalize on the existing Indian "moral economy" against the country's masculinization. There are many cultural environments within India where sex selection remains unthinkable, even in a context of fast social and economic progress.

Publicize Hardships being Experienced

Another line of advocacy follows the more functional argument related to the implications of future demographic disequilibrium, such as increased gender-based violence. The public needs to realise exactly how individual decisions can generate a collective calamity. But it is fair to say that catastrophic predictions may not be convincing for people who today often believe they are witnessing a shortage of males, rather than a surplus. And, in general, parents' investments in their children are based on their own experiences, rather than on speculative considerations such as population forecasts. Therefore, there is probably an urgent need to document in greater detail and publicize more widely the hardships faced by the younger male generations in different parts of India, where past sex-ratio imbalances have already resulted in severe gender imbalances among young adults.

Prioritize Sex Selection Now

Any mechanical transitional scenario, in which an excess masculinity of births corrects itself after a certain time span, seems overly optimistic. While there is no doubt that high SRBs are not demographically sustainable, families may not comprehend the full implications of their choices before the passage of several decades. In fact, the lag between skewed SRBs and their first tangible consequences on the marriage market and family structure is at least 25 years, during which time excess male births are going to significantly distort the age and sex pyramids. There is therefore no reason to be complacent about the current trends; the fight against pre-natal discrimination should be placed at the core of India's gender and demographic agenda.

6

Population Growth: Trends, Projections, Challenges and Opportunities

INTRODUCTION

Human beings evolved under conditions of high mortality due to famines, accidents, illnesses, infections and war and therefore the relatively high fertility rates were essential for species survival. In spite of the relatively high fertility rates it took all the time from evolution of mankind to the middle of the 19th century for the global population to reach one billion. The twentieth century witnessed an unprecedented rapid improvement in health care technologies and access to health care all over the world; as a result there was a steep fall in the mortality and steep increase in longevity. The population realised these changes and took steps to reduce their fertility but the decline in fertility was not so steep. As a result the global population has undergone a fourfold increase in a hundred years and has reached 6 billion.

DEMOGRAPHIC TRANSITION

Demographers refer to these changes from stable population with high fertility and mortality to a new stability in population due to low fertility and mortality patterns as demographic transition. Demographic transition occurs in four phases; of these the first three phases are characterized by population growth. In the first phase there is a fall in death rate and improvement in longevity; this leads to population growth. In the second phase there is a fall in birth rate but fall is less steep than fall in death rates and consequently there is population growth. In the third phase death rates plateau and replacement level of fertility is attained but the population growth continues because of the large size of population in reproductive age group.

The fourth phase is characterized by fall in birth rate to below replacement level and reduction in the proportion of the population in reproductive age group; as a result of these changes population growth ceases and population stabilizes. Experience in some of the developed countries suggest that in some societies even after attainment of stable population there may be a further decline in fertility so that there is a further reduction in the population-so called negative population growth phase of the demographic transition. Different countries in the world have entered the demographic transition at different periods of time; there are also substantial differences in the rate of demographic transition and time taken to achieve population stabilization.

Global Population Scenario			
Population in Billion		**Total Fertility Rate**	
1901	1.4	1969	6.0
1960	3.0	1999	3.0
1987	5.0		
1999	6.0		
Population growth		Population growth Rate	
1989–86 million		1969–2.4%	
1989–78 million		1999–1.8%	
Showing of population growth is due to:			
1. Global decline in fertility 2. Increase in mortality in some regions e.g. HIV related increase in mortality in subsahar as Africa			

GLOBAL POPULATION SCENARIO

In 1901 the world population was 1.6 billion. By 1960, it became 3 billion, and by 1987, 5 billion and in 1999, 6 billion. Currently, one billion people are added every 12-13 years. During the last decade there has been substantial decline in birth rate.

The reasons for decline vary from society to society; urbanization, rising educational attainment, increasing employment among women, lower infant mortality are some major factors responsible for growing desire for smaller families; increasing awareness and improved access to contraception have made it possible for the majority of the couple to achieve the desired family size.

In some countries slowing of the population growth has been due to an increase in mortality (*e.g.* HIV related mortality in sub-saharan Africa). As a result of all these the decline in the global population growth during the nineties is steeper than the earlier predictions.

Currently, the annual increment is about 80 million. It is expected to decrease to about 64 million by 2020-25 and to 33 million by 2045-50; 95% of the growth of population occurs in developing countries. Most demographers believe that the current accelerated decline in population growth will continue for the next few decades and the medium projections of Population Division of United Nations, that the global population will grow to 8.9 billion by 2050 is likely to be achieved.

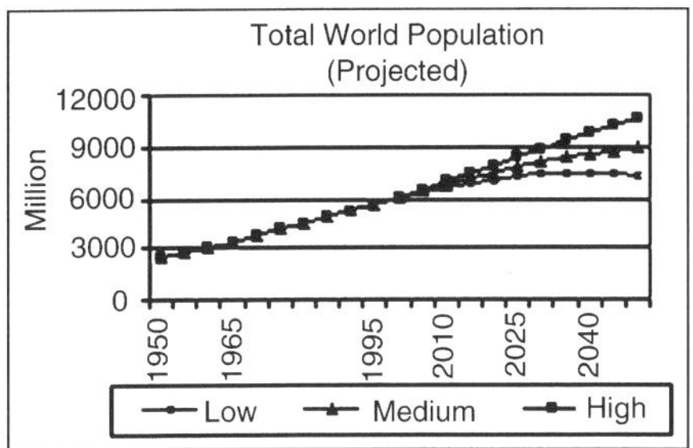

CHANGING AGE STRUCTURE OF THE POPULATION

During demographic transition along with the growth in number there are changes in the population age structure. While the importance of the population growth as a determinant of quality of life is universally understood, the profoundly serious consequences of changing age structure especially if it occurs too rapidly is not understood by many. Population pyramids graphically represent complex changes in age structure of the population so that it can be readily understood and interpreted.

The population pyramids for the global population, developed and developing countries is shown in Figure. Currently nearly half of the global population is below 25 years of age and one sixth are in the age group 15-24. Their choices, efforts and lifestyles will determine not only the population growth but also future improvement in the quality of life in harmony with global ecology.

In developed countries the reproductive age group population is relatively small; their fertility is low and the longevity at birth is high. Population profiles of these countries resemble a cylinder and not a pyramid.These countries have the advantages of having achieved a stable population but have to face the problems of having a relatively small productive workforce to support the large aged population with substantial non-communicable disease burden. Some of the developing countries have undergone a very rapid decline in the birth rates within a short period.

This enabled them to quickly achieve population stabilization but they do face the problems of rapid changes in the age structure and workforce which may be inadequate to meet their manpower requirements. In contrast the population in most of the developing countries (including India) consist of a very large proportion of children and persons in reproductive age. Because of the large reproductive age group (Population momentum) the population will continue to grow even when replacement level of fertility is reached (couples having only two children).

It is imperative that these countries should generate enough employment opportunities for this work force and utilise the human resources and accelerate their economic growth. Planners and policy makers in developing countries like India have to take into account the ongoing demographic changes (number and age structure of the population) so that available human resources are optimally utilised as agents of change and development to achieve improvement in quality of life.

DEMOGRAPHIC TRANSITION IN INDIA

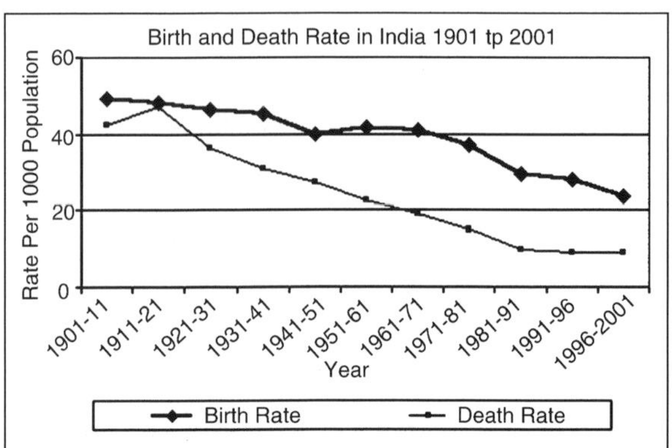

Over the last four decades there has been rapid fall in Crude Death Rate (CDR) from 25.1 in 1951 to 9.8 in 1991 and less steep decline in the Crude Birth Rate (CBR) from 40.8 in 1951 to 29.5 in 1991. The annual exponential population growth rate has been over 2% in the period 1961-90. During the nineties the decline in CBR has been steeper than that in the (CDR) and consequently, the annual population growth rate has fallen below 2%. The rate of decline in population growth is likely to be further accelerated during the next decade. The changes in the population growth rates have been relatively slow, steady and sustained. As a result the country was able to achieve a relatively gradual change in the population numbers and age structure.

The short and long term adverse consequences of too rapid decline in birth rates and change in age structure on the social and economic development were avoided and the country was able to adapt to these changes without massive disruptions of developmental efforts.

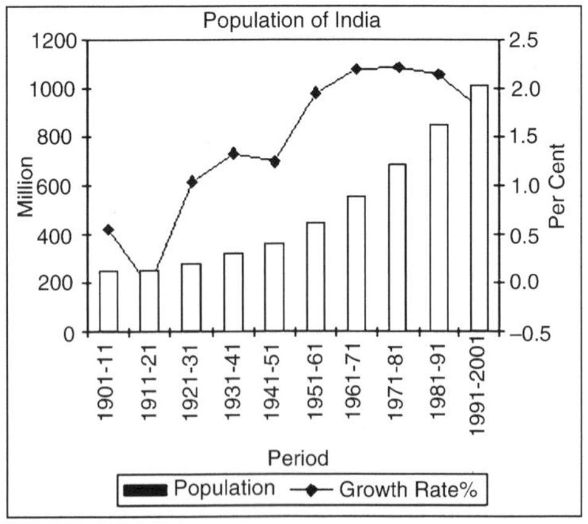

In spite of the uniform national norms set under the 100% Centrally Funded and Centrally Sponsored Scheme (CSS) of Family Welfare, there are substantial differences in the performance between States as assessed by IMR and CBR. Though the decline in CBR and IMR has occurred in all States, the rate of decline is slower in some States. At one end of the spectrum is Kerala with mortality and fertility rates nearly similar to those in some of the developed countries. At the other end, there are four large northern States with high Infant Mortality Rate and Fertility Rates. Though the decline in CBR, IMR and CDR has occurred in all States, the rate of decline was slower in some States like U.P. and Bihar. There are substantial differences in CBR and IMR not only between States but also between the districts in the same state.

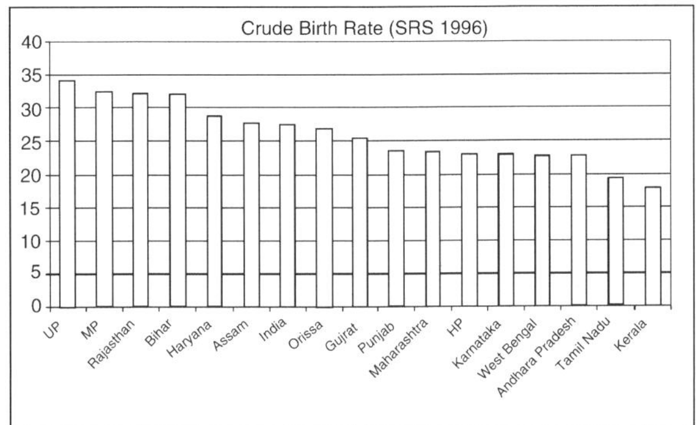

In view of these findings, the NDC Committee on Population recommended that efforts should be made to provide reproductive and child health services at district level and undertake decentralized area-specific micro planning and implementation of appropriate interventions. In response to this recommendation Dept of Family Welfare has abolished the practice of fixing targets for individual contraceptives by the Central Government from April 1996 and had initiated decentralized district based, planning (based on community need assessment), implementation, monitoring and midcourse corrections of FW programme.

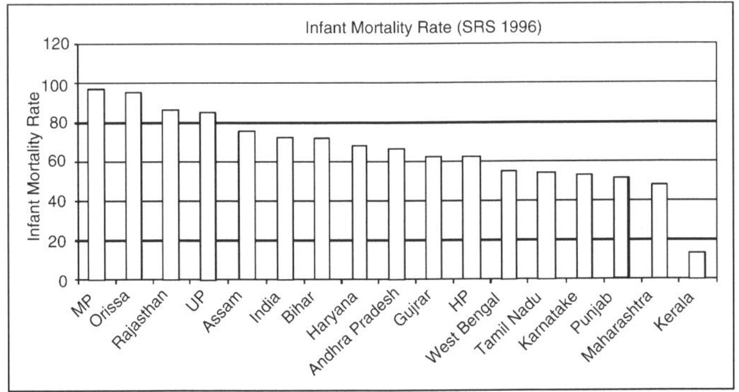

The experience of states with district based planning, implementation and the impact are being closely monitored.

CONSEQUENCES OF POPULATION GROWTH

ENVIRONMENTAL AND ECOLOGICAL CONSEQUENCES

The already densely populated developing countries contribute to over 95% of the population growth and rapid population growth could lead to environmental deterioration. Developed countries are less densely populated and contribute very little to population growth; however, they cause massive ecological damage by the wasteful, unnecessary and unbalanced consumption the consequences of which could adversely affect both the developed and the developing countries. The review on "Promotion of sustainable development: challenges for environmental policies" in the Economic Survey 1998-99 had covered in detail the major environmental problems, and policy options for improvement; the present review will only briefly touch upon some of the important ecological consequences of demographic transition.

In many developing countries continued population growth has resulted in pressure on land, fragmentation of land holding, collapsing fisheries, shrinking forests, rising temperatures, loss of plant and animal species. Global warming due to increasing use of fossil fuels (mainly by the developed countries) could have serious effects on the populous coastal regions in developing countries, their food production and essential water supplies.

The Intergovernmental Panel on Climate Change has projected that, if current greenhouse gas emission trends continue, the mean global surface temperature will rise from 1 to 3.5 degrees Celsius in the next century. The panel's best estimate scenario projects a sea-level rise of 15 to 95 centimeters by 2100. The ecological impact of rising oceans would include increased flooding, coastal erosion, salination of aquifers and coastal crop land and displacement of millions of people living near the coast. Patterns of precipitation are also likely to change, which combined with increased average temperatures, could substantially alter the relative agricultural productivity of different regions.

Greenhouse gas emissions are closely linked to both population growth and development. Slower population growth in developing countries and ecologically sustainable lifestyles in developed countries would make reduction in green house gas emission easier to achieve and provide more time and options for adaptation to climate change. Rapid population growth, developmental activities either to meet the growing population or the growing needs of the population as well as changing lifestyles and consumption patterns pose major challenge to preservation and promotion of ecological balance in India.

Some of the major ecological adverse effects reported in India include:

- Severe pressure on the forests due to both the rate of resource use and the nature of use. The per capita forest biomass in the country is only about 6 tons as against the global average of 82 tons.
- Adverse effect on species diversity:

- Conversion of habitat to some other land use such as agriculture, urban development, forestry operation. Some 70-80% of fresh water marshes and lakes in the gangetic flood plains has been lost in the last 50 years.
- Tropical deforestation and destruction of mangroves for commercial needs and fuel wood. The country's mangrove areas have reduced from 700,000 ha to 453,000 ha in the last 50 years.
- Intense grazing by domestic livestock
- Poaching and illegal harvesting of wildlife.
- Increase in agricultural area, high use of chemical fertilizers pesticides and weedicides; water stagnation, soil erosion, soil salinity and low productivity.
- High level of biomass burning causing large-scale indoor pollution.
- Encroachment on habitat for rail and road construction thereby fragmenting the habitat. Increase in commercial activities such as mining and unsustainable resource extraction.
- Degradation of coastal and other aquatic ecosystems from domestic sewage, pesticides, fertilizers and industrial effluents.
- Over fishing in water bodies and introduction of weeds and exotic species.
- Diversion of water for domestic, industrial and agricultural uses leading to increased river pollution and decrease in self-cleaning properties of rivers.
- Increasing water requirement leading to tapping deeper aquifers which have high content of arsenic or fluoride resulting health problems.
- Disturbance from increased recreational activity and tourism causing pollution of natural ecosystems with wastes left behind by people.

The United Nations Conference on Environment and Development acknowledged population growth, rising income levels, changing technologies, increasing consumption pattern will all have adverse impact on environment. Ensuring that there is no further deterioration depends on choices made by the population about family size, life styles, environmental protection and equity. Availability of appropriate technology and commitment towards ensuring sustainable development is increasing throughout the world.

Because of these, it might be possible to initiate steps to see that the natural carrying capacity of the environment is not damaged beyond recovery and ecological balance is to a large extent maintained. It is imperative that the environmental sustainability of all developmental projects is taken care of by appropriate inputs at the planning, implementation, monitoring and evaluation stages.

URBANIZATION

The proportion of people in developing countries who live in cities has almost doubled since 1960 (from less than 22 per cent to more than 40 per cent), while in more developed regions the urban share has grown from 61 per cent to 76 per cent. Urbanization is projected to continue well into the next century. By 2030, it is expected that nearly 5 billion (61 per cent) of the world's 8.1 billion people will live in cities. India shares this global trend towards urbanisation.

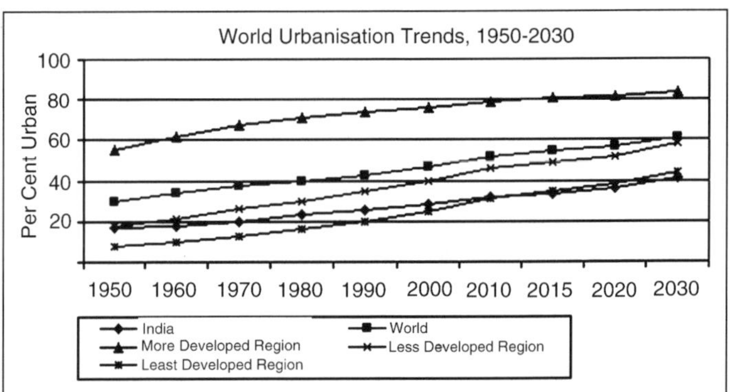

Globally, the number of cities with 10 million or more inhabitants is increasing rapidly, and most of these new "megacities" are in developing regions. In 1960, only New York and Tokyo had more than 10 million people. By 1999, the number of megacities had grown to 17(13 in developing countries). It is projected that there will be 26 megacities by 2015, (18 in Asia; of these five in India); more than 10 per cent of the world's population will live in these cities (1.7% in 1950). India's urban population has doubled from 109 million to 218 million during the last two decades and is estimated to reach 300 million by 2000 AD.

As a consequence cities are facing the problem of expanding urban slums. Like many other demographic changes, urbanization has both positive and negative effects. Cities and towns have become the engines of social change and rapid economic development. Urbanisation is associated with improved access to education, employment, health care; these result in increase in age at marriage, reduction in family size and improvement in health indices.

As people have moved towards and into cities, information has flowed outward. Better communication and transportation now link urban and rural areas both economically and socially creating an urban-rural continuum of communities with improvement in some aspects of lifestyle of both. The ever increasing reach of mass media communicate new ideas, points of reference, and available options are becoming more widely recognized, appreciated and sought.

This phenomenon has affected health care, including reproductive health, in many ways. For instance, radio and television programmes that discuss gender equity, family size preference and family planning options are now reaching formerly isolated rural populations. This can create demand for services for mothers and children, higher contraceptive use, and fewer unwanted pregnancies, smaller healthier families and lead to more rapid population stabilisation. But the rapid growth of urban population also poses some serious challenges.

Urban population growth has outpaced the development of basic minimum services; housing, water supply, sewerage and solid waste disposal are far from adequate; increasing waste generation at home, offices and industries, coupled with poor waste disposal facilities result in rapid environmental deterioration. Increasing automobiles add to air pollution. All these have adverse effect on ecology and health. Poverty persists in urban and peri-urban areas; awareness about the glaring inequities in close urban setting may lead to social unrest.

RURAL POPULATION AND THEIR DEVELOPMENT

Over seventy per cent of India's population still lives in rural areas. There are substantial differences between the states in the proportion of rural and urban population (varying from almost 90 per cent in Assam and Bihar to 61 per cent in Maharashtra). Agriculture is the largest and one of the most important sector of the rural economy and contributes both to economic growth and employment. Its contribution to the Gross Domestic Product has declined over the last five decades but agriculture still remains the source of livelihood for over 70 per cent of the country's population. A large proportion of the rural work force is small and consists of marginal farmers and landless agricultural labourers.

There is substantial under employment among these people; both wages and productivity are low. These in turn result in poverty; it is estimated that 320 million people are still living below the poverty line in rural India. Though poverty has declined over the last three decades, the number of rural poor has in fact increased due to the population growth. Poor tend to have larger families which puts enormous burden on their meagre resources, and prevent them from breaking out of the shackles of poverty. In States like Tamil Nadu where replacement level of fertility has been attained, population growth rates are much lower than in many other States; but the population density is high and so there is a pressure on land.

In States like Rajasthan, Uttar Pradesh, Bihar and Madhya Pradesh population is growing rapidly, resulting in increasing pressure on land and resulting land fragmentation. Low productivity of small land holders leads to poverty, low energy intake and under nutrition, and this, in turn, prevents the development thus creating a vicious circle. In most of the states non-farm employment in rural areas has not grown very much and cannot absorb the growing labour force. Those who are getting educated specially beyond the primary level, may not wish to do manual agricultural work.

They would like better opportunities and more remunerative employment. In this context, it is imperative that programmes for skill development, vocational training and technical education are taken up on a large scale in order to generate productive employment in rural areas. The entire gamut of existing poverty alleviation and employment generation programmes may have to be restructured to meet the newly emerging types of demand for employment. Rural poor have inadequate access to basic minimum services, because of poor connectivity, lack of awareness, inadequate and poorly functional infrastructure.

There are ongoing efforts to improve these, but with the growing aspirations of the younger, educated population these efforts may prove to be inadequate to meet the increasing needs both in terms of type and quality of services. Greater education, awareness and better standard of living among the growing younger age group population would create the required consciousness among them that smaller families are desirable; if all the felt needs for health and family welfare services are fully met, it will be possible to enable them to attain their reproductive goals, achieve substantial decline in the family size and improve quality of life.

WATER SUPPLY

In many parts of developed and developing world, water demand substantially exceeds sustainable water supply. It is estimated that currently 430 millions (8% of the global population) are living in countries affected by water stress; by 2020 about one fourth of the global population may be facing chronic and recurring shortage of fresh water. In India, water withdrawal is estimated to be twice the rate of aquifer recharge; as a result water tables are falling by one to three meters every year; tapping deeper aquifers have resulted in larger population groups being exposed to newer health hazards such as high fluoride or arsenic content in drinking water.

At the other end of the spectrum, excessive use of water has led to water logging and increasing salinity in some parts of the country. Eventually, both lack of water and water logging could have adverse impact on India's food production. There is very little arable agricultural land which remains unexploited and in many areas, agricultural technology improvement may not be able to ensure further increase in yield per hectare. It is, therefore, imperative that research in biotechnology for improving development of foodgrains strains that would tolerate salinity and those which would require less water gets high priority. Simultaneously, a movement towards making water harvesting, storage and its need based use part of every citizens life should be taken up.

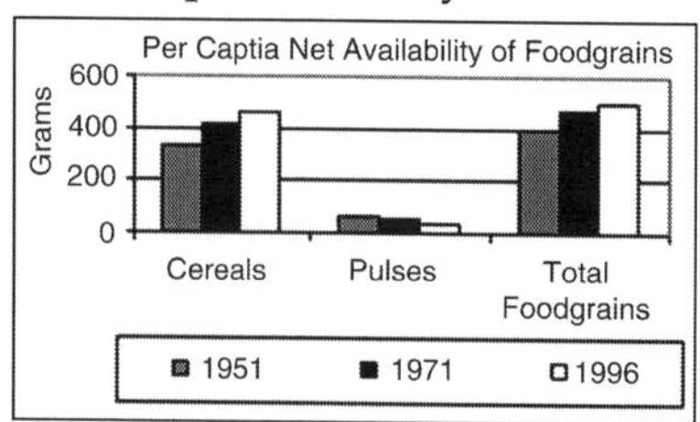

FOOD SECURITY

Technological innovations in agriculture and increase in area under cultivation have ensured that so far, food production has kept pace with the population growth. Evolution of global and national food security systems have improved access to food. It is estimated that the global population will grow to 9 billion by 2050 and the food production will double; improvement in purchasing power and changing dietary habits (shift to animal products) may further add to the requirement of food grains. Thus, in the next five decades, the food and nutrition security could become critical in many parts of the world especially in the developing countries and pockets of poverty in the developed countries.

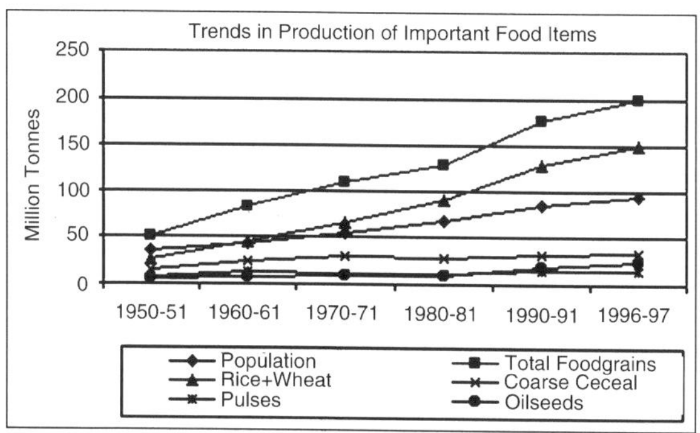

In India one of the major achievements in the last fifty years has been the green revolution and selfsufficiency in food production. Food grain production has increased from 50.82 in 1950-51 to 200.88 million tons in 1998-99. It is a matter of concern that while the cereal production has been growing steadily at a rate higher than the population growth rates, the coarse grain and pulse production has not shown a similar increase. Consequently there has been a reduction in the per capita availability of pulses (from 60.7 grams in 1951 to 34 grams per day in 1996) and coarse grains.

Table. Production of Food grains-Average Annual Growth

						(Million Tonnes)
Year	Rice	Wheat	Coarse Cereals	Pulses	Total Food Grains	Compound Annual Growth
			(Percent)			
1950-51	20.58	6.46	15.38	8.41	50.82	–
1960-61	34.58	11.00	23.74	12.70	82.02	3.22
1970-71	42.23	23.83	30.55	11.82	108.42	1.72
1980-81	52.63	36.31	29.02	10.63	129.59	2.08
1990-91	74.29	55.14	32.7	14.26	176.39	3.54
1997-98	82.3	65.9	31.1	13.1	192.4	1.66
1998-99*	84.50	70.63	30.58	15.2	200.88	
			*Estimated			

Over the last five decades there has been a decline in the per capita availability of pulses. During the last few years the country has imported pulses to meet the requirement. There has been a sharp and sustained increase in cost of pulses, so there is substantial decline in per capita pulses consumption among poorer segment of population. This in turn could have an adverse impact on their protein intake. The pulse component of the "Pulses and Oil Seeds Mission" need to receive a major thrust in terms of R&D and other inputs, so that essential pulse requirement of growing population is fully met. Rising cost of pulses had a beneficial effect also. Till eighties in central India wages of landless labourers were given in the form Kesari Dal which was cheaper than cereals or coarse grains.

Consumption of staple diet of Kesari Dal led to crippling disease of neuro lathyrism. Over the last three decades the rising cost of pulses has made Kesari Dal more expensive than wheat or rice and hence it is no longer given to labourers as wages for work done; as a result the disease has virtually disappeared from Central India.

Over years the coarse grain production has remained stagnant and per capita availability of coarse grain has under gone substantial reduction; there has been a shift away from coarse grains to rice and wheat consumption even among poorer segment of population. One of the benefits of this change is virtual elimination of pellagra which was widely prevalent among low income group population in Deccan Plateau whose staple food was sorghum. Coarse grains are less expensive than rice and wheat; they can thus provide higher calories for the same cost as compared to rice and wheat.

Coarse grains which are locally produced and procured if made available through TPDS at subsidised rate, may not only substantially bring down the subsidy cost without any reduction in calories provided but also improve "targetting"-as only the most needy are likely to access these coarse grains. Another area of concern is the lack of sufficient focus and thrust in horticulture; because of this, availability of vegetables especially green leafy vegetables and yellow/red vegetables throughout the year at affordable cost both in urban and rural areas has remained an unfulfilled dream. Health and nutrition education emphasizing the importance of consuming these inexpensive rich sources of micronutrients will not result in any change in food habits unless there is harnessing and effective management of horticultural resources in the country to meet the growing needs of the people at affordable cost. States like Tamil Nadu and Himachal Pradesh have initiated some efforts in this direction; similar efforts need be taken up in other states also.

NUTRITION

At the time of independence the country faced two major nutritional problems; one was the threat of famine and acute starvation due to low agricultural production and lack of appropriate food distribution system. The other was chronic energy deficiency due to poverty, low-literacy, poor access to safe-drinking water, sanitation and health care; these factors led to wide spread prevalence of infections and ill health in children and adults.

Kwashiorkor, marasmus, goitre, beri beri, blindness due to Vitamin-A deficiency and anaemia were major public health problems. The country adopted multi-sectoral, multi-pronged strategy to combat the major nutritional problems and to improve nutritional status of the population.

Chronic energy deficiency (CED)–current situation:

- While mortality has come down by 50% and fertility by 40% reduction in under nutrition is only 20%.
- There has been 50% decline in severe under-nutrition
- Reduction in mild under-nutrition is marginal
- India with less than 20% global children accounts for over 40% under nourished children
- Under nutrition in pregnant women and 6-24 months children has not declined
- Major causes of CED remains to be inadequate food intake, infections and poor caring practices..

During the last 50 years considerable progress has been achieved. Famines no longer stalk the country. There has been substantial reduction in moderate and severe undernutrition in children and some improvement in nutritional status of all segments of population. Kwashiorkor, marasmus, pellagra, lathyrism, beri beri and blindness due to severe Vitamin-A deficiency have become rare.

However, it is a matter of concern that milder forms of Chronic Energy Deficiency (CED) and micronutrient deficiencies continue to be widely prevalent in adults and children. In view of the fact that population growth in India will continue for the next few decades, it is essential that appropriate strategies are devised to improve food and nutrition security of families, identify individuals/families with severe forms of CED and provide them assistance to over come these problem

OPERATIONAL STRATEGY TO IMPROVE THE DIETARY INTAKE OF THE FAMILY AND IMPROVE NUTRITIONAL STATUS OF THE RAPIDLY GROWING ADULT POPULATION WOULD INCLUDE

- Ensuring adequate agricultural production of cereals, pulses, vegetables and other foodstuffs needed to fully meet the requirement of growing population.
- Improving in purchasing power through employment generation and employment assurance schemes;
- Providing subsidised food grains through TPDS to the families below poverty line.
- Exploring feasibility of providing subsidized coarse grains to families Below Poverty Line (BPL)

OPERATIONAL STRATEGIES TO IMPROVE HEALTH AND NUTRITIONAL STATUS OF THE GROWING NUMBERS OF WOMEN AND CHILDREN INCLUDE

- Pregnant and lactating women-screening to identify women with weight below 40 Kgs and ensuring that they/their preschool children receive food supplements through Integrated Child Development Services Scheme (ICDS); adequate antenatal intrapartum and neonatal care.
- *0-6 months infants-Nutrition education for*:
  - Early initiation of lactation
  - Protection and promotion of universal breast feeding
  - Exclusive breast feeding for the first six months; unless there is specific reason supplementation should not be introduced before 6 months
  - Immunisation, growth monitoring and health care.
- *Well planned nutrition education to ensure that the infants and children do*:
  - Continue to get breasted;
  - Get appropriate cereal pulse-vegetable based supplement fed to them at least 3-4 times a day–appropriate help in ensuring this through family/community/work place support;
  - Immunisation and health care.
- *Children in the 0-5 age group*:
  - Screen by weighment to identify children with moderate and severe undernutrition
  - Provide double quantity supplements through icds;
  - Screening for nutrition and health problems and appropriate intervention.
- *Primary school children*:
  - Weigh and identify those with moderate and severe chronic energy deficiency;
  - Improve dietary intake to these children through the mid-day meal.
- Monitor for improvement in the identified undernourished infants, children and mothers; if no improvement after 2 months refer to physician for identification and treatment of factors that might be responsible for lack of improvement;
- Nutrition education on varying dietary needs of different members of the family and how they can be met by minor modifications from the family meals. Intensive health education for improving the life style of the population coupled with active screening and management of the health problems associated with obesity.

POPULATION PROJECTIONS FOR INDIA AND THEIR IMPLICATIONS

Populations projections 1996-2016
The population will increase from 934 million in 1996 to 1264 million in 2016. *Between the periods 1996-2001 and 2011-2016 there will be a decline of:* • *CBR from:* 24.10 to 21.41 • *CDR from:* 8.99 to 7.48 • *NGR from:* 1.51% to 1.39% • IMR 1. *Male from:* 63 to 38 2. *Female from:* 64 to 39

Right from 1958 the Planning Commission has been constituting an Expert Group on Population Projections prior to the preparation of each of the Five Year Plans so that the information on the population status at the time of initiation of the Plan and population projections for future are available during the preparation of the Plan.

Population projections have been utilised not only for planning to ensure provision of essentials necessities such as food, shelter and clothing but also prerequisites for human development such as education, employment and health care.

Over the years there has been considerable refinement in the methodology used for population projections and substantial improvement in the accuracy of predictions. The projections made by the Standing Committee on Population Projection in 1988 for the year 1991 was 843.6 million; this figure was within 0.3% of the 846.3 million reported in the Census 1991.

In 1996, Technical Group on Population Projections, had work out the population projections for the country and the states for the period 1996 to 2016 on the basis of census 1991 and other available demographic data. Population pyramids for the period 1971 to 2016 are shown in Figure.

Economic Implications of Demographic Transition
The next two decades will witness: • Increase in the 15-59 age group from 519-800 million • Low dependency ration *Challenge is to ensure:* • Adequate investment in HRD • Appropriate employment with adequate emoluments for the labour force *Opportunity is to:* • Utilise available abundant human resources to accelerate economic development

ECONOMIC IMPLICATIONS

Population growth and its relation to economic growth has been a matter of debate for over a century. The early Malthusian view was that population growth is likely to impede economic growth because it will put pressure on the available resources, result in reduction in per capita income and resources; this, in turn, will result in deterioration in quality of life.

Contrary to the Malthusian predictions, several of the East Asian countries have been able to achieve economic prosperity and improvement in quality of life inspite of population growth. This has been attributed to the increase in productivity due to development and utilisation of innovative technologies by the young educated population who formed the majority of the growing population.

These countries have been able to exploit the dynamics of demographic transition to achieve economic growth by using the human resources as the engine driving the economic development; improved employment with adequate emoluments has promoted saving and investment which in turn stimulated economic growth. However, not all countries, which have undergone demographic transition, have been able to transform their economies. Sri Lanka in South Asia underwent demographic transition at the same time as South East Asian countries but has not achieved the economic transition.

It is now realised that population growth or demographic transition can have favourable impact on economic growth only when there are optimal interventions aimed at human resource development (HRD) and appropriate utilisation of available human resources.

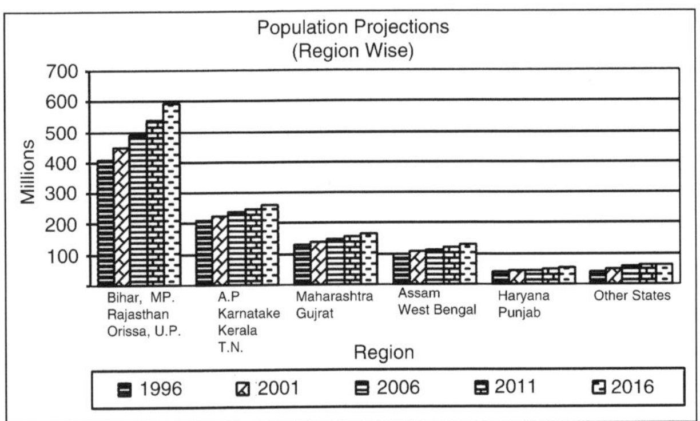

For India the current phase of demographic transition with low dependency ratio and high working age group population, represents both a challenge and an opportunity. The challenge is to develop these human resources through appropriate education and skill development and utilise them fully by giving them appropriate jobs with adequate emoluments; if this challenge is met through well planned schemes for HRD and employment generation which are implemented effectively, there will be improved national productivity and personal savings rates; appropriate investment of these savings will help the country to achieve the economic transition from low economic growth-low per capita income to high economic growth-high per capita income. It is imperative to make the best use of this opportunity so as to enable the country and its citizens to vault to the high income-high economic growth status and stabilize at that level.

INTERSTATE DIFFERENCES

The projected values for the total population in different regions is shown in Figure. There are marked differences between States in size of the population and population growth rates, the time by which replacement level of fertility is to be achieved and age structure of the population. If the present trend continues, most of the Southern and the Western States are likely to achieve TFR of 2.1 by 2010.

Urgent energetic steps to assess and fully meet the unmet needs for maternal and child health (MCH) care and contraception through improvement in availability and access to family welfare services are needed in the States of UP, MP, Rajasthan and Bihar in order to achieve a faster decline in their mortality and fertility rates. The five states of Bihar, Uttar Pradesh, Madhya Pradesh, Rajasthan and Orissa, which constitute 44% of the total population of India in 1996, will constitute 48% of the total population of India in 2016.

These states will contribute 55% of the total increase in population of the country during the period 1996-2016. In all the states performance in the social and economic sector has been poor. The poor performance is the outcome of poverty, illiteracy and poor development which co-exist and reinforce each other. The quality and coverage under health services is poor and the unmet need for FW services is about 30%. Urgent energetic steps are required to be initiated to assess and fully meet the unmet needs for maternal and child health (MCH) care and contraception through improvement in availability and access to family welfare services in the states of UP, MP, Rajasthan and Bihar in order to achieve a faster decline in their mortality and fertility rates. The performance of these states would determine the year and size of the population at which the country achieves population stabilisation.

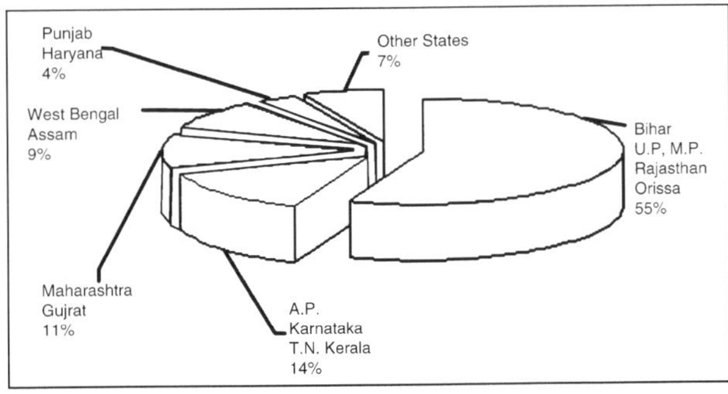

Fig. Share of Regions in Population Growth (1996-2016)

There are also marked differences between States in socio-economic development. Increasing investments and rapid economic development are likely to occur in the States where literacy rates are high; there is ready availability of skilled work force and adequate infrastructure. In these States, population growth rates are low.

If equitable distribution of the income and benefits generated by development is ensured, substantial increase in per capita income and improvement in quality of life could occur in these States in a relatively short time. In majority of States with high population growth rates, the performance in the social and economic sector has been poor. The poor performance could be the outcome of a variety of factors including paucity of natural, financial or human resources. Poverty, illiteracy and poor development co-exist and aggravate each other. In order to promote equity and reduce disparity between States, special assistance has been provided to the poorly performing States.

The benefits accrued from such assistance has to a large extent depended upon:

- The States' ability to utilise the available funds; improve quality & coverage of services and facilities, increase efficiency and improve performance
- Community awareness and ability to utilise the available services.

In spite of the additional assistance provided, improvement in infrastructure, agriculture and industry have been sub-optimal and the per capita income continues to be low in most of the poorly performing States. These States also have high birth rates and relatively low literacy rates. It is imperative that special efforts are made during the next two decades to break this vicious self perpetuating cycle of poor performance, poor per capita income, poverty, low literacy and high birth rate so that the further widening of disparities between States in terms of per capita income and quality of life is prevented.

The higher population growth rates and low per capita income in poorly performing States are likely to have a major impact on several social sector programmes. The health status of the population in these States is poor; the health sector programme will require inputs not only for improving infrastructure and manpower, but also increasing efficiency and improving performance. The Family Welfare Programme has to address the massive task of meeting all the unmet needs for MCH and contraception so that there is a rapid decline in mortality and fertility rates.

Due to high birth rate, the number of children requiring schooling will be large. The emphasis in the education sector on primary education is essential to ensure that the resource constraints do not result in an increase in either proportion or number of illiterates. Emphasis on prevocational and vocational training in schools will enable these children to acquire skills through which they will find gainful employment later.

MIGRATION

The available data from census shows that until 1991 both internal and international migration has been negligible. The Technical Group while computing the population projection upto 2016, has assumed that the component of migration between major States and from India will be negligible. This assumption may not be valid if there is further widening of the disparity between States in terms of economic growth and employment opportunity. Given the combination of high population growth, low literacy and lack of employment opportunities in the poorly performing States, there may be increasing rural to urban migration as well as interstate migration especially of unskilled workers.

Such migration may in the short run assist the migrants in overcoming economic problems associated with unemployment. However, the migrant workers and their families may face problems in securing shelter, education and health care. It is essential to build up a mechanism for monitoring these changes. Steps will have to be taken to provide for the minimum essential needs of the vulnerable migrant population.

LABOUR, EMPLOYMENT AND MANPOWER

Population, which is engaged in any economic activity (employed persons) and population seeking work (unemployed) constitute Labour Force. India has the second largest labour force in the world. Projection of labour force is pre-requisite ensuring optimal utilisation of available human resources. Manpower development is then taken up to provide adequate labour force, of appropriate skills and quality to different sectors so that there is rapid socioeconomic development and there is no mismatch between skills required and skills available. Planning also attempts to provide enabling environment for employment generation (both self employment and wage employment) in public, private and voluntary sectors in urban and rural areas.

Table. Population and Labour force Projections: 1997-2012.

	1997	2002	2007	2012
Population (Millions)	951.18	1028.93	1112.86	1196.41
Labour Force (Millions)	397.22	449.62	507.94	562.91

Labour force in India will be increasing by more than 10 million per annum during 1997-2012. It will be imperative to plan for and achieve adequate agricultural and industrial growth to absorb this work force. Most of the persons entering the labour force will be educated and have some skills. Increasing literacy and decreasing birth rates may result in more women seeking economically productive work outside home.

It will be important to generate appropriate and renumerative employment at places where labour force are available so as to reduce interstate and urban migration in search of employment. Attempts should be made to eliminate bonded labour, employment of children and women in hazardous industries and minimising occupational health hazards. Planners face the challenge to have sustained high economic growth rate in sectors that are labour-intensive to ensure adequate employment generation for productively utilising this massive work force.

If the massive work force of literate, skilled, aware men and women in age-group 20-60 years get fully employed and adequately paid they could trigger off a period of rapid economic development. As they have very few dependant children and elders there will be increased savings and investments at household level; this in turn will improve the availability of resources for accelerating economic growth. The current stage of demographic transition thus provides the country with the opportunity window for using human resources as the engine to power economic development and improving the quality of life of all the citizens.

SEX RATIO

The reported decline in the sex ratio during the current century has been a cause for concern. The factors responsible for this continued decline are as yet not clearly identified. However, it is well recognised that the adverse sex ratio is a reflection of the gender disparity. Higher childhood mortality in girl children is yet another facet of the existing gender disparities and consequent adverse effect on survival.

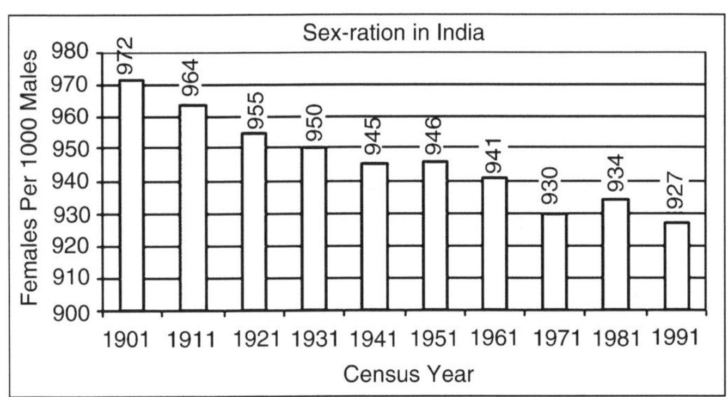

In the reproductive age group the mortality rates among women are higher than those among men. The continued high maternal mortality is one of the major factors responsible for this. Effective implementation of the Reproductive and Child Health Programme is expected to result in a substantial reduction in maternal mortality. At the moment, the longevity at birth among women is only marginally higher than that among men. However over the next decade life expectancy among women will progressively increase.

Once the reproductive age group is crossed, the mortality rates among women are lower as women outlive and outnumber men in the age group 65 and above. The needs especially of the widowed women have to be met so that quality of life does not deteriorate. The census 2001 will collect and report vital data on sex disaggregated basis; this will be of help in identifying and taking up appropriate interventions in correcting gender disparity; continued collection, collation, analysis and reporting of sex disaggregated data from all social sectors will also provide a mechanism to monitor whether girls and women have equal access to services.

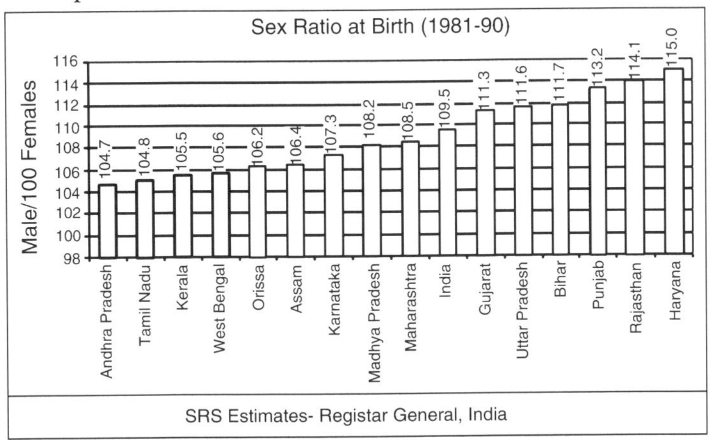

There are substantial differences in sex ratio at birth and in different age groups between states. The SRS based estimates of average sex ratio at birth for the period 1981-90 for the major States and India are given in Figure. The observed sex ratio of 110 is higher than the internationally accepted sex ratio at birth of 106. There are substantial differences among states in the reported sex ratio at birth. There had been speculations whether female infanticide, sex determination and selective female foeticide are at least in part responsible for this. The Government of India has enacted a legislation banning the prenatal sex determination and selective abortion. Intensive community education efforts are under way to combat these practices, especially in pockets from where female infanticide and foeticide have been reported.

INCREASING LONGEVITY

The projected populations of India in the three major age groups (less than 15, 15-59, 60 years or above) are shown in Figure.

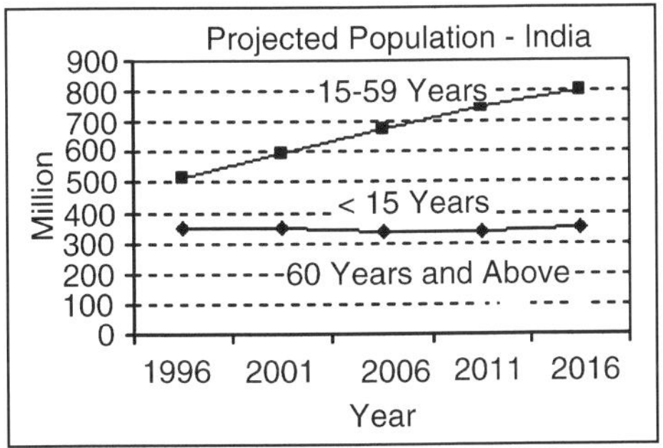

Over the coming decades the country will be facing a progressive increase both in the proportion and number of persons beyond 60 years of age. Over the next 20 years the population of more than 60 years will grow form 62.3 million to 112.9 million; the subsequent decades will witness massive increase in this age group. Increasing longevity will inevitably bring in its wake increase in the prevalence of non-communicable diseases. The growing number of senior citizens in the country poses a major challenge and the cost of providing socio-economic security and health care to this population has to be met. Currently several region and culture specific innovative interventions to provide needed care to this population are underway; among these are efforts to reverse the trend of break up of joint families. If these efforts succeed, it will be possible to provide necessary care for rapidly increasing population of senior citizens in the subsequent two decades within the resources of the family and the country.

Increasing longevity:

- The population of elderly (>60 years) will increase from 62.3 millions in 1996 to 112.9 million in 2016
- Improved health care had added "Years to life"
- Increased social sector investment is needed to add "Quality of life to years"

Majority of the people in their sixties will be physically and psychologically fit and would like to participate both in economic and social activities. They should be encouraged and supported to lead a productive life and contribute to the national development. Senior citizens in their seventies and beyond and those with health problems would require assistance. So far, the families have borne major share in caring for the elderly. This will remain the ideal method; however, there are growing number of elderly without family support; for them, alternate modes for caring may have to be evolved and implemented. Improved health care has "added years to life". The social sectors have to make the necessary provisions for improving the quality of life of these senior citizens so that they truly " add life to years."

HEALTH IMPLICATION OF THE DEMOGRAPHIC TRANSITION

It was earlier assumed that population growth during demographic transition will lead to overcrowding, poverty, undernutrition, environmental deterioration, poor quality of life and increase in disease burden. Experience in the last few decades have shown that this may not always be correct. India is currently in the phase of demographic transition when the increase in population is mainly among younger, better educated and healthy population with low morbidity and mortality rate.

The challenge for the health sector is to promote healthy life styles, improve access to and utilisation of health care so that the country can achieve substantial reduction in mortality and morbidity. Occupational health and environmental health programme need be augmented to ensure that working population remain healthy and productive.

If these challenges are fully met, it is possible to accelerate reduction in morbidity and mortality rate in this age group and improve health indices of the country. With growing number of senior citizens there may be substantial increase in health care needs especially for management of non-communicable diseases.

Increasing availability and awareness about technological advances for management of these problems, rising expectations of the population and the ever escalating cost of health care are some of the problems that the health care system has to cope with. Health care delivery systems will have to gear up to taking up necessary preventive, promotive, curative and rehabilitative care for growing population of senior citizens.

Age groups < 15 Years

There will be no increase in numbers.

Focus will be to improve:

- Quality and coverage of health and nutrition services and achieve improvement in health and nutrional status
- Improve access to education and skill development

Age groups < 15 Years

There will be no increase in numbers.

Focus will be to improve:

- Quality and coverage of health and nutrition services and achieve improvement in health and nutrional status
- Improve access to education and skill development

POPULATION PROJECTIONS AND THEIR IMPLICATIONS FOR THE FW PROGRAMME

There will be a marginal decline in the population less than 15 years of age (352.7 million to 350.4 million).

The health care infrastructure will therefore be not grappling with ever increasing number of children for providing care and they will be able to concentrate on:

- Improving quality of care;
- Focus on antenatal, intranatal and neonatal care aimed at reducing neonatal morbidity and mortality;
- Improve coverage and quality of health care to vulnerable and underserved adolescents;
- Promote intersectoral coordination especially with icds programme so that there is improvement in health and nutritional status;
- Improve coverage for immunization against vaccine preventable diseases.

Age groups 15-59 years
• There will be an increase from 519-800 million two decades *They will*: • Need wider spectrum of services • Expect better quality of services • Expect fulfillment of their felt need for MCH/FP care Opportunity is that if their felt needs are met through effective implementation of RCH programme, it is possible to accelerate demographic transition and achieve rapid population stabilization. Deptt. of family welfare is now implementing the RCH programme to meet these needs

The economic challenge is to provide needed funds so that these children have access to nutrition, education and skill development. The challenge faced by the health sector is to achieve reduction in morbidity and mortality rate in infancy and childhood, to improve nutritional status and eliminate ill-effects of gender bias.

Components of comprehensive RCH programme:

- Effective maternal and child health care
- Increased access to contraceptive care
- Safe management of unwanted pregnancies
- Nutritional services to vulnerable groups
- Prevention and treatment of RTI/STD
- Reproductive health services for adolescents
- Prevention and treatment of gynecological problems
- Screening and treatment of cancers, especially that of uterine cervix and breast

These services are bring provided in all the secondary and tertiary care hospitals. There will be a massive increase of population in the 15-59 age group. The persons in this age group will be more literate and have greater access to information; they will therefore have greater awareness and expectation regarding both the access to a wide spectrum of health care related services and the quality of these services.

Under the Reproductive and child health care programme efforts are underway to provide:

- Needed services for this rapid growing population
- To broaden the spectrum of services available and
- To improve quality and coverage of health care to women, children and adolescents, so that their felt needs for health care are fully met.
- To improve the participation of men in the planned parenthood movement.

The components of the comprehensive RCH services are given in the text box. While providing the package of services, efforts will have to be made to improve the quality of services, make services more responsive to users' needs, ensure that health workers and health care providers have the necessary skills and supplies they need and there is a strong and effective referral system to manage all the risk cases. Family welfare Programme is attempting to improve the logistics of supply of drugs and vaccine to make sure good quality drugs are available at appropriate time.

Simultaneously the IEC efforts are being directed to:

- Ensure responsible reproductive/sexual behaviour;
- Improve awareness about reproductive health needs;
- Promote community participation and optimal utilisation of available services

ESSENTIAL REPRODUCTIVE AND CHILD HEALTH SERVICES

Though it is desirable that the entire package of services indicated under comprehensive RCH care is made available to all those who need it, it will not be possible to immediately implement such a comprehensive package at primary health care level on a nationwide basis. After consultation with experts a package of essential reproductive health services for nationwide implementation at primary health care settings has been identified.

Essential components recommended for nationwide implementation include:

- Prevention and management of unwanted pregnancy,
- Services to provide antenatal, intra-natal and post-natal, and neo-natal care
- Services to promote child health and survival,
- Prevention and treatment of RTI/STD.

Most of these services are already being delivered under the Family Welfare Programme. However, there are wide variations in the quality and coverage of services not only between states but also between districts in the same state. The focus under RCH Programme is therefore on the improvement in the quality and coverage of the services over and above the existing level in all districts/states in an incremental manner so that there is over all improvement maternal and child health indices.

FAMILY WELFARE PROGRAMME IN INDIA

India, the second most populous country in the world, has no more than 2.5% of global land but is the home of 1/6th of the world's population. The prevailing high maternal, infant, childhood morbidity and mortality, low life expectancy and high fertility and associated high morbidity had been a source of concern for public health professionals right from the pre-independence period. The Bhore Committee Report (1946) which laid the foundation for health service planning in India, gave high priority to provision of maternal and child health services and improving their nutritional and health status. It is noteworthy that this report which emphasized the importance of providing integrated preventive, promotive and curative primary health care services preceded the Alma Ata declaration by over three decades.

Under the Constitution of India elimination of poverty, ignorance and ill health are three important goals. In 1951, the infant republic took stock of the existing situation in the country and initiated the first Five Year Development Plan. Living in a resource poor country with high population density, the Planners recognised in the census figures of 1951, the potential threat posed by population explosion and the need to take steps to avert it.

It was recognised that population stabilisation is an essential prerequisite for sustainability of development process so that the benefits of economic development result in enhancement of the well being of the people and improvement in quality of life. India became the first country in the world to formulate a National Family Planning Programme in 1952, with the objective of "reducing birth rate to the extent necessary to stabilise the population at a level consistent with requirement of national economy".

Thus, the key elements of health care to women and children and provision of contraceptive services have been the focus of India's health services right from the time of India's independence. Successive Five Year Plans have been providing the policy framework and funding for planned development of nationwide health care infrastructure and manpower. The Centrally Sponsored and 100% centrally funded Family Welfare Programme provides additional infrastructure, manpower and drugs, vaccines contraceptives and other consumables needed for improving health status of women and children and to meet all the felt needs for fertility regulation.

- Basic premises of the Family Welfare Programme are: Acceptance of FW services is voluntary,
  - FW programme will provide:
    i. Integrated Maternal and Child Health (MCH) & FP services
    ii. Effective IEC to improve awareness
    iii. Ensure easy and convenient access to FW services free of cost

PROGRESS UNDER THE FW PROGRAMME

Major achievements:

- A vast nation wide infrastructure and manpower fro providing FW services has been created
- There is increased access to and utilsation of FW services
- *These has been*:
  - Reduction in Crude Birth Rate (CBR) from 40.8 (1951 Census) to 27.4 in 1996 (SRS 96)
  - Reduction in Infant Mortality Rate (IMR) from 146 in 1951 t0 72 in 1996 (SRS)
  - Increase in couple protection Rate (CPR) from 10.4% (1970-71) to 45.4% (31.3.1997)

CONTRACEPTION

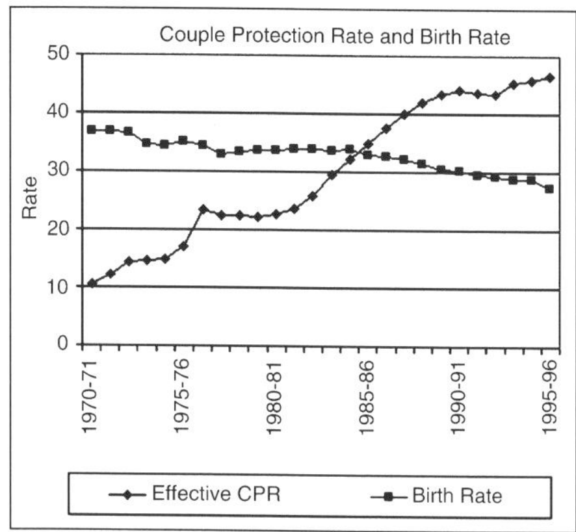

Over the last four decades there has been substantial improvement in the availability and utilization of the and access to FW services and a progressive increase in the acceptance of contraception and couple protection rates. In the initial fifteen years, the rise in the couple protection rate has been steep. The reduction in the CBR was however not commensurate with the increase in couple protection rates. In the last ten years, the rise in CPR is less steep, but the fall in CBR has been steeper than in the earlier years.

The age and parity of the acceptors of contraception, and the continuation rates of temporary methods of contraception are some of the important factors that determine birth rates. The trends in CPR and CBR over the last 25 years suggest that over the years there has been an improvement in the acceptance of appropriate contraception at appropriate time. Currently the FW Programme is focusing its attention on need assessment, balanced presentation of advantages and disadvantages about all the available methods of contraception counseling, provision of appropriate contraceptive at the right time and good follow up services. Effective implementation of the FW programme and ensuring that all the unmet needs for contraception are met will result in substantial improvement in CPR and enable rapid reduction in CBR.

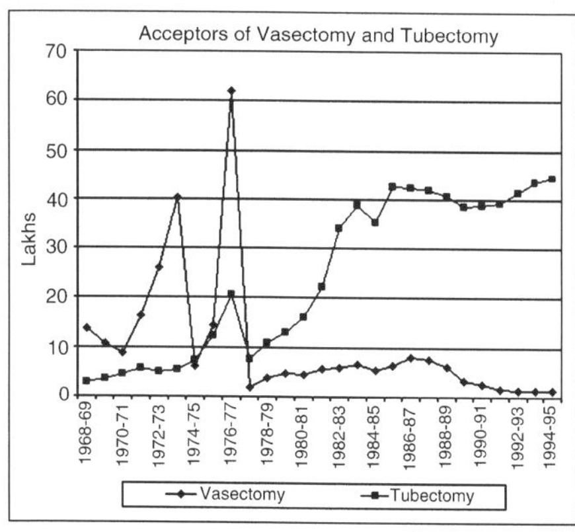

Over the last two decades there has been a steep fall in number of vasectomies. At the moment, over 97% of all sterilisations are tubectomies. If, over the next decade, attempts are made to repopularise vasectomy so that this safe, simple procedure forms at least 50% of all sterilizations, there will be a further improvement in access to sterilization in the primary health care settings, substantial reduction both in the morbidity/mortality associated with terminal methods of contraception and reduction in the cost of permanent methods of contraception. In addition this would be one of the efforts to improve participation of men in planned parenthood.

In the past demographers have assumed that access to a wide spectrum of spacing and permanent methods of contraception and achievement of contraceptive prevalence of atleast 60% are essential for achievement of replacement level of fertility. In Kerala and Tamil Nadu sterilisation is the most commonly utilised method of contraception; these States have been able to achieve replacement level of fertility (Total Fertility Rate (TFR) of 2.1) long before there was improved access to a wide spectrum temporary methods of contraception and Couple protection rate of 60% has been achieved. The National FW programme statistics as well as National Family Health Survey have shown in all the states in India sterilization is the most widely accepted method of contraception.

Given the fact that most couples in India complete their family by the time they are in their mid-20s and marriage is a stable institution, sterilisation is the most logical, safe and cost effective contraception to protect these young couples against unwanted pregnancies for the next two decades. There are substantial differences between states regarding the need for temporary and permanent methods of contraception.

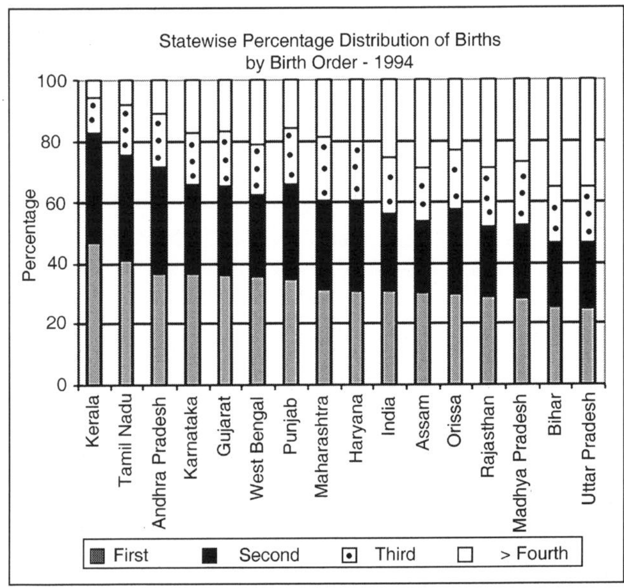

Percentage distribution of birth order in major states is shown in Figure. It is obvious in most of the poorly performing states over half of the women have two or more children and are likely to require permanent methods of contraception sooner or later. On the other hand in some of the better performing states increasing number of women may desire to postpone the first or second pregnancy and there may be a progressive increase in the need for spacing methods. Contraceptive need assessment, counseling, improved quality of initial and follow up care would go a long way in meeting the felt needs of contraception in the population and accelerate the decline in fertility.

MATERNAL AND CHILD HEALTH

Reduction in the infant and child mortality indices between 1951-1997 is shown in Figure. Even though the decline in IMR and CDR are substantial, it is noteworthy that maternal, perinatal, neonatal mortality rates continue to remain high. This is because the antenatal, intrapartum and neonatal care programmes have, till now, not aimed at screening of all pregnant women for risk factors, identification and appropriate referral of the 'at risk' individuals. Improvement in the contents and quality of antenatal and paediatric care at primary health care level is receiving focussed attention under the RCH programme.

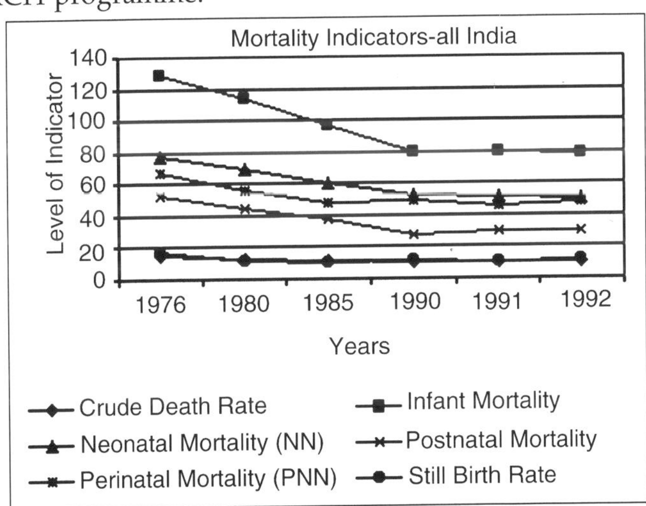

INTER-STATE/INTRA-STATE DIFFERENCES IN FERTILITY AND MORTALITY

The availability and utilisation of family welfare services is the critical determinant of performance in Family Welfare Programme, achievements in terms of reduction in IMR and CBR go hand in hand in most States. However, there are exceptions; both Punjab and Tamil Nadu have good primary health care infrastructure; IMR in both the States are identical and the age at marriage in these States is similar; TFR in Tamil Nadu is 2.1 and in Punjab it is 2.9. In Bihar, IMR is 72 and TFR is 4.6 but Assam with IMR of 75 has a TFR of 3.8. Efforts will have to be made to identify the factors responsible for poor achievements in terms of IMR and TFR and area specific remedial measures have to be planned and implemented in the States.

District wise data on CBR and IMR computed on the basis of Census 1991 show that there are marked differences in these indices not only between States but also between districts in the same State. Census 1991 has confirmed that even in Kerala there are districts where IMR and CBR are higher than national levels. There are districts in UP with IMR and CBR (Kanpur-Urban) lower than national levels.

The Family Welfare Programme, therefore, has been re-oriented to:

- Remove or minimise the inter and intra-state differences,
- Undertake realistic phc based decentralised area-specific microplanning tailored to meet the local needs and
- Involve panchayati raj institutions in microplanning and monitoring at local level to effective implementation of the programme and ensuring effective community participation.

Under the Reproductive Child Health programme efforts are under way to improve the quality and coverage of FW services in all states. In each state, the success achieved by the better performing districts will have be replicated in poorly performing districts; in addition efforts will have to be made to achieve incremental improvement in performance in all districts so that the performance in the state improves. States like Kerala and Tamil Nadu have achieved low CBR and IMR at relatively low cost.

On the other hand, States like Haryana and Punjab have not achieved any substantial reduction in CBR in spite of higher expenditure per eligible couple. In States like Bihar and Uttar Pradesh the expenditure is low and performance is poor. In between these extreme categories are States like Orissa and Andhra Pradesh with average or below average expenditure and average or below average performance in MCH or family planning.

In some States like Orissa and West Bengal the performance in family planning is better than the performance in MCH or vice versa. Deptt. of Family Welfare is attempting to implement the recommendation of the NDC Committee on Population, that factors responsible for observed differences in utilisation of funds as well as impact of the programme are to be studied and existing lacunae identified and rectified at the district level.

The last five decades have shown that different states used different approaches to achieve improvement in MCH care and improve performance in FW programme. Some of these efforts have been path breaking and have disproved many theories on the essential prerequisites for rapid achievement of decline fertility and mortality.

Some examples of these experiences are indicated below:

- Goa with relatively high income, literacy and good health care infrastructure was the first administrative unit to achieve the replacement level of fertility. This fitted the classical theory; Goa and Pondicherry have been having less than replacement level fertility for over a decade.
- Kerala, the first State to achieve replacement level of fertility did so in spite of relatively low per capita income proving that in the Indian context economic development is not an essential prerequisite for the achieving small family. High status of women, female literacy, age at marriage and low infant mortality were thought to be the factors behind the rapid fall in fertility in Kerala
- Tamil Nadu which was the second state to achieve replacement level of fertility did so in spite of low PCI, higher IMR and lower female literacy rate than Kerala. This is attributed to the strong social and political commitment, backed by good administrative support and ready availability of Family Welfare Services. There have been speculations whether the low PCI in the aware population desiring improvement in quality of care had also acted as factor that accelerated the decline in fertility.
- Andhra Pradesh is likely to achieve replacement level of fertility in the next two years. The State has shown a steep decline in fertility in spite of relatively lower age at marriage, low literacy and poorer outreach of primary health care infrastructure. It has been suggested that the major factors responsible for the success include caring attitude of the government and strong sustained movement to empower women.
- In the North-eastern States of Tripura, Manipur, Mizoram there is substantial difficulty in accessing primary health care facilities, but these States have achieved not only low fertility rates but also low infant mortality, suggesting thereby that a literate aware population can successfully overcome difficulties in access to and availability of primary health care infrastructure.

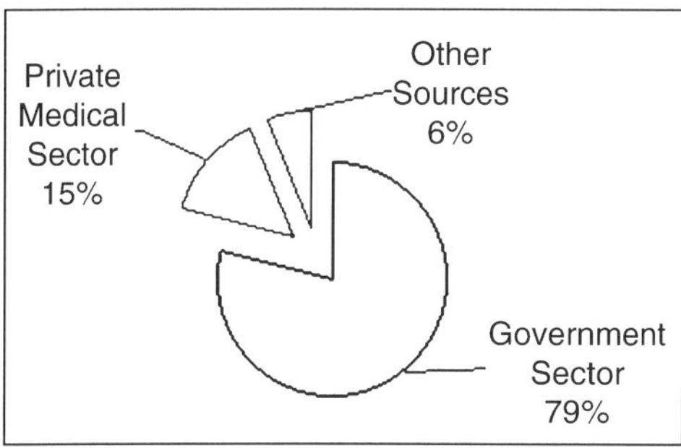

Fig. Sources of Family Planning Services

UNMET NEEDS FOR FAMILY WELFARE SERVICES

The National Family Health Survey (NFHS) 1992-93 had provided an independent nation wide evaluation of the progress and problems in delivery of Family Welfare services in the country. The survey confirmed that in spite of obvious constraints and inadequacies, the governmental network can, and does, provides most of the MCH and contraceptive care; Data from the NFHS showed that:

- There is universal awareness about contraception
- 40.6% of currently married women use contraceptives
- Wanted fertility is lower than the actual fertility
- There is a large unmet need for contraception:-
  - 11.0% for birth spacing methods and
  - 8.5% for terminal method.
- Unmet needs for health and contraceptive care exist in all regions and in all segments of the population irrespective of religion, caste, education and income status.

Lessons learnt during implementation of Family Welfare Programme:

- Governmental network provides most of the MCH and contraceptive care
- Adequate functional health infrastructure is an essential prerequisites for the success of the programme
- Providing efficient and effective integrated MCH and contraceptive care helps in building up rapport with the families
- IEC activities are powerful tools for promoting the small family norm;
- The population is conservative but responsible, responsive and mature; their response is slow but rational and sustained.

There is a popular belief that the population growth is due to poor performance in the health sector. This is not correct. The population growth that the country (and the world) had witnessed in the last five decades is mainly because of rapid reduction in the death rates due to health care and is inevitable during the frist three phases of demographic transition. India's progress in demographic transition has been a slow but sustained; unlike some other developing countries India's population growth never exceeded 2.2% even at its peak; the decline in population growth once started has been sustained. This orderly progression has been achieved through improving access to family welfare services and ensuring peoples participation.

Concern has been expressed by some groups that the RCH programme which essentially aims at improving quality and coverage of the already ongoing maternal and child health and contraceptive care may not be successful in accelerating the decline in fertility and help the country to achieve rapid population stabilization and that there is a need for new path breaking innovations.

Ongoing evaluations, however, do not suggest that there is a need for change in policy, strategy and programme content; all these studies have emphasized that there is a huge unmet need for services and there is an urgent need to improve access to good quality services to meet this need, the focus of the RCH initiative is on this task.

APPROACH TO FW PROGRAMME DURING THE NINTH PLAN

Reduction in Population growth is one of the major objectives in the Ninth Plan:

- *The current high population growth rate is due to*: The large size of the population in the reproductive age-group (estimated contribution 60%); higher fertility due to unmet need for contraception (estimated contribution 20%); and high wanted fertility due to prevailing high IMR (estimated contribution about 20%).
- *Rapid reduction in the population growth rate can be achieved by*: Meeting all the felt-needs for contraception; and reducing the infant and maternal morbidity and mortality so that there is a reduction in the desired level of fertility.
- *The Ninth Plan strategies for achieving these objectives are*: To assess the needs for reproductive and child health at PHC level and undertake area-specific micro planning; and To provide need-based, demand-driven high quality, integrated reproductive and child health care.
- *Efforts of the Family Welfare Programme are being directed towards*:
  - Bridging the gaps in essential infrastructure and manpower through a flexible approach and improving operational efficiency through investment in social, behavioural and operational research
  - Providing additional assistance to poorly performing districts identified on the basis of the 1991 census to fill existing gaps in infrastructure and manpower.
  - Ensuring uninterrupted supply of essential drugs, vaccines and contraceptives, adequate in quantity and appropriate in quality
  - Promoting male participation in the Planned Parenthood movement and increasing the level of acceptance of vasectomy.

Under the RCH Programme the focus is on enhancing the quality and coverage of family welfare services through:

- Increasing participation of general medical practitioners working in voluntary, private, joint sectors and the active cooperation of practitioners of ISM&H;
- Involvement of the Panchayati Raj Institutions for ensuring inter-sectoral coordination and community participation in planning, monitoring and management;
- Involvement of the industries, organised and unorganised sectors, agriculture workers and labour representatives.

GOALS TO BE ACHIEVED

The performance under the Family Welfare Programme will depend upon:

- Programme initiatives during the Ninth Plan
- Financial resources available;
- Capability and effectiveness of the infrastructure and manpower to carry out the programme;
- Literacy and economic status of the families particularly of the women;
- Policy support by opinion leaders and the society.

The Deptt. of Family Welfare has launched the RCH intiative during the Ninth Plan. Under the Special Action Plan an additional sum of ₹4700 crores had been provided to the Family Welfare Deptt. and the toal outlay provided the Department of Family Welfare was raised to ₹15120.20 crores for the Ninth Plan period to enable the Dept to implement the RCH programme. In view of the marked differences in the availability and utilisation of family welfare services and IMR CBR and CPR between States and districts within the states, a differential area specific approach to the implementation of Family Welfare Programme is being used.

State specific Expected Level of Achievement in terms of process and impact indicators have been worked out for effective monitoring of the programme. Projection of expected levels of achievement for process and impact indicators at the end of the Ninth Plan have taken into consideration the pace of improvement in these indicators during the Eighth Plan and the additional policy and programme measures envisaged to accelerate the pace of achievement during the Ninth Plan and the additional funding being provided under the Programme.

The State-specific projections have been worked out at two different levels of achievement, one on the basis of the assumption that the trend observed with regard to these parameters in the last 15 years will continue during the Ninth Plan period and the second on the assumption that the additional policy and programme initiatives provided during the Ninth Plan period will result in the acceleration of the pace and result in more substantial improvement during the Ninth Plan period. The expected levels of achievement under both these assumptions have been computed State wise The expected levels of achievement at the national level by the terminal year of Ninth Plan (2002) are given below:

Indicator	If current trend continues	If acceleration envisaged in the Ninth Five Year Plan is achieved
C B R	24/1000	23/1000
I M R	56/1000	50/1000
T F R	2.9	2.6
C P R	51%	60%
NNM R	35/1000	
M M R	3/1000	

The expected level of achievement for CBR at national level under these two sets of assumptions is 24 and 23/1000. If the target of 23/1000 is achieved there will be one million less births in 2002 AD alone. Similarly if the Programme achieves, the accelerated decline in IMR (from 56/1000-50/1000) over 140 thousand infant deaths will be averted in 2002 AD. These achievements may be the beginning of a major acceleration in pace of demographic transition and improving health status of the population. If the acceleration begun during the Ninth Plan is sustained the country may achieve replacement level of fertility by 2010, with the population of 1120 million; if this were done the country's population may stabilize by 2045.

SUMMARY

Demographic transition is a global phenomenon; population growth is inevitable in the initial phases of the transition. For India the current phase of the demographic transition is both a challenge and an opportunity. The challenge is to ensure human development and optimum utilisation of human resources. The opportunity is to utilise available human resources to achieve rapid economic development and improvement in quality of life. Over the last five decades the country has built up a massive healthcare infrastructure for delivery of FW services to the population in the Govt, private and voluntary sectors.

The RCH programme envisages wider range of services and improvement in quality of services provided. There is universal awareness about the need for these services. In the next two decades the population growth will be mainly among the young adults who will be more literate, aware and likely to make optimal use of available facilities. India is currently in the phase of demographic transition during which where it will be possible for the country to accelerate the pace of decline in fertility. If the population now has ready access to good quality services at affordable cost, it will be possible for them to meet all their needs, achieve the desired family size and enable the country to achieve population stabilsation rapidly.

Demographic transition does not occur in isolation. Simultaneously, there are ongoing economic transition, education transition, health transition and reproductive health transition. All these affect human development. If there is synergy between these transitions; the transitions can be completed rapidly; there will be substantial improvement in human development and economic development.

The focus of planners, programme implementers and the people during the next two decades will have to be in achieving the synergy so that India can achieve rapid population stabilization, improvement in economic social and human development.

7

Population Ageing Demography

DEMOGRAPHIC ASPECTS

The number of persons aged 60 years or older in the world is estimated to be 605 million in 2000. This number is projected to grow to nearly 2 billion by 2050, at which time it will be as large as the population of children. This historic crossover of an increasing share of older persons and a declining share of children will mark the first time that the number of children and older persons are the same.

Persons aged 60 or older currently comprise 10 per cent of the world population. The percentage is much higher in the more developed regions (20 per cent) than in the less developed regions (8 per cent), which are at an earlier stage of the demographic transition. It is especially low in the least developed countries (5 per cent). Among individual countries, the most aged are Greece and Italy, where 24 per cent of the population is aged 60 or older in 2000. Many European countries, as well as Japan, have percentages nearly as high.

By 2050, the older ages will make up a projected 22 per cent of the world population—33 per cent in the more developed regions, 21 per cent in the less developed regions and 12 per cent in the least developed countries.

SPEED OF AGEING

The growth of the older population often receives attention in connection with the developed countries. However, the tempo of ageing is more rapid in the less developed regions than in the more developed regions. Because rapid changes in age structure may be more difficult for societies to adjust to than change that is spread over a longer time horizon, the speed of population ageing has important implications for government policies, such as pension schemes, health care and economic growth.

Figure shows, for selected countries, the dates when the population reached, or is expected to reach, the point when 7, 14 and 21 per cent of the population was aged 65 or older. (Currently, 6.9 per cent of the world's population is aged 65 or older.) Typically, the transition from 7 to 14 per cent took longer for countries that reached the 7 per cent level at an earlier date. For example, France and Sweden, which reached the 7 per cent point before 1900, took 114 years and 82 years, respectively, to reach 14 per cent. That same transition required only 24 years in Japan, from 1970 to 1994.

Several developing countries shown in figure will also make a rapid transition from 7 to 14 per cent aged 65 or older. Brazil, Indonesia, the Republic of Korea and Tunisia are projected to make this transition in a time-span of under 25 years, and the two most populous countries, China and India, may require only 25 and 28 years, respectively.

Number of People:

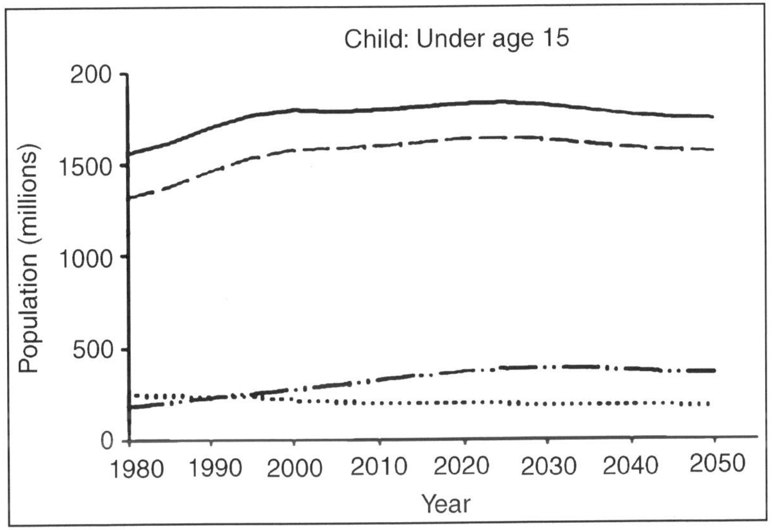

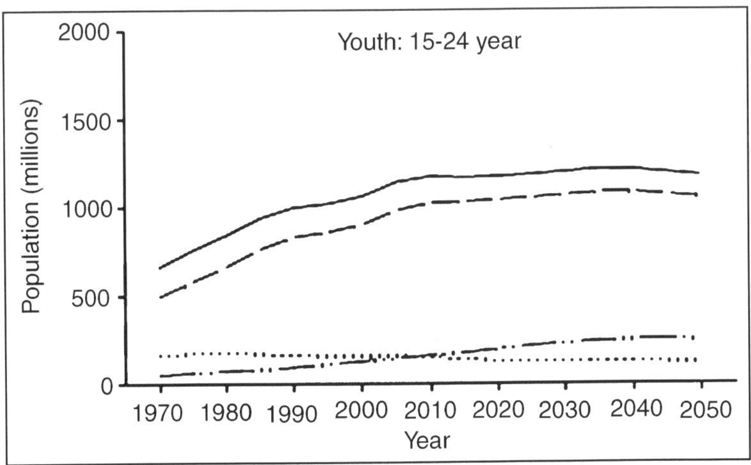

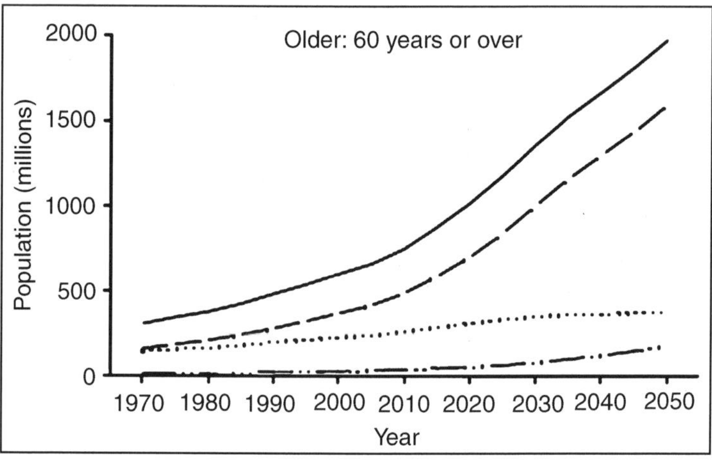

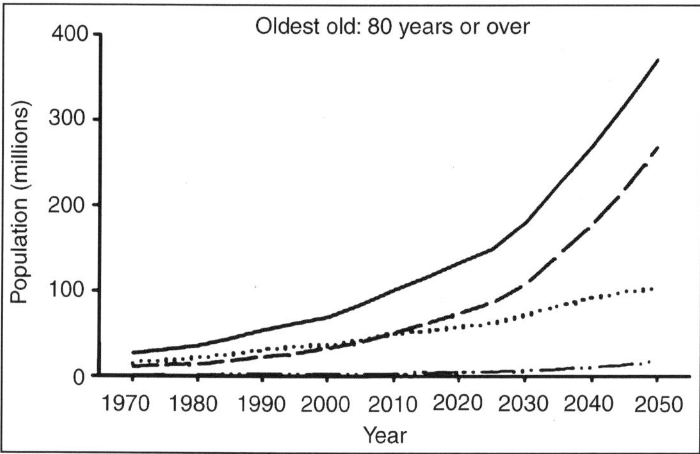

Average annual growth rate of the Population:

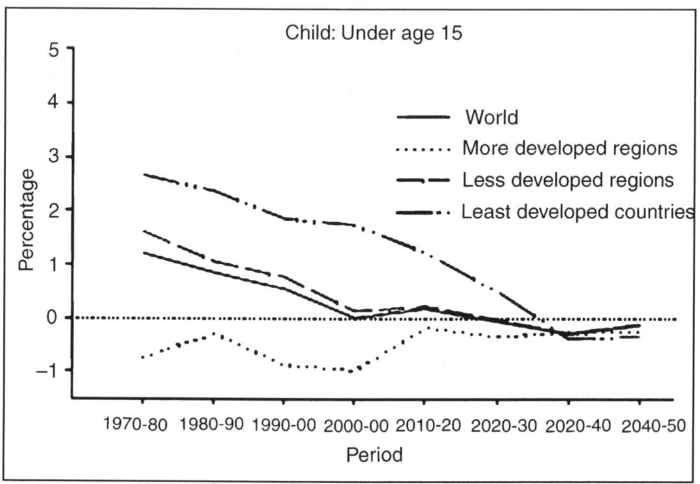

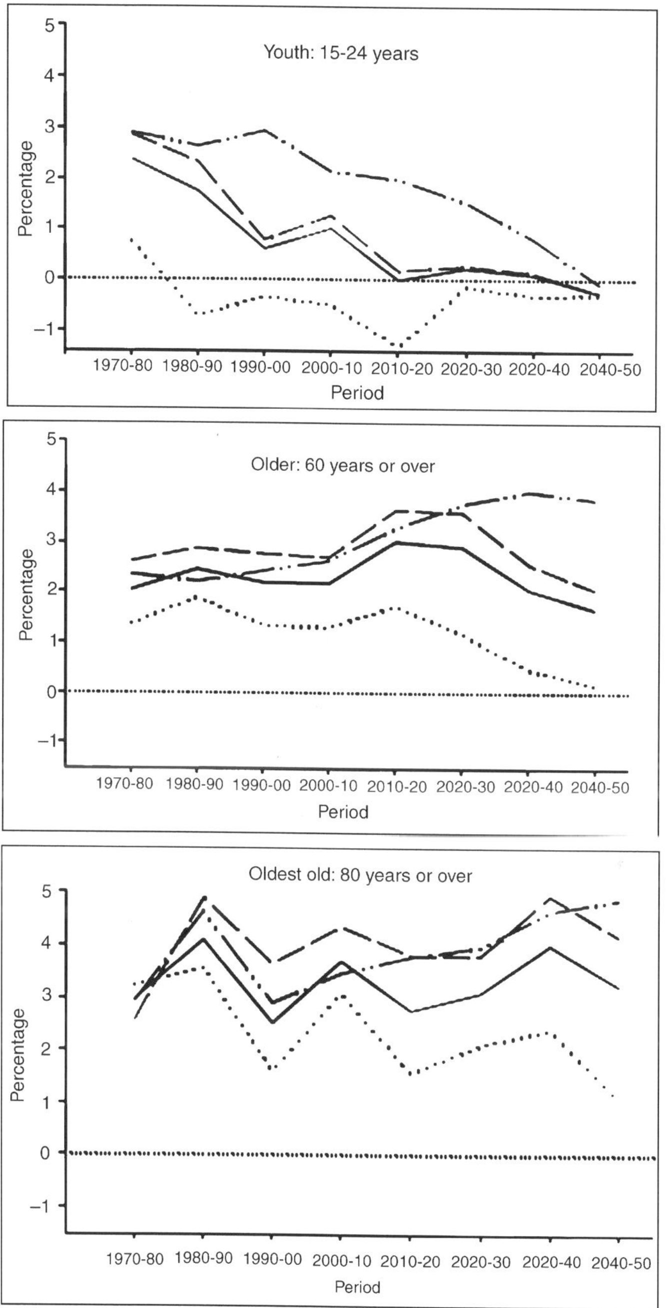

Fig. Growth in Population Size and Age-specific Annual Growth Rates, for the Child, Youth and Older Populations, 1970-2050

In many cases, it will take substantially less time for the transition from 14 to 21 per cent aged 65 years or older than it took to move from 7 to 14 per cent. Although no country has yet reached the point where 21 per cent of the population is aged 65 or older, some countries, including Italy and Japan, are expected to reach that point before 2015; in Japan, the transition from 14 to 21 per cent will have taken only 16 years, and in Italy, 23 years.

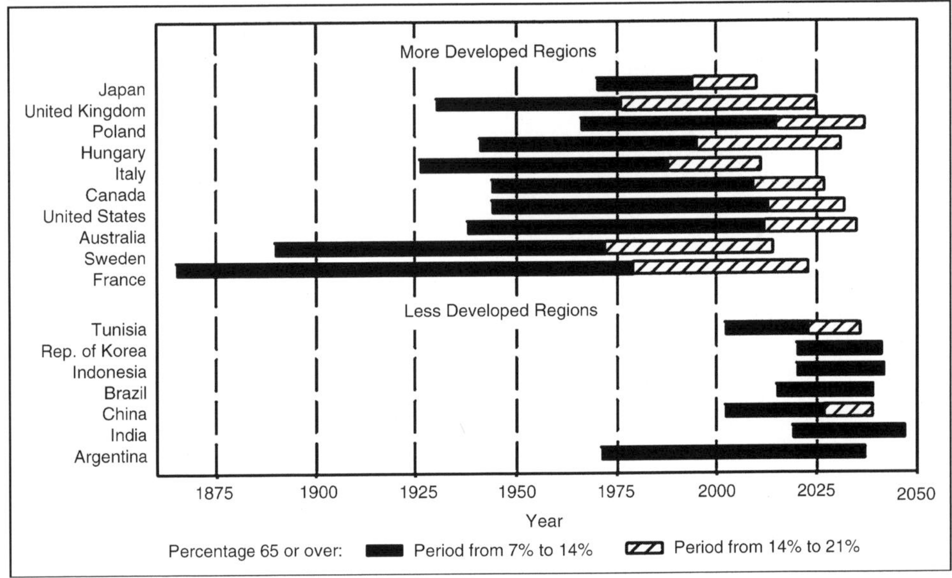

Fig. Time when the Percentage of the Population Aged 65 or Over Reached or will Reach 7, 14 and 21 Per cent: Selected Countries

Note: For countries where the percentage aged over 65 years will reach 21 per cent after 2050, only the period between attainment of the 7 and 14 per cent points is shown.

At a later date, Canada and the United States of America are also expected to make a rapid transition from 14 to 21 per cent aged 65 or older as the large "baby boom" cohorts enter the higher ages.

Thus, in the near future, some societies will be faced not only with older populations than have ever existed at the national level, but also with populations that are ageing at an extremely rapid pace.

AGEING AND GENDER

Population ageing is, in basic demographic respects, not "gender-neutral". The evolution to an older age structure changes the balance in numbers of men and women in the whole population.

Men's higher mortality over the life course means that women typically outnumber men at older ages, and the difference is quite large among the oldest old. At ages 60 or older, there were an estimated 81 men for every 100 women globally in 2000, and at ages 80 or older there were only 53 men for every 100 women.

The sex ratios of older age groups are lower in the more developed regions than in the less developed regions, since there are larger differences in life expectancy between the sexes in the more developed regions. In addition, the sex ratio in the oldest age groups in the more developed regions retains the effect of the heavy loss of males in some countries during the Second World War.

Table. Sex Ratios by Age in the More and Less Developed Regions, 2000 (Men per 100 Women)

Age	World	More developed regions	Less developed regions
For broad age groups			
Total	101	95	103
<15	106	105	106
15-59	103	101	104
60+	81	71	88
80+	53	44	64

Age	World	More developed regions	Less developed regions
For 5-Year groups, ages 60 or over			
60-64	94	87	97
65-69	89	82	93
70-74	81	72	86
75-79	69	59	78
80-84	60	51	69
85-89	48	41	59
90-94	36	32	46
95-99	27	23	37
100+	25	19	38

Given the age patterns of the sex ratio, the rapid growth of the elderly population and the increase in the proportion in older age groups imply a decrease in the sex ratio for the total population and a greater increase in the number of older women than of older men. Projected increases between 2000 and 2050 in the number of persons aged 60 or older are 636 million for men and 729 million for women in the world as a whole. Projected increases during the same period in the number of persons aged 80 or older are 116 million for men and 185 million for women.

Concomitant with dramatic improvements in average lifespan has been the widening differential over time between male and female longevity. By 1995-2000, the female advantage in life expectancy at birth has grown to almost eight years in more developed regions and three years in less developed regions. The advantage, however, diminishes during the life course and by age 60, the male-female differential has narrowed to four years in more developed regions and to only two years in less developed regions.

At current mortality rates (for 1995-2000), almost 40 per cent of girls and about one quarter of boys born can expect to survive to the "oldest old" ages, 80 years or older. While the increased likelihood of surviving to older ages is obviously due to mortality declines at younger ages, recent decades have also seen significant mortality improvements among the older population, including the oldest old, and these trends so far have been more beneficial to women than to men.

At older ages, women are less likely to be married and more likely to be widowed than are men, not only because they survive on average to higher ages, but also because most women marry men several years older than themselves. While more than three quarters (79 per cent) of older men are married, on a global basis, less than one half (43 per cent) of older women are married.

The longer-term effect of gender differences in marriage age on later widowhood is only one of many ways in which demographic, as well as economic and social circumstances in early life have diverging ramifications for men and women in old age.

DEMOGRAPHIC CAUSES OF POPULATION AGEING

The process of population ageing is determined primarily by trends in fertility rates and secondarily by mortality rates. Any population with a long history of high fertility has a "young" age structure, similar in its general features to the present age structure for the group of least developed countries. The average age of the population starts to rise when fertility rates decline.

For the period 1995-2000, 61 countries in the world, representing 44 per cent of the world's population, are at or below replacement fertility. By 2015, the world's population is projected to reach 7.2 billion, of which about two thirds will be living in countries at or below replacement fertility.

The impact of mortality decline is more variable, depending on whether the decline in mortality operates mainly at younger or at older ages. In fact, the first stages of mortality decline have usually particularly benefited infants and children, and have often served to make the population younger. However, changes in mortality may assume a greater importance for population ageing later in the demographic transition.

In countries where mortality rates at young ages are already low, further declines have tended to affect mainly the adult and older ages, and have contributed to population ageing. For example, Caselli and Vallin have demonstrated the growing impact of mortality change in population projections of France and Italy.

They concluded that even if Italian fertility remained at a very low level of 1.4 children per woman through the year 2040, more than half the increase in the proportion of the population aged 60 or older would be due to mortality change, and less than half to the earlier fertility trends.

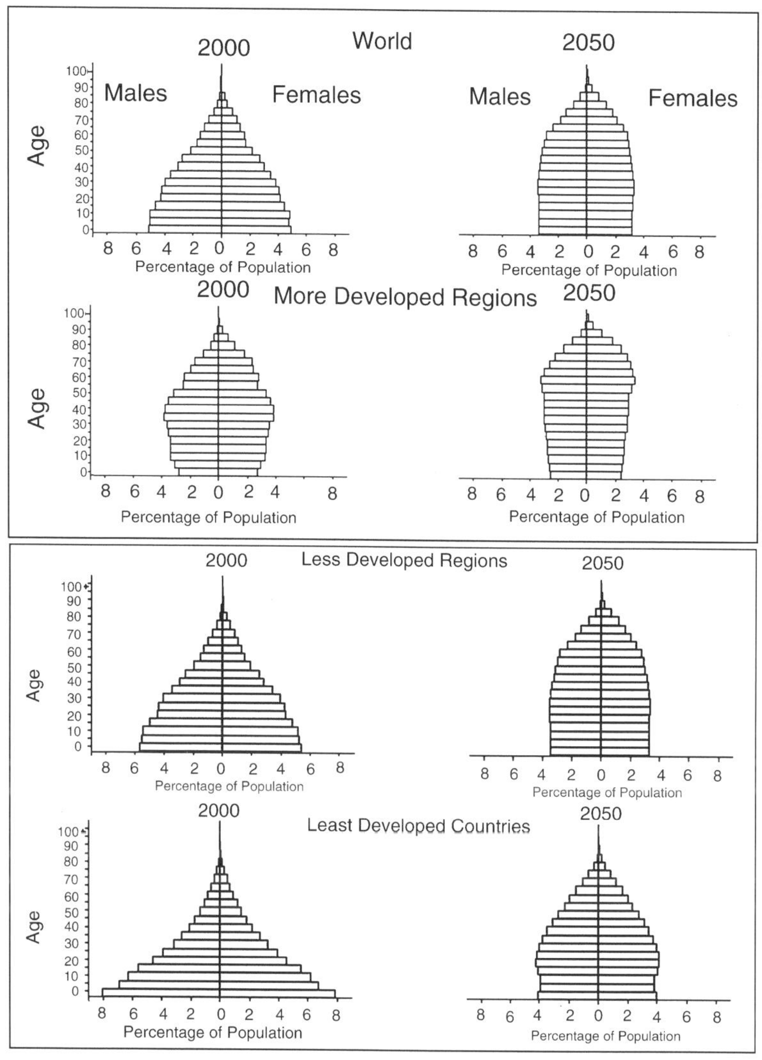

Fig. Population Pyramids: Age and Sex Distribution, 2000 and 2050

TRENDS IN DEPENDENCY RATIOS

Demographic dependency ratios are used as approximate indicators of the relative sizes of the nonworking-age and working-age populations.

The youth-dependency ratio (the number of children per 100 persons of labour force age, ages 15-64 years) and the elderly-dependency ratio (the number aged 65 years or older per 100 persons of labour force age) indicate the dependency burden on workers and how the type of dependency shifts from children to older persons during the demographic transition. The potential economic implications of falling or rising burdens of demographic dependency have been an area of active research. Since 1970, the youth-dependency ratio has been declining in all regions, while the over-65 dependency ratio is rising. Trends for the total ratio in different countries and regions depend upon the relative size and speed of these countervailing trends in the older and younger components. In general, the total dependency burden declined between 1970 and 2000. In the more developed regions, the total dependency ratio decreased over that period from 56 to 48 dependent-aged persons per 100 aged 15 to 64. The ratio will increase between the present and 2025 and is projected to rise further, to 70, by 2050.

Table. Trends in Age-dependency Ratios, by Region-1970 to 2050 (Percentage)

Region	1970	2000	2025	2050
Dependency ratio: Total				
World total	75	58	51	56
More developed regions	56	48	58	70
Less developed regions	84	60	50	54
Least developed countries	90	82	63	47
Africa	92	84	63	47
Asia	80	56	48	57
Europe	56	48	56	72
Latin America and the Caribbean	87	59	50	58
Northern America	62	51	59	64
Oceania	65	54	56	60
Under Age 15				
World total	66	47	36	31
More developed regions	41	27	25	26
Less developed regions	77	52	37	31
Least developed countries	84	77	56	35
Africa	86	78	56	35
Asia	73	47	33	30
Europe	39	26	23	25
Latin America and the Caribbean	79	50	35	32
Northern America	46	32	29	28
Oceania	53	39	33	30
Ages 65 or over				
World total	10	11	16	26
More developed regions	15	21	33	44
Less developed regions	7	8	13	23
Least developed countries	6	6	6	12
Africa	6	6	6	12
Asia	7	9	15	27
Europe	16	22	33	47
Latin America and the Caribbean	8	9	14	27
Northern America	16	19	30	36
Oceania	12	15	23	30

Note: The rations show the ratio of the numbers of persons aged under 15 years and over 65 years to the number aged 15 to 64 years, expressed as a percentage.

In the less developed regions, the overall dependency ratio in 1970 was 84, much higher than in the more developed regions, but it decreased rapidly to 60 by 2000, is projected to decline further to 50 by 2025 and then to increase slightly between 2025 and 2050.

The impact of demographic ageing is clearly visible in the old-age dependency ratio, which is increasing in both more and less developed regions during the period from 1970 to 2050. Between 2000 and 2050, the old-age dependency ratio will double in more developed regions and almost triple in less developed regions.

The amount and pace of change in demographic dependency ratios varies greatly between countries. Large swings in dependency ratios are typically initiated or accentuated by rapid fertility declines, but those effects take many years to play out.

Four examples are shown in figure to illustrate a range of situations and trends:

- Argentina has experienced a gradual fertility decline, with relatively minor fluctuations over a long period. It is projected to experience only minor changes in the total dependency ratio, which will remain near 60 over the entire period from 1970 to 2050.

In Italy, the total fertility rate plummeted after the mid-1970s to reach the unprecedentedly low level of 1.2 by the early 1990s. The total dependency ratio initially declined, but increases in the over-65 dependency ratio will dominate the trend into the future, and will produce an especially rapid rise in demographic dependency after 2020. The Republic of Korea experienced a rapid fertility decline after 1970, and the total dependency ratio fell to an unusually low level of 39 by 2000.

The overall ratio will not begin to rise appreciably until after 2015, but it will then increase rapidly. Kenya shows an extremely high child-dependency ratio, with a total dependency ratio of 115 in 1980. Kenya had one of the highest levels of fertility in the world, estimated at 8.1 children per woman during the period from 1960 to 1980, before beginning a rapid fertility decline, which is projected to continue. By 2000, Kenya's under-15 and over-65 ratios were similar to those seen in the Republic of Korea 30 years earlier.

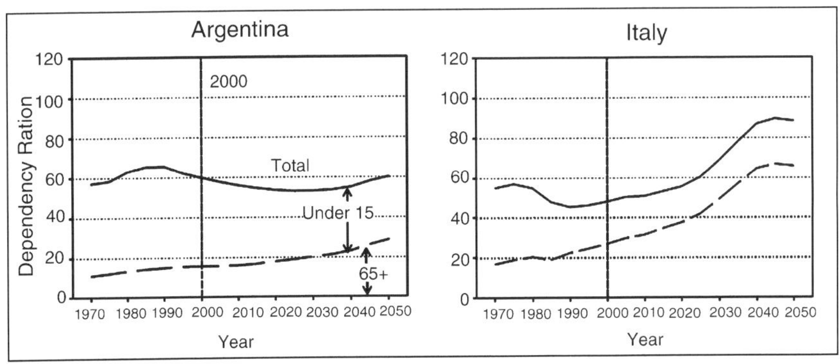

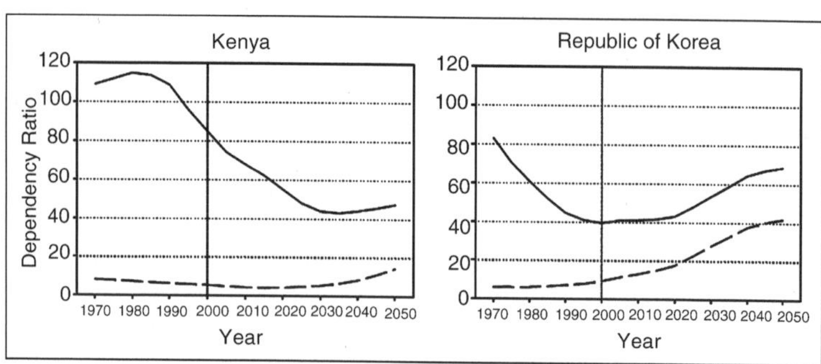

Fig. Estimated and Projected Trends in Age-dependency Ratios in Selected Countries (Persons Aged Under 15 or Over 65 Years Per 100 Persons Aged 15-64 Years)

URBANIZATION

Consistent with the global trend of urbanization, the older population is becoming more concentrated in urban areas. By 2000, the majority of the world's older persons (51 per cent) will live in urban areas; by 2025, this is expected to climb to 62 per cent of older persons. These figures, however, mask the large divergence between more and less developed regions. In the more developed regions, 74 per cent of older persons are urban dwellers, while in the less developed regions, which remain predominantly rural, slightly more than one third (37 per cent) of the elderly reside in urban areas. Despite the increasing urbanization of the older population, rural areas remain disproportionately older than urban areas in many countries as a result of migration of young persons to urban areas and the return migration of older persons to rural areas.

8

Development Goals and Population Challenges

INTRODUCTION

Part one of this report provides a global overview of demographic trends for major areas and selected countries. It reviews major population trends relating to population size and growth, urbanization and city growth, population ageing, fertility and contraception, mortality, including HIV/AIDS, and international migration. In addition, a section on population policies has been included, in which the concerns and responses of Governments to the major population trends are summarized.

The outcomes of the United Nations conferences convened during the 1990s set an ambitious development agenda reaffirmed by the United Nations Millennium Declaration in September 2000. The 1994 International Conference on Population and Development, being one of the major United Nations conferences of the decade, addressed all population aspects relevant for development and provided in its Programme of Action a comprehensive set of measures to achieve the development objectives identified. Given the crucial importance of population factors for development, the full implementation of the Programme of Action and the key actions for its further implementation will significantly contribute to the achievement of the universally agreed development goals, including those in the Millennium Declaration.

Part two discusses the relevance that particular actions contained in those documents have for the attainment of universally agreed development goals, including the Millennium Development Goals. It also describes the key population trends relevant for development and the human rights basis that underpins key conference objectives and recommendations for action. It is largely based on the discussion and documentation of the *Seminar on the Relevance of Population Aspects for the Achievement of the Millennium Development Goals*, held in New York from 17 to 19 November 2004.

The Seminar brought together representatives of the offices, funds, programmes and agencies of the United Nations system as well as experts to discuss the relevance of the ICPD Programme of Action for the attainment of the internationally agreed development goals. The demographic trends presented are based on the results of *World Population Prospects: The 2004 Revision,* the nineteenth round of official United Nations population estimates and projections prepared by the Population Division of the Department of Economic and Social Affairs of the Secretariat. The world demographic trends are based on population estimates and projections made separately for each country or area.

Projections of the population by age and sex are prepared by using the components method, which requires that explicit assumptions be made about future levels of fertility, mortality and international migration. Sets of countries are grouped into geographical regions and major areas, more developed regions and less developed regions, as well as into the group of least developed countries. Data on urban, city and rural population growth are derived from the Population Division publication *World Urbanization Prospects: The 2003 Revision.*

This publication presents estimates and projections of urban and rural populations for all countries of the world and of all urban agglomerations with 750,000 inhabitants or more in 2000. Data on contraceptive use are based on information from *World Contraceptive Use 2003* and *World Fertility Report 2003,* issued by the Population Division. The publications are part of the Population Division's ongoing monitoring of the use of family planning at the world level. The publications present, among other things, the most recent data available on current contraceptive practice, as well as recent trends in contraceptive use, for the countries and areas of the world. Data on international migration are derived from the Population Division publications *Trends in Total Migrant Stock: The 2003 Revision, International Migration Report 2002* and *World Economic and Social Survey 2004: International Migration.*

These publications present estimates of levels and trends of international migration for each country and area of the world. They also show the growth rate of migrant stock, the percentage of national populations that are international migrants and the percentage of migrants by sex. The estimates are derived mostly from data on the foreign-born enumerated by censuses.

The population policies of Governments presented in the present report are from *World Population Policies 2003,* also issued by the Population Division. The monitoring of national population policies at the international level has a long history that goes back to the World Population Plan of Action adopted at the United Nations World Population Conference held in Bucharest in August 1974. The policies examined cover the major population variables and are presented in a descriptive and concise format, focusing on analytical comparisons of countries and regions at present as well as over time. As is the case in the preparation of population estimates and projections, the monitoring of national population policies is guided by principles of objectivity and non-advocacy.

WORLD DEMOGRAPHIC TRENDS

POPULATION SIZE AND GROWTH

World population passed 6 billion persons at the end of the twentieth century and stands at 6.5 billion in 2005. It is currently growing at 1.2 per cent annually. The addition of the sixth billion took place in a 12-year period, namely, between 1987 and 1999, which is the shortest period within which the world has gained a billion persons. The addition of the next billion, the seventh, is expected to take about 13 years.

The population of the world is expected to increase by 2.6 billion during the next 45 years, from 6.5 billion today to 9.1 billion in 2050. However the realization of these projections is contingent on ensuring that couples have access to family planning and that efforts to arrest the current spread of the HIV/AIDS epidemic are successful in reducing its growth momentum.

The population of the more developed regions, currently estimated at slightly more than 1.2 billion persons, is anticipated to change little during the coming decades. However, some noteworthy demographic changes are expected to occur. In many countries, especially in Europe, populations are projected to decline, as fertility levels are expected to remain below replacement levels. Other developed countries will see their populations continue to grow because their fertility levels are closer to replacement levels and because of significant flows of international migration. The population of the less developed regions is projected to rise steadily, from about 5.3 billion persons today to 7.8 billion persons by mid-century.

That projection assumes continuing declines in fertility. In the absence of such declines, the population of the less developed regions could be substantially larger than projected. Particularly rapid growth is expected in the group of 50 countries classified as the least developed. By mid-century, for example, the population of the least developed countries could more than double in size.

The annual increment to world population during 2000-2005 has been estimated at 76 million persons. Six countries account for nearly half of that amount: India (22 per cent); China (11 per cent); and Pakistan, Nigeria, the United States of America and Bangladesh (about 4 per cent each). As a result of India's relatively rapid growth, it is expected to overtake China as the most populous country in the world by 2030. An additional 16 countries account for a quarter of the annual growth of the world's population. Among the 22 countries that together account for 75 per cent of the current world population growth, there is only one developed country, namely, the United States.

The growth of the United States population represents close to 4 per cent of world population growth; however, about 40 per cent of the population growth of the united states is the result of international migration.

Table. Countries Accounting for 75 Per cent of Population Growth in the

S. No	Country	Annual population increase 2000-2005 (millions)	Cumulated percentage
1	India	16.5	22
2	China	8.4	33
3	Pakistan	3.1	37
4	United States of America	2.8	40
5	Nigeria	2.8	44
6	Indonesia	2.7	48
7	Bangladesh	2.6	51
8	Brazil	2.5	54
9	Ethiopia	1.8	57
10	Dem. Republic of the Congo	1.5	59
11	Philippines	1.5	61
12	Mexico	1.4	63
13	Egypt	1.3	64
14	Afghanistan	1.2	66
15	Viet Nam	1.1	67
16	Turkey	1.0	69
17	Uganda	0.9	70
18	Iraq	0.7	71
19	Kenya	0.7	72
20	United Republic of Tanzania	0.7	73
21	Colombia	0.7	74
22	Sudan	0.7	75
	World	75.8	100

The world population growth rate has fallen from its peak of 2 per cent per year in the late 1960s to 1.2 per cent today. Nevertheless, United Nations population projections point to continued population growth during this century. The world population is expected to reach 7 billion persons by 2012, and 8 billion by 2027; the 9 billion mark should be reached just before 2050 (medium variant).

While world population is continuing to grow, considerable diversity exists in the expected population growth of countries. Though it is anticipated that the population of many countries will increase greatly in the coming decades, several countries are expected to grow little and quite a few are actually projected to experience a decline in their population size.

The contributions of the nine countries adding 100 million or more persons by mid-century are shown in table. India is expected to be the largest contributor to world population growth by far, adding around 570 million persons by 2050. After India comes Pakistan, which is projected to gain about 160 million more persons, followed by Nigeria, the Democratic Republic of the Congo and China, with an additional 141 million, 127 million and 118 million persons, respectively.

In contrast, the Russian Federation is expected to experience the largest decline in population, about 35 million persons; Ukraine, Japan and Italy follow, with projected decreases of 23 million, 15 million and 7 million persons, respectively.

Table. Top Nine Countries in Terms of Population Increase and T To OP Nine in Terms of Population Decrease from 2000 2050: Medium Variant

	Country	Population Change, 2000-2050 (Millions)
	A. Population Increase	
1	India	572
2	Pakistan	162
3	Nigeria	141
4	Dem. Republic of the Congo	127
5	China	118
6	Bangladesh	114
7	United States of America	111
8	Uganda	103
9	Ethiopia	102
	B. Population Decrease	
1	Russian Federation	–35
2	Ukraine	–23
3	Japan	–15
4	Italy	–7
5	Poland	–7
6	Romania	–5
7	Germany	–4
8	Belarus	–3
9	Bulgaria	–3

POPULATION AGEING

During the twentieth century, the proportion of older persons (those aged 60 years or over) continued to rise and this trend is expected to continue well into the twentyfirst century.

For example, the proportion of older persons was 8 per cent in 1950 and 10 per cent in 2005 and is projected to reach about 22 per cent by mid-century. As the twenty-first century began, the world population included approximately 600 million older persons, triple the number recorded 50 years earlier. By 2050, the world is expected to have some 2 billion older persons—once again, a tripling of the number in that age group within a span of 50 years. Globally, the population of older persons is growing by 2.0 per cent each year, considerably faster than the population as a whole. For at least the next 25 years, the older population is expected to continue growing more rapidly than other age groups. The growth rate of those aged 60 years or over will reach 3.1 per cent annually in the period 2010-2015. Such rapid growth will require far-reaching economic and social adjustments in most countries.

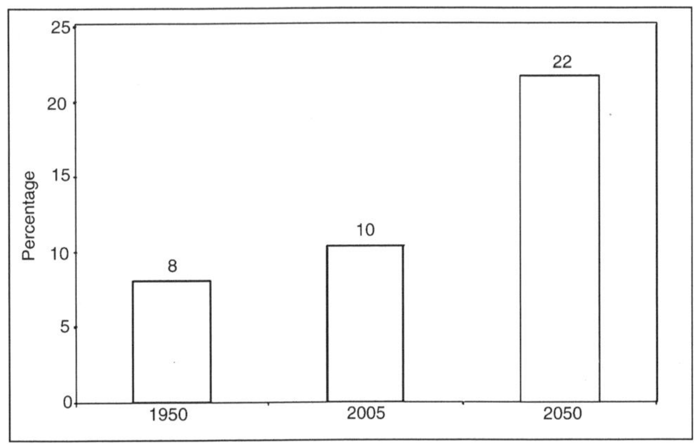

Fig. Proportion of Population Aged 60Years or Over: World, 1950-2050

The population of all countries will continue to age substantially. For example, the median age of the world will rise from 28 years today to 38 years in 2050. As already noted, the number of persons aged 60 years or over will rise from 10 per cent of the world population today to 22 per cent in 2050. The percentage aged 80 years or over will rise from just 1 per cent today to 4 per cent in 2050. Marked differences exist between regions in the number and proportion of older persons.

In the more developed regions, one fifth of the population was aged 60 years or over in the year 2005; by 2050, that proportion is expected to reach one third. In the less developed regions, 8 per cent of the population is currently over age 60; however, by 2050, older persons will make up one fifth of the population. As the pace of population ageing is much faster in the developing countries than in the developed ones, developing countries will have less time to adjust to the consequences of population ageing. Moreover, population ageing in the developing countries is taking place at much lower levels of socio-economic development than has been the case in the developed countries.

The older population is itself ageing. The fastest-growing age group in the world is the oldest old, those aged 80 years or over. Their number is currently increasing at a rate of 4.2 per cent per year and they constitute more than one eighth of the total number of older persons. By the middle of the century, one fifth of older persons will be aged 80 years or over. The potential support ratio (PSR) indicates the dependency burden on potential workers.

The impact of demographic ageing is visible in the PSR, which has fallen and will continue to fall. From 1950 to 2005, the PSR fell from 12 to 9 people in the working ages per each person aged 65 years or over. By mid-century, the PSR for the world is projected to fall to four working-age persons for each person aged 65 years or over. PSRs have important implications for social security schemes, particularly traditional systems in which current workers pay for the benefits of current retirees.

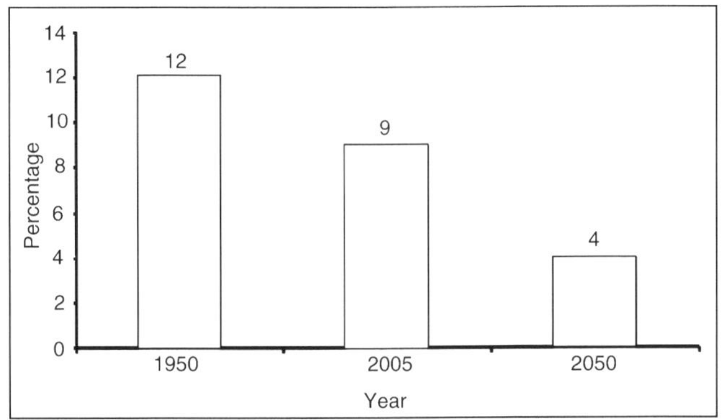

Fig. Potential Support Ration (PSR): World, 1950-2050

The majority of older persons are women, as life expectancy for women is higher than that for men. In 2005, there were 67 million more women than men aged 60 years or over and, at the oldest ages (80 years or above), there were almost twice as many women as men. The declines in fertility reinforced by increasing longevity have produced and will continue to produce unprecedented changes in the age structure of all societies, notably the historic reversal in the proportions of young and older persons. The profound, pervasive and enduring consequences of population ageing present opportunities as well as challenges for all societies.

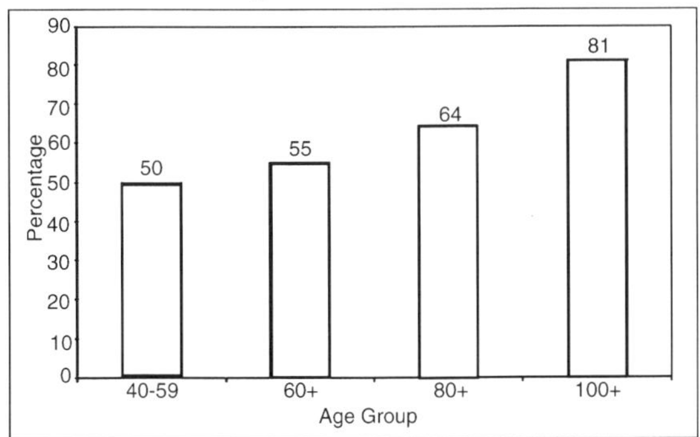

Fig. Proportion of Women Among Persons Aged 40-59, 60+, 80+ and 100+ years: World, 2005

FERTILITY AND CONTRACEPTION

Fertility has declined substantially over the last several decades in all areas of the world. Around 30 years ago, for example, the total fertility rate—that is to say, the average number of children a woman would bear if fertility rates remained unchanged during her lifetime—was close to five children per woman at the world level. By the end of the twentieth century, the fertility rate had declined to slightly less than three children per woman.

In 2000-2005, 84 countries or areas exhibited fertility levels at or below replacement level. These countries accounted for about 45 per cent of the world's population, or 2.8 billion persons in 2003. Because their levels of fertility are low and are expected to remain low during the coming decades, the populations of those countries are projected to grow relatively little by mid-century, and in a number of countries population is expected to decline.

The remaining countries of the world, with a combined population of about 3.5 billion persons, exhibit total fertility levels above replacement level. Forty-two countries have fertility levels at or above five children per woman in 2000-2005. As a consequence, the population of that group of countries is expected to grow markedly in the coming decades.

Among the developing countries, the pace of fertility decline during the recent past has varied significantly. Although by 2000-2005 most countries in the less developed regions are already far advanced in the transition from high to low fertility, there are some 13 countries that exhibit sustained high fertility and for which either there is no recent evidence about fertility trends or the available evidence does not indicate the onset of sustained fertility decline. In those countries, even though fertility is projected to decline after 2005, it is not expected to reach replacement level by the period 2045-2050.

The high fertility of those countries will lead to rapid population growth. All but the Congo belong to the group of the least developed countries. The continuation of rapid population growth presents serious challenges to the future development of those countries. Contraceptive use increased markedly over the past decade. At the global level, contraceptive prevalence increased from 54 per cent in 1990 to 59 per cent in 1995 and to an estimated 63 per cent in 2000. The fastest increases were in Africa and Latin America and the Caribbean where contraceptive prevalence increased by more than 1 percentage point per year, on average.

The increase was less rapid in Asia where prevalence increased by 0.8 percentage points per year between 1990 and 2000. Modern methods account for a large proportion of current contraceptive use, especially in the less developed regions where they account for 90 per cent of contraceptive use compared with 81 per cent in the more developed regions. The three methods most used are female sterilization, the intrauterine device (IUD) and the pill, with prevalence levels of 21 per cent, 14 per cent and 7 per cent, respectively. These three methods account for two thirds of use worldwide. Traditional methods are more popular in the developed countries than in the developing countries: they are used by 13 per cent of married couples in the more developed countries compared with just 6 per cent in the developing countries. The most used traditional methods include rhythm (periodic abstinence) and withdrawal.

In the world as a whole, those methods are used by about 7 per cent of married women. Short-acting and reversible methods are more popular in the developed countries, whereas longer-acting methods are more popular in the developing countries. In the developed countries, contraceptive users rely mostly on pills (16 per cent of married women) and condoms (13 per cent). In contrast, female sterilization and IUDs, used by 23 per cent and 15 per cent of married women, respectively, dominate in the developing countries.

MORTALITY, INCLUDING HIV/AIDS

During the twentieth century, mortality experienced the most rapid decline in the history of humanity. Although the sustained reduction of mortality had started in the eighteenth century, it gained momentum in the early part of the twentieth century as better hygiene, improved nutrition and medical practices based on scientific evidence became the rule in the more advanced countries. Despite the setbacks brought about by the First and Second World Wars, by the period 1950-1955, mortality had declined markedly in the more developed regions.

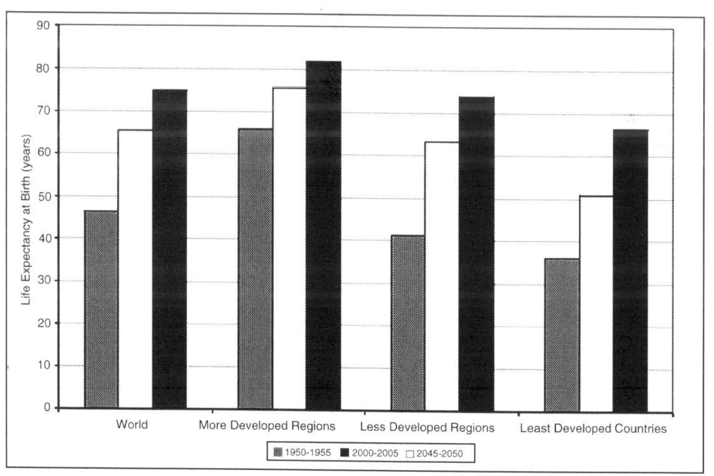

Fig. Life Expectancy at Birth for the World, the More Developed Regions, the Less Developed Regions and the Least Developed Countries, 1950-1955, 2000-2005 and 2045-2050

For example, by the middle of the twentieth century, average life expectancy at birth had reached 66 years, ranging from 63 years in Southern Europe to 70 years in Australia and New Zealand. The century also marked an important turning point in the less developed regions. With the expanded use of antibiotics, vaccines and insecticides, mortality in the developing world began to decline rapidly.

For example, life expectancy at birth for the less developed regions increased by slightly more than 50 per cent from 1950-1955 to 2000-2005, rising from about 41 to 63 years. As a result, the mortality differentials between the less developed and the more developed regions narrowed. By the period 2000-2005, the difference in life expectancy between the two groups amounted to 12 years instead of 25 years, the difference observed in the period 1950-1955.

There remains, however, a group of countries—the least developed—where the reduction of mortality has lagged behind. While mortality declined in the least developed countries, it did not keep pace with mortality improvements in the less developed regions. For example, the difference between the life expectancy for the least developed countries and that for the less developed regions as a whole increased from 5 years in the period 1950-1955 to 12 years in the period 2000-2005.

A major reason for such an increase is that the 50 countries classified as least developed include 26 that are highly affected by the HIV/AIDS epidemic. Until fairly recently it was expected that mortality would continue declining in all countries, especially in those that were still experiencing moderate to high mortality levels because of their late start in the transition to low mortality.

However, two developments have made it necessary to adjust those expectations: HIV/AIDS and the shocks from socio-economic transformations in countries with economies in transition. The emergence of the virus that causes acquired immunodeficiency syndrome (AIDS) and the worldwide pandemic that it has generated have already produced marked increases in mortality in the countries most affected by the disease. It is estimated that by the end of 2003, about 58 million persons had been infected by the virus and about 38 million were still alive.

Some 92 per cent of those infected with HIV are living in the developing countries, with sub-Saharan Africa experiencing the highest prevalence rates. In addition, the number of countries where HIV prevalence has become significant has been growing rapidly in Asia and Latin America and the Caribbean.

While it is not yet certain that the spread in those regions will follow the pattern observed in Africa, rapid and effective responses may be required to avert the devastation that Africa is already experiencing.

It has also become evident that mortality has tended to stagnate or even to increase in certain countries with economies in transition, most of which exhibited fairly low mortality in the period 1950-1955. The causes for the slowdown or reversal of the transition to low mortality are multiple and complex, but they have no doubt been exacerbated by the momentous social and economic transformations resulting from the political changes taking place in the former communist countries since 1985. As a result of those developments and in the light of the increases in mortality that have occurred in countries affected by conflict or civil strife, considerable uncertainty exists about the future path of mortality.

It seems less certain than a decade or two ago that mortality will necessarily decrease in all countries in future. Nevertheless, mortality has declined more rapidly than expected in a number of developed countries, so that the possibility of further medical and technological breakthroughs that may increase the human lifespan cannot be ruled out, opening up the prospect of a future where expectations of life at birth of above 85 or 90 years will be a reality in certain populations.

With regard to gender differences in mortality, by the end of the twentieth century, female life expectancy was higher than male life expectancy in all regions, although the difference between the two was relatively small in Western Africa and South-central Asia. However, even in those regions, there was a marked gain in life expectancy for females in relation to males.

In the period 1950-1955, South-central Asia had been the only region where females had a lower life expectancy than males. Female life expectancy increased more than male life expectancy during the last half-century in three major areas: Asia, Europe and Latin America and the Caribbean. In contrast, in Africa, Northern America and Oceania, the female advantage remained relatively unchanged or declined.

Table. Life Expectancy at Birth by Sex, and Sex Differentials, for the World and Major Areas, 1950-1955 and 2000-2005

Major area or region	Male (years)		Female (years)		Difference between female and male life expectancy at birth (years)	
	1950-1955	2000-2005	1950-1955	2000-2005	1950-1955	2000-2005
World	45.3	63.2	48.0	67.7	2.8	4.5
More developed regions	63.5	71.9	68.5	79.3	5.0	7.4
Less developed regions	40.3	61.7	42.0	65.2	1.7	3.5
Least developed regions	35.4	50.1	36.8	52.0	1.4	1.9
Less developed regions without the least developed countries	41.1	64.2	42.8	68.0	1.7	3.8
Europe	62.9	69.6	67.9	78.0	5.0	8.4
Northern America	66.1	74.8	71.9	80.2	5.8	5.4
Oceania	58.1	71.7	62.9	76.2	4.8	4.5
Africa	37.1	48.2	39.7	49.9	2.6	1.7
Asia	40.7	65.4	42.2	69.2	1.4	3.8
Latin America and the Caribbean	49.7	68.3	53.1	74.9	3.4	6.6

In Europe, life expectancy of females made the greatest gains with respect to that of males, whereas in Africa life expectancy of males made the greatest gains with respect to that of females. Generally, the female advantage in life expectancy increased from 1950-1955 to 2000-2005. Over the past half century, a major part of the reduction of mortality has occurred in childhood. Overall levels of life expectancy are strongly determined by mortality at young ages, especially when mortality is high. Consequently, the marked increases in life expectancy that have occurred since 1950 at the world level reflect in large part sharp drops of mortality in childhood. Future reductions of mortality are expected to result in the virtual elimination of deaths at young ages in many countries. However, certain regions and countries are expected to fare better than others in achieving such a goal. Another aspect of mortality trends that needs consideration is the changing age distribution of deaths.

In contrast with the period 1950-1955, when 43 per cent of all deaths took place before age 5 and just 26 per cent occurred above age 60, by the period 2000-2005, 20 per cent of all deaths took place by age 5 and 50 per cent occurred among persons aged 60 years or over. By mid-century, it is expected that only 5 per cent of all deaths will occur before age 5 and that 79 per cent of all deaths will be those of persons aged 60 years or over.

Most regions of the world are projected to see continuing improvements in their mortality rates and, as a result, an increase in their expectations of life to levels that were, until recently, unprecedented in human history. However, for the least developed countries, even the substantial improvements expected by mid-century are unlikely to eliminate the gap in respect of mortality existing between them and the rest of the world. Moreover, given the setbacks that have occurred recently in many of those countries, it may not be at all certain that the projected improvements will be achieved.

INTERNATIONAL MIGRATION

About 175 million persons, representing about 3 per cent of the world population in 2000, resided in a country other than the one in which they had been born. The number of migrants more than doubled between 1960 and 2000. Sixty per cent of the world's migrants reside in the more developed regions, while 40 per cent reside in the less developed regions. Most of the world's migrants live in Europe (56 million), Asia (50 million) and Northern America (41 million).

The volume of international migration is nearly equal for men and women. In 2000, females constituted almost 49 per cent of all migrants, up from 47 per cent in 1960. While women and girls were slightly more numerous than males among migrants in 2000 in the more developed regions, they accounted for just under 45 per cent of all migrants in the less developed regions.

At the regional level, female migrants are more numerous than male migrants in Europe, Latin America and the Caribbean, Northern America and Oceania, but remain underrepresented in many parts of Africa and Asia.

Table. Proportion Female Among the Stock of International Migrants, by Major Area, 1960 and 2000

Major area	1960	2000
World	46.7	48.6
Developed countries	48.7	51.0
Developed countries excluding USSR	48.7	50.6
Developing countries	45.3	44.6
Africa	42.3	46.7
Asia	46.4	43.3
Latin America and the Caribbean	44.7	50.2
Northern America	49.8	50.3
Oceania	44.4	50.5
Europe	48.5	51.0
USSR (former)	48.0	52.1

Almost 1 of every 10 persons living in the more developed regions was an international migrant in 2000. In contrast, nearly 1 of every 70 persons in the developing countries was a migrant. With 35 million migrants, the United States was the single largest recipient, followed by the Russian Federation with 13 million and Germany with 7 million. The four countries with the highest proportion of international migrants were: the United Arab Emirates (68 per cent), Kuwait (49 per cent), Jordan (39 per cent) and Israel (37 per cent).

Between 1995 and 2000, the more developed regions of the world gained nearly 13 million migrants from the less developed regions, around 2.6 million migrants per year. Net migration accounted for two thirds of the population growth in the more developed regions. The largest gains took place in Northern America, which absorbed about 1.4 million migrants annually, followed by Europe with an annual net gain of over 1 million. At the end of 2003, the number of refugees in the world stood at 15 million, of whom approximately 10 million were under the mandate of the Office of the United Nations High Commissioner for Refugees (UNHCR) and 5 million under the mandate of the United Nations Relief and Works Agency for Palestine Refugees in the Near East. The largest numbers of refugees were found in Asia (8 million) and in Africa (3 million).

Three million refugees were in the developed countries and 12 million in the developing countries. The remittances sent back to the home country by migrants represent an important aspect of international migration. Those moneys are a major source of foreign exchange earnings for some countries and an important addition to gross domestic product (GDP). For example, in 2000, remittances from abroad constituted more than 10 per cent of GDP for countries such as Albania, Bosnia and Herzegovina, Cape Verde, El Salvador, Jamaica, Jordan, Nicaragua, Samoa and Yemen.

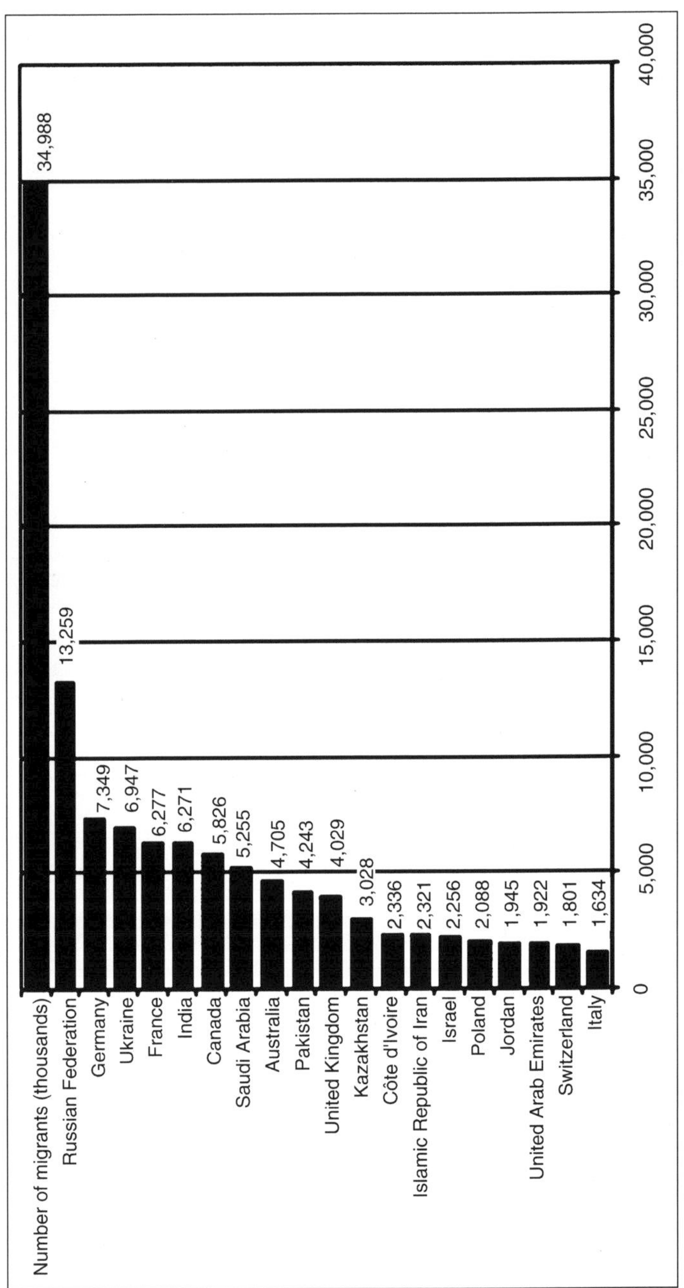

Fig. Countries with the Largest International Migrant Stock, 2000

POPULATION POLICIES

Continued high rates of population growth remain an issue of policy concern for many countries of the developing world. About half of the countries in the less developed regions consider their rate of population growth to be too high. The proportion of such countries encompass much of Africa (77 per cent) and the proportion is significant in Oceania (56 per cent). Concern with rapid population growth is lower among the countries of Asia (36 per cent) and Latin America and the Caribbean (36 per cent). Nearly 60 per cent of the countries in the less developed regions consider fertility too high and, in the group of 50 least developed countries, close to 80 per cent report fertility as too high.

The latter proportion has been rising steadily since the mid-1970s. At that time, about 1 out of 3 of the least developed countries thought its fertility was too high. Adolescent fertility is also a concern for Governments, particularly in the less developed regions. Almost two thirds of the countries in those regions and one third of the countries in the more developed regions view this as a major concern. Government support for policies and programmes that affect fertility has increased steadily during the last quarter-century: about 90 per cent of countries provide either direct or indirect support for family planning programmes and contraceptives. The practice of limiting access to contraceptives has nearly vanished. Low fertility has become a concern for an increasing number of countries in recent years, particularly in more developed regions. More than half the countries in those regions consider fertility to be too low, up from one fifth in the mid-1970s.

Of the 39 countries that consider fertility too low, 27 were in Europe and 9 in Asia. Governments' views of their country's mortality level are split according to development level. About 70 per cent of the countries in the more developed regions consider the level of life expectancy to be acceptable, compared with 35 per cent of the less developed countries and 4 per cent of the least developed countries. Some segments of the population—most notably infants and children under age 5—continue to register unacceptably high mortality levels and are considered problem groups for many countries.

Maternal mortality is another serious concern, particularly in the less developed countries. In the less developed regions, 1 country in 5 reports the level of maternal mortality to be acceptable, as compared with three fourths of the countries in the more developed regions. Only two of the least developed countries consider the level of maternal mortality to be acceptable. During the 20 years since HIV/AIDS was identified as a disease, the pandemic has emerged as one of the leading causes of adult mortality in many countries, particularly in the less developed regions of the world.

More than 80 per cent of the countries in those regions have reported that AIDS is a major concern, as have nearly 90 per cent of the least developed countries. Concern has also been substantial in the more developed regions, where three quarters of the countries view AIDS as a major concern. Developed and developing countries show a similar inclination towards restricting immigration. Among developed and developing countries, one third have policies aimed at lowering their immigration levels. In comparison, in the mid-1970s, 18 per cent of the developed countries and 3 per cent of the developing countries had adopted such policies. Concerning emigration, both the developed and the developing countries show similar trends in their views and policies. About 3 out of 4 countries, whether developed or developing, view their level of emigration as satisfactory, whereas 1 country in 4 has policies aimed at lowering emigration.

For many years, Governments have expressed concern about the spatial distribution of their populations. This concern often arises from high levels of migration from rural to urban areas, urban sprawl and the uncontrolled growth of primate cities and metropolitan areas. Governments in the past have attempted to change distribution in a variety of ways, inter alia, through building new capitals, encouraging growth in small and medium-sized cities rather than in large ones, creating regional development zones, controlling the movement of people to cities and limiting urban sprawl by curbing development. Most of those attempts have failed to achieve their objectives, and population distribution remains an area of major concern to a significant number of Governments, particularly in the less developed regions.

SUMMERY

World population has reached 6.5 billion and is currently growing at about 1.2 per cent annually. The 7 billion mark is projected to be reached in 2012, just seven years from now. Long-range population projections suggest that the world's population could ultimately stabilize at about 9 billion people. While world population is continuing to grow, considerable diversity exists in the expected population growth of countries.

The population of many countries, particularly in Africa and Asia, will increase greatly in the coming decades. In contrast, owing to below-replacement fertility levels, some developed countries are expected to experience significant population decline. The world's urban population is increasing rapidly, and is expected to increase from today's 3.2 billion persons to about 5 billion in 2030. Half the world's population is expected to live in urban areas by 2007. The number of very large urban agglomerations is increasing. Tokyo, Mexico City, New York–Newark, Mumbai (Bombay), São Paulo and Delhi all have more than 15 million persons. However, about half of all urban-dwellers live in small settlements with fewer than 500,000 inhabitants. The proportion of older persons is expected to continue rising well into the twenty-first century.

As the pace of population ageing is much faster in the developing countries than in the developed ones, developing countries will have less time to adjust to the consequences of population ageing. Moreover, population ageing in the developing countries is taking place at much lower levels of socio-economic development. Most developed countries exhibit fertility levels at or below the replacement level. Although most developing countries are far advanced in the transition from high to low fertility, some developing countries, mainly in Africa, still exhibit high fertility.

Contraceptive use has increased significantly over the past decade, from 54 per cent in 1990 to 63 per cent in 2000. Short-acting and reversible methods are more popular in the developed countries, whereas longer-acting methods are more popular in the developing countries. During the twentieth century, mortality experienced the most rapid decline in the history of humanity, owing to better hygiene, improved nutrition and medical practices based on scientific evidence. Until recently, it was expected that mortality would continue declining in all countries.

However, HIV/AIDS has already produced marked increases in mortality in Africa, the region most affected by the disease. About 175 million persons reside in a country other than the one in which they were born. The number of migrants more than doubled between 1960 and 2000; 60 per cent of the world's migrants reside in the more developed regions. Affecting countries of origin, transit and destination, international migration is in the forefront of national and international agendas.

Developed and developing countries differ significantly with regard to their population concerns. High mortality, particularly infant and child mortality, maternal mortality and mortality related to HIV/AIDS, is the most significant population concern for developing countries. The most significant demographic concern of the developed countries relates to low fertility and its consequences, including population ageing and the shrinking of the working-age population.

In sum, the current population picture is one of dynamic population change, reflected in new and diverse patterns of childbearing, mortality, migration, urbanization and ageing. The continuation and consequences of these population trends present opportunities as well as challenges for all societies in the twenty-first century.

ACHIEVING THE INTERNATIONALLY AGREED DEVELOPMENT GOALS

POPULATION TRENDS RELEVANT FOR DEVELOPMENT

The goal of development is to improve the quality of life of all people. In that sense, population is at the core of development. In 2005, 759 million, or 12 per cent, of the 6.5 billion inhabitants of the world live in the least developed countries. Between 2005 and 2015, the least developed countries as a whole are expected to absorb a quarter of all population growth in the world. High fertility levels characterize the majority of the least developed countries. Consequently, their populations are still young, with 42 per cent of their inhabitants being children under age 15.

Levels of extreme poverty in most of the least developed countries are high: over 20 per cent of their overall population live in extreme poverty, surviving on less than US$ 1 per day, and in 10 of them that proportion is higher than 40 per cent. Although fertility levels have started to decline in some of the least developed countries, the desired number of children remains high.

Nevertheless, in the majority of the least developed countries, the number of children that women have surpasses the number desired, suggesting that universal provision of family planning services could result in a reduction of unwanted fertility. The rest of the developing world, whose population amounts to 4.5 billion, includes the two population giants: China, with 1.3 billion people, and India, with 1.1 billion. In China, fertility is already well below 2 children per woman, whereas in India it is about 3 children per woman.

The process of population ageing is therefore more advanced in China, where 8 per cent of the population are aged 65 years or over. In India, the equivalent proportion is 5 per cent. However, China has a smaller proportion of children (21 per cent) than India (32 per cent) and China's dependency ratio, that is to say, the number of children and elderly persons per 10 persons of working age, is 5 compared with India's dependency ratio, which is 6. In both countries, the proportion of persons living in extreme poverty is significant, but the proportion in China (17 per cent) is about half that in India (35 per cent).

Most countries of Latin America and the Caribbean are already far advanced in the transition to low fertility. Average fertility in the region is currently 2.5 children per woman. Children under age 15 account for 30 per cent of the population and persons aged 65 years or over account for 6 per cent. There are about 6 dependants (children and the elderly) per every 10 adults of working age and that ratio is expected to continue declining as fertility falls even further. Although levels of extreme poverty tend to be below 10 per cent in most of Latin America and the Caribbean, countries in Central America tend to have higher levels of extreme poverty and most Latin American countries are characterized by the prevalence of very unequal income distributions.

A major concern in the region is therefore the reduction of this inequality. Population trends vary considerably in the remaining developing countries, with current fertility ranging from less than 1.5 children per woman in Armenia, Georgia and the Republic of Korea to over 5 children per woman in the Congo and Nigeria. On average, these countries have a fertility of about 3.1 children per woman, higher than that in Latin America and the Caribbean but similar to that of India. Because of their higher average fertility, the proportion of children in their population stands at 33 per cent, whereas the proportion of elderly amounts to just 5 per cent. The number of dependants per 10 adults of working age is 6, lower than the equivalent value of 8 for the least developed countries. That is, just as the latter would, the higher-fertility countries in this group would most likely benefit from increased efforts to reduce unwanted fertility. The countries in this group located in sub-Saharan Africa tend to have high levels of extreme poverty, often surpassing 20 per cent.

Levels of extreme poverty tend to be lower in the Asian and North African countries in this group. In developed countries, fertility declined much earlier than in the developing world and has been very low (below 2 children per woman) since the 1980s. Consequently, population declined in 17 developed countries during 2000-2005 and during 2005-2015 will do so in 25 of them, including Italy, the Russian Federation and Ukraine. Furthermore, population ageing is more advanced in developed countries, where over 15 per cent of the population is aged 65 years or over and just 17 per cent is under age 15.

The dependency ratio in the developed world is currently under 5 children and elderly persons per 10 adults of working age but it is rising and is expected to reach 7 by 2050. Rising dependency ratios are also expected in China over the next 40 years but not in India, Latin America and the Caribbean and the rest of the developing world taken as a whole. In all groups and regions, however, the proportion of elderly is expected to rise as the proportion of children falls with declining fertility. The expected reductions in fertility are consistent with the continued implementation of the Programme of Action of the International Conference on Population and Development and would be less likely to materialize in certain regions if the objective of providing family planning services to all who needed and wanted them was not met.

The world today encompasses, therefore, countries at all stages of the demographic transition, that is to say, the transition from a regime of high fertility and high mortality producing low population growth to one where both fertility and mortality are low and produce again low rates of population change. The fact that, during the transition, mortality reductions usually precede fertility reductions leads to a period of rapid population growth. The end of that period of rapid growth has been reached or is within reach of about two fifths of humanity today.

Another two fifths of the world population is already advanced on the path to lower population growth, but the remaining fifth is still growing very rapidly, largely because it has barely begun the transition to low fertility. Furthermore, for all the countries that are highly affected by the HIV/AIDS epidemic, the transition to lower mortality has been interrupted, and the epidemic is having major detrimental effects on both population trends and socio-economic development. Bearing this context in mind is therefore crucial in assessing to what extent the implementation of the Programme of Action can contribute to the achievement of the agreed development goals, since its recommendations for action are not equally relevant for all countries.

IMPORTANCE OF HUMAN RIGHTS

Respect for human rights underpins the attainment of development because if a person's human rights are not safeguarded and respected that person's well-being is undermined. Furthermore, a number of objectives and recommendations contained in the Programme of Action are justifiable not only because they lead to development or have positive impacts on the socio-economic status of people, but because they are an expression of the fundamental rights of the individual. For instance, article 26 of the Universal Declaration of Human Rights states that "(e)veryone has the right to education" and that "(e)lementary education shall be compulsory".

Both the Programme of Action and the Millennium Development Goals reaffirm this right in setting out the goal of achieving universal primary education for both girls and boys by 2015. Similarly, article 24 of the Convention on the Rights of the Child calls for a reduction of infant and child mortality; appropriate prenatal and post-natal care for mothers; and the development of preventive health care, guidance for parents and family planning education and services. The Programme of Action contains specific recommendations and goals to make these rights a reality, goals that are consistent with those included in the Millennium Development Goals with regard to the reduction of mortality in childhood and the improvement of maternal health. A key aspect of the Programme of Action is its emphasis on measures to advance gender equality and equity and the empowerment of women as a matter of right.

As with education, this goal is important in itself and need not be justified in terms of its likely impact on development. The Programme of Action underscores that the "human rights of women and the girl child are an inalienable, integral and indivisible part of universal human rights". Such a recognition is also reflected in the Millennium Development Goal of promoting gender equality and the empowerment of women. In sum, implementing the Programme of Action in all its aspects would not only contribute to the attainment of a number of universally agreed development goals but also ensure that all people enjoy fully certain key human rights.

ACHIEVING SUSTAINABLE DEVELOPMENT AND ENSURING ENVIRONMENTAL SUSTAINABILITY

The key development goal for the international community is to achieve sustainable development as a means to ensure human well-being, equitably shared by all people today and in the future. The Programme of Action also has this as an overriding goal. According to the Programme of Action, the achievement of sustainable development requires that the interrelationships between population, resources, the environment and development be fully recognized, properly managed and brought into a harmonious, dynamic balance.

Because population is expected to increase substantially, especially in developing countries, the Programme of Action recognizes the usefulness of achieving a lower population growth as early as possible. It notes that in many countries, slower population growth has bought more time to adjust to future population increases, improving the ability of those countries to combat poverty, protect and repair the environment, and set the conditions for sustainable development. Even the difference of a single decade in the transition to stabilization levels of fertility can have a considerable positive impact on quality of life.

Consequently, the Programme of Action calls for the formulation of development strategies that realistically reflect the short-term, medium-term and long-term implications of population dynamics by integrating population into development and environment programmes that take into account patterns of production and consumption and seek to bring about population trends consistent with the achievement of sustainable development and the improvement of the quality of life.

The Programme of Action notes that, to ensure the economic well-being of growing populations, investment in human resource development must be given priority, by increasing access to, inter alia, information, education, skill development and employment opportunities. It particularly underscores that existing inequities and barriers to women in the workforce should be eliminated and that women's access to productive resources, and ownership of land, and their right to inherit property, should be promoted and strengthened. It encourages Governments and the private sector to foster job creation in all sectors by expanding trade and investment on an environmentally sound basis, increasing investment in human resource development, and developing democratic institutions and good governance.

Full implementation of these measures would contribute significantly to promoting development. One of the major development goals is to ensure environmental sustainability, particularly by integrating the principles of sustainable development into country policies and programmes, so as to reverse the loss of environmental resources. The Programme of Action recognizes that meeting the basic human needs of growing populations is dependent on a healthy environment and it provides guidance on how to address the human dimensions of pressures on the environment. However, it also recognizes that "(d)emographic factors, combined with poverty and lack of access to resources in some areas, and excessive consumption and wasteful production patterns in others, cause or exacerbate problems of environmental degradation and resource depletion and thus inhibit sustainable development".

To prevent or reverse these outcomes, the Programme of Action supports the objectives and actions agreed to in Agenda 21 and recommends that Governments "(i)mplement policies to address the ecological implications of inevitable future increases in population numbers and changes in concentration and distribution, particularly in ecologically vulnerable areas and urban agglomerations".

This recommendation, in conjunction with the call for the integration of "demographic factors into environment impact assessments and other planning and decision-making processes aimed at achieving sustainable development", is fully consistent with the Millennium Development Goals and underscores the importance of population aspects in the pursuit of sustainable development. In this regard, although the Programme of Action recognizes that further increases in population numbers are inevitable, particularly in the poorer and most vulnerable countries, the implementation of its call for universal access to family planning services is expected to contribute to a reduction in the growth of the world's population.

ERADICATION OF POVERTY

The Programme of Action recognizes that "(w)idespread poverty remains the major challenge to development efforts. Poverty is often accompanied by unemployment, malnutrition, illiteracy, low status of women, exposure to environmental risks and limited access to social and health services... including family planning. All these factors contribute to high levels of fertility, morbidity and mortality, as well as to low economic productivity. Poverty is also closely related to inappropriate spatial distribution of population, to unsustainable use and inequitable distribution of such natural resources as land and water, and to serious environmental degradation". The Programme of Action stresses that sustained economic growth in the context of sustainable development is essential to eradicating poverty, which in turn will contribute to slowing population growth and to achieving early population stabilization.

In addition, research carried out during the 1990s has shown that changes in the age distribution of a population resulting from declining fertility can help accelerate economic growth. As fertility declines, the proportion of the population comprising children (persons under age 15) also declines, whereas the proportion of the population of working age increases, resulting in a decreasing dependency ratio (defined as the average number of children and elderly persons per 10 persons of working age). Provided jobs are available for the rising number of workers, a country can reap the benefits of increased production and lower costs associated with the decreasing proportion of dependants.

This so-called demographic bonus can thus contribute significantly to economic growth and poverty reduction in contexts where governance facilitates human resource development and employment creation. The experience of the newly industrializing countries in Asia provides an example of this outcome. However, over the long run, the demographic bonus dissipates as the population continues to age and the dependency ratio rises again because of increasing proportions of elderly persons. Implementation of the Programme of Action, particularly of measures to ensure that family planning services are affordable, acceptable and accessible to all who need and want them, can help reduce unwanted fertility, especially in the high-fertility countries of today, and thus trigger the process that gives rise to the demographic bonus.

Because most of those high-fertility countries are among the least developed countries where levels of extreme poverty are high, the advantages that can be brought by the demographic bonus can also contribute to the reduction of poverty. However, realizing those advantages requires that economic growth be possible in the countries involved and that it be accompanied by substantial job growth. Not all countries experiencing a decline of fertility have seen economic growth increase markedly as a result of the demographic bonus.

Many of the countries in Latin America, for instance, have experienced slow economic growth despite being fairly advanced in the transition to low fertility. Most of them are middle-income countries where levels of extreme poverty are low. Relative poverty, however, is significant. Consequently, in addition to the positive effects that the demographic bonus might still have on economic growth, measures adopted to improve income distribution—for instance, income-generation and employment strategies directed to the poor, as suggested by the Programme of Action—would be of benefit to these countries.

The Programme of Action also recognizes that high priority should be given "to meeting the needs, and increasing the opportunities, for information, education, jobs, skill development and relevant reproductive health services, of all underserved members of society", who generally include the poor in both urban and rural areas. Its full implementation would therefore contribute to the reduction of inequalities within societies. Compared with the objectives of the Programme of Action regarding poverty eradication, the Millennium Development Goal target relative to the eradication of extreme poverty is more modest, calling for a 50 per cent reduction, between 1990 and 2015, of the proportion of people living on less than US$ 1 a day. The countries most likely to contribute to the attainment of this goal at the global level, China and India, are both beneficiaries of the demographic bonus.

Countries whose fertility is still high and where the proportion of the population living in extreme poverty is also substantial would benefit from reductions of fertility brought about by the prevention of unwanted births, which the Programme of Action aims to achieve, but they cannot expect to attain the Millennium Development Goal target without implementing other macroeconomic measures to raise economic growth, create jobs and increase the income share of the poor. Implementation of the Programme of Action can also contribute to the reduction of poverty by preventing pregnancy among young adolescents, reducing maternal mortality, and slowing the spread of HIV. Single adolescent women who become pregnant are more likely to drop out of school, thus compromising their future earning capacity and becoming more likely to end in poverty.

Maternal mortality and the mortality of parents due to HIV/AIDS often lead to or exacerbate poverty. The Programme of Action also acknowledges that international migration can have significant positive impacts on development, especially through remittances. Remittances have become the second largest source of foreign exchange for developing countries, following foreign direct investment (FDI). Furthermore, remittance levels are double those of official development assistance (ODA). Remittances benefit both the families that receive them and their communities through multiplier effects and may therefore contribute to the reduction of extreme poverty even if the very poor do not migrate.

REDUCTION OF HUNGER

Because poverty and malnutrition often go together, sustained economic growth broadly shared is also necessary to reduce hunger, particularly in the least developed countries. The Programme of Action acknowledges the importance of attaining food security at all levels and calls for measures to strengthen food, nutrition and agricultural policies and programmes, and fair trade relations. The Millennium Development Goal target of reducing by half, between 1990 and 2015, the proportion of people suffering from hunger is consistent with this call.

Because there is no shortage of food worldwide, combating hunger implies providing people with the means of acquiring food. Fair trade is necessary to achieve this objective, since agricultural subsidies in developed countries distort world prices and hurt farmers in developing countries, thereby contributing to high rural poverty in the latter. In sub-Saharan Africa, where population growth has surpassed increases in agricultural productivity, food availability per capita has dropped, leading to rises in malnutrition and hunger. In that region, increases in agricultural productivity, reductions in population growth, improved governance and economic growth would together serve to reduce poverty and hunger.

Implementation of other recommendations in the Programme of Action—including improvements in education and gender equality, the achievement of better child health, the implementation of policies to address the impact of HIV/AIDS and urban poverty, and the provision of reproductive health services that reduce both unwanted fertility and maternal mortality—can also contribute to reducing hunger. Studies have shown that a mother's low educational attainment is the factor most consistently related to malnutrition among children in developing countries. With more education, as called for in the Programme of Action, women are better able to ensure the health and proper nutrition of their children. Enhancing the status of women, particularly by providing them with access to income and resources, can also result in better intra-household distribution of food, thus preventing female malnutrition. Lastly, measures to prevent the spread of HIV are crucial in forestalling the potentially devastating effects that the HIV/AIDS epidemic, by debilitating or reducing the agricultural labour force, can have on agricultural productivity.

ACHIEVEMENT OF UNIVERSAL PRIMARY EDUCATION

The Programme of Action stresses the importance of achieving universal education by 2015, especially of girls and calls for the extension of education for all to the secondary and higher levels. Thus, the goals regarding education set by the Programme of Action are similar to, but more ambitious than, the target for Millennium Development Goal 2, which is to ensure that universal primary education is achieved by 2015.

By calling for the extension of education to the secondary level as well, the Programme of Action, if fulfilled, would accrue substantial benefits that could contribute to the attainment of other development goals, including the reduction of poverty and hunger through the effects that improvements in human capital might bring; the reduction of child mortality, of maternal mortality and of the spread of HIV; the promotion of gender equality and the empowerment of women; and the facilitation of sustainable development and possibly the conservation of natural resources.

Gaining more education would also enhance the ability of young persons to use information technologies. Improving educational attainment, particularly of girls, would also have an impact on population dynamics, since education is known to influence demographic behaviour with respect to nuptiality, fertility, health and migration. Education also affects the intergenerational formation of human capital, with the education of mothers influencing the educational attainment of children.

Conversely, high fertility and rapid population growth have hindered the achievement of universal primary education in many developing countries, especially the least developed. Early marriage and pregnancy among adolescent women often curtail their education. Implementation of the Programme of Action, by preventing early marriage and pregnancy as well as unwanted births, would contribute to achieving universal primary education.

GENDER EQUALITY AND THE EMPOWERMENT OF WOMEN

Both the Programme of Action and the United Nations Millennium Declaration call for the achievement of gender equality and the empowerment of women, recognizing that both are important in combating poverty, hunger and disease and in achieving sustainable development. However, the Programme of Action sets a broader agenda and provides more detailed guidance on how to achieve that goal, not only focusing on measures to improve the status of women but also including recommendations on the involvement and participation of men in realizing gender equality.

With regard to women, the Programme of Action stresses the importance of increasing their equal participation and equitable representation at all levels of the political process; of improving their ability to earn income in occupations beyond the range of traditional ones so as to achieve economic self-reliance; and of ensuring their equal access to the labour market and social security systems; of ensuring their equal rights to buy, hold and sell property and land, obtain credit and negotiate contracts in their own name, and exercise their right to inheritance.

The Programme of Action also underscores the need to eliminate all practices that discriminate against women and all forms of violence against women or girls. Furthermore, it points out repeatedly that actions to enhance the welfare of people should be particularly tailored to meeting the needs of women and girls. With respect to education, the Programme of Action states that "(e)ducation is one of the most important means of empowering women with the knowledge, skills and self-confidence necessary to participate fully in the development process". It therefore urges countries to ensure the widest and earliest possible access of girls and women to secondary and higher levels of education, as well as to vocational education and technical training.

It also calls for the closing of the gender gap in primary and secondary education by 2005 providing guidelines on measures to keep girls and adolescents in school. Its implementation would therefore result in the elimination of gender disparities in primary and secondary education as called for by the Millennium Development Goals.

Acknowledging that "full participation and partnership of both women and men are required in productive and reproductive life, including shared responsibilities for the care and nurturing of children and maintenance of the household", the Programme of Action puts considerable emphasis on the gender aspects of reproductive life, especially in relation to the maintenance of reproductive health and access to reproductive health-care services, including family planning. For women, having access to affordable, acceptable and convenient reproductive health-care services is essential to having control over their reproductive lives and to ensuring that the timing of their pregnancies fits with their family, education and work plans.

Realizing the reproductive rights of women is therefore essential for their empowerment. However, according to the objectives stressed by the Programme of Action, both women and men should "have access to the information, education and services needed to achieve good sexual health and exercise their reproductive rights and responsibilities" and it is also important "to emphasize men's shared responsibility and promote their active involvement in responsible parenthood, sexual and reproductive behaviour, including family planning; prenatal, maternal and child health; prevention of sexually transmitted diseases, including HIV; prevention of unwanted and high-risk pregnancies; shared control and contribution to family income, children's education, health and nutrition; and recognition and promotion of the equal value of children of both sexes".

In essence, full implementation of the Programme of Action entails both the empowerment of women in all spheres of life and a greater involvement of men in the exercise of reproductive rights and responsibilities. The achievement of gender equality in those terms would not only be consistent with the improvement of the status of women as called for in the Beijing Platform for Action, but also contribute to enhancing economic growth and reducing poverty through the growing and more productive participation of women in the economy; to reducing child mortality and improving maternal health because of the increasing education and decisionmaking power of women; and to reducing the transmission of HIV by improving the willingness of men and women to accept responsibility for their own and their partner's sexual health.

IMPROVEMENT OF HEALTH

Good health is essential for the well-being of individuals and societies. In countries where poor health is common, labour productivity suffers. High rates of morbidity and mortality are still common in many low-income countries, especially those highly affected by infectious diseases such as HIV/AIDS, malaria and tuberculosis. A major goal of the international community is to provide access to primary health-care services to all and to reduce the risks of contracting the major infectious diseases.

The Programme of Action calls upon all countries to provide primary health care to all and to make efforts to ensure a longer and healthier life for their populations. It sets quantitative goals urging high-mortality countries to achieve a life expectancy at birth greater than 70 years by 2015 and the rest to achieve a life expectancy at birth greater than 75 years by the same date. Achievement of those goals would imply that major progress had been made in combating the major causes of death in poor countries and in providing adequate sanitation and health services to most people on the planet. The full implementation of the Programme of Action would ensure access to health-care services for all people and especially for the most underserved and vulnerable groups.

Reducing Mortality in Childhood

The Programme of Action urged that by 2000, under-five mortality should be reduced by one third or to a maximum of 70 deaths per 1,000 births in all countries, and that under-five mortality should decline to below 45 deaths per 1,000 births in all countries by 2015 a goal consistent with the United Nations Millennium Declaration's goal of reducing under-five mortality by two thirds between 1990 and 2015.

The measures proposed to achieve this goal are summarized in the key actions for the further implementation of the Programme of Action as follows: Governments should continue to support reductions in child mortality "by strengthening infant and child health programmes that emphasize improved prenatal care and nutrition, including breastfeeding, unless it is medically contraindicated, universal immunization, oral rehydration therapies, clean water sources, infectious disease prevention, reduction of exposure to toxic substances, and improvements in household sanitation; and by strengthening maternal health services, quality family-planning services to help couples to time and space births, and efforts to prevent transmission of HIV/AIDS and other sexually transmitted diseases".

Clearly, implementation of these measures would contribute to the attainment of the goals set. Other measures included in the Programme of Action whose implementation would also contribute to the reduction of child mortality are: the reduction of poverty; the increase of educational attainment, especially among women; the improvement of maternal health; the promotion of the empowerment and equality of women; and the reduction of the spread of HIV/AIDS. These measures, which are consistent with several of the goals contained in the United Nations Millennium Declaration, illustrate the synergies existing between the mutually reinforcing development goals and actions recommended by the Programme of Action.

Improving Maternal Health

Ensuring women's health is a major concern of the Programme of Action. In that respect, its implementation would contribute to realizing the basic right contained in article 12 of the Convention on the Elimination of All Forms of Discrimination against Women, which states:

- States Parties shall take all appropriate measures to eliminate discrimination against women in the field of health care in order to ensure, on a basis of equality of men and women, access to health-care services, including those related to family planning.
- States Parties shall ensure to women appropriate services in connection with pregnancy, confinement and the post-natal period, granting free services where necessary, as well as adequate nutrition during pregnancy and lactation."

To realise this right, the Programme of Action calls for an expansion of "the provision of maternal health services in the context of primary health care. These services, based on the concept of informed choice, should include education on safe motherhood, prenatal care that is focused and effective, maternal nutrition programmes, adequate delivery assistance that avoids excessive recourse to Caesarean sections and provides for obstetric emergencies; referral services for pregnancy, childbirth and abortion complications; post-natal care; and family planning. All births should be assisted by trained persons, preferably nurses and midwives, but at least by trained birth attendants".

In addition, the Programme of Action urges countries to reduce maternal mortality by one half between 1990 and 2000, and by a further one half by 2015. This goal is equivalent to that of reducing the maternal mortality ratio by 75 per cent between 1990 and 2015 as called for by the United Nations Millennium Declaration, that is to say, implementation of the Programme of Action would fulfil the Millennium Declaration goal. A key preventive measure to reduce a woman's lifetime probability of dying from pregnancy-related causes is to ensure access to family planning to avoid unwanted pregnancies.

In addition, the presence of a trained attendant at delivery and access to emergency obstetric care are essential to preventing deaths occurring because of complications during delivery. Providing access to quality services for the management of complications arising from abortion and offering post-abortion counselling, education and family planning services so as to help prevent repeat abortions are also measures needed to reduce the risks of maternal death.

The avoidance of early marriage and of pregnancy among very young women is also conducive to the reduction of maternal mortality as are strategies to reduce the spread of HIV. The Programme of Action calls for all these actions and also notes that, to enhance the effectiveness of programmes for the improvement of maternal health, it is important to engage men's support. The implementation of all these measures and the achievement of lower maternal mortality, particularly among the vulnerable and underserved population groups, would improve not only the health of women, but also that of their children, and the well-being of their families, thus contributing to reducing child mortality and malnutrition.

Combating HIV/AIDS, Malaria and Other Diseases

The Programme of Action recognizes that infectious and parasitic diseases continue to be a major affliction of large numbers of people. To combat them, it suggests that developing countries be assisted in producing generic drugs for their domestic markets so as to ensure the wide availability and accessibility of such drugs. This recommendation is complementary to the call in the United Nations Millennium Declaration for the pharmaceutical industry to make essential drugs more widely available to and affordable by all who need them in developing countries.

In addition, the Programme of Action calls upon all countries to ensure "a safe and sanitary living environment for all population groups through measures aimed at avoiding crowded housing conditions, reducing air pollution, ensuring access to clean water and sanitation, improving waste management, and increasing the safety of the workplace". Although no explicit mention is made of the provision of insecticidetreated netting to protect humans against the bite of the mosquito that transmits malaria, such measures would also be necessary to combat the spread of that disease. Both access to adequate treatment and the implementation of preventive measures to avoid infection are necessary in order to reduce the spread of diseases such as malaria and tuberculosis, and implementation of the Programme of Action would contribute towards making this a reality.

With respect to HIV/AIDS, the Programme of Action underscores the disastrous consequences of the epidemic for individuals, communities and entire nations. It therefore emphasizes the need for measures to prevent the spread of HIV and to treat and support those infected. One of its objectives is therefore "(t)o ensure that HIV-infected individuals have adequate medical care and are not discriminated against; to provide counselling and other support for people infected with HIV and to alleviate the suffering of people living with AIDS and that of their family members, especially orphans; to ensure that the individual rights and the confidentiality of persons infected with HIV are respected; and to ensure that sexual and reproductive health programmes address HIV infection and AIDS".

This objective, if achieved, would palliate the negative effects of the disease. Whereas the Programme of Action does not include quantitative targets regarding HIV/AIDS, the key actions for its further implementation do, by calling for a reduction by 2005 of global HIV prevalence among persons aged 15-24 and for a 25 per cent reduction in that prevalence in the most affected countries.

It also calls for a 25 per cent reduction by 2010 of global HIV prevalence among those aged 15-24. Achievement of these goals would therefore contribute directly to the goal included in the United Nations Millennium Declaration of having halted or begun to reverse the spread of HIV by 2015. Reducing the prevalence of HIV/AIDS would also contribute to the achievement of other development goals, including the reduction of poverty, the reduction of child mortality and the reduction of maternal mortality. To combat the spread of HIV, the Programme of Action attaches "high priority to information, education and communication campaigns to raise awareness and emphasize behavioural change. Sex education and information should be provided to both those infected and those not infected, and especially to adolescents".

It also suggests that "(w)herever possible, reproductive health programmes, including family-planning programmes, should include facilities for the diagnosis and treatment of common sexually transmitted diseases", since the latter are known to be factors facilitating infection by HIV. Emphasis is given to the promotion of responsible sexual behaviour, including voluntary sexual abstinence, and its inclusion in education and information programmes. Wide availability of affordable condoms and drugs for the prevention and treatment of sexually transmitted diseases is recommended, and action to control the quality of blood products and equipment decontamination is stressed.

All these measures plus making information, education and counselling for responsible sexual behaviour and effective prevention of sexually transmitted diseases, including HIV, integral components of all reproductive and sexual health services and facilitating the distribution of condoms through those services would contribute significantly to the control of the epidemic. The Programme of Action stresses the importance of providing young people and adolescents of both sexes with the information and education needed to prevent the transmission of sexually transmitted diseases, and the need to ensure that adolescent and adult men take responsibility for their own sexual health and the prevention of sexually transmitted diseases.

Full implementation of these measures, together with the provisions aimed at improving the status of women and empowering them, would greatly contribute to reducing the transmission of HIV in contexts where the subordination of women to men and the weak economic position of women have constituted a factor promoting the spread of the disease, particularly among women.

CHALLENGES OF CHANGING POPULATION AND AGE DISTRIBUTIONS

Improving Livelihoods in an Urbanizing World

Over the next 15 years, the growth in the world population will be absorbed mainly by urban areas of developing countries, and the world's population will become more urban than rural. As a result, extreme poverty, which has until now been more common in rural than in urban areas, will become increasingly an urban phenomenon.

In most developing countries, where urban-dwellers have better access to education and health services than do rural inhabitants, rural-urban migration is a means of improving the access of migrants to such services and of improving their livelihoods. Nevertheless, the rapid pace of urbanization has strained the capacity of Governments to provide adequate services to urban-dwellers and the number of persons living in slums has been rising, amounting to about 900 million today. In this light, the goal of improving the lives of 100 million slum-dwellers by 2020, one of the goals set forth in the United Nations Millennium Declaration, is a modest one. Although not all slum-dwellers are poor, those having the greatest needs are among the poor and underserved populations focused on by the Programme of Action when it stresses the importance of providing underserved groups with "information, education, jobs, skill development and reproductive health services". To achieve improvement of the lives of slum-dwellers, programmes aimed specifically at improving their access to basic services are necessary. The Programme of Action provides guidance on the types of improvements required and, implicitly, recognizes the importance of targeting programmes to satisfy the particular needs of underserved population groups.

It also calls upon Governments "to respond to the needs of all citizens, including urban squatters, for personal safety, basic infrastructure and services, to eliminate the health and social problems" in urban agglomerations and "to improve the plight of the urban poor ... by facilitating their access to employment, credit, production, marketing opportunities, basic education, health services, vocational training and transportation". A full implementation of these recommendations would certainly contribute to improving the lives of slum-dwellers.

Population Ageing

The number and proportion of older people are expected to continue increasing over the foreseeable future, leading to population age distributions unprecedented in human history. Given the social and economic implications of such changes, "(i)t is essential to integrate the evolving process of global ageing within the larger process of development", as stated in paragraph 9 of the Madrid International Plan of Action on Ageing, 2002, adopted by the Second World Assembly on Ageing, held in Madrid from 8 to 12 April 2002. The Programme of Action of the International Conference on Population and Development recognizes that elderly people constitute a valuable and important component of a society's human resources and recommends a series of measures to ensure that elderly persons are able to work and live independently as long as possible or as desired.

These measures include the development of social security systems that ensure greater intergenerational and intragenerational equity and solidarity; facilitating the use of the skills and abilities of older persons for the benefit of society; valuing and recognizing the contribution that elderly people make to families and society; and strengthening formal and informal support systems for elderly people, with special attention to the needs of elderly women. These measures contribute to empowering elderly persons and promoting their full participation in society, as called for by the International Plan of Action on Ageing.

DEVELOPING A GLOBAL PARTNERSHIP FOR DEVELOPMENT

The Programme of Action gives considerable attention to the ways and means by which its recommendations may be implemented. In particular, it includes cost estimates for the major components of basic national programmes on population and reproductive health, programmes aimed at providing reproductive health services to all who need them. The Programme of Action acknowledges that domestic resources provide the largest portion of the funds needed, estimating that only about a third of those costs would come from external sources.

The least developed countries and other low-income developing countries would require a greater share of external resources on a concessional and grant basis. Recalling that international cooperation has been essential for the implementation of population and development programmes in the past, the Programme of Action notes that international cooperation has become increasingly important and varied because "countries that formerly attached minimal importance to population issues now recognize them at the core of their development challenge. International migration and AIDS, for instance ... are currently high-priority issues in a large number of countries".

Consequently, the Programme of Action encourages Governments to build partnerships with multilateral and donor agencies, civil society and the private sector, as appropriate, for the purpose of undertaking projects or developing programmes for the implementation of its recommendations. It also calls upon the international community to support South-South collaborative arrangements and facilitate direct South-South cooperation.

At the programme level, it recommends national capacity-building for population and development and transfer of appropriate technology and know-how to developing countries. It also reiterates the call for the international community to "strive for the fulfilment of the agreed target of 0.7 per cent of gross national product for overall official development assistance and endeavour to increase the share of funding for population and development programmes commensurate with the scope and scale of activities required to achieve the objectives and goals" of the Programme of Action.

The implementation of these recommendations would not only ensure the achievement of those goals and objectives but also contribute to building the global partnership for development called for in the United Nations Millennium Declaration.

SUMMERY

Population is at the core of development, and population trends are a key element of the context in which development takes place. Consequently, measures directed towards influencing demographic behaviour and population dynamics, such as those contained in the Programme of Action of the International Conference on Population and Development and the key actions for its further implementation, would, if fully implemented, contribute significantly to the achievement of universally agreed development goals, including those in the United Nations Millennium Declaration. Implementation of the Programme of Action, particularly of measures to ensure that all couples and individuals have the number of children they desire and the information, education and means to do so, would contribute to accelerating the transition to low fertility in developing countries that still have high fertility levels, and would produce slower population growth, which in turn would improve the ability of those countries to adjust to future population increases, to combat poverty, to protect and repair the environment, and to set the conditions for sustainable development. Even the difference of a single decade in the transition to stabilization levels of fertility can have a considerable positive impact on quality of life.

Furthermore, reduction of fertility gives rise to the "demographic bonus" whereby the proportion of the population of working age increases relative to that of children and the elderly, a change that can contribute significantly to economic growth and poverty reduction in contexts where governance facilitates human resource development and employment creation. Implementation of other recommendations included in the Programme of Action regarding the provision of education to all, especially girls and women, and increased investment in human resource development would also contribute to ensuring the benefits of the demographic bonus.

Fulfilment of the goals and objectives of the Programme of Action would ensure the achievement of equivalent goals included in the United Nations Millennium Declaration, particularly reduction of child mortality and maternal mortality, universal access to primary education, parity in access to secondary and higher education between boys and girls, reductions in the spread of HIV, and achievement of gender equality and women's empowerment. Because of synergies between these goals and other universally agreed development goals, further benefits would be reaped. For instance, implementation of the Programme of Action would lead to both the empowerment of women in all spheres of life and a greater involvement of men in the exercise of reproductive rights and responsibilities. These achievements would contribute to enhancing economic growth and reducing poverty, reducing child mortality and improving maternal health, and reducing the spread of HIV. Similarly, improvements in education, particularly of girls, would contribute to reducing poverty, hunger, child and maternal mortality, and the spread of HIV, as well as promote gender equality.

Furthermore, a better-educated population would likely change its demographic behaviour with respect to nuptiality, fertility, health and migration in ways leading to greater well-being. The Programme of Action offers guidance on ways of addressing the major challenges of the future, including increasing urbanization and population ageing, so that its fulfilment would contribute to the attainment of the objectives set both by the United Nations Millennium Declaration and by the Second World Assembly on Ageing. The Programme of Action also focuses special attention on the needs of vulnerable groups, including children and youth, the elderly, the poor, the disabled and indigenous populations, and stresses the need to provide support and protection to families, especially single-parent families, and to vulnerable family members, such as orphans and widows.

Consequently, full implementation of the Programme of Action would benefit all segments of society, particularly the most vulnerable, and lead to less inequality. It would also promote the equal participation and sharing of responsibility of women and men in all areas of family and community life. Implementation of the Programme of Action depends crucially on building a partnership for global development where all actors, including Governments, multilateral and donor agencies, civil society and the private sector, cooperate to realise its goals and objectives. In this way, it would validate the importance of the goals included in the United Nations Millennium Declaration and contribute to underscoring that international cooperation is essential for the implementation of population and development programmes, particularly in the least developed and other low-income developing countries.

9

Population Dynamics

AN OVERVIEW

India is often described as a collection of many countries held together by a common destiny and a successful democracy. Its diverse ethnic, linguistic, geographic, religious, and demographic features reflect its rich history and shape its present and future. No fewer than 16 languages are featured on Indian rupee notes. It is also only the second country to achieve a population of 1 billion. While it is an emerging economic power, life remains largely rooted in its villages. Only a small fraction of Indians are benefiting from the country's expanding industrial and information sectors. India has more people than Europe, more than Africa, more than the entire Western Hemisphere.

India's population will exceed that of China before 2030 to become the world's most populous country, a distinction it will almost certainly never lose. Just one group, Indian boys below age 5, numbers 62 million—more than the total population of France. India's annual increase of nearly 19 million contributes far more to annual world population growth than any other country. This Population Bulletin presents a demographic portrait of the diverse country of India in the early years of the 21st century and offers insight into some of the forces driving continued growth.

A RICH HISTORY

Although the region has a rich and ancient history, present-day India is a relatively new nation. India gained independence from British rule in 1947, after decades of struggle against the former colonial power. The country was then partitioned into primarily Hindu India and Muslim Pakistan. The eastern part of Pakistan is today's Bangladesh. In the largest mass migration ever recorded, millions of Hindus left Pakistan to resettle in India, as millions of Muslims moved from India to Pakistan.

The upheaval of the partition also unleashed a period of horrific violence between Hindus and Muslims, and sporadic conflicts between Hindus and Muslims and between India and Pakistan continue to this day. At independence, India consisted of provinces defined by the British, along with more than 500 princely states whose territory was ultimately taken over by the new Indian government. Boundaries for today's states were largely drawn along language lines after independence. In the 21st century, India is a federal republic comprised of 28 states and seven union territories. States and union territories are split into 593 districts and 5,564 subdistricts. New states are created periodically to ease the burden of governing as their populations grow or to provide separate states for ethnic and tribal groups.

Three new states were created in 2000 when Jharkhand was split from Bihar, Chhattisgarh was cut from Madhya Pradesh, and a few mountain districts were carved out of Uttar Pradesh to form the state of Uttaranchal. Part of Kashmir, along the northwestern border with Pakistan, is occupied by Pakistan, although India considers it Indian territory. Disputes over this territory have spawned intense political battles and terrorism.

India's 1.2 million square miles equals about one-third the land area of the United States. In the far north, India is dominated by the grand sweep of the Himalayas, Hindu Kush, and Patkai mountain ranges, which soon give way to the vast and fertile Indo-Gangetic plain of the north, fed by such major rivers as the Ganges and Yamuna.

Here are located many of India's most populous states such as Haryana, Delhi, Uttaranchal, Uttar Pradesh, Bihar, Jharkhand, and West Bengal. Moghuls invaded from Afghanistan in the 16th century, leaving a mark on the architecture, food, and dress of northern India still discernable today. Hindi, India's official language of government, is spoken in much of the north, and the area from Rajasthan to Bihar is often referred to as the "Hindi Belt."

This region, which contains just over 40 per cent of the national population, is known for high birth and death rates, low literacy levels, and endemic rural poverty. Mountain ranges divide north from south, marking the beginning of the Deccan Plateau that makes up much of southern India. The north/south division also marks enormous socioeconomic differences.

In contrast to high illiteracy, rapid population growth, and poor health common in the north, the southern states of Kerala, Karnataka, and Tamil Nadu are known for high literacy levels, long life expectancy, and low birth rates. Throughout history, the south had more contact with an outside world attracted by its profitable spice trade. Trade and interaction with foreign people encouraged literacy and introduced a diversity of religions.

Although Hinduism predominates throughout the region, Kerala, on the southwestern coast, has one of the highest proportions of both Christians and Muslims in India. That state has also historically been one of India's most advanced in terms of women's rights and education levels. Northeast India, barely connected to the rest of the country by a narrow strip of land known as the Siliguri, or "Chicken's Neck," consists of seven smaller states, some carved out of the state of Assam, which are ethnically closer to Southeast Asia than to the rest of India.

POPULATION CHANGE

The Indian subcontinent has long been one of the world's most populous regions, but as in many of today's developing countries, population growth took off in the 20th century. India began the century with a population of about 238 million and ended it with 1 billion.

Table. Population Size and Growth, India, 1901–2001

Census year	Population	Growth over decade		Multiple of 1901 population
		Number	Per cent	
1901	238,396,327	—	—	1.0
1911	252,093,390	1,3697,063	5.7	1.1
1921	251,321,213	–772,177	–0.3	1.1
1931	278,977,238	27,656,025	11.0	1.2
1941	318,660,580	39,683,342	14.2	1.3
1951	361,088,090	42,427,510	13.3	1.5
1961	439,234,771	78,146,681	21.6	1.8
1971	548,159,652	108,924,881	24.8	2.3
1981	683,329,097	135,169,445	24.7	2.9
1991	846,421,039	163,091,942	23.9	3.6
2001	1,028,737,436	182,316,397	21.5	4.3

India added another 100 million by 2006, when its population reached an estimated 1.1 billion. This phenomenal growth followed a century of relatively stable population size, according to most historical estimates. Scholars differ in the historical estimates of the region's population, but many assume that the population was roughly 200 million in the early 1800s. India's population total remained more or less static during the 19th century, reflecting a slender balance of births over deaths. Growth slowly accelerated in the late 1800s. By 1871, India's population had reached 255 million.

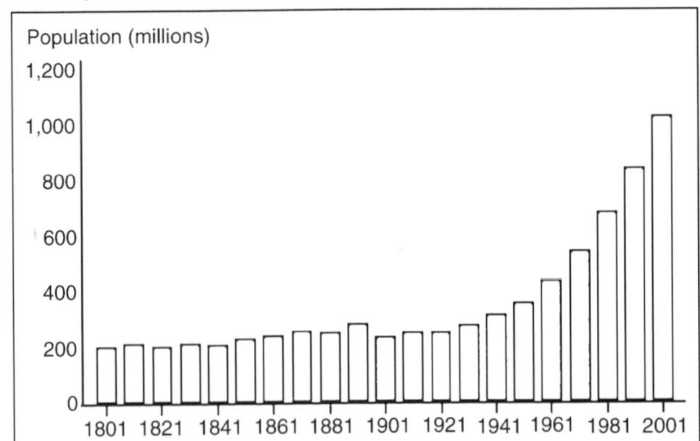

Fig. India's Populations Growth, 1801-2001

The first population census was conducted in 1872, and a census has been taken every decade since.

POPULATION STATISTICS IN INDIA

The Census of India—Counting 1 Billion People

Often called the largest administrative exercise in the world, India's census is a truly monumental exercise that involves 2 million enumerators and supervisors. In the year before the census, enumerators canvass the entire country listing every dwelling—whether a house or temporary structure. This list serves as a basis for planning enumerator assignments and other organizational needs. The 2001 Census population questionnaire featured 23 questions for people in households, including a new question on women's work as an economic activity. In 2001, provisional population totals were released only three weeks after the census date—March 1—an amazing feat considering the size of the country. The Indian censuses have very good coverage by global standards.

After the 1991 Census, the Registrar General's office estimated that the census undercount was about 1.8 per cent of the population. Detailed data from the census highlight the fact that many Indians do not know their exact birth year and often report an approximate age rounded to a "0" or "5." This rounding causes pronounced heaping of census data by age, as seen in the bars jutting out from the population pyramid at ages ending in 0, and to a lesser extent, ages ending in 5.

Census data also reveal that females, particularly in younger ages, are often missing from census figures. In Uttar Pradesh in 2001, the number of females below age 25 is about 6 million fewer than what would be expected in a "normal" age-sex distribution. Somc of this female deficit reflects sex-selective abortions by parents who want to avoid having a girl and the omission of female household members from the census count.

The Sample Registration System Monitors Change

India is one of a few developing countries that publish annual birth and death rates. Since the 1970s, its Sample Registration System has collected data on births and deaths from sample villages and from sample census blocks in urban areas. India publishes annual estimates of birth, death, and infant mortality rates; life expectancy; and other key measures for the nation and most states. Less detail is provided for smaller states because of insufficient sample sizes. The quality of SRS estimates has improved over the years, and the SRS provides valuable data for officials and planners who rely on population data. In 2004, the SRS covered 7,597 sample units comprising 1.3 million households and 6.7 million people.

National Family Health Surveys Enrich India's Demographic Data

The National Family Health Surveys, a part of the global Demographic and Health Survey programme, have provided a wealth of information on a wide variety of sociodemographic topics. The NFHS produce measures of fertility, contraceptive use, childbearing desires, the status of women, infant mortality, immunization coverage, use of iodized salt, reproductive health, knowledge of HIV and AIDS, housing, and other valuable data. The first two surveys were taken in 1992–1993 and 1998–1999. With a sample size of nearly 90,000 women of childbearing age, the NFHS provides detailed analyses down to the state level. A third NFHS being conducted in 2006 has an even larger sample size, will include men, and will test participants for HIV infection.

India's population growth pattern is typical for a high-fertility and high-mortality country in that population grew quite slowly, even declining in the early 20th century. High birth rates were counterbalanced by high death rates, along with periodic famines, outbreaks of lethal diseases such as cholera and smallpox, and endemic parasitic diseases such as malaria. But epidemics and famines receded in the first half of the 20th century. The year 1921 is often referred to as the "Year of the Great Divide," because it marked the shift from a pattern of relatively static population size to one of steady and often rapid increase.

As the mid-20th century approached, growth began to accelerate as the more serious threats to public health waned: Death rates fell but birth rates remained high. India's population growth rate peaked between the 1971 and 1981 censuses, but growth in absolute numbers has not yet peaked.

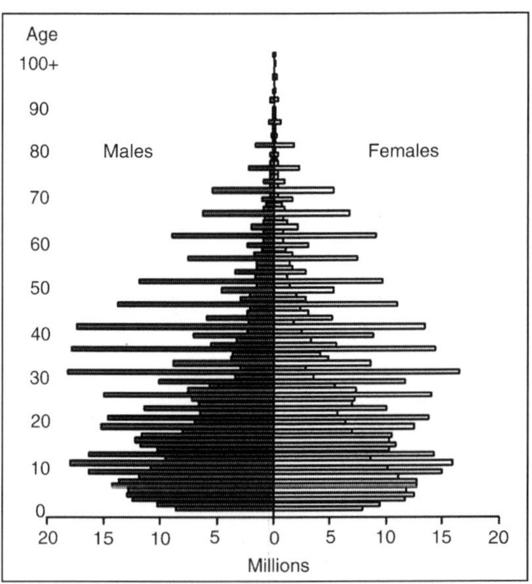

Fig. India's Population by Sex and Single Years of Age, 2001 Census

The country added 16 million people annually in the 1980s and 18 million annually in the 1990s until the present. India's population growth slowed as the birth rate gradually declined beginning in the late 1960s. Since the early 1970s, the birth rate has fallen from just under 40 births per 1,000 population to 24 per 1,000 in 2004. This decline reflected the concerted effort by the government to slow population growth.

MORTALITY

India's mortality has declined at a sluggish rate.

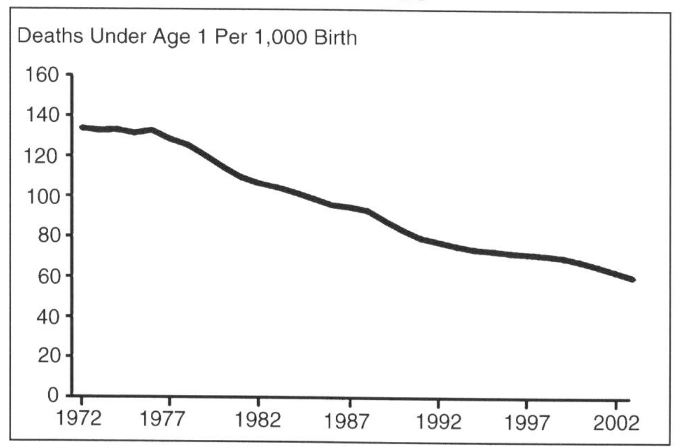

Fig. Infant Mortality Rate in India, 1971-1973 to 2002-2004

In the early 1970s, the infant mortality rate was about 130 deaths to infants under age 1 per 1,000 live births. By 2004, the IMR declined to about 58. In recent years, the pace of improvement has quickened. Maternal mortality has also declined since the 1970s, although at 540 maternal deaths per 100,000 births in 2000, the rate remains higher than in many other less-developed countries, and nearly 10 times higher than in China. Declining death rates, especially among infants and young children, boosted the average life expectancy for Indians from about 50 years in the early 1970s to 63 years for the 1999–2003 period. The national average is similar to levels in neighbouring Bangladesh, Nepal, and Pakistan.

Table. Life Expectancy at Birth in Years, India and Selected States, 1999–2003

State	Both sexes	Male	Female	Change since 1970–1975 Both sexes
India	62.7	61.8	63.5	13.0
Kerala	73.6	70.9	76.0	11.6
Punjab	68.6	67.6	69.6	10.7
Maharashtra	66.4	65.2	67.6	12.6
Tamil Nadu	65.4	64.3	66.5	15.8
Rajasthan	61.3	60.7	61.8	12.9
Uttar Pradesh	59.3	59.6	58.7	16.3
Orissa	58.7	58.6	58.7	13.0
Madhya Pradesh	57.1	57.2	56.9	9.9

Yet, life expectancies are above 70 years in some Indian states such as Kerala, and other Asian countries, including Sri Lanka and Thailand, and are 80 or above in Singapore and Japan, suggesting there is considerable room for improvement in India.

A substantial fall in mortality could boost population growth unless accompanied by further declines in the birth rate. Life expectancy at birth varies by nearly 20 years among Indian states, ranging from 57 years in Madhya Pradesh to 74 in Kerala. These vast differences reflect a large gap among states in education and access to health services.

AGE AND SEX PROFILE

The history of high birth rates has kept India's population relatively young: In 2005, about 36 per cent of the population was below age 15 and just 4 per cent was age 65 or older. The broad-based age and sex population "pyramid" taken from United Nations projections shows this youthfulness clearly.

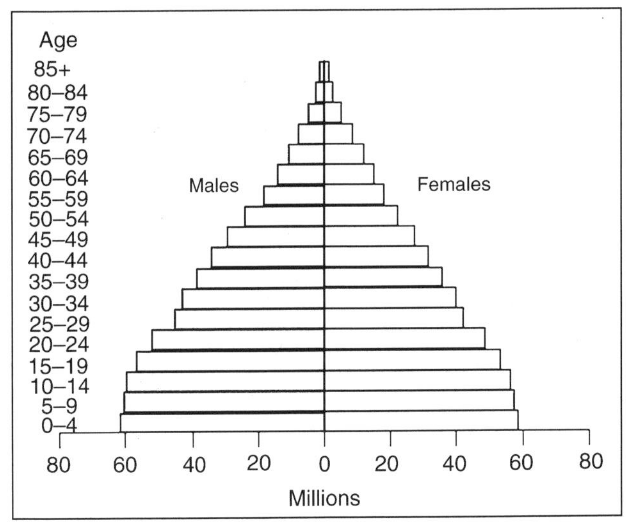

Fig. India's Population by Age and Sex, 2005

More than half the population is below age 25. The young population virtually guarantees further growth, as these young people produce their own families, who will also require additional schools, jobs, and housing.

SEX RATIO AT BIRTH

One of the most striking features of India's population profile is its abnormally high ratio of males to females, particularly at young ages.

While about 105 boys are born for every 100 girls in most countries, the ratio is about 113 per 100 in India, and it ranges up to 129 per 100 in some states. This skewed ratio has been increasing.

Table. Ratio of Boys Per 100 Girls at Birth, India and Selected States, 2001–2003

State	Total	Urban	Rural
India	113	115	113
Tamil Nadu	105	110	103
Karnataka	106	105	106
Assam	111	109	111
Kerala	112	107	114
Haryana	124	131	123
Punjab	129	131	128

Note:

Globally, the average sex ratio at birth is 105 boys to 100 girls

The overriding explanation is the abortion of female fetuses. While abortion has been legal in India since 1972, sex-selective abortion has been illegal since 1994. However, the government has not effectively enforced the ban. The practice has increased, especially in wealthier states, such as Haryana and Punjab, and in urban areas, where couples are more likely to have access to the prenatal tests to determine their fetus' sex. The government has redoubled efforts to enforce the ban in recent years in the face of growing alarm at the frequency of female feticide. Efforts to stem the practice of sex-selective abortion include a broader campaign to improve the status of women and to encourage parents to value daughters as well as sons. In districts where son preference is especially strong, initiatives involve medical professionals, religious leaders, schools, television shows, and politicians.

A "Save a Girl Child" campaign highlights the achievements and value of young girls. This desire to enhance the value of daughters was behind the government's decision to choose a baby girl as India's official "billionth baby," born in Safdarjung Hospital in New Delhi on May 11, 2000. Some states are initiating their own campaigns. cDelhi is launching a "Girl Child Protection Scheme" campaign under which 5,000 rupees will be deposited in the name of every girl born in a government hospital or maternity home. The money and accrued interest will be given to the girl when she reaches 18 and completes a specified level of education. The Punjab government will give a reward of 250,000 rupees to communities that achieve a target sex ratio among recorded births. Jalahmazra village in Nawashahr, Punjab, received this reward in 2006.

GEOGRAPHIC DIVERSITY

The Indian population is heavily concentrated in the broad fertile northern plains. Historically higher birth rates in the northern states continue to shift a larger share of India's population growth northward. Four northern states—Bihar, Madhya Pradesh, Rajasthan, and Uttar Pradesh—often referred to as the "BIMARU" states, accounted for 40 per cent of India's population, but 47 per cent of the country's population growth between 1991 and 2001. Uttar Pradesh, with 166 million people in 2001, is by far India's most populous state and is larger than Pakistan and Bangladesh.

Table. Population Size and Growth of States and Union Territories, 1991–2001

State/union territory	Total population		Percent change	Percent of national population
	1991	2001	1991–2001	2001
India	846,421,039	1,028,737,436	21.5	100
Uttar Pradesh	132,061,653	166,197,921	25.9	16.2
Maharashtra	78,937,187	96,878,627	22.7	9.4
Bihar	64,530,554	82,998,509	28.6	8.1
West Bengal	68,077,965	80,176,197	17.8	7.8
Andhra Pradesh	66,508,008	76,210,007	14.6	7.4
Tamil Nadu	55,858,946	62,405,679	11.7	6.1
Madhya Pradesh	48,566,242	60,348,023	24.3	5.9
Rajasthan	44,005,990	56,507,188	28.4	5.5
Karnataka	44,977,201	52,850,562	17.5	5.1
Gujarat	41,309,582	50,671,017	22.7	4.9
Orissa	31,659,736	36,804,660	16.3	3.6
Kerala	29,098,518	31,841,374	9.4	3.1
Jharkhand	21,843,911	26,945,829	23.4	2.6
Assam	22,414,322	26,655,528	18.9	2.6
Punjab	20,281,969	24,358,999	20.1	2.4
Haryana	16,463,648	21,144,564	28.4	2.1
Chhattisgarh	17,614,928	20,833,803	18.3	2.0
Delhi	9,420,644	13,850,507	47.0	1.4
Jammu & Kashmir	7,837,051	10,143,700	29.4	1.0
Uttaranchal	7,050,634	8,489,349	20.4	0.8
Himachal Pradesh	5,170,877	6,077,900	17.5	0.6
Tripura	2,757,205	3,199,203	16.0	0.3
Meghalaya	1,774,778	2,318,822	30.7	0.2
Manipur	1,837,149	2,293,896	24.9	0.2
Nagaland	1,209,546	1,990,036	64.5	0.2
Goa	1,169,793	1,347,668	15.2	0.1

State/union territory	Total population		Percent change	Percent of national population
	1991	2001	1991–2001	2001
Arunachal Pradesh	864,558	1,097,968	27.0	0.1
Pondicherry*	807,785	974,345	20.6	0.1
Chandigarh*	642,015	900,635	40.3	0.1
Mizoram	689,756	888,573	28.8	0.1
Sikkim	406,457	540,851	33.1	0.1
Andaman & Nicobar Islands*	280,661	356,152	26.9	–
Dadra & Nagar Haveli*	138,477	220,490	59.2	–
Daman & Diu*	01,586	158,204	55.7	–
Lakshadweep*	51,707	60,650	17.3	–

* Union Territory—Less than 0.1 per cent

Fertility decline has been most dramatic in southern states, and those states contribute less and less to India's annual population growth. Andhra Pradesh, Karnataka, Kerala, and Tamil Nadu accounted for 22 per cent of the country's population in 2001, but contributed only 14 per cent of its population growth. This disparity is certain to increase.

INDIA LIVES IN ITS VILLAGES

Although many Westerners associate Indian life with teeming megacities, as the country's registrar general said in 2005, "India lives in its villages." A large majority of Indians live in relatively small localities and are engaged in farming or some activity related to farming. In 2001, the average Indian lived in a village of about 4,200 people; 72 per cent of India's total population was classified as rural, and 58 per cent of workers were engaged in agriculture.

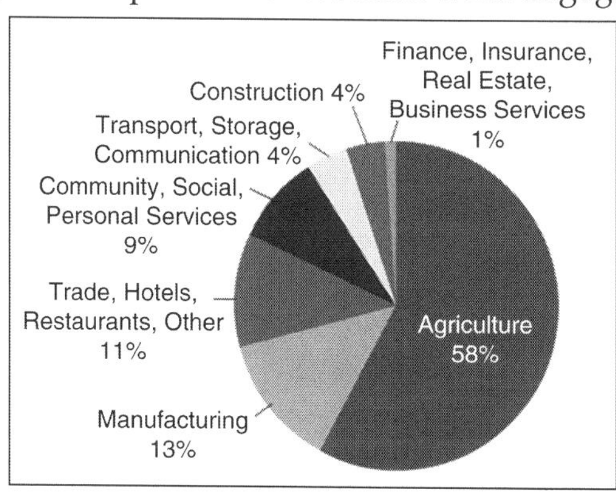

Fig. Indian Workers by Sector, 2001

Just 11 per cent of Indians lived in large cities of 1 million or more residents.

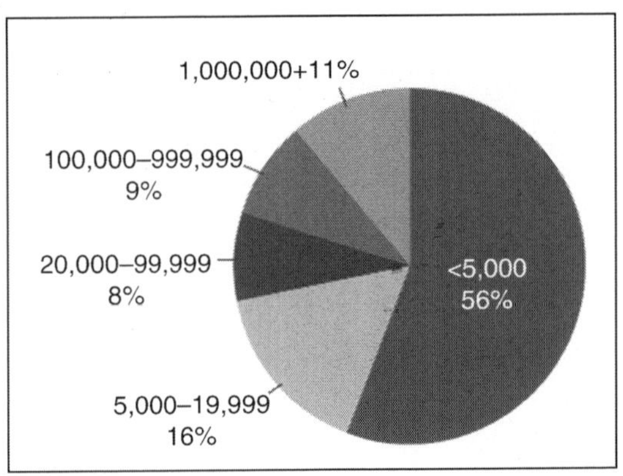

Fig. India's Population by Size of City or Place, 2001

Many Indians who live in relatively populated areas are classified as rural because their communities are highly dependent on agriculture and lack the population density required for the official urban designation. In general, India classifies communities as urban if they have at least 5,000 people; a population density of at least 400 people per square kilometer; and less than 25 per cent of the male labour force engaged in agriculture.

Accordingly, many of the 16 per cent of Indians living in places with 5,000 to 19,999 people are classified as rural. Throughout most of India, rural residents have lower educational levels, higher mortality and fertility, higher poverty, and fewer modern amenities than urban residents. Rural-to-urban migration has been much slower than in Latin America and in other world regions. Most Indians live their entire lives within a relatively limited geographic area.

URBAN INDIA

Before 1951, defining an urban area was left entirely to the discretion of local authorities, leading some demographers to joke that "in the pre-independence era, some princely states of India, in order to lay a claim to respectability, were inclined to treat any habitation with a lamppost as an urban centre." The definition of an urban place in India has varied, but now is similar to that used in most other developing countries. In addition to the criteria, some places—centers of government, for example—are officially designated as urban regardless of their other characteristics.

As in other countries of South Asia, India's urban population has grown relatively slowly for the last century. The percentage of Indians living in urban areas rose from 11 per cent in 1901 to 28 per cent in 2001. Rural areas added significantly more people than urban areas between 1991 and 2001: 114 million compared with 69 million.

Table Urban and Rural Population in India, 1901–2001

Census year	Population in thousands		Change over decade (thousands)		
	Urban	Rural	Urban	Rural	Percent Urban
1901	25,855	212,541	—	—	10.8
1911	25,948	226,145	93	13,604	10.3
1921	28,091	223,230	2,143	–2,915	11.2
1931	33,463	245,515	5,371 22,285	12.0	
1941	44,162	274,498	10,700	28,984	13.9
1951	62,444	298,644	18,282	24,146	17.3
1961	78,937	360,298	16,493	61,654	18.0
1971	109,114	439,046	30,177	78,748	19.9
1981	159,463	523,867	50,349	84,821	23.3
1991	217,611	628,810	58,148	104,943	25.7
2001	286,120	742,618	68,509	113,808	27.8

INDIAN MEGACITIES

The world has about 20 megacities—urban areas with 10 million or more people. Three are in India: Delhi, Kolkata, and Mumbai.

Table. Indian Urban Areas with 2 Million or More Residents, 2001

Urban agglomeration (U.A.)/city	State	Population (millions)
Greater Mumbai U.A.	Maharashtra	16.4
Kolkata U.A.	West Bengal	13.2
Delhi U.A.	Delhi	12.9
Chennai U.A.	Tamil Nadu	6.6
Hyderabad U.A.	Andhra Pradesh	5.7
Bangalore U.A.	Karnataka	5.7
Ahmedabad U.A.	Gujarat	4.5
Pune U.A.	Maharashtra	3.8
Surat U.A.	Gujarat	2.8
Kanpur U.A.	Uttar Pradesh	2.7
Jaipur Municipal Corporation	Rajasthan	2.3
Luchnow U.A.	Uttar Pradesh	2.2
Nagpur U.A.	Maharashtra	2.1

Delhi is one of the world's oldest cities and has been India's capital since 1911. Kolkata, Mumbai, and Chennai (Madras) were established under colonial rule. Kolkata was founded as a port for the British East India Company while Mumbai was founded by Portuguese colonialists. India's fourth-largest city,

Chennai, in the southern state of Tamil Nadu, was another British creation, beginning as Ft. George. Delhi is the world's fastest-growing megacity, adding nearly one-half million people per year.

Although the city has long since expanded beyond the original inhabited area, it still has room to grow both within its borders and in adjacent suburbs. Mumbai, located on a long peninsula in Maharashtra state, has had to build up rather than out and available land is now virtually nonexistent. Large cities have sprung up across the bay on the mainland, expanding the greater Mumbai area. With its tall buildings and status as a financial capital, downtown Mumbai gives some visitors the feel of a Manhattan. At partition, Kolkata became the capital of the Indian state of West Bengal, while the eastern half of Bengal became East Pakistan and, in 1971, Bangladesh.

When Kolkata—the commercial center of Bengal province—was cut off from the rest of its population, Bangladesh was left largely dependent on subsistence agriculture, and remains one of the world's poorest countries today. Other major cities include Bangalore, the capital of Karnataka state with its gleaming Indian headquarters of such companies as IBM and Intel; and Hyderabad, capital of Andhra Pradesh state and another important center of India's growing computer industry.

SLUM POPULATIONS

More than 40 million urban Indians live in areas classified as slums—a number roughly equal to the population of Spain. Slums are defined as any area designated as such by a state or local government or any "compact area of at least 300 population or about 60 to 70 households of poorly built, congested tenements in unhygienic environment usually with inadequate infrastructure and lacking in proper sanitary and drinking water facilities." India conducted a systematic enumeration of the urban slum population for the first time during the 2001 Census, pegging the slum population at 42.6 million, or about 14.9 per cent of the national urban population.

The largest slum populations are in major cities, Mumbai (6.5 million slum dwellers), Delhi (1.9 million), Kolkata (1.5 million), Chennai (0.8 million), and Nagpur (0.7 million). Even the "hi-tech" cities of Bangalore and Hyderabad have 1 million slum residents between them. By far the largest percentage of population living in slums is in Mumbai, a shocking 54 per cent. Next are Faridabad (46 per cent slum dwellers) and Meerut (44 per cent), both in the Delhi National Capital Region, followed by Kolkata at 32 per cent. Six million children under age 7 lived in slums in 2001, with 1.6 million in Maharashtra state alone.

Most inhabitants of slums came to the city in hopes of earning some income, no matter how meager. Other slum dwellers may, in fact, have paying jobs but live in the slums because of a severe shortage of other housing. Nearly three-fourths of slum residents are literate (73 per cent), just below the 81 per cent literacy reported among the general population in states reporting slums. Slightly more than one-half of men living in slums were reported as working, about the same as among the general population.

Yet women who live in slums are less likely than the average to be working: just 12 per cent of women compared with 26 per cent among women in the total population of those states in 2001. Slums are by definition illegal, usually rising on a piece of empty government or private land in less desirable places near railway lines or drainage canals. They may obtain some services, such as electricity and sanitation, and may eventually be annexed as an integral part of the city. In other cases, city governments may remove the slums, relocating residents to the city fringe and allocating them about 250 square feet (20 to 25 square meters) of land per household. These relocated slums often develop into full-scale towns with brick houses and shops. Some slums simply become too large to move and become permanent parts of the city.

SOCIO-ECONOMIC CHARACTERISTICS

India's society is deeply rooted in religion, language, and tradition. Religion and conflicts among religious and cultural groups are fundamental forces in Indian life that bear on economic and educational disparities, the division of political power, the traditional role of women, and on the demographic profile of the country. At the 2001 Census, just over 80 per cent of Indians practiced Hinduism, one of the world's oldest religions. Muslims are second, with 13 per cent.

The balance consists of Christians, Sikhs, Buddhists, Jains, and others, such as Parsis. The ongoing conflicts between the Hindu majority and Muslim minority—which occasionally erupt in violence—fuel fears about the long-term effects of demographic changes that could shift the balance of the two groups in some states. Muslims have higher fertility and are growing at a slightly faster rate than Hindus. While a relatively small minority nationally, Muslims make up one-quarter or more of the population in Kerala, West Bengal, Assam, and Jammu and Kashmir, as shown by 2001 Census results. With higher fertility and a more rapid growth rate, the Muslim percentage is slowly increasing nationally. Between 1991 and 2001, the Muslim percentage in India increased from 12 per cent to 13 per cent. The Muslim percentage increased slightly more in many states, for example, it rose from 23 per cent to 25 per cent in Kerala, from 28 per cent to 31 per cent in Assam, and from 18 per cent to 19 per cent in Uttar Pradesh. Hinduism has been a unifying force throughout India's history.

With its many holy days, festivals, and caste system, it defines life for the great majority of Indians. Several other religions, although with much smaller percentages of the population, have also had an important influence in some regions. Sikhs, for example, whose religion branched off from Hinduism, are native to Punjab state. They are generally credited with turning that region's marginal crop land into "India's granary." The importance of Hindu traditions is manifested in India's deeply rooted caste system, which continues to play a key role in the organization and stratification of Indian society.

The system, which was largely based upon occupation, has four main divisions: Brahmin (priests, teachers), Kshatriya (kings, warriors), Vaishya (merchants, landowners, craftsmen), and Shudra (laborers, artisans). The "Untouchables" are the lowest caste, who usually performed menial jobs. Mahatma Gandhi attempted to remove discrimination against this group by referring to them as Harijans or Children of God.

Today, Untouchables are called by the label they themselves prefer, Dalits, or "the oppressed." The discriminatory aspects of the caste system have been under assault since India's independence in 1947, but the system has been difficult to dislodge, particularly because of its deep roots in ancient texts at the basis of Hinduism, such as the Vedas, and the belief that the creator of the universe, Brahma, also created the four main divisions. Still, the Indian government has attempted to lower caste boundaries and to redress the effects of discrimination against the Dalits.

In 1947, well before the landmark civil rights laws in the United States, India established a system whereby a percentage of public-sector jobs and university slots were reserved for certain castes of Dalits. The castes identified were known as Scheduled Castes (SCs) and recognized only among Hindus and Sikhs. The reservation of jobs and university seats was also extended to specific tribal groups that had suffered from discrimination. STs were not necessarily Hindu or associated with a caste, but had a long history of poverty and low educational attainment.

In 2006, 15 per cent of job vacancies and university seats were reserved for SCs and nearly 8 per cent for STs. The reservation policy is not without controversy, in part because of concerns that STs and SCs are not adequately prepared for these positions, and that they prevent morequalified candidates from getting jobs or university seats. Many ST and SC youths grow up in poverty, with limited educational resources, and find it hard to compete with more-educated students in the university setting. A recent Times of India article noted that 2,000 of the 9,000 places reserved for SC/STs in prestigious Delhi University remained unfilled at a time when India is trying to expand the number of qualified graduates.

But the significance of these groups is apparent when we consider that they represent one-fourth of the country's population. In addition to SCs and STs, a large group of lower castes who had not previously benefited from the scheduled caste system, other backward classes are now seeking similar accommodation. While the caste system has not been eliminated, it plays a somewhat reduced role among the educated elite. It is quite common to see the phrase "caste no bar" in advertisements in the matrimonial section of newspapers placed by the parents of prospective brides and grooms.

LITERACY AND EDUCATION

Mass education and literacy are a hallmark of modern society. In India, the goal of free and compulsory education through age 14 is provided for under Article 45 of the Constitution. Literacy is defined as the ability to read and write any language, regardless of level of education. In the census, literacy is based on the response of whoever answers the enumerator's questions, nearly always a male household head. Thus, the census figures may overstate the functional literacy levels of the population. In 1999, there was a network of more than 1.1 million educational institutions, from primary through preuniversity level, with more than 5.4 million teachers and a student enrollment of 186 million.

Still, the national literacy rate at the time of the 2001 Census had reached only 65 per cent—75 per cent for males and 54 per cent for females—a gender gap of 22 percentage points. Among the states, literacy for both sexes in 2001 was highest in Kerala at 91 per cent of the population above age 6 and lowest in Bihar at 47 per cent. For females, the highest literacy was also in Kerala, 88 per cent, and the lowest in Bihar, 33 per cent. Given the low literacy among Indians at independence, the government has made great progress in educating the population, particularly in the past two decades. The percentage of the population who were literate rose from 16 per cent to 65 per cent between 1951 and 2001, but this total belies the substantial and persistent gap between men and women.

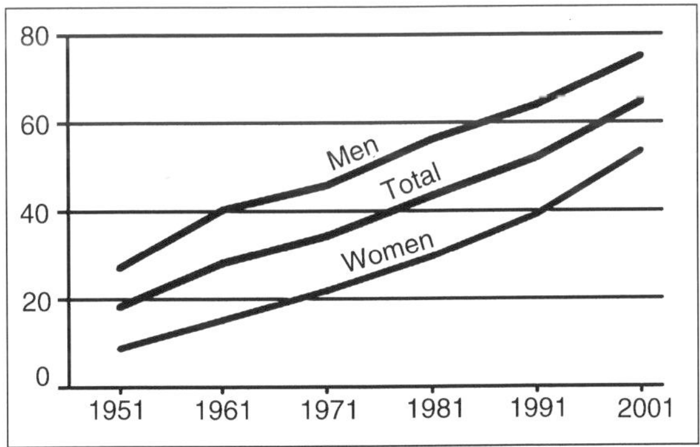

Fig. Per cent of Indians who are Literate, by Sex, 1951–2001

Between 1981 and 1991 the number of illiterate Indians declined, and they were outnumbered by literates for the first time in India's history.

WOMEN'S ROLES AND MARRIAGE

The gender gap in literacy highlights another important aspect of Indian society and tradition: the generally low status of women. Within a family, girls receive less nutrition and medical care than boys, undermining their health and sometimes leading to premature death. Surveys show that girls are less likely than boys to be immunized against major childhood diseases. And, as literacy figures demonstrate, girls were traditionally less likely to go to school. Marriage is universal in India.

Most Indian marriages are arranged by parents, leaving little choice to the couples themselves. Unlike contemporary Western cultures, marriage is seen as more of a family or social duty than a romantic liaison, and the selection of mate and marriage ceremonies are important social and religious events. The practice of dowry was outlawed in 1961, yet it remains widespread and appears to be gaining importance as a status symbol among wealthier Indians. The amount of the dowry can become a contentious issue for a new bride when her inlaws feel it was insufficient and pressure the bride to secure more from her parents.

Dowry-related violence is a major problem in India and is grossly underreported. In extreme cases, brides are hounded until they commit suicide; or young wives are murdered in suspect "kitchen fires," freeing the husband to seek another bride with another dowry. While the universality of marriage has not changed, age at marriage has risen significantly. The minimum legal age at marriage was set at 18 for women and 21 for men in 1929, but most Indian women married before age 17 until fairly recently. In 1961, about 20 per cent of girls ages 10 to 14 and 71 per cent of women ages 15 to 19 had already been married. By 2001, a remarkable social transformation had taken place. The rate for 10-to-14-year-olds had dropped to near zero and the rate for the 15-to-19 group had fallen by nearly two-thirds. The age at marriage affects fertility, because it affects the number of years a woman is at risk of getting pregnant. A rising age at marriage is associated with lower fertility, because women spend fewer years exposed to the risk of pregnancy. The shift in marriage patterns of recent decades favours further decline in India's birth rate. The decline in adult mortality can have the opposite effect on fertility rates.

With increased longevity for both men and women, fewer women die or are widowed at younger ages, exposing them to the risk of pregnancy for longer periods. The major factor in India's fertility decline in recent decades, however, has been an increase in the use of family planning. Indians have been slow to adopt family planning, and the issue has been fraught with political and social controversy, as explained in the next section. But contraceptive use and family planning are gaining wider acceptance, especially among more-educated women.

POPULATION POLICIES

India justifiably claims to be the first country to adopt an official policy to slow population growth, beginning with the country's first Five Year Plan in 1952. In the 1950s, the country was experiencing accelerated population growth created by declining death rates and high birth rates—a situation shared by many developing countries in that period. Death rates had fallen as these countries gained better public sanitation, widespread immunization of children, and expanded medical care. But birth rates remained high, pushing population growth to unprecedented heights.

Initial efforts to implement a family planning programme were rather limited, with a budget of US$1.35 million. The programme began by setting up family planning clinics with the expectation that people would seek out the clinics on their own. But the goal of reducing birth rates through family planning was hampered both by deep-seated traditions that favoured larger families and by the enormous challenge of bringing services to a vast, largely rural population. In the second Five Year Plan, expenditures for family planning were increased and the idea of incorporating family planning into community-based development programmes were introduced. Home visits by family planning workers was expanded in the 1960s to reach even more people. The population programme gained status when it was brought under the new Ministry of Health and Family Planning in 1966. The government's concern about the country's population growth was heightened in the 1970s when successive censuses had shown that the rate was rising, despite the policies and investments in family planning.

This concern set the stage for the family planning program's most controversial period. This took place during the National Emergency declared by Prime Minister Indira Gandhi in 1975, partly to thwart her political opposition. With financial support from the central government and the political backing of Mrs. Gandhi's popular son Sanjay, many states adopted coercive measures along with quota systems that resulted in the establishment of the infamous sterilization camps. In the 1976–1977 programme year, 8.3 million sterilizations, primarily vasectomies, were performed, up from 2.7 million the year before. The abuses and negative publicity generated by the Emergency compromised the reputation of the government family planning programme, and family planning services were suspended.

By the 1977–1978 programme year, the number of sterilizations had plummeted to 0.9 million. The slow decline in India's fertility rate of the previous decade stopped. To distance itself from the negative image of the Emergency, the name of the ministry responsible for family planning was changed to the Ministry of Health and Family Welfare, and remains so to this day. The backlash against the involuntary sterilizations was partly responsible for the defeat of Mrs.

Gandhi's party in the next elections. Successive governments—including Mrs. Gandhi herself, who returned to power in 1980 and served until her assassination in 1984—have been careful to emphasize the voluntary nature of the programme. Following the 1994 International Conference on Population and Development in Cairo, India announced that it was adopting a "target-free" approach in its population policy. This change reflected the spirit of the

Cairo conference, which called for greater emphasis on a full programme of reproductive health that would be less concerned with specific demographic goals. In reality, this new approach has been applied differently in different areas of the country. In some cases, local clinics found it hard to operate without specific quotas, such as the number of women accepting family planning or for condoms distributed. Some states, such as Andhra Pradesh, continued to offer incentives such as cash or goods such as transistor radios, for women to agree to sterilization.

In the 1998-1999 period, 67 per cent of women ages 25 to 29 in Andhra Pradesh had been sterilized, a remarkably high percentage for women under age 30. The failure of some states to lower their birth rates also has undermined their political clout in the national legislature. Seats in India's parliament are apportioned among the states according to population size. But giving the rapidly growing northern states more seats was viewed as rewarding them for poor performance in lowering birth rates and contradicting the government's policy to reduce population growth. Accordingly, the Indian Supreme Court has repeatedly frozen the allocation of seats to the population distribution as of 1971. In 2000, the year population reached 1 billion, the government promulgated its first National Population Policy, NPP 2000.

This policy contained a comprehensive sociodemographic programme covering 14 topics such as reducing infant and maternal mortality, promoting later marriage, universal immunization of children, and preventing the spread of HIV. The policy maintains a commitment to couples' "voluntary and informed choice" of reproductive health services so that replacement level fertility of two children per woman could be achieved by 2010. The need for a separate national population policy had been identified as early as 1983, but was not realised for 17 years. This long delay at least partly reflected fears of a political backlash against family planning, as there had been after the Emergency. More recently, a debate has been underway regarding elected officials leading by example, willingly or unwillingly, in the practice of family planning. In a number of states, including Maharashtra, people with more than two children are banned from any elective office from state assemblies to five-member village councils. There has been an outcry against this policy as inequitable and too strict, and charges that it will increase, not reduce, female feticide. In the wake of the controversy, Himachal Pradesh state withdrew its twochild limit for elected officials in 2005.

FAMILY PLANNING AND FERTILITY

Despite the obstacles, family planning use did slowly rise in India, from 13 per cent of couples in 1970 to 53 per cent for the 2002–2004 period. Given the logistical problems of supplying information and services to more than 250 million women of reproductive age, this increase is a remarkable achievement. Women's knowledge of contraception is nearly universal, although knowledge of traditional methods such as rhythm and withdrawal is less common. Most Indian women know about female sterilization, but other modern methods, such as intrauterine devices or the pill, are much less well known. Female sterilization remains the most common method of family planning.

Table. Contraceptive Methods Used in India, 1992–1993 to 2002–2004

	Percent of married women ages 15–49 using contraception		
	1992–93	**1998–99**	**2002–04**
Any method	40.6	48.2	53.0
Any modern method	36.3	42.8	45.7
Pill	1.2	2.1	3.5
IUD	1.9	1.6	1.9
Condom	2.4	3.1	4.8
Female sterilization	27.3	34.2	34.3
Male sterilization	3.4	1.9	0.9
Any traditional method	4.3	5.0	7.3
Periodic abstinence	2.6	3.0	4.1
Withdrawal	1.4	2.0	2.7
Other	0.2	0.4	0.5
Not using a method	59.4	51.8	47.0

Female sterilization rose from 27 per cent to 34 per cent of contraceptive methods used between NFHS-1 and the Reproductive and Child Health Survey of 2002–2004. Among women familiar with them, "spacing" methods such as the pill and IUD are widely mistrusted for fear of side effects, and female sterilization is often viewed as the best alternative.

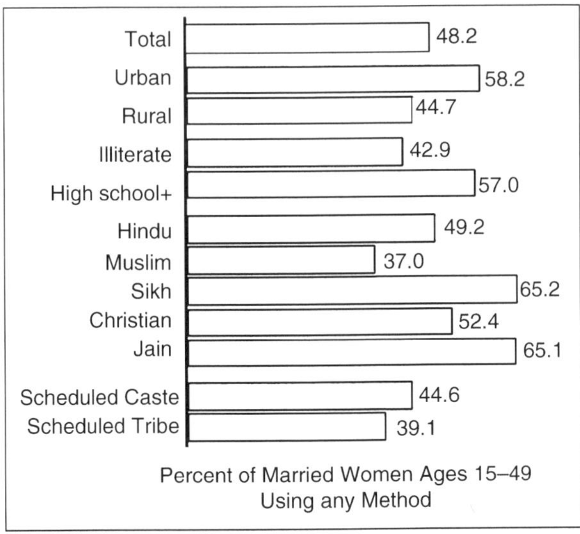

Fig. Contraceptive Use by Selected Indicators, 1998–1999

Male sterilization is unpopular; prevalence recorded in the NFHS and other surveys has been declining as older husbands who had been sterilized in the 1970s during the Emergency age out of the sample of women ages 15 to 49. In NFHS-2, for example, 8 per cent of husbands ages 45 to 49 had been sterilized, compared with only 1 per cent of those ages 30 to 34. Contraceptive use is higher in urban than rural areas and increases with a woman's educational attainment.

Among religious groups surveyed in NFHS-2, Sikhs and Jains had the highest use, 65 per cent, followed by Christians at 52 per cent and Hindus at 49 per cent. Muslims have the lowest rate of contraceptive use at 37 per cent. Contraceptive use was also well below the national average among women from the scheduled tribes in 1999, but not for women in scheduled castes. Contraceptive prevalence varies widely among the states. The RCH survey reported the highest level of use in West Bengal, Himachal Pradesh, and Kerala, with between 69 per cent and 74 per cent of married women ages 15 to 49 using a family planning method. The three lowest states were Jharkhand, Uttar Pradesh, and Bihar, with between 31 per cent and 38 per cent of women using family planning.

FERTILITY TRENDS

Since 1950, fertility in India has decreased by about half, from just under six children per woman to about three. The total fertility rate or average total number of children a woman would have given current birth rates, was 2.3 or fewer in seven states in 2003. Two states, Kerala and Tamil Nadu, had TFRs below 2.0, close to the level of the United States and other developed countries, and below the replacement level of 2 children per woman. In most states, however, the TFR was well above replacement level, and it ranged up to 4.2 in Bihar and 4.4 in Uttar Pradesh. Although there are still considerable differences in state-level TFRs, the rate has declined by just over 2 children per woman in most of the states.

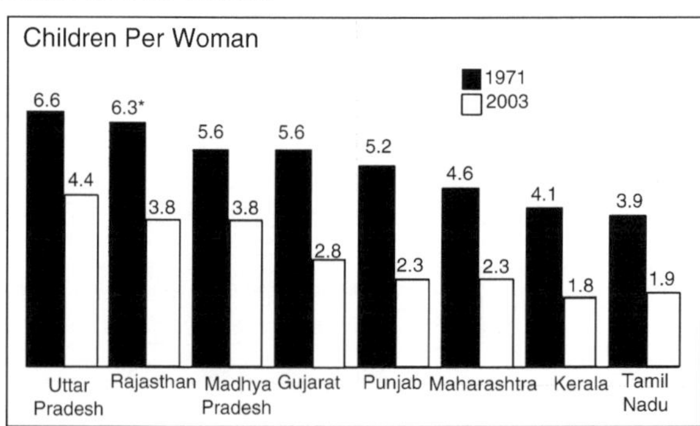

Fig. Total Fertility Rate, Selected States, 1971 and 2003

In percentage terms, however, the declines were greatest in Kerala and other lower-fertility states. The TFR was a full child higher among rural than urban women in 2003, 3.2 to 2.2. In the NFHS-2 survey, the TFR was highest for Muslim women (3.6), followed by Hindus (2.8), Christians (2.4), Sikhs (2.3), and Jains (1.9). Probably reflecting their lower educational and income levels, scheduled classes and tribes had relatively high TFRs: 3.2 among SCs and 3.1 for STs in 1998-1999.

Fertility decline in the 1990s was greater among older than younger women, a typical pattern for a population with declining fertility. Past trends in birth rates can offer some insight into the future, an important issue given that fertility trends are the primary factor determining India's future population size.

As a population transitions from high to low fertility, fertility often declines rapidly to a moderately low rate, then the pace of decline slows as the TFR approaches the replacement level of two children per woman. But the pattern of decline can vary significantly within countries, as illustrated by the trends in the birth rate for two low-fertility states and two high-fertility states between 1971 and 2004.

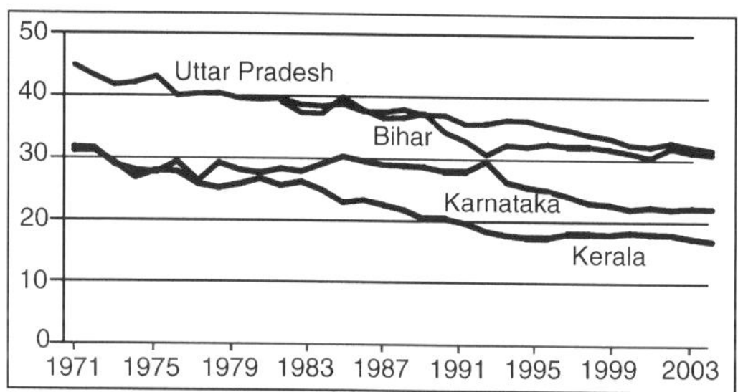

Fig. Birth Rates in Four Indian States, 1971–1973 to 2002–2004

Karnataka and Kerala began at the same level in 1971, when they were already among India's low-fertility states. The rates appeared to plateau during the 1970s—an apparent rejection of family planning after the excesses of the Emergency. But Karnataka's birth rate was stagnant through the 1980s, while Kerala's plummeted.

The gap between the two states has narrowed during the early 1990s, but both have plateaued, with no sign that Karnataka's birth rate will fall as low as Kerala's. The TFR in Kerala was down to 2.0 as early as 1988, and fell to 1.8 in 2003, while Karnataka's was still 2.3 in 2001. The two high-fertility states shown, Bihar and Uttar Pradesh, also exhibit somewhat different patterns. Fertility declined fairly steadily but slowly in Uttar Pradesh, but it is difficult to guess how much further it will fall. There has been no significant fertility decrease since the early 1990s in Bihar.

HIV AND AIDS

India is a low-prevalence HIV/AIDS country, with an estimated 0.9 per cent of the adult population ages 15 to 49 infected with HIV. While the rate is relatively low, India has the world's largest number of people of all ages with

HIV: 5.7 million in 2005. South Africa is estimated to have a similar, but slightly lower number of HIV-infected people: 5.5 million. South Africa's population is much smaller than India's but an estimated one-fifth of South African adults are infected with HIV. China, the only country larger than India, has just 0.1 per cent of adults infected with HIV, and an estimated 650,000 people of all ages.

These estimates, from the Joint United Nations Programme on HIV/AIDS have a margin of error because it is impossible to precisely measure the number of HIV-infected people. The estimates of HIV prevalence, and the relative ranking of countries, have always been controversial. India uses a network of "sentinel sites" to evaluate the extent of HIV-infection, a practice followed in most developing countries that lack accurate data on disease. Most sites are at sexually transmitted disease and antenatal care clinics in government hospitals.

People visiting sexually transmitted disease clinics are considered a high-risk group, while those visiting ANCs are considered low-risk. Often, HIV prevalence among women at ANCs is used as a surrogate for overall HIV prevalence in a country. But the women visiting ANC clinics are not statistically representative of the entire population, and coverage is fairly thin in many Indian states. More accurate estimates of HIV infection among the general population are expected when the results of the 2005–2006 NFHS-3 become available. HIV-testing of respondents was an important component of NFHS-3, and will provide the first nationally representative prevalence estimates for India and for some severely affected states.

COMBATING HIV AND AIDS

India reacted to the earliest cases of HIV, discovered in 1986 in the port cities of Chennai and Mumbai, by establishing the National AIDS Control Programme. The initial budget was insufficient for the task and the programme did not gain momentum until about 1992. State AIDS Cells set up to manage the programme at the local level proved cumbersome, and the programme languished. But an experimental programme established in 1994—the Tamil Nadu State AIDS Control Society—was so successful that it has become the model for other states. State AIDS Control Societies based on the Tamil Nadu programme—which drew members from all government departments and from nongovernmental organizations—have been established in 32 states and union territories. HIV is spreading largely through sexual activity, although intravenous drug use plays a major role in the two high-prevalence northeastern states of Nagaland and Manipur.

Four other states—Andhra Pradesh, Karnataka, Maharashtra, and Tamil Nadu—are considered to be high-prevalence states because the prevalence measured at ANC sites has been 1.0 or above. HIV-prevention campaigns are often aimed at truckers—who spend long periods away from home and on the road. The prevalence is higher along major highways. Commercial sex workers, another high-risk group, are more difficult to locate because so many do not operate from fixed locations.

HIV programmes in India have been expanding geographically, and include more testing and counseling centers, a new antiretroviral treatment programme, and expanded publicity. TV spots with popular sports figures and actors, as well as newspaper advertisements and billboards, are attempting to spread information about how to avoid HIV infection and to reduce the intense discrimination faced by HIV-positive people in India. More people know about HIV/AIDS than in the past.

In the 2001 Behavioural Surveillance Survey, about 82 per cent of men and 70 per cent of women had heard of HIV/AIDS—a figure that has undoubtedly increased over the past five years because of widespread publicity campaigns. But the knowledge gap between urban and rural populations is probably still substantial, even if it has narrowed. In Bihar, for example, just 22 per cent of rural women had heard of HIV/AIDS in 2001, compared with 63 per cent of urban women.

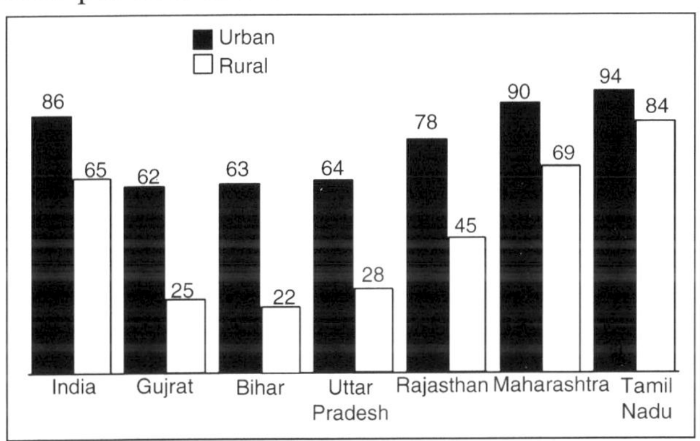

Fig. Per cent of Women Ages 15–49 Who Have Heard of HIV/AIDS, India and Selected States, 2001

The government's campaign, assisted by major support from foreign governments and foundations, has continued to expand, but given the size and diversity of India's population, few countries face a bigger challenge in fighting HIV.

INDIA'S FUTURE POPULATION

India's future population size will largely depend upon the future course of the birth rate, particularly in the heavily populated north. UN projections offer one view of India's population future. The low variant sees India growing from 1.1 billion in 2006 to 1.3 billion in 2050.

This projection, however, makes the unrealistic assumption that the country's total fertility rate will quickly decline from about 3.0 in 2005 to 2.10

in the 2010–2015 period, and then continue downward to 1.35 by 2030–2035. The medium variant assumes that a TFR of 2.1 children would be reached by 2020–2025 and then level off at 1.85 by 2030–2035, resulting in a 2050 population of 1.6 billion.

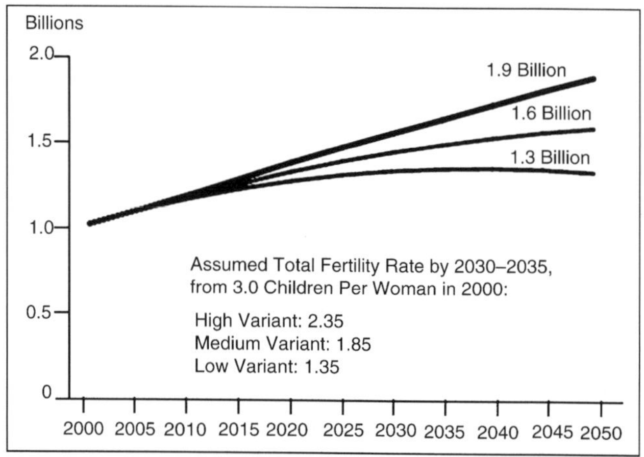

Fig. India's Population Projected to 2050: Three Scenarios

Finally, the high variant assumes that the TFR would fall from 3.0 to 2.35 by 2030–2035, remaining stationary thereafter. The high variant yields a population of 1.9 billion in 2050. Any consideration of India's population future raises a number of important questions. Will the "two child family" concept take hold throughout the entire country Or will other factors such as the preference for sons and deeply rooted family traditions counter the notion in many parts of the country?

CONCLUSION

Few countries are as complex as India. A visitor to Delhi or Bangalore might leave with the impression that India is rapidly becoming a middle-class country with a consumer-oriented lifestyle. But India remains an essentially rural country steeped in centuries-old social and religious traditions. In its modern cities, large proportions of the population live in officially classified slums. Still, progress on many fronts has been remarkable, if uneven, particularly in light of its vast population. Agricultural production quadrupled during a remarkable transformation of its agricultural sector in the 1960s and 1970s, which, along with expanded transportation and communications networks, have made famines nearly obsolete. Nonetheless, almost 50 per cent of Indian children are malnourished.

The expansion of the health care system has raised life expectancy at birth to 63 years from less than 40 years in 1950. But less than half of births are attended by skilled health personnel, and maternal mortality is still high. During the 20th century, India's population growth awoke from the doldrums as real progress was made against disease and hunger. The quarter-billion of 1900 became the 1 billion of 2000. Slowing such unheard-of growth became a national priority from the nation's beginning, and India can count many successes in that effort.

But India's wide social diversity has resulted in very different demographic situations—persistently high fertility in the Hindi Belt compared with below-replacement fertility in Kerala, for example. Success in one area has not been matched by success in others. India's future population size will depend upon what happens in the heavily populated north. In 2000, India's population reached 1 billion. Now the question of 2 billion arises. Will India become the world's first population "double billionaire?" Such a development is well within mathematical possibility. That is one of India's most compelling future issues.

10

Population and its Aspects

ANTHROPOLOGY

The classification of mankind into a number of permanent varieties or races, rests on grounds which are within limits not only obvious but definite. Whether from a popular or a scientific point of view, it would be admitted that a Negro, a Chinese, and an Australia, belong to three such permanent varieties of men, all plainly distinguishable from one another and from any European. Moreover, such a division takes for granted the idea which is involved in the word race, that each of these varieties is due to special ancestry, each race thus representing an ancient breed or stock, however these breeds or stocks may have had their origin.

The anthropological classification of mankind is thus zoological in its nature, like that of the varieties or species of any other animal group, an the character on which it is based on in great measure physical, though intellectual and traditional peculiarities, such as moral habit and language, furnish important aid. Among the best-marked race-characters are the following:— The colour of the skin has always been held as specially distinctive.

The coloured race-portraits of ancient Egypt remain to prove the permanence of complexion during a lapse of a hundred generations, distinguishing coarsely but clearly the types of the red-brown Egyptian, the yellow-brown Canaanite, the comparatively fair Libyan, and the Negro. These broad distinctions have the same kind of value as the popular terms describing white, yellow, brown, and black races, which often occur in ancient writings, and are still used. But for scientific purposes greater accuracy is required, and this is now satisfactorily attained by the use of Dr. Broca's graduated series of colours as a standard.

The varieties of the human skin may be followed from the fairest hue of the Swede and the darker tint of the Provencal, to the withered-leaf brown of the Hottentot, the chocolate brown of the Mexican, and the brown-black of the West African. The colour of the eyes and hair is also to be defined accurately by Broca's table. This affords, however, less means of distinction, from the extent in which dark tints of hair and iris are common to races whose skins are more perceptibly different; yet some varieties are characteristic, such as the blue eyes and flaxen hair of that fair race of Northern Europe. As to the hair, its structure and arrangement is a better indication of race than its tint.

The fair differs in quantity between scantiness of the body of the Mongol and profusion on the body of the Aino; while as to the arrangement on the scalp, the tufts of the Bushman contrast with the more equal distribution on the European head. The straight hair of the North American or Malay is recognizable at once as different from the waving or curling hair of the European, and both from the naturally frizzed hair of the Negro.

These marked differences are due to the structure of the hair, wick, examined in sections under the microscope, varies from the circular section proper to the straight-haired races, to the more or less symmetrically oval or reniform sections belonging to races with curled and twisted hair. Stature is by no means a general criterion of race, and it would not, for instance, be difficult to choose groups of Englishmen, Kafirs, and North American Indians, whose mean height should hardly differ.

Yet in many cases it is a valuable means of distinction, as between the tall Patagonians and the stunted Fuegians, and even as a help in minuter problems, such as separating the Teutonic and Keltic ancestry in the population of England. Proportions of the limbs, compared in length with the trunk, have been claimed as constituting peculiarities of African and American races; and other anatomical points, such as the conformation of the pelvis, have speciality. But inferences of this class have hardly attained to sufficient certainty and generality to be set down in the form of rules. The conformation of the skull is second only to the colour of the skin as a criterion for the distinction of race.

The principal modes of estimating the differences of skulls are the following:-The proportions of the two diameters are estimated on the principle employed by Retzius: taking the longer diameter from front to back as 100, if the shorter or cross diameter falls below 80, the skull may be classed as long; while if it exceeds 80, the skull may be classed as broad; or a third division may be introduced between these as intermediate, comprehending skulls with a proportionate breadth of 75 to 80, or thereabout. The percentage of breadth to length measured in this manner is known as the cephalic index; thus, the cephalic index of a Negro or Australian may be as low as 72, and that of a Tatar as high as 88, while the majority of Europeans have an index not departing in either direction very far from 78.

The cephalic height is measured in the same way as a percentage of the length. The back view of the skull is distinguished as rounded, pentagonic, &c., and the base view of the skull shows the position of the occipital foramen and the zygomatic arches. The position of the jaws is recognized as important, races being described as prognathous when the jaws project, far, as in the Asutralian or Negro, in contradistinction to the orthognathous type, which is that of the ordinary well-shaped European skull. On this distinction in great measure depends the celebrated "facial angle," measured by Camper as a test of low and high races; but this angle is objectionable as resulting partly from the development of the forehead and partly from the position of the jaws. The capacity of the cranium is estimated in cubic measure by filling it with sand, &c., with the general result that the civilized white man is found to have a larger brain than the barbarian or savage.

Classification of races on cranial measurements has long been attempted by eminent anatomists, such as Blumenbach and Retzius, while the later labours of Von Baer, Welcker, Davis, Broca, Busk, Lucae, and many others, have brought the distinctions to extreme minuteness. In certain cases great reliance may be placed on such measurements. Thus the skulls of an Asutralian and a Negro would be generally distinguished by their narrowness and the projection of the jaw from that of any Englishman; while, although both the Australian and Negro are thus dolichocephalic and prognathous, the first would usually differ perceptibly from the second in its upright sides and strong orbital ridges.

The relation of height to breadth may furnish a valuable test; thus both the Hafir and the Bushman are dolichocephalic, with an index of about 72, but they differ in the index of height, which may be 73 and 71 respectively, in the one case more than the width and in the other less. It is, however, acknowledged by all experienced craniologists, that the shape of the skull may vary so much within the same tribe, and even the same family, that it must be used with extreme caution, and if possible only in conjunction with other criteria of race.

The general contour of the face, in part dependent on the form of the skull, varies much in different races, among whom it is loosely defined as oval, lozenge-shaped, pentagonal, &c. Of particular features, some of the most marked contrast to European types are seen in the oblique Chinese eyes, the broad-set Kamchadal cheeks, the pointed Arab chin, the snub Kirghis nose, the fleshy protuberant Negro lips, and the broad Kalmuk ear. Taken altogether, the features have a typical character which popular observation seizes with some degree of correctness, as in the recognition of the Jewish countenance in a European city.

The state of adaptation in which each people stands to its native climate forms a definite race-character. In its extreme form this is instanced in the harmful effect of the climate of India on children of European parents, and the corresponding danger in transporting natives of tropical climates to England. Typical instances of the relation of race-constitutions to particular diseases are seen in the liability of Europeans in the West Indies to yellow fever, from which Negroes are exempt, and in the habitation by tribes in India of so-called "unhealthy districts," whose climate is deadly to Europeans, and even to natives of neighbouruing regions. Even the vermin infesting different races of men are classified by Mr. A. Murray as distinct.

The physical capabilities of different races are known to differ widely, but it is not easy to discriminate here between hereditary race-differences and those due to particular food and habit of life. A similar difficulty has hitherto stood in the way of any definite classification of the emotional, moral and intellectual characters of races. Some of the most confident judgment which have been delivered on this subject have been dictated by prejudice or willful slander, as in the many lamentable cases in which slave-holders and conquerors have excused their ill-treatment of subject and invaded races on the ground of their being creatures of bestial nature in mind and morals.

Two of the best-marked contrasts of mental type recorded among races are Mr. A. R. Wallace's distinction between the sky, reserved, and impassive Malay and the sociable and demonstrative Papuan and the very similar difference pointed out by Spix and Martius between the dull and morose natives of the Brazilian forests, an the lively sensuous African Negroes brought into contact with them. In general, however, descriptions of national or racial character are so vitiated by the confusion of peculiarity of natural character with stage of civilization, that they can only be made use of with the greatest reserve.

Were the race-character indicated in the foregoing paragraphs constant in degree or even in kind, the classification of races would be an easy task. In fact it is not so, for every division of mankind presents in every character wide deviations from a standard. Thus the Negro race, well marked as it may seem at the first glance, proves on closer examination to include several shades of complexion and features, in some districts varying far from the accepted Negro type; while the examination of a series of native American tribes shows that, notwithstanding their asserted uniformity of type, they differ in stature, colour, features, and proportions of skull. Detailed anthropological research, indeed, more and more justifies Blumenbach's words, that "innumerable varieties of mankind run into one another by insensible degrees."

This state of things, due partly to mixture and crossing of races, and partly to independent variation of types, makes the attempt to arrange the whole human species within exactly bounded divisions an apparently hopeless task. It does not follow, however, that the attempt to distinguish special races should be given up, for there at least exist several definable types, each of which so far prevails in a certain population as to be taken as its standard. M. Quetelet's plan of defining such types will probably meet with general acceptance as the scientific method proper to this branch of anthropology.

It consists in the determination of the standard, or typical "mean man" of a population, with reference to any particular quality, such as stature, weight, complexion, &c. In the case of statute, this would be done by measuring a sufficient number of men, and accounting how many of them belong to each height on the scale. If it be thus ascertained, as it might be in an English district, that the 5 ft. 7 in. men form the most numerous group, while the 5 ft. 6 in. and 5 ft. 8 in. men are less in number, and the 5 ft. 5 in. and 5 ft. 9 in. still fewer, and so on until the extremely small number of extremely short or tall individuals of 5 ft. or 7 ft. is reached, it will thus be ascertained that the stature of the mean or typical man is to be taken as 5 ft. 7 in.

The method is thus that of selecting as the standard the most numerous group, on both sides of which the groups decrease in number as they vary in type. Such classification may show the existence of two or more types in a community, as, for instance, the population of a Californian settlement made up of Whites and Chinese might show two predominant groups corresponding to these two racial types. It need hardly be said that this method of determining the mean type of a race, as being that of its really existing and mist numerous class, is altogether superior to the ere calculation of an average, which may actually be represented by comparatively few individuals, and those the exceptional ones.

For instance, the average stature of the mixed European and Chinese population just referred to might be 5 ft. 6 in—a worthless and, indeed, misleading result. The measurement and description of the various races of men are now carried to great minuteness so that race classification is rapidly improving as to both scope and accuracy. Even where comparatively loose observations have been made, it is possible, by inspection of considerable number of individuals, to define the prevalent type of a race with tolerable approximation to the real mean or standard man. It is in this way that the subdivision of mankind into races, so far as it has been done to any purpose, has been carried out by anthropologists.

These classifications have been numerous, and though, regarded as system's most of them are now seen at the first glance to be unsatisfactory, yet they have been of great value in systematizing knowledge, and are all more or less based on indisputable distinctions. Blumenbach's division, though published nearly a century ago has had the greatest influence. He reckon five races, *viz.*, Caucasian, Mongolian, Ethiopian, American, Malay. The ill-chosen name of Caucasian, used by Blumenbach to denote what may be called white men, is still current; it brings into one race peoples such as the Arabs and Swedes, although these are scarcely less different than the Americans and Malays, who are set down as two distinct races.

Again, two of the best-marked varieties of mankind are the Australians and the Bushmen, neither of whom, however, seem to have a natural place in Blumebach's series. The yet simpler classification by Cuvier into Caucasian, Mongol, and Negro, corresponds in some measure with a division by mere complexion into white, yellow, and black races; but neither this threefold division, nor the ancient classification into Semitic, Hamitic, and Japhetic nations can be regarded as separating the human types either justly or sufficiently. Schemes which set up a larger number of distinct races, such as the eleven of Pickering, the fifteen of Bory de St Vincent, and the sixteen of

Desmoulins, have the advantage of finding niches for most well-defined human varieties; but no modern naturalist would be likely to adopt any one of these as it stands.

In criticism of Pickering's system, it is sufficient to point out that he divides the white nations into two races, entitled the Arab and the Abyssinian Agassiz, Nott, Crawfurd, and others who have assumed a much larger number of races or species of man, are not considered to have satisfactorily defined a corresponding number of distinguishable types. On the whole, Professor Huxley's recent scheme probably approaches more nearly than any other to such a tentative classification as may be accepted in definition of the principal varieties of mankind, regarded from a zoological point of view, though anthropologists may be disposed to erect into separate races several of his widely-differing sub-races. He ditinsguishes four principal types of mankind, the Australioid, Negroid, Mongoloid, and Xanthochoroic, adding a fifth variety, the Melanochroic.

The special points of the Australioid are a chocolate-brown skin, dark brown or black eyes, black hair, narrow skull, brow-ridges strongly developed, projecting jaw, coarse lips, and broad nose. This type is best represented by the natives of Australia, and next to them, by the indigenous tribes of Southern India, the so-called coolies. The Egyptians to some degree approach this type; they are, however, held by good authorities to be a modified African race. The Negroid type is primarily represented by the Negro of Africa, between the Sahara and the Cape district, including Madagascar.

The skin varies from dark brown to brown-black, with eyes of similar dark hue, and hair usually black, and always crisp or woolly. The skull is narrow with orbital ridges not prominent, prognathous, with depressed nasal, bones, causing the nose to be flat as well as broad; and the lips are coarse and projecting. Two important families are classed in this system as special modifications of the Negroid type. First, the Bushman of South Africa is diminutive in stature, and of yellowish-brown complexion; the Hottentot is supposed to be the result of crossing between the Bushman and ordinary Negroid.

Second, the Negritos of the Andaman Islands, the peninsula of Malacca, the Philippines and other islands, to New Caledonia and Tasmania, are mostly dolichocephalism, with dark skins and woolly hair. In various districts they tend towards other types, and show traces of mixture. The Mongoloid type prevails over the vast area lying east of a line drawn from Lapland to Siam. Its definition includes a short, squat build, a yellowish brown complexion, with black eyes and black straight hair, a broad skull, usually without prominent brow-ridges, flat small nose, and oblique eyes. The dolichocephalic Chinese and Japanese in other respect correspond.

Various other important branches of the human species are brought into connection with the Mongoloid type, though on this view the differences they present raise difficult problems of gradual variations, as well as of mixture of race; these are the Dyak-Malays, the Polynesians, and the Americans. The Xanthochroi, or fair whites-tall, with almost colourless skin, blue or grey eyes, hair from straw colour to chesnut, and skulls varying as to proportionate width-are the prevalent inhabitants of Northern Europe, and the type may be traced into North Africa, and eastward as far as Hindostan. On the south and west it mixes with that of the Melanochroi, or dark whites, and on the north and east with that of the Mongoloids. The Melanochroi, or dark whites, differ from the fair whites in the darkening of the complexion to brownish and olive, and of the eyes and hair to black, while the stature is somewhat lower and the frame lighter.

To this class belong a large part of those classed as Kelts, and of the populations of Southern Europe, such as Spaniards, Greeks, and Arabs, extending as far as India; while endless intermediate grades between the two white types testify to ages of intermingling. Professor Huxley is disposed to account for the Melanochroi as themselves the result of crossing between the Xanthochroi and the Australioids. Whatever ground there may be for his view, it is obviously desirable to place them in a class by themselves, distinguishing them by an appropriate name.

In determining whether the races of mankind are to be classed as varieties of one species, it is important to decide whether every two races can unite to produce fertile offspring. It is settled by experience that the most numerous and well-known crossed races, such as the Mulattos, descended from Europeans and Negroes-the Mestizos, from Europeans and American indigenes—the Zambos, from these American indigenes and Negroes, &c., are permanently fertile. They practically constitute sub-races, with a general blending of the characters of the two parents, and only differing from fully established races in more or less tendency to revert to one or other of the original types.

It has been argued, on the other hand, that not all such mixed breeds are permanent, and especially that the cross between European and Australian indigenes is almost sterile; but this assertion, when examined with the care demanded by its bearing on the general question of hybridity, has distinctly broken down. On the whole, the general evidence favours the opinion that any two races may combine to produce a new sub-race, which again may combine with any other variety.

Thus, if the existence of a small number of distinct races of mankind be taken as a starting-point, it is obvious that their crossing would produce an indefinite number of secondary varieties, such as the population of the world actually presents. The working out in detail of the problem, how far the differences among complex, nations, such as those of Europe, may have been brought about by hybridity, is still, however, a task of almost hopeless intricacy.

Among the boldest attempts to account for distinctly-marked population as resulting from the intermixture of two races, are Professor Huxley's view that the Hottentots are hybrid between the Bushmen and the Negroes, and his more important suggestion, that the Melnochroic peoples of Southern Europe are of mixed Xanthochoric and Australioid stock.

The problem of ascertaining how the small number of races, distinct enough to be called primary, can have assumed their different types, has been for years the most disputed field of anthropology, the battle-ground of the rival schools of monogenists and polygenists. The one has claimed all mankind to be descended from one original stock, and generally from a single pair; the other has contended for the several primary races being separate species of independent origin. It is not merely as a question of natural history that the matter has been argued.

Biblical authority has been appealed to, mostly on the side of the monogenists, as recording the descent of mankind from a single pair. On the other hand, however, the polygenists not less confidently claim passages from which they infer the existence of non-Adamite, as well as Adamite races of man. Nor have political considerations been without influence, as where, for instance, one American school of ethnologists have been thought to have formed, under the bias of a social system recognizing slavery, their opinion that the Negro and the white man are of different species.

Of the older school of scientific monogenists, Blumenbach and Prichard are eminent representatives, as is Quatrefages of the more modern. The great problem of the monogenist theory is to explain by what course of variation the so different races of man have arisen from a single stock. In ancient times little difficulty was left in this, authorities such as Aristotle and Vitruvius seeing in climate and circumstance the natural cause of racial differences, the Ethiopian having been blackened by the tropical sun, &c. Later and closer observations, however, have shown such influences to be, at any rate, far slighter in amount and slower in operation than was once supposed. M. de Quatrefages brings forward his strongest arguments for the variability of races under change of climate, &c, instancing the asserted alteration in complexion, constitution, and character of Negroes in America, and Englishmen in America and Australia.

But although the reality of some such modification is not disputed, especially as to stature and constitution, its amount is not enough to upset the counter-proposition of the remarkable permanence of type displayed by races ages after they have been transported to climates extremely different from that of their former home. Moreover, physically different races, such as the Bushmen and Negroids in Africa, show no signs of approximation under the influence of the same climate; while on the other hand, the coast tribes of Tierra del Fuego and forest tribes of tropical Brazil continue to resemble one another, in spite of extreme differences of climate and food. Mr. Darwin, than whom no naturalist could be more competent to appraise the variation of a species, is moderate in his estimation of the changes produced on races of man by climate and mode of life within the range of history. The slightness and slowness of variation in human races having become known, a great difficulty of the monogenist theory was seen to lie in the shortness of the chromology with which it was formerly associated.

Inasmuch as several well-marked races of mankind, such as the Egyptian, Phoenician, Ethiopian, &c., were much the same three or four thousand years ago as now, their variation from a single stock in the course of any like period could hardly be accounted for without a miracle.

This difficulty was escaped by the polygenist theory, which, till a few years since, was gaining ground. Two modern views have, however, intervened which have tended to restore, though under a new aspect, the doctrine of a single human stock. One has been the recognition of man having existed during a vast period of time which made it easier to assume to continuance of very slow natural variation as having differenced even the white man and the Negro among the descendants of a common progenitor.

The other wise is that of the evolution or development of species, at the present day so strongly upheld among naturalists. It does not follow necessarily form a theory of evolution of species that mankind must have descended from a single stock, for the hypothesis of development admits of the arguments, that several simious species may have culminated in several races of man.

The general tendency of the development theory, however, is against constituting separate species where the differences are moderate enough to be accounted for a due to variation from a single type. Mr. Darwin's summing up of the evidence as to unity of type throughout the races of mankind is as distinctly a monogenist argument as those of Blumenbach, Prichard or Quatrefages-"Although the existing races of man differ in many respects, as in colour, hair, shape of skull, proportions of the body, &c., yet, if their whole organization be take into consideration, they are found to resemble each other closely in a multitude of points.

Many of these points are of so unimportant, or of so singular a nature, that it is extremely improbable that they should have been independently acquired by aboriginally distinct species or races.

The same remark holds good with equal or greater force with respect to the numerous points of mental similarity between the most distinct races of man... Now, when naturalists observe a close agreement in numerous small details of habits, tastes, and dispositions between two or more domestic races, or between nearly allied natural forms, they use this fact as an argument that all are descended from a common progenitor, who was thus endowed; and consequently, that all should be classed under the same species.

The same argument may be applied with much force to the races of man." A suggestion by Mr. A.R. Wallace has great importance in the application of the development theory to the origin of the various races of man; it is aimed to meet the main difficulty of the monogenist school, how races which have remained comparatively fixed in type during the long period of history, such as the white man and the Negro, should have, in even a far longer period, passed by variation from a common original.

Mr. Wallace's view is substantially that the remotely ancient representatives of the human species, being as yet animals too low in mind to have developed those arts of maintenance and social ordinances by which man holds his own against influences from climate and circumstance, were in their then wild state much more plastic than now to external nature; so that "natural selection" and other causes met with but feeble resistance in forming the permanent varieties or races of man, whose complexion and structure still remain fixed in their descendants.

On the whole, it may be asserted that the doctrine of the unity of mankind now stands on a firmer basis than in previous ages. It would be premature to judge how far the problem of the origin of races may be capable of exact solution; but the experience of the last few years countenances Mr. Darwin's prophecy, that before long the dispute between the monogenists and the polygenists will die a silent and unobserved death.

POPULATION SIZE, DISTRIBUTION AND GROWTH

Populations are dynamic entities. Over time they grow or decline, they become younger or older and their geographic distribution changes. Such changes are the cumulative effects of the events that people undergo during their lives, namely births, deaths and migrations. One of the concerns in demography is to trace out the consequence of changes in individual-level behaviour for aggregate processes. The combination of these individual events shapes the population of each country, and, though partially predictable, the outcome is sometimes surprising.

While no other century has witnessed such rapid and accelerating population growth as did the twentieth, population declines have been observed in several countries during the past decade or so. Such declines are foreseen to become the rule rather than the exception in some regions of the world, while in other regions the population will continue to grow, albeit at a more moderate pace.

POPULATION SIZE AND DISTRIBUTION

In the year 2005, the world population is estimated to have reached 6.5 billion, more than two and a half times the level in 1950; according to the medium-variant projection of the 2004 Revision, it is expected to reach 9.1 billion in 2050.

The less developed regions, with 5.3 billion people in 2005, account for the vast majority of the world population (81.3 per cent). The more developed regions have an estimated population of 1.2 billion, or 18.7 per cent of the world population. More and more of the world's inhabitants are coming to reside in the less developed regions, increasing from 67.7 per cent in 1950 to a projected 86.4 per cent in 2050.

Table. Population, by Development Group and Major Aarea, Estimates and Medium Variant, 1950, 2005 and 2050

	Population (millions)			Percentage distribution		
Development group or major area	1950	2005	2050	1950	2005	2050
World	2 519	6 465	9 076	100.0	100.0	100.0
More developed regions...............	813	1 211	1 236	32.3	18.7	13.6
Less developed regions...........	1 707	5 253	7 840	67.7	81.3	86.4
Least developed countries	201	759	1 735	8.0	11.7	19.1
Other less developed countries	1 506	4 494	6 104	59.8	69.5	67.3
Africa	224	906	1 937	8.9	14.0	21.3
Asia	1 396	3 905	5 217	55.4	60.4	57.5
Europe	547	728	653	21.7	11.3	7.2
Latin America and the Caribbean........	167	561	783	6.6	8.7	8.6
Northern America.............	172	331	438	6.8	5.1	4.8
Oceania..............	13	33	48	0.5	0.5	0.5

Within the less developed regions in 2005, the least developed countries account for about 0.8 billion and other less developed countries for 4.5 billion. The share of the least developed countries is projected to grow from 8.0 per cent in 1950 to 19.1 per cent in 2050. Asia, with a population of 3.9 billion in 2005, is by far the most populous major area; its share of the world population stays fairly stable over time, rising and falling slightly in the neighbourhood of 55-60 per cent between 1950 and 2050. The population shares of two other major areas,however, have shifted considerably since 1950, and this shifting is expected to continue.

Europe's population represented 21.7 per cent of the world population in 1950, a figure that was reduced by almost half by 2005, to 11.3 per cent. Europe's share of the world population is projected to decline furthermore, to 7.2 per cent in 2050. At the same time, Africa's share of the world population has been increasing, from 8.9 per cent in 1950 to 14.0 per cent in 2005, and is projected to reach 21.3 per cent in 2050, close to Europe's share in 1950. The social and economic disadvantages afflicting least developed countries are often vividly expressed in basic demographic indicators.

In assessing the challenges to international development that are presented by these countries, it should be remembered that they account for a relatively small share of the world population: 11.7 per cent in 2005. The other less developed countries, which include China and India, the two most populous countries collectively account for 69.5 per cent of the world population. Most of the world's population is found in a small set of very populous countries. A mere 4.8 per cent of all countries, that is, the 11 largest countries, each with an estimated population of 100 million or more in the year 2005, lay claim to 60.9 per cent of the world population.

The vast majority of the world's countries are actually relatively small in terms of their population size—of all countries, 77.2 per cent have populations under 20 million (with almost one third of all countries having fewer than 1 million). Taken as a group, these small countries account for only 11.6 per cent of the world population, while countries with populations from 20 million to 100 million include 18.0 per cent of all countries and 27.5 per cent of all population. Taken together, the 11 largest countries are home to more than 3.9 billion people.

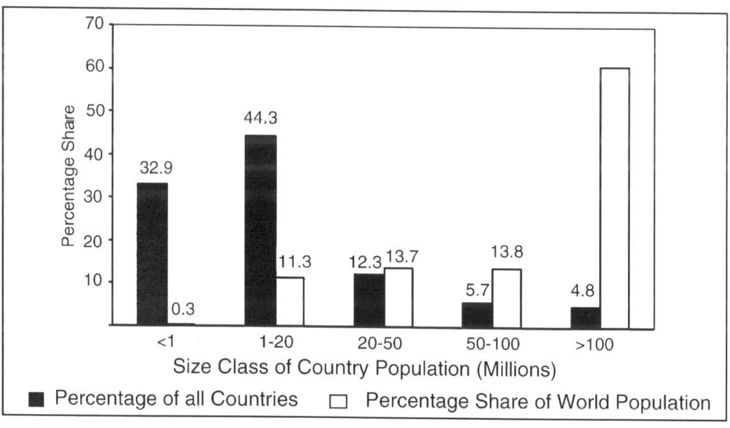

Fig. Distribution of Countries and Areas, by Percentage in Each Population Size Class and by Percentage Share of World Population in Each Population Size Class, 2005

Jointly, China and India account for more than 37 per cent of the world population in 2005, with estimated populations of 1.3 billion and 1.1 billion, respectively. A further 9 countries account for almost a quarter of the earth's population, namely, the United States of America, Indonesia, Brazil, Pakistan, the Russian Federation, Bangladesh, Nigeria, Japan and Mexico. Eight of the 11 most populous countries are considered to be less developed, leaving only

3 in the more developed regions (the United States of America, with a population of 298 million; the Russian Federation, with 143 million; and Japan, with 128 million).

These large, more-developed countries account for almost 9 per cent of the world population, a considerable share but far below that of China and India. The concentration of world population in large countries has been lessening, and this trend is projected to continue. In 1950, the combined populations of some 21 countries accounted for three-quarters of the population of the globe, a number that increased to 24 countries in 2005.

By 2050, according to the mediumvariant projection, 28 countries will be needed to reach that same share. Inevitably, several countries are projected to change ranks over thenext 45 years. India and China will likely trade places at the very top of the population rankings, Nigeria is expected to rise from 9th to 6th in rank, and the Russian Federation will likely fall from 7th to 17th. In addition, three least developed countries—Bangladesh, the Democratic Republic of the Congo and Ethiopia—will be among the ten most populous countries. Population growth would be substantially greater in the absence of fertility decline.

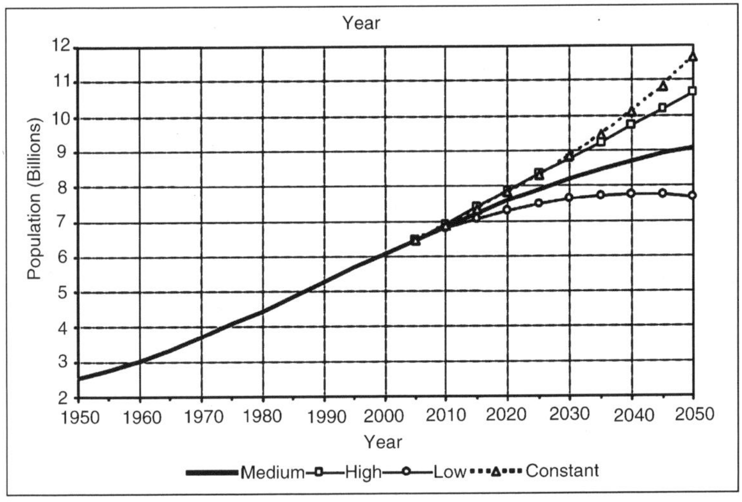

Fig. World Population, Estimates and Projection Variants, 1950–2050

If fertility were to be held constant at its current level for every country, the world population would reach a total of 11.7 billion persons by the year 2050, almost doubling its present size. The extent of growth is all the more impressive when one considers that an assumed constant fertility fixes a number of countries at below-replacement fertility levels. Alternatively, if total fertility were to adhere to the high-fertility variant, usually half a child above what is assumed in the medium-variant projection but generally declining over time, the world total would reach 10.6 billion in 2050. Under the low-fertility assumption, by contrast, with total fertility rates usually set at half a child below the medium variant, world population would reach 7.7 billion, far lower but still representing an addition of 1.2 billion persons to the world's current total. Evidently, the pace and depth of fertility decline will continue to have an important impact on world population levels and trends. Anticipated mortality trends will also influence the overall population.

The basic projection variants assume a single course of mortality change, usually a continuous decline, for each country. If mortality rates were held constant at their current levels, however, under the medium fertility variant world population would rise to 8.1 billion persons in 2050, about 1 billion less than the projected levels. Although there are important differences across these projection variants, in one respect they all agree: an era of substantial world population growth lies ahead. The estimated and projected world population levels are the product of divergent trends across the more developed and less developed regions.

For the more developed regions, it seems that an era of population decline may not be too far into the future. According to the medium-variant projection, the aggregate population of this region will rise from the year 2005 estimate of 1.21 billion persons to a peak of 1.25 billion around 2030, and will then fall to 1.24 billion by the end of the projection period, yielding a net addition of only about 25 million. Only the high fertility variant suggests continued growth in the populations of the more developed regions. Note that if current levels of fertility were to be maintained, as assumed in the constant fertility variant, the populations of the more developed regions would fall below the medium-variant projection. Likewise, the path of fertility decline will make an important difference to the futures of the other less developed countries, a group that includes China, India, Indonesia, Brazil, Pakistan and other populous nations.

The medium-variant projection for these countries indicates continued population growth, with their total rising from 4.5 billion persons in 2005 to 6.1 billion in 2050. Continuation of current fertility rates would add an expected 1.6 billion persons to the total population of these countries (relative to the medium variant), whereas the expected total would be only 632 million above the current population if the low fertility variant were to prevail. To sum up, for all less developed regions combined, constant fertility would imply total populations of 10.5 billion in 2050, well above the 7.8 billion produced by the medium variant. Under most projection scenarios, population decline will occur in the more developed regions at some point in the projection period

The anticipated trend at the aggregate level, however, masks differences at the national and regional level. Some developed countries are expected to continue to grow, but others may experience population declines. Overall, among all countries with a population of at least 100,000 in the year 2000, according to the results of the medium variant, 44 countries are expected to experience a reduction in population between 2005 and 2050, the majority of them located in the more developed regions. The prospects for population decline in selected countries and regions of the more developed world are quite striking. The most substantial population decline relative to present levels is likely to occur in Eastern Europe, which is projected to lose about 25 per cent of its current total population by 2050.

The Russian Federation, which constitutes approximately 48 per cent of Eastern Europe's population in 2005, is projected to decline by some 22 per cent. Other Eastern European countries, such as Ukraine, Belarus and Bulgaria, are also expected to experience a substantial decline in their population size. The least developed countries comprise 50 countries that are located mainly in Africa and Asia, plus small island developing States1 from Oceania and the Caribbean. Jointly, these countries have recorded relatively higher fertility and mortality levels than the more developed regions and the other less developed countries, a trend that is expected to continue in the coming decades.

Since the 1970s, the least developed countries have experienced, on average, the highest population growth rates in the world. Even though they represent a relatively small share of the world population, just under 12 per cent in 2005, it is expected that the overall population increment in those countries will account for 37 per cent of all world population growth during the period 2005-2050. Though fertility has been declining in most countries of this group, averaging on the whole about 5 children per woman in 2000-2005, mortality trends have not shown encouraging signs since the late 1980s. Continued population growth in already fragile economies will exacerbate problems of resource allocation for education and health care. Southern Europe and Japan will likely see declines of about 7 and 12 per cent, respectively, by 2050.

Little change is anticipated in the total populations of Western Europe, while an increase in the order of 10 per cent is projected for Northern Europe, even though some countries within that region will experience substantial declines (*e.g.*, Latvia, Lithuania and Estonia). In both Northern and Western Europe, immigration is likely to play an important role in maintaining or slightly increasing the population size. Population declines or only slight increases are also projected between 2005 and 2050 in some less developed countries, for example, those in the Southern Africa region, which are among the countries most highly affected by the HIV/AIDS epidemic. Among these countries, only Namibia is thought likely to experience substantial continued population growth, mainly because of its relatively high fertility.

During the period 2000-2005, the estimates show that 16 countries across the world experienced a reduction in population of more than 5,000 persons, ranging from 37 thousand in Estonia to close to more than 3 million in the Russian Federation. Except for Serbia and Montenegro, all countries included in this group are located in Eastern and Northern Europe or are successor States of the former USSR. Losses will be greater and more widespread by 2045-2050.

During the last five years of the projection period, 31 countries are expected to experience population declines of 100,000 persons or more (up from 9 countries in 2000-2005), with an additional 15 countries losing more than 25,000 persons or more. Comparing 2000-2005 with 2045-2050, countries newly experiencing declines in 2045-2050 are located in Asia, Southern and Western Europe and also include Cuba and Mexico. Among the five countries that are expected to lose the largest absolute amount of population in 2045-2050, three are from Eastern Asia: China, Japan and the Republic of Korea. As in 2000-2005, the Russian Federation and Ukraine are expected to be among the countries with the biggest declines.

POPULATION GROWTH RATES

Throughout the course of human history, and partially as a consequence of high mortality levels, population growth rates were on average quite low. It was probably not until the seventeenth and eighteenth centuries that annual growth rates as high as 0.5 per cent were being sustained. From then until the dawn of the twentieth century, annual population growth at the rate of half a percentage point was the norm. But improvements in sanitary measures as well as access to antibiotics during the twentieth century, among other factors, led to a reduction in mortality levels.

Consequently, population growth accelerated to historically unprecedented rates, reaching levels of around 2 per cent annually in 1965–1970. Since that historic peak, world population growth has greatly decelerated, and if the medium projections made in the 2004 Revision come to pass, the world will be returning to the 0.5 per cent rate of growth. The rapid growth of the twentieth century may come to be seen as an extraordinary but historically isolated phenomenon. The annual population growth rate2 of the world is now estimated at 1.21 per cent. At present, the growth rate of the more developed regions stands at 0.30 per cent per annum—about half of the norm in the eighteenth and nineteenth centuries—whereas the growth rate for the least developed countries is 2.40 per cent, far above the historical norm.

The other less developed countries have an intermediate position with a growth rate of 1.27 per cent. Growth rates in all three regions are projected to decline over time under the medium-variant projection, but only the more developed regions are thought likely to enter an era of population decline during the projection period. By 2050, the combined population of the more developed regions will have been declining in absolute terms for 20 years, whereas the least developed countries will still be growing at a rate of 1.30 per cent annually. An inspection of growth rate trajectories for the major areas of the world shows that two will be sharply distinguishable from the others.

Population growth rates in Africa are expected to be the highest throughout the projection period, falling to 1.21 per cent in 2045–2050, while those for Europe are projected to be the lowest, reaching-0.37 per cent by the end of the projection period. Growth rates of the other major areas—Asia, Latin America and the Caribbean, Northern America and Oceania—are expected to converge to between 0.19 and 0.45 per cent in 2 045-2050. Noticeably, most of the convergence in terms of growth rates between these major areas actually occurred between 1950 and 2005, while growth rates from Africa and Europe actually diverged from those of the rest of the world.

At the country level, among the ten countries with the highest population growth rates in 2000-2005, five are from Africa and five from Asia, with values ranging from around 3.40 per cent in Niger, Uganda and Chad to 6.51 per cent in the United Arab Emirates.

Most countries included in the list have relatively high fertility levels, the main cause of such growth, but the soaring growth rates in the countries from the Arabic Peninsula (United Arab Emirates, Qatar and Kuwait) are largely due to international migration. By 2045-2050, all countries with the highest projected growth rates are in Africa, except for Afghanistan. Nevertheless, the anticipated growth rates are much lower than current ones, ranging from 1.75 per cent in Burkina Faso to 2.39 per cent in Uganda.

At the other end of the spectrum, the countries with the lowest rates of population change in 2000-2005 (*i.e.*, fastest rates of decline) are all from Eastern and Northern Europe or are successor States of the former USSR. Estimates of growth rates range from about-0.4 per cent in Romania, Lithuania and Armenia to about-1.10 per cent in Georgia and Ukraine. A few of these countries will continue to have some of the lowest rates of change in the world by 2045-2050, joined mainly by members of the small island developing States1.

HUMAN MIGRATION

According to the International Organization for Migration's World Migration Report 2010, the number of international migrants was estimated at 214 million in 2010. If this number continues to grow at the same pace as during the last 20 years, it could reach 405 million by 2050. While some modern migration is a byproduct of wars (for example, emigration from Iraq and Bosnia to the US and UK), political conflicts (for example, some emigration from Zimbabwe to the UK), and natural disasters (for example, emigration from Montserrat to the UK following the eruption of the island's volcano), contemporary migration is predominantly economically motivated. In particular, there are wide disparities in the incomes that can be earned for similar work in different countries of the world. There are also at any given time some jobs in some high-wage countries for which there is a shortage of appropriately skilled/qualified citizens.

Some countries (*e.g.* UK and Australia) operate points systems that give some lawful immigration visas to some non-citizens who are qualified for such 'shortage' jobs. Non-citizens therefore have an economic incentive to obtain the necessary skills/qualifications in their own countries and then apply for, and migrate to take up, these job vacancies. International migration similarly motivated by economic disparities and opportunities occurs within the EU, where legal barriers to migration between member countries have been wholly or partially lifted. Countries with higher prevailing wage levels, such as France, Germany, Italy and the UK are net recipients of immigration from lower-wage member countries such as Greece, Hungary, Lithuania, Poland and Romania.

Some contemporary economic migration occurs even where the migrant becomes illegally resident in their destination country and therefore at major disadvantage in the employment market. Illegal immigrants are, for example, known to cross in significant numbers, typically at night, from Mexico into the US, from Mozambique into South Africa, from Bulgaria and Turkey into Greece, and from north Africa into Spain and Italy. The pressures of human migrations, whether as outright conquest or by slow cultural infiltration and resettlement, have affected the grand epochs in history and in land (for example, the decline of the Roman Empire); under the form of colonization, migration has transformed the world (such as the prehistoric and historic settlements of Australia and the Americas). Population genetics studied in traditionally settled modern populations have opened a window into the historical patterns of migrations, a technique pioneered by Luigi Luca Cavalli-Sforza.

Forced migration has been a means of social control under authoritarian regimes yet free initiative migration is a powerful factor in social adjustment and the growth of urban populations. In December 2003, The Global Commission on International Migration (GCIM) was launched with the support of Secretary-General of the United Nations Kofi Annan and several countries, with an independent 19-member Commission, a threefold mandate and a finite life-span ending December 2005. Its report, based on regional consultation meetings with stakeholders and scientific reports from leading international migration experts, was published and presented to Kofi Annan on 5 October 2005.

Different types of migration include:

- Seasonal human migration mainly related to agriculture and tourism.
- Rural to Urban, more common in developing countries as industrialization takes effect (urbanization)
- Urban to Rural, more common in developed countries due to a higher cost of urban living (suburbanization)
- International migration

PRE-MODERN MIGRATIONS

Historical migration of human populations begins with the movement of Homo erectus out of Africa across Eurasia about a million years ago. Homo sapiens appear to have occupied all of Africa about 150,000 years ago, moved out of Africa 70,000 years ago, and had spread across Australia, Asia and Europe by 40,000 years BC. Migration to the Americas took place 20,000 to 15,000 years ago, and by 2,000 years ago, most of the Pacific Islands were colonized. Later population movements notably include the Neolithic Revolution, Indo-European expansion, and the Early Medieval Great Migrations including Turkic expansion. In some places, substantial cultural transformation occurred following the migration of relatively small elite populations, for example from Brittonic to English culture between the 4th and 7th centuries CE in what had been Roman Britain.

Early humans migrated due to many factors such as changing climate and landscape and inadequate food supply. The evidence indicates that the ancestors of the Austronesian peoples spread from the South Chinese mainland to Taiwan at some time around 8,000 years ago. Evidence from historical linguistics suggests that it is from this island that seafaring peoples migrated, perhaps in distinct waves separated by millennia, to the entire region encompassed by the Austronesian languages. It is believed that this migration began around 6,000 years ago. Indo-Aryan migration from the Indus Valley to the plain of the River Ganga in Northern India is presumed to have taken place in the Middle to Late Bronze Age, contemporary to the Late Harappan phase in India (ca. 1700 to 1300 BC). From 180 BC, a series of invasions from Central Asia followed, including those led by the Indo-Greeks, Indo-Scythians, Indo-Parthians and Kushans in the north-western Indian subcontinent.

From about 750 BC, the Greeks began 250 years of expansion, settling colonies in several places including Sicily and Marseille. In Europe two waves of migrations dominate demographic distributions, that of the Celtic people, and the later Migration Period from the North and East, both being examples of general cultural change sparked by primarily elite and warrior migration. Other examples are small movements like that of the Magyars into Pannonia (modern-day Hungary). Turkic peoples spread from their homeland in modern Turkestan across most of Central Asia into Europe and the Middle East between the 6th and 11th centuries. Recent research suggests that Madagascar was uninhabited until Austronesian seafarers from Indonesia arrived during the 5th and 6th centuries AD. Subsequent migrations from both the Pacific and Africa further consolidated this original mixture, and Malagasy people emerged.

Desertification in the Sahara led to the descendants of the ancient Egyptians of the Pharaonic period becoming the Dogon people of Mali. Before the expansion of the Bantu languages and their speakers, the southern half of

Africa is believed to have been populated by Pygmies and Khoisan speaking people, today occupying the arid regions around the Kalahari Desert and the forest of Central Africa. By about 1000 AD Bantu migration had reached modern day Zimbabwe and South Africa. The Banu Hilal and Banu Ma'qil were a collection of Arab Bedouin tribes from the Arabian Peninsula who migrated westwards via Egypt between the 11th and 13th centuries. Their migration strongly contributed to the arabization and islamization of the western Maghreb, which was until then dominated by Berber tribes. Ostsiedlung was the medieval eastward migration and settlement of Germans. The 13th century was the time of the great Mongol and Turkic migrations across Eurasia.

Between the 11th and 18th centuries, the Vietnamese expanded southward in a process known as nam tièn (southward expansion). Manchuria was separated from China proper by the Inner Willow Palisade, which restricted the movement of the Han Chinese into Manchuria during the Qing Dynasty, as the area was off-limits to the Han until the Qing started colonizing the area with them later on in the dynasty's rule.

The Age of Exploration and European Colonialism led to an accelerated pace of migration since Early Modern times. In the 16th century perhaps 240,000 Europeans entered American ports. In the 19th century over 50 million people left Europe for the Americas. The local populations or tribes, such as the Aboriginal people in Canada, Brazil, Argentina, Australia, Japan and the United States, were usually far overwhelmed numerically by the settlers.

MODERN MIGRATIONS

Industrialization

While the pace of migration had accelerated since the 18th century already (including the involuntary slave trade), it would increase further in the 19th century. Manning distinguishes three major types of migration: labour migration, refugee migrations, and urbanization. Millions of agricultural workers left the countryside and moved to the cities causing unprecedented levels of urbanization. This phenomenon began in Britain in the late 18th century and spread around the world and continues to this day in many areas.

Industrialization encouraged migration wherever it appeared. The increasingly global economy globalized the labour market. The Atlantic slave trade diminished sharply after 1820, which gave rise to self-bound contract labour migration from Europe and Asia to plantations. Overpopulation, open agricultural frontiers, and rising industrial centers attracted voluntary migrants. Moreover, migration was significantly made easier by improved transportation techniques.

Transnational labour migration reached a peak of three million migrants per year in the early twentieth century. Italy, Norway, Ireland and the

Quongdong region of China were regions with especially high emigration rates during these years. These large migration flows influenced the process of nation state formation in many ways. Immigration restrictions have been developed, as well as diaspora cultures and myths that reflect the importance of migration to the foundation of certain nations, like the American melting pot. The transnational labour migration fell to a lower level from 1930s to the 1960s and then rebounded.

The United States experienced considerable internal migration related to industrialization, including its African American population. From 1910–1970, approximately 7 million African Americans migrated from the rural Southern United States, where blacks faced both poor economic opportunities and considerable political and social prejudice, to the industrial cities of the Northeast, Midwest and West where relatively well paid jobs were available.

This phenomenon came to be known in the United States as its own Great Migration. With the demise of legalized segregation in the 1960s and greatly improved economic opportunities in the South in the subsequent decades, millions of blacks have returned to the South from other parts of the country since 1980 in what has been called the New Great Migration.

World War I

The twentieth century experienced also an increase in migratory flows caused by war and politics. Muslims moved from the Balkan to Turkey, while Christians moved the other way, during the collapse of the Ottoman Empire. 400,000 Jews moved to Palestine in the early twentieth century. The Russian Civil War caused some 3 million Russians, Poles and Germans to migrate out of the Soviet Union. World War II and decolonization also caused migrations.

World War II

The Jewish communities across Europe, the Mediterranean and the Middle East were formed from voluntary and involuntary migrants. After the Holocaust (1938 to 1945), there was increased migration to the British Mandate of Palestine, which became the modern state of Israel as a result of the United Nations Partition Plan for Palestine. Provisions of the Potsdam Agreement from 1945 signed by victorious Western Allies and the Soviet Union led to one of the largest European migrations, and the largest in the 20th century. It involved the migration and resettlement of close to or over 20 million people.

The largest affected group were 16.5 million Germans expelled from Eastern Europe westwards. The second largest group were Poles, millions of whom were expelled westwards from eastern Kresy region and resettled in the so-called Recovered Territories. Hundreds of thousands of Poles, Ukrainians, Lithuanians, Latvians, Estonians and some Belarusians, were expelled eastwards from Europe to the Soviet Union. Finally, many of the several hundred thousand Jews remaining in Eastern Europe after the Holocaust migrated outside Europe to Israel and the United States.

India

In 1947, upon the Partition of India, large populations moved from India to Pakistan and vice versa, depending on their religious beliefs. The partition was promulgated in the Indian Independence Act 1947 as a result of the dissolution of the British Indian Empire. The partition displaced up to 12.5 million people in the former British Indian Empire, with estimates of loss of life varying from several hundred thousand to a million. Muslim residents of the former British India migrated to Pakistan (including East Pakistan which is now Bangladesh), whilst Hindu and Sikh residents of Pakistan and Hindu residents of East Pakistan (now Bangladesh) moved in the opposite direction.

In modern India, estimates based on industry sectors mainly employing migrants suggest that there are around 100 million circular migrants in India. Caste, social networks and historical precedents play a powerful role in shaping patterns of migration. Migration for the poor is mainly circular, as despite moving temporarily to urban areas, they lack the social security which might keep them there more permanently. They are also keen to maintain a foothold in home areas during the agricultural season.

Research by the Overseas Development Institute identifies a rapid movement of labour from slower to faster growing parts of the economy. Migrants can often find themselves excluded by urban housing policies and migrant support initiatives are needed to give workers improved access to market information, certification of identity, housing and education. Some people usually move from the Thar Desert, over to Dharvi in Mumbai, whilst shortly living in small towns/cities along the way

HISTORICAL THEORIES

Ravenstein

Certain laws of social science have been proposed to describe human migration. The following was a standard list after Ravenstein's proposals during the time frame of 1834 to 1913.

The laws are as follows:

- Every migration flow generates a return or countermigration.
- The majority of migrants move a short distance.
- Migrants who move longer distances tend to choose big-city destinations
- Urban residents are often less migratory than inhabitants of rural areas.
- Families are less likely to make international moves than young adults.

- Migration stage by stage
- Urban Rural difference
- Migration and Technology
- Economic condition

Lee

Lee's laws divides factors causing migrations into two groups of factors: Push and pull factors. Push factors are things that are bad about the country that one lives in and pull factors are things that attract one to another area.

Push Factors:

- Not enough jobs
- Few opportunities
- Primitive conditions
- Desertification
- Famine or drought
- Political fear or persecution
- Poor medical care
- Loss of wealth
- Natural disasters
- Death threats
- Lack of political or religious freedom
- Pollution
- Poor housing
- Landlord/tenant issues
- Bullying
- Discrimination
- Poor chances of marrying
- Condemned Housing

Pull Factors:

- Job opportunities
- Better living conditions
- Political and/or religious freedom
- Enjoyment
- Education
- Better medical care
- Attractive climates
- Security
- Family links
- Industry
- Better chances of marrying

Climate Cycles

The modern field of climate history suggests that the successive waves of Eurasian nomadic movement throughout history have had their origins in climatic cycles, which have expanded or contracted pastureland in Central Asia, especially Mongolia and the Altai. People were displaced from their home ground by other tribes trying to find land that could be grazed by essential flocks, each group pushing the next further to the south and west, into the highlands of Anatolia, the plains of Hungary, into Mesopotamia or southwards, into the rich pastures of China.

Other Models

Migration occurs because individuals search for food, sex and security outside their usual habitation. Idyorough is of the view that towns and cities are a creation of the human struggle to obtain food, sex and security. Migration occurs because individuals search for food, sex and security outside their usual habitation. To produce food, security and human reproduction of its species, human beings must, out of necessity, move out of their usual habitation and enter into indispensable social relationships that are cooperative or antagonistic.

Human beings also develop tools/equipment to enable them interact with nature to produce the desired food and security. The improved relationship (cooperative relationships) among human beings and improved technology further conditioned by the push and pull factors all interact together to cause or bring about migration and higher concentration of individuals into towns and cities. The higher the technology of production of food and security and the higher the cooperative relationship among human beings in the production of food and security and in the reproduction of the human species the higher would be the push and pull factors in the migration and concentration of human beings in towns and cities.

Countryside, towns and cities do not just exist but they do so to meet the human basic needs of food, security and the reproduction of the human species. Therefore, migration occurs because individuals search for food, sex and security outside their usual habitation. Social services in the towns and cities are provided to meet these basic needs for human survival and pleasure.

- Zipf's Inverse distance law (1956)
- Gravity model of migration and the Friction of distance
- Buffer Theory
- Stouffer's Theory of intervening opportunities (1940)
- Zelinsky's Mobility Transition Model (1971)
- Bauder's Regulation of labour markets (2006) "suggests that the international migration of workers is necessary for the survival of industrialized economies...[It] turns the conventional view of international migration on its head: it investigates how migration regulates labour markets, rather than labour markets shaping migration flows."

THEORIES FOR MIGRATION FOR WORK IN THE 21ST CENTURY

Migration for work in the 21st century has become a popular way for individuals from impoverished developing countries to obtain sufficient income for survival. This income is sent home to family members in the form of remittances, and has become an economic staple in a number of developing countries, namely the Philippines and Latin America structure. There are a number of theories to explain the international flow of capital and people from one country to another.

Neoclassical Economic Theory

This is the oldest theory of migration, and states that the main reason for labour migration is wage difference between two geographic locations. These wage differences are usually linked to geographic labour demand and supply. It can be said that areas with a shortage of labour but an excess of capital have a "high" relative wage while areas with a high labour supply and a dearth of capital have a "low" relative wage.

Labour tends to flow from low wage areas to high wage areas. Often, with this flow of labour comes changes in the sending as well as the receiving country. Neoclassical economic theory is best used to describe transnational migration because it is not confined by international immigration laws and similar governmental regulations.

Dual Labour Market Theory

Dual labour market theory states that migration is mainly caused by "pull" factors in more developed countries. This theory assumes that the labour markets in these developed countries consist of two segments: Primary, which requires high skilled labour and secondary which is very labour-intensive but requires low-skilled workers.

This theory assumes that migration from less developed countries into more developed countries is a result of a "pull" created by a need for labour in the developed countries in their secondary market. Migrant workers are needed to fill the lowest rung of the labour market because the native laborers don't want to do these jobs as they present a lack of mobility. This creates a need for migrant workers. Furthermore, the initial dearth in available labour pushes wages up, making migration even more enticing.

The New Economics of Labour Migration

This theory states that migration flows and patterns cannot be explained solely at the level of individual workers and their economic incentives, rather wider social entities must be considered as well. One such social entity is the household. Migration can be viewed as a result of risk-aversion on the part of a household that has insufficient income. The household, in this case, is in need of extra capital which can be achieved through remittances sent back by family members who participate in migrant labour abroad. These remittances can also have a broader effect on the economy of the sending country as a whole as they bring in capital.

Relative Deprivation Theory

Relative Deprivation Theory states that awareness of the income difference between neighbours or other households in the migrant-sending community is an important factor in migration. The incentive to migrate is a lot higher in areas that have a high level of economic inequality. In the short run, remittances may increase inequality, but in the long run they may actually decrease it.

There are two stages of migration for a worker: first, they invest in human capital formation, and then they try to capitalize on their investments. In this way, successful migrants may use their new capital to provide for better schooling for their children, and better homes for their families. Successful high-skilled emigrants may serve as an example for neighbours and potential migrants who hope to achieve that level of success.

world systems theory

World Systems Theory looks at migration from a global perspective. It explains that interaction between different societies can be an important factor in social change within societies.Trade with one country, which causes economic decline in another, may create incentive to migrate to a country with a more vibrant economy. It can be argued that even after decolonization the economic dependence of former colonies still remains on mother countries. This view of international trade is controversial, however, and some argue that free trade can actually reduce migration between developing and developed countries.

It can be argued that the developed countries import labour-intensive goods which causes an increase in employment of unskilled workers in the less developed countries decreasing the outflow of migrant workers. The export of capital-intensive goods from rich countries to poor countries also equalizes income and employment conditions thus also slowing migration. In either direction, this theory can be used to explain migration between countries that are geographically far apart.

POPULATION PROBLEMS OF DEVELOPED AND DEVELOPING COUNTRIES

The global rate of human population growth peaked around 1963, but the number of people living on Earth—and sharing finite resources like water and food—has grown by more than two-thirds since then, topping out at over 6.6 billion today. Human population is expected to exceed nine billion by 2050. Environmentalists don't dispute that many if not all of the environmental problems—from climate change to species loss to overzealous resource extraction—are either caused or exacerbated by population growth. "Trends such as the loss of half of the planet's forests, the depletion of most of its major fisheries, and the alteration of its atmosphere and climate are closely related to the fact that human population expanded from mere millions in prehistoric times to over six billion today," says Robert Engelman of Population Action International.

POPULATION GROWTH CAUSES MULTIPLE ENVIRONMENTAL PROBLEMS

According to Population Connection, population growth since 1950 is behind the clearing of 80 per cent of rainforests, the loss of tens of thousands of plant and wildlife species, an increase in greenhouse gas emissions of some 400 per cent and the development or commercialization of as much as half of the Earth's surface land. The group fears that in the coming decades half of the world's population will be exposed to "water-stress" or "water-scarce" conditions, which are expected to "intensify difficulties in meeting…consumption levels, and wreak devastating effects on our delicately balanced ecosystems."

IS ACCESS TO CONTRACEPTION AN ENVIRONMENTAL IMPERATIVE

In less developed countries, lack of access to birth control, as well as cultural traditions that encourage women to stay home and have babies, lead to rapid population growth. The result is ever increasing numbers of poor people across Africa, the Middle East, Southeast Asia, and elsewhere who suffer from malnourishment, lack of clean water, overcrowding, inadequate shelter, and AIDS and other diseases.

HIGH-CONSUMPTION LIFESTYLES EXACERBATE PROBLEMS OF POPULATION GROWTH

And while population numbers in most developed nations are leveling off or diminishing today, high levels of consumption make for a huge drain on resources. Americans, who represent only 4 per cent of world population, consume 25 per cent of all resources. Industrialized countries also contribute far more to climate change, ozone depletion and overfishing than developing countries. And as more and more residents of developing countries get access to Western media, or immigrate to the United States, they want to emulate the consumption-heavy lifestyles they see on their televisions and read about on the Internet.

U.S. POLICY CHANGES COULD HELP CONTROL POPULATION GROWTH WORLDWIDE

Given the overlap of population growth and environmental problems, many would like to see a change in U.S. policy on global family planning. In

2001, President George W. Bush instituted what some call the "global gag rule," whereby foreign organizations that provide or endorse abortions are denied U.S. funding support. Environmentalists consider that stance to be shortsighted, because support for family planning is the most effective way to check population growth and relieve pressure on the planet's environment

Index

M

N

O

P

R

S

U

W